W9-BBC-104

STUDIES OF THE GREEK POETS

AGENTS IN AMERICA

THE MACMILLAN COMPANY

66 FIFTH AVENUE, NEW YORK

STUDIES

OF THE

GREEK POETS

BY

JOHN ADDINGTON SYMONDS

Im Ganzen, Guten, Schönen
Resolut zu leben

VOL. I

THIRD EDITION

LONDON

ADAM AND CHARLES BLACK

1902

First Edition published—1st Series, 1873 ; 2nd Series, 1876
Second Edition published 1879
Third Edition published 1893. Reprinted 1902

TO

HENRY GRAHAM DAKYNS

My dear Graham,

It is about thirty years since I first set hand to the studies which compose these volumes. Our friendship, *Eheu Posthume*, has lasted during all this period.

It is twenty years since I first wrote a dedication of the *Studies of Greek Poets* to yourself. I now come again and ask you to accept this third edition.

I have rearranged the original studies in chronological order, adding one upon the newly-discovered Mimiambi of Herondas. I have also made certain additions of translated poems, which perhaps will form a feature of novelty. But, otherwise, I have left the substance of the book unaltered. I felt that it would be impossible to rehandle the style without entirely destroying its specific quality.

You know in what way the two Series of *Studies of Greek Poets* grew up. Some of the earliest were the recreations of my leisure hours during enforced sojourns upon the shores of the Riviera. Then came the Lectures which I delivered to the Sixth Form of Clifton College, at a bright and happy period of my life. Others have been composed from time to time, as inclination prompted, or as it seemed desirable to fill in gaps and to complete the scheme.

From a work of this kind unity of style and symmetry of plan are not to be expected. I hope that a certain freshness of feeling and spontaneity of expression may make up for what is deficient in systematic treatment.

Anyhow, pray accept the book again as a sign of my unalterable affection after the lapse of what is counted as a generation in the life of humanity.

JOHN ADDINGTON SYMONDS.

Venice, 560 Zattere, *March* 19, 1893.

NOTE

I wish to express my sincere thanks to Mr. Walter Headlam, of King's College, Cambridge, for the assistance he gave me in revising the English version of *Herondas*. I may take occasion here to mention Mr. Headlam's scholarly translation into English verse of *Fifty Poems of Meleager* (Macmillan, 1890).

CONTENTS

CHAPTER I

CHAPTER II

CHAPTER III

CHAPTER IV

CHAPTER V

CHAPTER VI

CHAPTER VII

CHAPTER XII

CHAPTER XIII

CHAPTER I

THE PERIODS OF GREEK LITERATURE

Language and Mythology—The Five Chief Periods of Greek Literature—
The First Period : Homer—Religion and State of the Homeric Age
—Achilles and Ulysses—Second Period : Transition—Breaking up
of the Homeric Monarchies—Colonisation—the Nomothetæ—Ionians
and Dorians—Development of Elegiac, Iambic, Lyric Poetry—
Beginning of Philosophy—Third Period : Athenian Supremacy—
Philosophy at Athens—the Fine Arts—the Drama—History—Sparta
and Athens—Pericles and Anaxagoras—Fourth Period : Hegemony
of Sparta—Enslavement of Hellas—Demosthenes—Alexander and
Achilles—Aristotle—the Hellenisation of the East—Menander—the
Orators—Fifth Period : Decline and Decay—Greek Influence upon
the World—Alexandria—the Sciences—Theocritus—the University of
Athens—Sophistic Literature—Byzantium— Hellas and Christendom.

THE most fascinating problems of history are veiled as closely The mystery
from our curiosity as the statue of Egyptian Isis. Nothing is of national
character.
known for certain about the emergence from primitive barbarism of the great races, or about the determination of
national characteristics. Analogies may be adduced from the
material world; but the mysteries of organised vitality remain impenetrable. What made the Jew a Jew, the Greek a
Greek, is as unexplained as what daily causes the germs of
an oak and of an ash to produce different trees. All we
know is that in the womb of the vague and infinitely distant

past, the embryos of races were nourished into form and individuality by means of the unseen cord which attaches man to nature, his primitive mother. But the laws of that rudimentary growth are still unknown; "the abysmal deeps of Personality" in nations as in men remain unsounded: we cannot even experimentalise upon the process of ethnical development.

Language and Mythology. Those mighty works of art which we call languages, in the construction of which whole peoples unconsciously co-operated, the forms of which were determined not by individual genius, but by the instincts of successive generations acting to one end inherent in the nature of the race :—those poems of pure thought and fancy, cadenced not in words but in living imagery, fountain-heads of inspiration, mirrors of the mind of nascent nations, which we call Mythologies :—these surely are more marvellous in their infantine spontaneity than any more mature production of the races which evolved them. Yet we are utterly ignorant of their embryology : the true science of Origins is as yet not even in its cradle.

Experimental philologers may analyse what remains of early languages, may trace their connections and their points of divergence, may classify and group them. But the nature of the organs of humanity which secreted them is unknown, the problem of their vital structure is insoluble. Antiquarian theorists may attempt to persuade us that Myths are decayed, disintegrated, dilapidated phrases, the meaning of which had been lost to the first mythopœists. But they cannot tell us how these splendid flowers, springing upon the rich soil of rotting language, expressed in form and colour to the mental eye the thoughts and aspirations of whole races, and presented a measure of the faculties to be developed during long ages of expanding civilisation. If the boy is father of the man, Myths are the parents of philosophies, religions, polities.

To those unknown artists of the prehistoric age, to the language-builders and myth-makers, architects of cathedrals not raised with hands but with the Spirit of man for Humanity to dwell therein, poets of the characters of nations, sculptors of the substance of the very soul, melodists who improvised the themes upon which subsequent centuries have written variations, we ought to erect our noblest statues and our grandest temples. The work of these first artificers is more astonishing in its unconsciousness, more effective in its spontaneity, than are the deliberate and calculated arts of sculptor, painter, poet, philosopher, and lawgiver of the historic periods.

Some such reflections as these are the natural prelude to the study of a literature like that of the Greeks. Language and Mythology form the vestibules and outer courts to Homer, Pheidias, Lycurgus.

It is common to divide the history of Greek literature into three chief periods : the first embracing the early growth of Poetry and Prose before the age in which Athens became supreme in Hellas—that is, anterior to about 480 B.C.; the second coinciding with the brilliant maturity of Greek genius during the supremacy of Athens—that is, from the termination of the Persian war to the age of Alexander; the third extending over the Decline and Fall of the Greek spirit after Alexander's death—that is, from 323 B.C., and onwards, to the final extinction of Hellenic civilisation. There is much to be said in favour of this division. Indeed, Greek history falls naturally into these three sections. But a greater degree of accuracy may be attained by breaking up the first and last of these divisions, so as to make five periods instead of three. After having indicated these five periods in outline, we will return to the separate consideration of them in detail and in connection with the current of Greek history.

Stages in the history of the Greek mind.

The first may be termed the Heroic, or Prehistoric, or Legendary period. It ends with the first Olympiad, 776 B.C., and its chief monuments are the epics of Homer and Hesiod. The second is a period of transition from the Heroic or Epical to that of artistic maturity in all the branches of literature.

In this stage history, properly so-called, begins. The Greeks try their strength in several branches of composition. Lyrical, Satirical, Moral, and Philosophical poetry supplant the Epic. Prose is cultivated. The first foundations of the Drama are laid. The earliest attempts at science emerge from the criticism of old mythologies. The whole mind of the race is in a ferment, and, for the moment, effort and endeavour are more apparent than mastery and achievement. This period extends from 776 to 477 B.C., the date of the Athenian league. The third period is that of the Athenian Supremacy. Whatever is great in Hellas is now concentrated upon Athens. Athens, after her brilliant activity during the Persian war, wins the confidence and assumes the leadership of Greece. Athens is the richest, grandest, most liberal, most cultivated, most enlightened state of Hellas. To Athens flock all the poets and historians and philosophers. The Drama attains maturity in her theatre. Philosophy takes its true direction from Anaxagoras and Socrates. The ideal of history is realised by Thucydides. Oratory flourishes under the great statesmen and the demagogues of the Republic. During the brief but splendid ascendency of Athens, all the masterpieces of Greek literature are simultaneously produced with marvellous rapidity. Fixing 413 B.C. as the date of the commencement of Athenian Decline, our fourth period, which terminates in 323 B.C. with the death of Alexander, is again one of transition. The second period was transitional from adolescence to maturity. The fourth is transitional from maturity to old age. The creative genius of the Greeks is now less active. We have indeed the great names of Plato, Aristotle, and Demosthenes, to give splendour to this stage of national existence. But the sceptre has passed away from the Greek nation proper. Their protagonist, Athens, is in slavery. The civilisation which they had slowly matured, and which at Athens had been reflected in the masterpieces of Art and Literature, is now spread abroad and scattered over

the earth. Asia and Egypt are Hellenised. The Greek spirit
is less productive than it has been; but it is not less vigorous.
It still asserts itself as the greatest in the world; but it does
so, relying more upon its past acquirements than on any seeds
of power that remain to be developed in the future. The
fifth period, the longest of all, is one of decline and decay.
It extends from 323 B.C. to the final extinction of classical
civilisation. Two chief centres occupy our attention—Athens,
where the traditions of art and philosophy yet linger, where
the Stoics and Epicureans and the sages of the New Academy
still educate the world and prepare a *nidus* for the ethics
of Christianity—and Alexandria, where physical science is
cultivated under the Ptolemies, where mystical theology
flourishes in the schools of the Neoplatonists, where libraries
are formed and the labour of literary criticism is conducted
on a gigantic scale, but where nothing new is produced except
the single, most beautiful flower of Idyllic poetry and some
few epigrams. In this fifth period, Rome and Byzantium,
where the Greek spirit, still vital, overlives its natural decay
upon a foreign soil, close the scene.

In these five periods—periods of superb adolescence, early
manhood, magnificent maturity, robust old age, and senility—
we can trace the genius of the Greeks putting forth its vigour
in successive works of art and literature, concentrating its
energy at first upon its own self-culture, then extending
its influence in every direction, and controlling the education
of humanity, finally contenting itself with pondering and
poring on its past, with mystical metaphysics and pedantic
criticism. Yet even in its extreme decadence the Hellenic
spirit is still potent. It still assimilates, transmutes, and
alchemises what it works upon. Coming into contact with
the new and mightier genius of Christianity, it forces even
that first-born of the Deity to take form from itself. One
dying effort of the Greek intellect, if we may so speak, is to
formulate the dogma of the Trinity and to impress the doctrine

Analogy between the life of nations and of men.

of the Logos upon the author of the Gospel of St. John. The analogy between the history of a race so undisturbed in its development as the Greek, and the life of a man, is not altogether fanciful. A man like Goethe, beautiful in soul and body, exceedingly strong and swift and active and inquisitive in all the movements of his spirit, first lives the life of the senses and of physical enjoyment. His soul, "immersed in rich foreshadowings of the world," has scarcely begun to think consciously in the first period. But he feels the glory of existence, the strivings of inexhaustible energy, the desire of infinite expansion. The second period is one of *Sturm und Drang*. New things are learned: much of the beautiful physical activity is sacrificed; he discovers that life involves care and responsibility as well as pleasure; he concentrates his mental faculty on hard and baffling study, in which at first he halts and falters. Then he goes forth to the world and wins great fame, and does the deeds and thinks the thoughts by which he shall be known to all posterity. His physical and mental faculties are now in perfect harmony; together they offer him the noblest and most enduring pleasures. But after a while his productiveness begins to dwindle. He has put forth his force, has fully expressed himself, has matured his principles, has formed his theory of the world. Our fourth period corresponds to the early old age of such a man's life. He now applies his principles, propagates his philosophy, subordinates his fancy, produces less, enjoys with more sobriety and less exhilaration, bears burdens, suffers disappointments, yet still, as Solon says, "learns always as he grows in years." Then comes the fifth stage. He who was so vigorous and splendid, now has but little joy in physical life; his brain is dry and withering; he dwells on his old thoughts, and has no faculty for generating new ones: yet his soul contains deep mines of wisdom; he gives counsel and frames laws for younger generations. And so he gradually sinks into the grave. His acts remain: his life is written.

The great name of Homer covers the whole of the first period of Greek Literature. It is from the Homeric poems alone that we can form a picture to our imagination of the state of society in prehistoric Hellas. The picture which they present is so lively in its details, and so consistent in all its parts, that we have no reason to suspect that it was drawn from fancy. Its ideal, as distinguished from merely realistic, character is obvious. The poet professes to sing to us of heroes who were of the seed of gods, whose strength exceeded tenfold the strength of actual men, and who filled the world with valiant deeds surpassing all that their posterity achieved. Yet, in spite of this, the *Iliad* and the *Odyssey* may be taken as faithful mirrors of a certain phase of Greek society, just as the *Nibelungen Lied*, the romances of Charlemagne, and the tales of the Round Table reflect three stages in the history of feudalism. We find that in this earliest period of Greek history the nation was governed by monarchs each of whom claimed descent from a god. Thus the kings exercised their power over the people by divine right; but at the same time a necessary condition of their maintaining this supremacy was that they should be superior in riches, lands, personal bravery, and wisdom. Their subjects obeyed them, not merely because they were Διογενεῖς (of kinship with Zeus), or because they were Fathers of the people, but also, and chiefly, because they were the ablest men, the men fitted by nature to rule, the men who could be depended upon in an emergency. The king had just so much personal authority as he had ability to acquire or to assert. As soon as this ability failed, the sceptre departed from him. Thus Laertes overlives his royalty; and the suitors of Penelope, fancying that Ulysses is dead, take no heed of Telemachus, who ought to rule in his stead, because Telemachus is a mere lad; but as soon as the hero returns, and proves his might by stringing the bow, the suitors are slain like sheep. Again, Achilles, while acknowledging the sway of Agamemnon, quarrels with him openly, proving his equality and right to such independence as he can assert for himself. The bond between the king in the Heroic age and his chieftains was founded on the personal superiority of the suzerain, and upon the necessity felt for the predominance of one individual in warfare and council. The chiefs were grouped around the monarch like the twelve peers round Charlemagne, or like the barons, whose turbulence Shakspere has described in *Richard II.* The relation of the Homeric sovereign to his princes was, in fact, a feudal one. Olympus repeats the same form of government. There Zeus is monarch simply because he wields the thunder. When Heré wishes to rebel, Hephæstus advises her to submit, because Zeus can root up the world, or hurl them all from the crystal parapet of heaven. Such, then, is the society of kings and princes in Homer. They stand forth in brilliant relief against the background, gray, and misty, of the common people. The masses of the nation, like the Chorus in Tragedy, kneel passive, deedless, appealing to heaven, trembling at the strokes of fate, watching with anxiety the action of the heroes. Meanwhile the heroes enact their drama for themselves. They assume responsibility. They do and suffer as their passions sway them. Of these the greatest, the most truly typical, is Achilles. In Achilles, Homer summed up and fixed for ever the ideal of the Greek character. He presented an imperishable picture of their national youthfulness, and of their ardent genius, to the Greeks. The "beautiful human heroism" of Achilles, his strong personality, his fierce passions controlled and tempered by divine wisdom, his intense friendship and love that passed the love of women, above all, the splendour of his youthful life in death made perfect, hovered like a dream above the imagination of the Greeks, and insensibly determined their subsequent development. At a later age this ideal was destined to be realised in Alexander. The reality fell below the ideal: for *rien n'est si beau que la fable, si triste que la vérité.* But the life of Alexander is the most convincing proof of the importance of Achilles in the history of the Greek race.

If Achilles be the type of the Hellenic genius, radiant, adolescent, passionate; as it still dazzles us in its artistic beauty and unrivalled physical energy; Ulysses is no less a true portrait of the Greek as known to us in history—stern in action, ruthless in his hatred, pitiless in his hostility ; subtle, vengeful, cunning ; yet at the same time the most adventurous of men, the most persuasive in eloquence, the wisest in counsel, the bravest and coolest in danger. The *Græculus esuriens* of Juvenal may be said to be the caricature in real life of the idealised Ulysses. And what remains to the present day of the Hellenic genius in the so-called *Greek nation* descends from Ulysses rather than Achilles. If the Homeric Achilles has the superiority of sculpturesque and dramatic splendour, the Homeric Ulysses beats him on the ground of permanence of type.

Achilles and Ulysses.

Homer, then, was the Poet of the Heroic age, the Poet of Achilles and Ulysses. Of Homer we know nothing, we have heard too much. Need we ask ourselves again the question whether he existed, or whether he sprang into the full possession of consummate art without a predecessor? That he had no predecessors, no scattered poems and ballads to build upon, no well-digested body of myths to synthesise, is an absurd hypothesis which the whole history of literature refutes. That, on the other hand, there never was a Homer, —that is to say, that some diaskeuast, acting under the orders of Pisistratus, gave its immortal outline to the colossus of the *Iliad*, and wove the magic web of the *Odyssey*—but that no supreme and conscious artist working toward a well-planned conclusion conceived and shaped these epics to the form they bear, appears to the spirit of sound criticism equally ridiculous. The very statement of this alternative involves a contradiction in terms ; for such a diaskeuast must himself have been a supreme and conscious artist. Some Homer did exist. Some great single poet intervened between the lost chaos of legendary material and the cosmos of artistic beauty which we now possess. His work may have been tampered with in a thousand ways, and religiously but inadequately restored. Of his age and date and country we may know nothing. But this we do *know*, that the fire of moulding, fusing, and controlling genius in some one single brain has made the *Iliad* and *Odyssey* what they are.[1]

Imperson-
ality of the
Epic.

The Epic poet merges his personality in his poems, the words of which he ascribes to the inspiration of the Muse. The individual is nowhere, is forgotten in the subject and suppressed, while the luminous forms of gods and heroes move serenely across the stage, summoned and marshalled by the maidens of Helicon. In no other period of Greek literature shall we find the same unconsciousness of self, the same immersion in the work of Art. In this respect the poetry of the Heroic age answers to the condition of prehistoric Hellas, where as yet the elements of the Greek race remain still implicit in the general mass and undeveloped. We hear in Homer of no abrupt division between Dorians and Ionians. Athens and Sparta have not grown up into prominence as the two leaders of the nation. Argos is the centre of power ; but Phthiotis, the cradle of the Hellenes, is the home of Achilles. Ulysses is an islander. In the same way, in Homer the art of the Greeks is still a mere potentiality. The artistic sentiment, indeed, exists in exquisite perfection ; but it is germinal, not organised and expanded as it will be. We hear of embroidery for royal garments, of goldsmith's work for shields and breastplates, of stained ivory trappings for chariots and horses. But even here the poet's imagination had probably outrun the fact. What he saw with his fancy, could the

---

[1] I do not mean to assert by this that *one* poet composed both epics, but that each bears upon it the mark of unity in conception and execution. Whether the same poet produced both is a different question, and I am inclined to regard the *Odyssey* as a later work.

heroic artisans have fashioned with their tools? Is not the
shield of Achilles, like Dante's pavement of the Purgatorial
staircase, a forecast of the future? Architecture and Sculpture at any rate can scarcely be said to exist. Ulysses builds
his own house. The statues of the gods are fetishes. But,
meanwhile, the foundation of the highest Greek art is being
laid in the cultivation of the human body. The sentiment of
beauty shows itself in dances and games, in the races of naked
runners, in rhythmic processions, and the celebration of religious rites. This was the proper preparation for the after-
growth of Sculpture. The whole race lived out its sculpture
and its painting, rehearsed, as it were, the great works of
Pheidias and Polygnotus in physical exercise before it learned
to express itself in marble or in colour. The public games,
which were instituted in this first period, further contributed
to the cultivation of the sense of Beauty, which was inherent
in the Greeks.

The second period is one of transition—in Politics, in
Literature, in the Fine Arts. Everywhere the old landmarks
are being broken up, and the new ones are not yet fixed. The
Heroic monarchies yield first of all to oligarchies, and then to
tyrannies; the tyrannies in their turn give place to demo-
cracies, or to constitutional aristocracies. Argos, the centre
of Heroic Hellas, is the first to change. Between 770 and
730 B.C. Pheidon usurps the sovereign power, and dies, leaving
no dynasty behind him.[1] Between 650 and 500 we find
despots springing up in all the chief Greek cities. At Corinth
the oligarchical family of the Bacchiadæ are superseded by
the tyrants Cypselus and Periander. At Megara the despot
Theagenes is deposed and exiled. At Sicyon the Orthagoridæ
terminate in the despot Cleisthenes, whose reign is marked

(margin note: Transition from monarchy through tyranny to constitutional law.)

---

[1] The date of Pheidon is in truth unfixed. According to recent
calculations, he may have celebrated the 28th and not the 8th Olympiad.
The involved alteration in his date would bring him into closer connection
with the other despots.

by an attempt to supersede the ancient Doric order of government by caste. At Mitylene, Pittacus becomes a constitutional autocrat, or dictator for the public safety. At Samos, Polycrates holds a post of almost Oriental despotism. At Athens, we find the great family of the Pisistratidæ, who supersede the dynastic tyranny in commission of the house of Codrus. What is the meaning of these changes? How does the despot differ from the Heroic monarch, who held, as we have seen, his power by divine right, but who also had to depend for his ascendency on personal prowess? Gradually the old respect for the seed of Zeus died out. Either the royal families abused their power, or became extinct, or, as in the case of Athens and Sparta, retained hereditary privileges under limitations. During this decay of the Zeus-born dynasties, the cities of Greece were a prey to the quarrels of great families; and it often happened that one of these obtained supreme power—in which case a monarchy, based not on divine right, but on force and fear, was founded; or else a few of the chief houses combined against the State, to establish an oligarchy. The oligarchies, owing their authority to no true, legal, or religious fount of honour, were essentially selfish, and were exposed to the encroachments of the more able among their own families. The cleverest man in an oligarchy tended to draw the power into his own hands; but in this he generally succeeded by first flattering, and then intimidating the people. Thus in one way or another the old type of dynastic government was superseded by despotisms, more or less arbitrary, tending to the tyranny of single individuals, or to the coalition of noble houses, and bringing with them the vices of greed, craft, and servile cruelty. The political ferment caused a vast political excitement. Party strove against party; and when one set gained the upper hand, the other had to fly. The cities of Hellas were filled with exiles. Diplomacy and criticism occupied the minds of men. Personal cleverness became the one essential point in politics. But two permanent advantages were secured by this anarchy to the Greeks. The one was a strong sense of the equality of citizens ; the other a desire for established law, as opposed to the caprice of individuals and to the clash of factions in the State. This then is the first point which marks the transitional period. The old monarchies break up, and give place to oligarchies first, and then to despotism. The tyrants maintain themselves by violence and by flattering the mob. At last they fall, or are displaced, and then the states agree to maintain their freedom by the means of constitutions and fixed laws. The despots are schoolmasters, who bring the people to *Nomos* (established laws and constitutions) as their lord.

Three other general features distinguish this period of transition. The first is Colonisation. In the political disturbances which attend the struggle for power, hundreds of citizens were forced to change their residence. So we find the mother cities sending settlers to Italy, to Sicily, to Africa, to the Gulf of Lyons, to Thrace, and to the islands. In these colonies the real life and vigour of Hellas show themselves at this stage more than in the mother states. It is in Sicily, on the coast of Magna Græcia, on the sea-board of Asia Minor, in the islands of the Ægean, that the first poets and philosophers and historians of Greece appear. Sparta and Athens, destined to become the protagonists of the real drama of Hellas, are meanwhile silent and apparently inert. Secondly, this is the age of the Nomothetæ. Thebes receives a constitution from the Corinthian lovers and lawgivers Philolaus and Diocles. Lycurgus and Solon form the states of Sparta and Athens. It is not a little wonderful to think of these three great cities, successively the leaders of historic Hellas, submitting to the intellect each of its own lawgiver, taking shape beneath his hands, cheerfully accepting and diligently executing his directions. Lastly, it is in this period that the two chief races of the Greeks—the Ionians and the Dorians—

The Greek colonies.

Lawgivers.

Ionians and Dorians.

emerge into distinctness. Not only are Athens and Sparta fashioned to the form which they will afterwards maintain; but also in the colonies two distinct streams of thought and feeling begin to flow onwards side by side, and to absorb, each into its own current, those minor rivulets which it could best appropriate.

Hesiod.

What happens to literature in this period of metamorphosis, expansion, and anarchy? We have seen that Homer covers the whole of the first period of literature; and in the Homeric poems we saw that the interests of the present were subordinated to a splendid picture of the ideal past, that the poet was merged in his work, that the individual joys and sorrows of the artist remained unspoken, and that his words were referred immediately to the Muse. All this is now to be altered. But meanwhile between the first and second period a link is made by Hesiod. In his *Works and Days* he still preserves the traditions of the Epic. But we no longer listen to the deeds of gods and heroes; and though the Muse is invoked, the poet appears before us as a living, sentient, suffering man. We descend to earth. We are instructed in the toils and duties of the beings who have to act and endure upon the prosaic stage of the world, as it exists in the common light of the present time. Even in Hesiod there has therefore been a change. Homer strung his lyre in the halls of princes who loved to dwell on the great deeds of their god-descended ancestors. Hesiod utters a weaker and more subdued note to the tillers of the ground and the watchers of the seasons. In Homer we see the radiant heroes expiring with a smile upon their lips as on the Æginetan pediment. In Hesiod we hear the low sad outcry of humanity. The inner life, the daily loss and profit, the duties and the cares of men are his concern. Homer, too, was never analytical. He described the world without raising a single moral or psychological question. Hesiod poses the eternal problems: What is the origin and destiny of mankind? Why should we toil pain-

fully upon the upward path of virtue? How came the gods
to be our tyrants? What is Justice? How did evil and pain
and disease begin? After Hesiod the Epical impulse ceases.
Poets, indeed, go on writing narrative poems in hexameters.
But the Cycle, so called by the Alexandrian critics, produced
about this time, had not innate life enough to survive the
wear and tear of centuries. We have lost the whole series,
except in the tragedies which were composed from their
materials. Literature had passed beyond the stage of the
heroic Epic. The national ear demanded other and more
varied forms of verse than the hexameter. Among the *Development of*
Ionians of Asia Minor was developed the pathetic melody of *Lyric,*
Elegiac, and
the Elegiac metre, which first apparently was used to express *Iambic*
verse.
the emotions of love and sorrow, and afterwards came to be
the vehicle of moral sentiment and all strong feeling. Callinus
and Tyrtæus adapted the Elegy to songs of battle. Solon
consigned his wisdom to its couplets, and used it as a trumpet
for awakening the zeal of Athens against her tyrants. Mimnermus confined the metre to its more plaintive melodies, and
made it the mouthpiece of lamentations over the fleeting
beauty of youth and the evils of old age. In Theognis the
Elegy takes wider scope. He uses it alike for satire and
invective, for precept, for autobiographic grumblings, for
political discourses, and for philosophical apophthegms. Side
by side with the Elegy arose the various forms of Lyric poetry.
The names of Alcæus and Sappho, of Alcman, Anacreon, Simonides, Bacchylides, Stesichorus, Arion instantly suggest themselves. But it must be borne in mind that Lyric poetry in
Greece at a very early period broke up into two distinct
species. The one kind gave expression to strong personal
emotion and became a safety-valve for perilous passions: the
other was choric and complex in its form; designed for public
festivals and solemn ceremonials, it consisted chiefly of odes
sung in the honour of gods and great men. To the former or
personal species belong the lyrics of the Ionian and Æolian

families; to the latter, or more public species, belong the so-called Dorian odes. Besides the Elegy and all the forms of lyric stanza, the Iambic, if not invented in this period, was now adapted of set purpose to personal satire.[1] Archilochus is said to have preferred this metre, as being the closest in its form to common speech, and therefore suited to his unideal practical invective. From the lyric Dithyrambs of Arion, sung at festivals of Dionysus, and from the Iambic satires of Archilochus, recited at the feasts of Demeter,[2] was to be developed the metrical structure of the drama in the third period. As yet, it is only among the Dorians of Sicily and of Megara that we hear of any mimetic shows, and these of the simplest description.

Emergence of philo-sophy.

In this period the first start in the direction of philosophy was made. The morality which had been implicit in Homer, and had received a partial development in Hesiod, was condensed in proverbial couplets by Solon, Theognis, Phocylides, and Simonides. These couplets formed the starting-points for discussion. Many of Plato's dialogues turn on sayings of Theognis and Simonides. Many of the sublimer flights of meditation in Sophocles are expansions of early Gnomes. Even the Ethics of Aristotle are indebted to their wisdom. The ferment of thought produced by the political struggles of this age tended to sharpen the intellect and to turn reflection inwards. Hence we find that the men who rose to greatest eminence in statecraft as tyrants or as lawgivers, are also to be reckoned among the primitive philosophers of Greece. The aphorisms of the Seven Sages, two of whom were Nomothetæ, and several of whom were despots, contain the kernel of much

---

[1] The *Margites* and *Eiresione*, attributed by the Greeks to Homer, contain possibly the earliest fragments of Iambic verses.

[2] Satire, it is well known, was permitted at some of the festivals of Demeter; and the legend of the maid Iambë, who alone could draw a smile from Demeter, after she had lost Persephone, seems to symbolise the connection of Iambic recitations with the cultus of this goddess.

that is peculiar in Greek thought. It is enough to mention these : μηδὲν ἄγαν· μέτρον ἄριστον· γνῶθι σεαυτόν· καιρὸν γνῶθι· ἀνάγκῃ δ᾽ οὐδὲ θεοὶ μάχονται, which are the germs of subsequent systems of ethics, metaphysics, and theories of art.[1] Solon, as a patriot, a modeller of the Athenian constitution, an elegiac poet, one of the Seven Sages, and the representative of Greece at the court of Crœsus, may be chosen as the one most eminent man in a period when literature and thought and politics were to a remarkable extent combined in single individuals.

Meanwhile philosophy began to flourish in more definite shape among the colonists of Asia Minor, Italy, and Sicily. The criticism of the Theogony of Hesiod led the Ionian thinkers, Thales, Anaximenes, Anaximander, Heraclitus, to evolve separate answers to the question of the origin of the universe. The problem of the physical ἀρχή, or starting-point, of the world occupied their attention. Some more scientific theory of existence than mythology afforded was imperatively demanded. The same spirit of criticism, the same demand for accuracy, gave birth to history. The Theogony of Hesiod and the Homeric version of the Trojan war, together with the genealogies of the Heroes, were reduced to simple statements of fact, stripped of their artistic trappings, and rationalised after a rude and simple fashion by the annalists of Asia Minor. This zeal for greater rigour of thought was instrumental in developing a new vehicle of language. The time had come at length for separation from poetry, for the creation of a prose style which should correspond in accuracy to the logical necessity of exact thinking. Prose accordingly was elaborated with infinite difficulty by these first speculators from the elements of common speech. It was a great epoch in the history of European culture when men ceased to produce their thoughts in the fixed cadences

Creation of Prose.

[1] Nothing overmuch : measure is best : know thyself : know the right moment : against necessity not even gods fight.

of verse, and consigned them to the more elastic periods of prose. Heraclitus of Ephesus was the first who achieved a notable success in this new and difficult art. He for his pains received the title of ὁ σκοτεινός, the obscure; so strange and novel did the language of science seem to minds accustomed hitherto to nothing but metre. Yet even after his date philosophy of the deepest species was still conveyed in verse. The Eleatic metaphysicians Xenophanes and Parmenides— Xenophanes, who dared to criticise the anthropomorphism of the Greek Pantheon, and Parmenides, who gave utterance to the word of Greek ontology, τὸ ὄν, or Being, which may be significantly contrasted with the Hebrew I am—wrote long poems in which they invoked the Muse, and dragged the hexameter along the pathway of their argument upon the entities, like a pompous sacrificial vestment. Empedocles of Agrigentum, to whom we owe the rough and ready theory of the four elements, cadenced his great work on Nature in the same sonorous verse, and interspersed his speculations on the Cycles of the Universe with passages of brilliant eloquence.

Apparition of personality in Art.

Thus the second period is marked alike by changes in politics and society, and by a revolution in the spirit of literature. The old Homeric monarchies are broken up. Oligarchies and tyrannies take their place. To the anarchy and unrest of transition succeeds the demand for constitutional order. The colonies are founded, and contain the very pith of Hellas at this epoch: of all the great names we have mentioned, only Solon and Theognis belong to Central Greece. The Homeric Epos has become obsolete. In its stead we have the greatest possible variety of literary forms. The Elegiac poetry of morality and war and love; the Lyrical poetry of personal feeling and of public ceremonial; the Philosophical poetry of metaphysics and mysticism; the Iambic, with its satire; Prose, in its adaptation to new science and a more accurate historical investigation; are all built up upon the ruins of the Epic. What is most prominent in the spirit of this second period is the emergence of private interests and individual activities. No dreams of a golden past now occupy the minds of men. No gods or heroes fill the canvas of the poet. Man, his daily life, his most crying necessities, his deepest problems, his loves and sorrows, his friendships, his social relations, his civic duties—these are the theme of poetry. Now for the first time in Europe a man tells his own hopes and fears, and expects the world to listen. Sappho simply sings her love; Archilochus, his hatred; Theognis, his wrongs; Mimnermus, his *ennui ;* Alcæus, his misfortunes ; Anacreon, his pleasure of the hour; and their songs find an echo in all hearts. The Individual and the Present have triumphed over the Ideal and the Past. Finally, it should be added that the chief contributions to the culture of the fine arts in this period are Architecture, which is carried to perfection ; Music, which receives elaborate form in the lyric of the Dorian order ; and Sculpture, which appears as yet but rudimentary upon the pediments of the temples of Ægina and Selinus.

Our third period embraces the supremacy of Athens from the end of the Persian to the end of the Peloponnesian war. The Persian war. It was the struggle with Xerxes which developed all the latent energies of the Greeks, which intensified their national existence, and which secured for Athens, as the central power on which the scattered forces of the race converged, the intellectual dictatorship of Hellas. No contest equals for interest and for importance this contest of the Greeks with the Persians. It was a struggle of spiritual energy against brute force, of liberty against oppression, of intellectual freedom against superstitious ignorance, of civilisation against barbarism. The whole fate of humanity hung trembling in the scales at Marathon, at Salamis, at Platæa. On the one side were ranged the hordes of Asia, tribe after tribe, legion upon legion, myriad by myriad, under their generals and princes. On the other side stood forth a band of athletes, of Greek citizens, each one himself a prince and general. The countless masses of the herd-like Persian host were opposed to a handful of resolute men in whom the force of the spirit of the world was concentrated. The triumph of the Greeks was the triumph of the spirit, of the intellect of man, of light dispersing darkness, of energy repelling a dead weight of matter. Other nations have shown a temper as heroic as the Greeks. The Dutch, for instance, in their resistance against Philip, or the Swiss in their antagonism to Burgundy and Austria. But in no other single instance has heroism been exerted on so large a scale, in such a fateful struggle for the benefit of mankind at large. Had the Dutch, for example, been quelled by Spain, or the Swiss been crushed by the House of Hapsburg, the world could have survived the loss of these athletic nations. There were other mighty peoples, who held the torch of liberty and of the spirit, and who were ready to carry it onward in the race. But if Persia had overwhelmed the Greeks upon the plains of Marathon or in the straits of Salamis, that torch of spiritual liberty would have been extinguished. There was no runner in the race to catch it up from the dying hands of Hellas, and to bear it forward for the future age. No : this contest of the Greeks with Persia was the one supreme battle of history ; and to the triumph of the Greeks we owe whatever is most great and glorious in the subsequent achievements of the human race.

Supremacy of Athens.

Athens rose to her full height in this duel. She bore the brunt of Marathon alone. Her generals decided the sea-fight of Salamis. For the Spartans it remained to defeat Mardonius at Platæa. Consequently the olive-wreath of this more than Olympian victory crowned Athens. Athens was recognised as Saviour and Queen of Hellas. And Athens, who had fought the battle of the Spirit—by Spirit we mean the greatness of the soul, liberty, intelligence, civilisation, culture, everything which raises men above brutes and slaves, and makes them free beneath the arch of heaven—Athens who had fought and won this battle of the Spirit, became immediately the recognised impersonation of the Spirit itself. Whatever was superb in human nature found its natural home and sphere in Athens. We hear no more of the colonies. All great works of Art and Literature now are produced in Athens. It is to Athens that the sages come to teach and to be taught. Anaxagoras, Socrates, Plato, the three masters of philosophy in this third period, are Athenians. It is, however, noticeable and significant that Anaxagoras, who forms a link between the philosophy of the second and third period, is a native of Clazomenæ, though the thirty years of his active life are spent at Athens. These thinkers introduce into speculation a new element. Instead of inquiries into the factors of the physical world or of ontological theorising, they approach all problems which involve the activities of the human soul, the presence in the universe of a controlling Spirit. Anaxagoras issues the famous apophthegm, νοῦς πάντων κρατεῖ: "intelligence disposes all things in the world." Socrates founds his ethical investigation upon the Delphian precept, γνῶθι σεαυτόν: or, "the proper study of mankind is man." Plato, who belongs chronologically to the fourth period, but who may here be mentioned in connection with the great men of the third, as synthesising all the previous speculations of the Greeks, ascends to the conception of an ideal existence which unites Truth, Beauty, and Goodness in one scheme of universal order.

At the same time Greek art rises to its height of full maturity. Ictinus designs the Parthenon, and Mnesicles the Propylæa; Pheidias completes the development of Sculpture in his statue of Athene, his pediment and friezes of the Parthenon, his chryselephantine image of Zeus at Olympia, his marble Nemesis upon the plain of Marathon. These were

Architecture and Sculpture.

the ultimate, consummate achievements of the sculptor's skill; the absolute standards of what the statuary in Greece could do. Nothing remained to be added. Subsequent progression——for a progression there was in the work of Praxiteles — was a deflection from the pure and perfect type.

Rise of the Drama.

Poetry, in the same way, receives incomparable treatment at the hands of the great dramatists. As the Epic of Homer contained implicitly all forms of poetry, so did the Athenian Drama consciously unite them in one supreme work of art. The energies aroused by the Persian war had made action and the delineation of action of prime importance to the Greeks. We no longer find the poets giving expression to merely personal feeling, or uttering wise saws and moral precepts, as in the second period. Human emotion is indeed their theme; but it is the phases of passion in living, acting, and conflicting personalities which the Drama undertakes to depict. Ethical philosophy is more than ever substantive in verse; but its lessons are set forth by example and not by precept—they animate the conduct of whole trilogies. The awakened activity of Hellas at this period produced the first great drama of Europe, as the Reformation in England produced the second. The Greek Drama being essentially religious, the tragedians ascended to Mythology for their materials. Homer is dismembered, and his episodes or allusions, together with the substance of the Cyclic poems, supply the dramatist with plots. But notice the difference between Homer and Æschylus, the Epic and the Drama. In the latter we find no merely external delineation of mythical history. The legends are used as outlines to be filled in with living and eternally important details. The heroes are not interesting merely as heroes, but as the types and patterns of human nature, as representatives on a gigantic scale of that humanity which is common to all men in all ages, and as subject to the destinies which control all human affairs.

Mythology has thus become the text-book of life, interpreted by the philosophical consciousness. With the names of Æschylus, Sophocles, Euripides, must be coupled that of Aristophanes. His Comedy is a peculiarly Athenian product —the strongest mixture of paradox and irony and broad buffoonery and splendid poetry, designed to serve a serious aim, the world has ever seen. Here the many-sided, flashing genius of the Ionian race appears in all its subtlety, variety, suppleness, and strength. The free spirit of Athens runs riot and proclaims its liberty by license in the prodigious saturnalia of the wit of Aristophanes.

It remains to be added that to this period belong the histories of Herodotus, the Halicarnassean by birth, who went to Thurii as colonist from Athens, and of Thucydides, the Athenian general; the lyrics of Pindar the Theban, who was made the public guest of Athens; the eloquence of Pericles, and the wit of Aspasia. This brief enumeration suffices to show that in the third period of Greek Literature was contained whatever is most splendid in the achievements of the genius of the Greeks, and that all these triumphs converged and were centred upon Athens. *History.*

The public events of this period are summed up in the struggle for supremacy between Athens and Sparta. The race which had shown itself capable of united action against the common foe, now develops within itself two antagonistic and mutually exclusive principles. The age of the despots is past. The flowering-time of the colonies is over. The stone of Tantalus in Persia has been removed from Hellas. But it remains for Sparta and Athens to fight out the duel of Dorian against Ionian prejudices, of Oligarchy against Democracy. Both states have received their definite stamp, or permanent $\mathring{\eta}\theta o\varsigma$—Sparta from semi-mythical Lycurgus; Athens from Solon, Cleisthenes, and Pericles. Their war is the warfare of the powers of the land with the powers of the sea, of Conservatives with Liberals, of the rigid principle *Struggle between Athens and Sparta.*

of established order with the expansive spirit of intellectual and artistic freedom. What is called the Peloponnesian war—that internecine struggle of the Greeks—is the historical outcome of this deep-seated antagonism. And the greatest historical narrative in the world, that of Thucydides, is its record. To dwell upon the events of this war would be superfluous. Athens uniformly exhibits herself as a dazzling, brilliant, impatient power, led astray by the desire of novelty, and the intoxicating sense of force in freedom. Sparta proceeds slowly, coldly, cautiously; secures her steps; acts on the defensive; spends no strength in vain; is timid, tentative, and economical of energy; but at the decisive moment she steps in and crushes her antagonist. Deluded by the wandering fire of the inspiration of Alcibiades, the Athenians venture to abandon the policy of Pericles and to contemplate the conquest of Syracuse. A dream of gigantic empire, in harmony with their expansive spirit, but inconsistent with the very conditions of vitality in a Greek state, floated before their imaginations. In attempting to execute it, they over-reached themselves and fell a prey to Sparta. With the fall of Athens, faded the real beauty and grandeur of Greece. Athens had incarnated that ideal of loveliness and sublimity. During her days of prosperity she had expressed it in superb works of art and literature, and in the splendid life of a free people governed solely by their own intelligence. Sparta was strong to destroy this life, to extinguish this light of culture. But to do more she had no strength. Stiffened in her narrow rules of discipline, she was utterly unable to sustain the spiritual vitality of Hellas, or to carry its still vigorous energy into new spheres. It remained for aliens to accomplish this.

Pericles.   Just before passing to the fourth period of comparative decline, we may halt a moment to contemplate the man who represents this age of full maturity. Pericles, called half in derision by the comic poets the Zeus of Athens, called after-

wards, with reverence, by Plutarch, the Olympian—Pericles
expresses in himself the spirit of this age.   He is the typical
Athenian, who governed Athens during the years in which
Athens governed Greece, who formed the taste of the
Athenians at the time when they were educating the world
by the production of immortal works of beauty.   We have
seen that the conquest of the Persians was the triumph of
the spirit, and that after this conquest the spirit of humanity
found itself for the first time absolutely and consciously free
in Athens.   This spirit was, so to speak, incarnated in Pericles.
The Greek genius was made flesh in him, and dwelt at Athens.
In obedience to its dictates, he extended the political liberties
of the Athenians to the utmost, while he controlled those
liberties with the laws of his own reason.   In obedience to
the same spirit, he expended the treasures of the Ionian
League upon the public works, which formed the subsequent
glory of Hellas, and made her august even in humiliation.
" That," says Plutarch, " which now is Greece's only evidence
that the power she boasts of and her ancient wealth are no
romance or idle story, was his construction of the public and
sacred buildings."   It was, again, by the same inspiration that
Pericles divined the true ideal of the Athenian commonwealth.
In the Funeral Oration he says : " We love the beautiful, but
without ostentation or extravagance ; we philosophise without
being seduced into effeminacy ; we are bold and daring ; but
this energy in action does not prevent us from giving to ourselves a strict account of what we undertake.   Among other
nations, on the contrary, martial courage has its foundation
in deficiency of culture ; we know best how to distinguish
between the agreeable and the irksome ; notwithstanding
which we do not shrink from perils."   In this panegyric of
the national character, Pericles has rightly expressed the real
spirit of Athens as distinguished from Sparta.   The courage
and activity of the Athenians were the result of open-eyed
wisdom, and not of mere gymnastic training.   Athens knew

that the arts of life and the pleasures of the intellect were superior to merely physical exercises, to drill, and to discipline.

Anaxagoras.   While fixing our thoughts upon Pericles as the exponent of the mature spirit of free Hellas, we owe some attention to his master, the great Anaxagoras, who first made Reason play the chief part in the scheme of the universe.   Of the relations of Anaxagoras to his pupil Pericles, this is what Plutarch tells us : " He that saw most of Pericles, and furnished him most especially with a weight and grandeur of sense, superior to all arts of popularity, and in general gave him his elevation and sublimity of purpose and of character, was Anaxagoras of Clazomenæ, whom the men of those times called by the name of Nous, that is, mind or intelligence ; whether in admiration of the great and extraordinary gift he displayed for the science of nature, or because he was the first of the philosophers who did not refer the first ordering of the world to fortune or chance, nor to necessity or compulsion, but to a pure, unadulterated intelligence, which in all other existing mixed and compound things acts as a principle of discrimination, and of combination of like with like."   Thus we may say, without mysticism, that at the very moment in history when the intelligence of mankind attained to freedom, there arose a philosopher in Anaxagoras to proclaim the freedom and absolute supremacy of intelligence in the universe ; and a ruler in Pericles to carry into action the laws of that intelligence, and to govern the most uncontrollably free of nations by Reason.   When Pericles died, Athens lost her Zeus, her head, her real king.   She was left a prey to parties, to demagogues, to the cold encroaching policy of Sparta.   But Pericles had lived long enough to secure the immortality of what was greatest in his city, to make of Athens in her beauty " a joy for ever."

Fall of Athens.   " If the army of Nicias had not been defeated under the walls of Syracuse ; if the Athenians had, acquiring Sicily, held the balance between Rome and Carthage, sent garrisons to the

Greek colonies in the south of Italy, Rome might have been all that its intellectual condition entitled it to be, a tributary, not the conqueror, of Greece; the Macedonian power would never have attained to the dictatorship of the civilised states of the world." Such is the exclamation of Shelley over the fall of Athens. But, according to the Greek proverb, to desire impossibilities—in the past as in the present—is a sickness of the soul. No Greek state could have maintained its ἦθος (specific character in customs, institutions, and political temperament) while it ruled a foreign empire; nor is the right to govern measured by merely intellectual capacity. The work of Greece was essentially spiritual and not political. The chief sign of weakness which meets us in the fourth period is in the region of politics. After the humiliation of Athens, Sparta assumed the leadership of Greece. But she shamefully misused her power by betraying the Greek cities of Asia to the Persians, while her generals and harmosts made use of their authority for the indulgence of their private vices. Nothing in the previous training of the Spartan race fitted them for the control of nations with whose more liberal institutions and refined manners they could not sympathise. Their tyranny proved insupportable, and was at last reduced to the dust by the Thebans under Pelopidas and Epaminondas. But Thebes had neither the wealth nor the vigour to administer the government of Hellas. Therefore the Greek states fell into a chaos of discord, without leadership, without a generous spirit of mutual confidence and aid; while at the same time the power of the Macedonian kingdom was rapidly increasing under the control of Philip. An occasion offered itself to Philip for interfering in the Greek affairs. From that moment forward for ever the cities of Greece became the fiefs of foreign despots. The occasion in question was a great one. The Phocians had plundered the Delphian temple, and none of the Greeks were strong enough to punish them. The act of the Phocians was parricidal in its sacrilege, suicidal in short-sightedness.

Sparta, Thebes, Macedon.

Defiling the altar of the ancestral god, on whose oracles the
states had hitherto depended for counsel, and destroying, with
the sanctity of Delphi, the sacred symbol of Greek national
existence, they abandoned themselves to desecration and dishonour.   With as little impunity could a king of Judah have
robbed the temple and invaded the Holiest of Holies.   But
neither Spartans, nor Athenians, nor yet Thebans arose to
avenge the affront offered to their common nationality.   The
whole of Greece proper lay paralysed, and the foreigner
stepped in—Philip, whom in their pride they had hitherto
called the Barbarian.   He took up the cause of Phœbus and
punished the children of the Delphian god for their impiety.
It was clearly proved to the states of Hellas that their independence was at an end.   They submitted.   Greece became the
passive spectator of the deeds of Macedonia.   Hellas, who had
been the hero, was now the chorus.   It was Alexander of
Macedon who played the part of Achilles in her future drama.

Demos-
thenes.

One man vindicated the spirit of Greek freedom against this
despotism.   The genius of Athens, militant once more, but
destined not to triumph, incarnates itself in Demosthenes.
By dint of eloquence and weight of character he strives to
stem the tide of dissolution.   But it is in vain.   His orations
remain as the monuments of a valiant but ineffectual resistance.   The old intelligence of Athens shines, nay, fulminates,
in these tremendous periods; but it is no longer intelligence
combined with power.   The sceptre of empire has passed from
the hands of the Athenians.

Alexander
the Great.

Still, though the states of Greece are humiliated, though we
hear no more of Ionians and Dorians, but only of Macedonians,
yet the real force of the Greek race is by no means exhausted
in this fourth period.   On the contrary, their practical work
in the world is just beginning.   Under the guidance of
Alexander, the Greek spirit conquers and attempts to civilise
the East.   The parallel between Alexander and Achilles, as
before hinted, is more than accidental.   Trained in the study

of Homer as we are in the study of the Bible, he compared his
destinies with those of the great hero, and formed himself
upon the type of Pelides. At Troy he pays peculiar reverence
to the tomb of Patroclus. He celebrates Hephæstion's death
with Homeric games and pyres up-piled to heaven. He carries
Homer with him on war-marches, and consults the *Iliad* on
occasions of doubt. Alexander's purpose was to fight out to
the end the fight begun by Achilles between West and East,
and to avenge Greece for the injuries of Asia. But it was
not a merely military conquest which he executed. Battles
were the means to higher ends. Alexander sought to subject
the world to the Greek spirit, to stamp the customs, the
thoughts, the language, and the culture of the Greeks upon
surrounding nations. Poets and philosophers accompanied his
armies. In the deserts of Bactria and Syria and Libya he
founded Greek cities. During the few years of his short life
he not only swept those continents, but he effaced the past and
inaugurated a new state of things throughout them ; so that, in
subsequent years, when the Romans, themselves refined by
contact with the Greeks, advanced to take possession of those
territories, they found their work half done. The alchemising
touch of the Greek genius had transformed languages, cities,
constitutions, customs, nay, religions also, to its own likeness.
This fourth period, a period of transition from maturity to
decay, is the period of Alexander. In it the Greek spirit,
which had been gathering strength through so many generations,
poured itself abroad over the world. What it lost in intensity
and splendour, it gained in extension. It was impossible even
for Greeks, while thus impressing their civilisation on the whole
earth, to go on increasing in the beauty of their life and art at
home.

Some of the greatest names in Art, Philosophy, and Liter- Aristotle.
ature still belong to this fourth period. The chief of all is
Aristotle, *il maestro di color che sanno*, "the master of those who
know," the absorber of all previous and contemporary know-

ledge into one coherent system, the legislator for the human intellect through eighteen centuries after his death. It is worth observing that Aristotle, unlike Socrates and Plato, is not a citizen of Athens, but of the small Thracian town Stageira. Thus, at the moment when philosophy lost its essentially Hellenic character and became cosmopolitan in Aristotle, the mantle devolved upon an alien. Again Aristotle was the tutor of Alexander. The two greatest men of the fourth period are thus brought into the closest relations. In pure literature the most eminent productions of this period are the orations of Æschines, Demosthenes, Isocrates ; and the comedies of Menander. It is not a little significant that we should have retained no authentic fragment of the speeches of Pericles—except in so far as we may trust Thucydides,—while the studied Rhetoric of these politically far less important orators should have been so copiously preserved. The reign of mere talk was imminent. Oratory was coming to be studied as an art, and practised, not as a potent instrument in politics, but as an end in itself. Men were beginning to think more of how they spoke than of what they might achieve by speaking. Besides, the whole Athenian nation, as dikasts and as ecclesiasts, were interested in Rhetoric. The first masters of eloquence considered as a fine art were therefore idolised. Demosthenes, Æschines, Isocrates, combined the fire of vehement partisans and impassioned politicians with the consummate skill of professional speech-makers. After their days Rhetoric in Greece became a matter of frigid display—an ἀγώνισμα ἐς τὸ παράχρημα (off-hand declamation). In the comedies of Menander, as far as we may judge of them from fragments and critiques, and from their Latin copies, a very noticeable change in the spirit of literature is apparent. The so-called New Comedy, of which he was the representative, is the product of a meditative and inactive age. The great concerns of the world, and of human life seen in its profoundest depth, which formed the staple of Aristophanes, have been

Orators and Rhetoricians.

abandoned.   We are brought close to domesticities: the
events of common life occupy the stage of Menander.   The
audience of Aristophanes listened with avidity to comedies of
which politics upon the grandest scale were the substance.
Menander invited his Athenians to the intrigues of young
men, slaves, and hetairai, at warfare with niggardly parents.
Athens has ceased to be an empress.   She has become a
garrulous housewife.   She contents herself with amusements,—
still splendid with intelligence and dignified with wisdom, but
not weighty with the consciousness of power, nor throbbing
with the pulses of superabundant youthfulness and vigour.

In the Fine Arts this fourth period was still inventive. *Painting and Sculpture.*
Under Alexander painting, which had received its Hellenic
character from Polygnotus and Zeuxis, continued to flourish
with Apelles.   Indeed, it may be fairly said that while Art in
the Heroic period was confined to the perfecting of the human
body, in the second period it produced Architecture, in the
third Sculpture, and in the fourth Painting—this being apparently the natural order of progression in the evolution of
the fine arts.   Lysippus, meanwhile, worthily represents the
craft of the statuary in Alexander's age; while the coins and
gems of this time show that the glyptic and numismatic arts
were at their zenith of technical perfection.   Of Greek Music,
in the absence of all sure information, it is difficult to speak.
Yet it is probable that the age of Alexander witnessed a new
and more complex development of orchestral music.   We
hear of vast symphonies performed at the Macedonian court.
Nor is this inconsistent with what we know about the history
of Art: for music attains independence, ceases to be the
handmaid of Poetry or Dancing, only in an age of intellectual
reflectiveness.   When nations have expressed themselves in
the more obvious and external arts, they seek through harmonies and melodies to give form to their emotions.

The fifth, last, and longest period is one of Decline and *Decadence of Hellas.*
Decay.   But these words must be used with qualification when

we speak of a people like the Greeks. What is meant is that the Greeks never recovered their national vigour or produced men so great as those whom we have hitherto been mentioning. The Macedonian empire prepared the way for the Roman : Hellenic civilisation put on the garb of servitude to Rome and to Christianity. Henceforth we must not look to Greece proper for the more eminent achievements of the still surviving spirit of the Greeks. Greek culture in its decadence has become the heritage of the whole world. Syrians, Egyptians, Phrygians, Romans, carry on the tradition inherited from Athens. Hellas is less a nation now than an intellectual commonwealth, a society of culture holding various races in communion. The spiritual republic established thus by the Greek genius prepares the way for Christian brotherhood ; the liberty of the children of the Muses leads onward to the freedom of the sons of God.

Alexandrian age.

In this period, the chief centres are first Alexandria and Athens, then Rome and Byzantium. The real successors of Alexander were his generals. But the only dynasty founded by them which rises into eminence by its protection of the arts and literature was the Ptolemaic. At Alexandria, under the Ptolemies, libraries were formed and sciences were studied. Euclid the geometer, Aratus the astronomer, Ptolemy the cosmographer, add lustre to the golden age of Alexandrian culture. Callimachus at the same time leads a tribe of learned poets and erudite men of letters. Dramas meant to be read, like Lycophron's *Cassandra ;* epics composed in the study, like the *Argonautica* of Apollonius Rhodius, form the diversion of the educated world. Meanwhile the whole genus of parasitic *littérateurs* begin to flourish : grammarians, who settle and elucidate texts with infinite labour and some skill ; sophists and rhetoricians, whose purpose in life it is to adorn imaginary subjects and to defend problematical theses with conceits of the fancy and ingenious subtleties of reasoning. A young man writing to his mistress, a dinner-seeker who has failed to get an invitation, Themistocles at the Persian court, celebrated statues, philosophical puzzles—everything that can be wordily elaborated, is grist for their mill. The art of writing without having anything particular to say, the sister art of quarrying the thoughts of other people and setting them in elaborate prolixities of style, are brought to perfection. At the same time, side by side with these literary moths and woodlice, are the more industrious ants,—the collectors of anecdotes, compilers of biographies, recorders of quotations, composers of all sorts of commonplace books, students of the paste-brush and scissors sort, to whom we owe much for the preservation of scraps of otherwise lost treasures. Into such mechanical and frigid channels has the life of literature passed. Literature is no longer an integral part of the national exist-ence, but a form of polite amusement. The genius of Hellas has nothing better to do than to potter about like a dilettante among her treasures.

The only true poets of this period are the Sicilian Idyllists. Idyllists. Over the waning day of Greek poetry Theocritus, Bion, and Moschus cast the sunset hues of their excessive beauty. Genuine and exquisite is their inspiration; pure, sincere, and true is their execution. Yet we agree with Shelley, who compares their perfume to "the odour of the tuberose, which overcomes and sickens the spirit with excess of sweetness." In the same way the erotic epigrammatists, though many of them genuine poets, especially the exquisite Meleager of Gadara, in the very perfection of their peculiar quality of genius offer an unmistakable sign of decay. It is the fashion among a certain class of modern critics to rave about the art of Decadence, to praise the hectic hues of consumption and even the strange livors of corruption more than the roses and the lilies of health. Let them peruse the epigrams of Meleager and of Straton. Of beauty in decay sufficient splendours may be found there.

While Alexandria was thus carrying the poetic tradition

of Hellas to its extremity in the Idyll and the Epigram—carving cherrystones after the sculptor's mallet had been laid aside—and was continuing the criticism which had been set on foot by Aristotle, Athens persisted in her function of educating Europe. She remained a sort of university, in which the doctrines of Plato and Aristotle were adequately developed, though not in the most comprehensive spirit, by a crowd of Peripatetic and Academic sages, and where the founders of the Epicurean and Stoic schools gave a new direction to thought. It was during the first vigour of the Epicurean and Stoic teaching that the spirit of Hellas came into contact with the spirit of Rome. Hence Lucretius, Cicero, the Satirists—whatever, in fact, Rome may boast of philosophy, retains the tincture of the ethics of her schoolmasters. Rome, as Virgil proudly said, was called to govern—not to write poems or carve statues—but to quell the proud and spare the abject. Still she caught, to some extent, the æsthetic manners of her captive. Consequently, long after the complete political ascendency of Rome was an established fact, and geographical Greece had become an insignificant province, the Hellenic spirit led the world. And some of its latest products are still dazzling in beauty, marvellous in ingenuity, Titanic in force. A few names selected from the list of Græco-Roman authors will be more impressive than much description. Plutarch of Chæronea, in the first century, the author of the great biographies; Lucian, the Syrian, in the second century, the master of irony and graceful dialogue and delicate description; Epictetus, the Phrygian slave, in the second century, who taught the latest form of Stoicism to the Romans, and had for his successor Marcus Aurelius; Philostratus of Lemnos, the rhetorician and author of the life of Apollonius; Plotinus, Porphyrius, and Proclus, the revivers of Platonic philosophy under a new form of mysticism at Alexandria during the third and fourth centuries; Longinus, the critic, who adorned Palmyra in the third century;

Heliodorus of Emesa, Achilles Tatius, Longus, Musæus, the erotic novelists and poets of the fourth and fifth centuries; these, not to mention the Christian fathers, are a few of the great men whom Greece produced in this last period. But now notice how miscellaneous in nationality and in pursuit they are. One only is a Greek of the old stock—Plutarch, the Bœotian. One is a slave from Phrygia. Another is a Roman Emperor. A fourth is a native of the desert city of Tadmor. Two are Syrians. One is a Greek of the Ægean. Another is an Egyptian. From this we may see how the genius of the Greeks had been spread abroad to embrace all lands. No fact better illustrates the complete leavening of the world by their spirit.

But considering that this fifth period may be said to cover six centuries, from the death of Alexander to about 300 after Christ,—for why should we continue our computation into the dreary regions of Byzantine dulness?—it must be confessed that it is sterile in productiveness and inferior in the quality of its crop to any of the previous periods. Subtle and beautiful is the genius of Hellas still, because it *is* Greek; strong and stérn it is in part, because it has been grafted on the Roman character; its fascinations and compulsions are powerful enough to bend the metaphysics of the Christian faith. Yet, after all, it is but a shadow of its own self. _{Decline of Greek spirit.}

After the end of the fourth century the iconoclastic zeal and piety of the Christians put an end practically to Greek art and literature. Christianity was at that time the superior force in the world; and though Clement of Alexandria contended for an amicable treaty of peace between Greek culture and the new creed, though the two Gregories and Basil were, to use the words of Gibbon, "distinguished above all their contemporaries by the rare union of profane eloquence and orthodox piety," though the Bishops of the Church were selected from the ranks of scholars trained by Libanius and other Greek Sophists, yet the spirit of Christianity proved fatal to the spirit of Greek art. Early in the fifth century the

Christian rabble at Alexandria, under the inspiration of their ferocious despot Cyril, tore in pieces Hypatia, the last incarnation of the dying beauty of the Greeks. She had turned her eye backwards to Homer and to Plato, dreaming that haply even yet the gods of Hellas might assert their power and resume the government of the world, and that the wisdom of Athens might supplant the folly of Jerusalem. But it was a vain and idle dream. The genius of Greece was effete. Christianity was pregnant with the mediæval and the modern world. In violence and bloodshed the Gospel triumphed. This rending in pieces of the past, this breaking down of temples and withering of illusions, was no doubt necessary. New wine cannot be poured into old bottles. No cycle succeeds another cycle in human affairs without convulsions and revolutions that rouse the passions of humanity. It is thus that

> "God fulfils Himself in many ways,
> Lest one good custom should corrupt the world."

Yet even in this last dire struggle of the spirit of Pagan art with the spirit of Christian faith, when Beauty had become an abomination in the eyes of the Holiest, on the ruins, as it were, of the desecrated fanes of Hellas, weeds lovely in their rankness flourished. While Cyril's mobs were dismembering Hypatia, the erotic novelists went on writing about Daphnis, and Musæus sang the lamentable death of Leander. Nonnus was perfecting a new and more polished form of the hexameter. These were the last, the very swan's notes, of Greek poetry. In these faint and too melodious strains the Muse took final farewell of her beloved Hellas. And when, after the lapse of 1000 years, the world awoke upon the ruins of the past, these were among the first melodies which caught its ear. One of the three first Greek books issued from the Aldine press about the year 1493, and called by Aldus the "precursors," was the poem of Hero and Leander. It was reprinted at Paris in

1507 by De Gourmont, at Alcala, in Spain, in 1514, and at Cologne in 1517 by Hirschhorn. Our Marlowe in the sixteenth century translated Musæus. The French Amyot translated Longus, and bequeathed to his nation a voluminous literature of pastorals founded upon the tale of Chloe. Tasso and Guarini, in Italy, caught the same strain ; so that the accents of the modern Renaissance were an echo of the last utterances of dying Greece. The golden age of pastoral innocence, the *bell' età dell' oro*, of which the Alexandrians had been dreaming in the midst of their effete and decaying civilisation, fascinated the imagination of our immediate ancestors, when, four centuries ago, they found the Sun of Art and Beauty shining in the heavens, new worlds to conquer, and indefinite expansions of the spirit to be realised.

CHAPTER II

MYTHOLOGY

The Notion of a Systematic Pantheon—Homer and Hesiod—Mythology before Homer—Supposed Conditions of the Mythopœic Age—Vico—The Childhood of the World—Goethe's Boyhood—Mythology is a Body of Rudimentary Thought, penetrated with the Spirit of the Nation—Different Views of the Greek Myths—Grote—Relics of a Primitive Revelation—The Symbolic Hypothesis—Rationalism and Euemerus—Fetishism—Poetic Theory—The Linguistic Theory—Comparative Philology—Solar Theory—The Myth of Herakles—Its Solar Interpretation—Its Ethical Significance—Summary of the Points suggested with regard to Mythology—Mediæval Myths—The Action of the Greek Intelligence upon Mythology—In Art—In Philosophy—Persistence of the National Polytheism—Homer Allegorised at Alexandria—Triumph of Christianity—The Greek Pantheon in the Middle Ages—Greek Mythology recovers Poetic and Artistic Value in the Renaissance.

The Greek Pantheon.

IT has been remarked with justice that, when we use the word Mythology, we are too apt to think of a Pantheon, of a well-defined hierarchy of gods, and demigods, and heroes, all fabulous indeed, but all arranged in one coherent system. This conception of Greek Mythology arises partly from the fact that we learn to know it in dictionaries, compiled from the works of authors who lived long after the age in which myths were produced, and partly from the fact that the conditions under which myth-making was a possibility are so far removed from us as to be almost unintelligible. Yet there is some truth in what, upon the whole, is an erroneous view. Although the Greek myths, in their origin, were not a well-digested system, still they formed a complete body of national thought, on which the intelligence of the Greek race, in its art and its religion, was continually working, until it took the final form in which we have it in our dictionaries. What remained in the Pantheon of Apollodorus and Hyginus, remained there by no freak of accident. What was omitted by Homer and by Hesiod was omitted by no operation of blind chance. The spirit of the Greeks was concerned in the purification and the preservation of their myths, and the unity of that spirit constitutes the unity of their mythology.

Two great poets gave to Greek mythology the form which it maintained in the historic period. Herodotus says that "Homer and Hesiod named the gods, and settled their genealogies for the Hellenes." What this means is, that at a certain prehistoric epoch, the epoch of Epic poetry, mythology had passed from the primitive and fluid state, and had become the subject-matter of the arts. Between the mythopœic liberty of creation and the collections of the grammarians was interposed the poetry, the sculpture, and the religious ritual of the historic Greeks. What we have to deal with at the present moment is, not mythology as it appears in art, but the genesis of the myths conceived as a body of Greek thought and fancy in their infantine or rudimentary stages. *Homer and Hesiod.*

What was mythology before Homer? How did it come into existence? How were the Greeks brought to believe that there was a supreme father of gods and men called Zeus, a wise patroness of arts and sciences called Pallas, a pure and glorious and far-darting deity called Phœbus? There is no one who does not acknowledge something sublime and beautiful in this part of the Greek mythology. Even those who do not care to comprehend the growth of these conceptions, admit that the genius of the race shone with splendour peculiar to itself in their creation. *The myths before Homer's time.*

To this question must be counterpoised another. What are we to think about the many repulsive, grotesque, and hideous

Indecent
myths.

elements of Greek mythology—the incest and adultery of Zeus,
the cannibalism of Cronos, the profligacy of Aphrodite, the
cruelty of Phœbus? When thought began to be conscious
of itself in Greece these abominations moved the anger of
the philosophers. Xenophanes, Heraclitus, Pythagoras, Pindar,
and Plato, in succession, recognised that the mythical fables
were incompatible with the notion of deity, and rejected them
forthwith. Modern students have been so disgusted by the
same indecencies that some of them have abandoned Greek
mythology as hopeless, while others have taken refuge in
the extraordinary paradox that myths are a disease of language. These methods of dealing with the problem are alike
unphilosophical. It is impossible for the historian to
reject what formed the groundwork of religious and artistic
thought in Greece. It is childish to represent the human
mind as a sort of bound Mazeppa, stretched helpless on
the wild horse, Language, which carries it away into the
wilderness.

Mythopœic
imagination.

In order to understand the two questions which have been
propounded, we must make a demand upon our imagination,
and endeavour to return, in thought at least, to the conditions
of a people in the mythopœic age—the age, that is to say, in
which not only were myths naturally made, but all the thinking of a nation took the form of myths. We must go back to
a time when there were no written records, when there were
no systems of thought, when language had not been subjected
to analysis of any kind, when abstract notions were unknown,
when science had not begun to exist, when history was impossible, and when the whole world was a land of miracles.
There was no check then laid upon fancy, because nothing as
yet was conceived as thought, but everything existed as sensation. In this infancy the nation told itself stories, and believed
in them. The same faculties of the mind which afterwards
gave birth to poetry and theology, philosophy and statecraft,
science and history, were now so ill-defined and merely germinal

that they produced but fables. Yet these faculties were vigorous and vivid. The fables they produced were infinite in number and variety, beautiful, and so pregnant with thought under the guise of fancy that long centuries scarcely sufficed for disengaging all that they contained. In dealing with Greek mythology it must be remembered that the nation with whose mythopœic imagination we are concerned, was the Greek nation. It had already in itself all Hellas, as the seed enfolds the plant.

A famous passage in Vico's work *Della Metafisica Poetica* may here be paraphrased, in order to make the conditions under which we must imagine myths to have arisen more intelligible:[1] "Poetry, which was the first form of wisdom, began with a system of thought, not reasoned or abstract, as ours is now, but felt and imagined, as was natural in the case of those primitive human beings who had developed no reasoning faculties, but were all made up of senses in the highest physical perfection, and of the most vigorous imaginations. In their total ignorance of causes they wondered at everything; and their poetry was all divine, because they ascribed to gods the objects of their wonder, and thought that beings like themselves but greater could alone have caused them. Thus they were like children, whom we notice taking into their hands inanimate things, and playing and talking with them as though they were living persons. When thunder terrified them, they attributed their own nature to the phenomenon; and, being apt to express their most violent passions by howls and roarings, they conceived heaven as a vast body, which gave notice of its anger by lightnings and thunderings. The whole of nature, in like manner, they imagined to be a vast animated body, capable of feeling and passion." Vicò then proceeds to point out how difficult it is for us who, through long centuries, have removed ourselves as far as possible from the life of the instincts, senses, and imagination, whose language has become

Vico's theory of myths.

[1] The original is quoted in the notes to Grote, vol. i. p. 474.

full of abstract terms, whose conception of the universe has been formed by science, whose thought is critical and reflective, and who have been educated in a rational theology, to comprehend the attitude of primitive humanity in its personifying stage of thought.

The childhood of humanity.

In this childhood of the world, when the Greek myths came into existence, the sun was called a shepherd, and the clouds were his sheep; or an archer, and the sunbeams were his arrows.   It was easier then to think of the sea as a husky-voiced and turbulent old man, whose true form none might clearly know, because he changed so often and was so secret in his ways, who shook the earth in his anger, and had the white-maned billows of the deep for horses, than to form a theory of the tides.   The spring of the year became a beautiful youth, beloved by the whole earth, or beloved like Hyacinthus by the sun, or like Adonis by the queen of beauty, over whom the fate of death was suspended, and for whose loss annual mourning was made.   Such tales the Greeks told themselves in their youth; and it would be wrong to suppose that deliberate fiction played any part in their creation.   To conceive of the world thus was natural to the whole race; and the tales that sprang up formed the substance of their intellectual activity.   Here, then, if anywhere, we watch the process of a people in its entirety contributing to form a body of imaginative thought, projecting itself in a common and unconscious work of art.   Nor will it avail to demur that behind the Greeks there stretched a dim and distant past, that many of their myths had already taken shape to some extent before the separation of the Aryan families.   That is now an ascertained fact, the bearings of which will have to be discussed further on in this chapter.   For the moment it is enough to reply that, not the similarities, but the differences, brought to light by the study of comparative mythology, are important for the historian of each several race.   The raw material of silk may interest the merchant or the man of

science; the artist cares for the manufactured fabric, with its
curious patterns and refulgent hues.

In order further to illustrate the conditions of the mytho-   Goethe's
pœic age, a passage from the *Dichtung und Wahrheit* of Goethe   boyhood.
might be quoted. If it is not a mere fancy to suppose that
the individual lives, to some extent at least, in his own self
the life of humanity, and therefore to conclude that the childhood of the world can be mirrored in the childhood of a man,
a poet like Goethe is precisely fitted, by the record of his
own boyhood, to throw light upon the early operations of
the human mind. For, in one sense of the term, the mythopœic faculty never dies with poets; in their own persons they
prolong the youth and adolescence of the race, retaining the
faculty, now lost to nearly all, of looking on the universe as
living. Goethe, then, relates that when he was at school at
Frankfort, he used to invent stories about himself and the
places he frequented, half consciously, and half by a spon-
taneous working of his fancy. These stories he told to his
schoolfellows so vividly that they accepted them as fact. "It
greatly rejoiced them," he says, "to know that such wonderful things could befall one of their own playmates; nor was
it any harm that they did not understand how I could find
time and space for such adventures, as they must have been
pretty well aware of all my comings and goings, and how I
was occupied the whole day." He goes on to recount one of
these marvellous narratives. The scene of it was laid in
Frankfort, in a street familiar to his schoolfellows. Down
this street, which had a long blank wall surmounted by trees,
he supposed himself to have been walking one day, and to
have found a door in the wall, not noticed by him on any
previous occasion. His curiosity being aroused, he knocked
at the door, and after some delay was admitted. Inside he
found a garden full of wonders, fountains, and fair nymphs,
exotic shrubs, and quaint old men, magicians, knights, sylphs,
and all the proper furniture of a romance. Goethe's comrades,

the first time that they heard him describe this enchanted pleasure-ground in glowing terms, already more than half believed in its existence; "and," says the poet, "each of them visited alone the place, without confiding it to me or to the others, and discovered the nut-trees," but none found the door. Still, they did not disbelieve what Goethe told them, but preferred to imagine that the magic door had once at least been seen by him, and opened for him only, though it remained invisible and closed for them. And herein they were literally right, for Goethe trod an enchanted ground of poetry which few can hope to win. The story proved so fascinating that he had to tell it over and over again, always repeating the same order of events, until, he says, "by the uniformity of the narrative I converted the fable into truth in the minds of my hearers."

How myths arose.

This, then, may be used as an illustration of the mythopœic faculty. All that was needed for the growth of myths was imagination on the one side and receptive fancy on the other. It did not, probably, require a Goethe to make a myth, though we may still believe that the greatest and best myths owed their form to the intervention at some period of unknown and unacknowledged Goethes. When the logical faculty was in abeyance, when the critical faculty had not been aroused, when sympathy was quick, language fertile, fancy exuberant, and belief sincere, there was nothing to check mythopoetry. The nation had to make the step from boyhood to adolescence before the impulse ceased; nor was there any education from without in a fixed body of systematised knowledge to coerce its freedom. Forming the first activity of the intellect, it held in solution, as it were, the rudiments of religion and morality, of psychological reflection, of politics, geography, and history. Had there been any one to ask the myth-maker: Who told you this strange tale? what is your authority for imposing it upon us? he would have answered: The goddess told me, the divine daughter of

memory, as I walked alone. And this he would sincerely and
conscientiously have believed; and those who heard him
would have given credence to his words; and thus his
intuitions became their intuitions. Creative faculty and credence, insight and sympathy, two forms of the same as yet
scarcely divided operation of the mind, gave permanence to
myths. What the fathers received they transmitted to their
sons. Successive generations dealt freely with them, moulding and remodelling, within the limits set upon the genius of
the race. Hundreds may have been produced simultaneously,
and among them must have raged a fierce struggle for existence, so that multitudes perished or were hopelessly defaced,
just as in the animal and vegetable kingdom whole species
disappear or survive only in fragments and fossils.

It cannot be too often repeated that the power which
presided over the transmission of the myths was the spirit of
the people : an inherent selective instinct in the nation determined which of them should ultimately survive; and thus a
body of legend, truly national, was formed, in which the
nation saw itself reflected. When, therefore, we say that
Greek Mythology is Hellenic and original, we are admitting
this unconscious, silent, steady, irresistible faculty of the mind
to fashion gods in its own image, to come to a knowledge of
itself in its divinities, to create a glorified likeness of all that it
admires in its own nature, to deify its truest and its best, and to
invest its thought with an imperishable form of art. Nor will
it here again avail to demur that Zeus was originally the open
sky, Pallas the dawn, Phœbus and Artemis the sun and moon.
The student of the Greeks accepts this information placidly
and gratefully from the philologer; but he passes immediately
beyond it. For him Zeus, Pallas, Phœbus, Artemis are no
longer any more the sky and dawn, the sun and moon.
Whatever their origin may have been, the very mythopœic
process placed them in quite a different and more important
relation to Greek thought when it handed them over to

National
genius.

Hesiod and Homer, to Pindar and Æschylus, to Pheidias and Polygnotus.

Conditions of early thought.

To discuss the bearings of the linguistic and solar theories of mythology may be reserved for another part of this chapter. It is enough, at this point, to bear in mind that there was nothing in the consciousness of the prehistoric Greeks which did not take the form of myth. Consequently their mythology, instead of being a compact system of polytheism, is really a whole mass of thought, belonging to a particular period of human history, when it was impossible to think except by pictures, or to record impressions of the world except in stories. That all these tales are religious or semi-religious—concerned, that is to say, with deities—must be explained by the tendency of mankind at an early period of culture to conceive the powers of nature as persons, and to dignify them with super-human attributes. To the apprehension of infantine humanity everything is a god. Viewed even as a Pantheon, reduced to rule and order by subsequent reflection, Greek Mythology is, therefore, a mass of the most heterogeneous materials. Side by side with some of the sublimest and most beautiful conceptions which the mind has ever produced, we find in it much that is absurd and trivial and revolting. Different ages and conditions of thought have left their products embedded in its strange conglomerate. While it contains fragments of fossilised stories, the meaning of which has either been misunderstood or can only be explained by reference to barbaric customs, it also contains, emergent from the rest and towering above the rubbish, the serene forms of the Olympians. Those furnish the vital and important elements of Greek mythology. To perfect them was the work of poets and sculptors in the brief, bright, blooming time of Hellas; yet, when we pay these deities homage in the temple of the human spirit, let us not forget that they first received form in the mythopœic age— the age of "the disease of language," as Max Müller whimsically states it.

In order to comprehend a problem so complex as that Complexity approaching it from one point of view, but must sift opinion, of the problem. which is offered by mythology we must not be satisfied with submit our theory to the crucible in more than one experiment, and, after all our labour, be content to find that much remains still unexplained. Therefore, it will not do to accept without further inquiry the general description of the mythopœic faculty which has just been advanced. After examining the various methods which may be adopted for dealing with the myths, and welcoming the light which can be thrown upon the subject from different quarters, it will, perhaps, be possible to return to the original position with a fuller understanding of the problem. If nothing else be gained by this process, it is, at least, useful to be reminded that intricate historical questions cannot be settled by one answer alone ; that a variety of agencies must be admitted ; and that the domination of a favourite hypothesis is prejudicial to the end which serious inquiry has in view.

Regarding the Greek myths in their totality as a thickly- The tufted jungle of inexplicable stories, and presupposing the historian's point of activity of the mythopœic faculty to be a play of irrational view. fancy, it is possible for the political historian to state them as he finds them, and then to pass on and to disregard them. This is, practically speaking, what Grote has done, though the luminous and exhaustive treatment of mythology in his six-teenth chapter proves his complete mastery of the subject from the philosophic point of view. Solely occupied with history, and especially interested in political history, when he has once recognised " the uselessness of digging for a supposed basis of truth " in legends which relate to "a past which was never present," he is justified in leaving them alone. The strong political bias which concentrates attention upon the develop-ment of constitutions and the history of States, while it throws the æsthetic activity of the race into the background, sufficiently accounts for this negative relation to the myths.

Its value for our purpose consists in the recognition that mythology must not be confounded with history.

Theory of primitive revelation.

Another method of dealing with mythology requires a passing notice, and a brief dismissal. It has not unfrequently been suggested at uncritical periods of culture, and by uncritical minds in our own age, that the Greek myths are the degradation of primitive truth revealed to mankind by God. As they are Christians who advance this view, the essential dogmas of Christianity are sought for in the Greek Pantheon. The three persons of the Trinity, the personality of the devil, the Divine Redeemer, and so forth, are read into the sagas of Kronos, and Prometheus, and Phœbus. To bring arguments against a theory so visionary, and so devoid of real historical imagination, would be superfluous. Otherwise it might be questioned how a primitive revelation, after undergoing such complete disintegration and debasement, blossomed forth again into the æsthetical beauty which no one can deny to be the special property of the Greek race. According to the terms of the hypothesis, a primal truth was first degraded, so as to lose its spiritual character; and then, from this corruption of decay, arose a polytheism eminently artistic, which produced works of beauty in their kind unsurpassable, but in their essence diverse from the starting-point of revelation. Moreover, the very dogmas which these visionaries detect in Greek mythology, had a historical development posterior to the formation of the Greek Olympus. It was, for instance, the Greek genius in its old age which gave the substantiality of thought to the doctrine of the Trinity. The only good to be got from the consideration of this vain method is the conviction that a problem like that of Greek mythology must be studied in itself and for itself. Whatever its antecedents may have been, its outgrowth in poetry, philosophy, and sculpture —in other words, its realised or permanent manifestation—is not Christian, and has nothing but general human elements in common with Christianity.

A third hypothesis for the explanation of Greek myths, Theory of symbolism. which used to find much favour with the learned, may be stated thus. Myths were originally invented by priests and sages, in order to convey to the popular mind weighty truths and doctrines which could not be communicated in abstract terms to weak intelligences. Thus, each myth was a dark speech uttered in parables. The first fatal objection to this theory is that it does not fulfil its own conditions. To extract a body of doctrine from the vast majority of the myths is not possible. Moreover, it is an inversion of the natural order to assume that priests and sages in a very early age of culture should have been able to arrive at profound truth, and clever enough to clothe it in parable, and yet that, as the nation grew in mental power, the truths should have been forgotten, and the symbols which expressed them have been taken as truth in and for itself. Without, however, entering into a discussion of this hypothesis in detail, it is enough to point out that it implies the same incapacity for realising the early conditions of society as that which is involved in Locke's and Adam Smith's theory of the Origin of Language. It presupposes fully-developed intelligence, whereas we are concerned precisely with the first and germinal commencement of intelligence. At the same time there is a certain foundation for the symbolic theory. Just in the same way as all language is unconsciously metaphorical, so all myths are parabolical, inasmuch as they involve the operation of thought seeking to express itself externally. The mistake lies in maintaining that the parabolic form was deliberately used in the prehistoric period. Its deliberate employment must rather be confined to the age of self-conscious thinking. Thus the myths by which Plato illustrated his philosophy, the Empedoclean parable of Love and Hate, the Choice of Herakles invented by the sophist Prodicus, are purposely symbolical. It is also worth noticing that, among genuine myths, those which seem to justify this hypothesis are of comparatively late origin, or are immediately concerned with psychological questions—such, for example, as the myths of Cupid and Psyche and of Pandora and Epimetheus.

A fourth way of dealing with mythology is to rationalise it, by assuming that all the marvellous stories told about the gods and heroes had historical foundation in the past. Myths, according to this method, become the reminiscences of actual facts, the biographies of persons, which in course of time have lost their positive truth. In order to recover and reconstitute that truth, it is necessary to reduce them to prose. Thus Hecatæus, who was one of the earliest among the Greeks to attempt this interpretation, declared that Geryon was a king of Epirus, and that Cerberus was a serpent haunting the caverns of Cape Tænarus. Herodotus, in like manner, explained the sacred black dove of Dodona by saying that she was a woman, who came from Egyptian Thebes, and introduced a peculiar cult of Zeus into Hellas. After the same fashion, Python, slain by Phœbus, was supposed to have been a troublesome freebooter. Æolus was changed into a weather-wise seaman, the Centaurs into horsemen, Atlas into an astronomer, Herakles into a strong-limbed knight-errant. It was when the old feeling for the myths had died out among the learned, when physical hypotheses were adopted for the explanation of the heavens and the earth instead of the religious belief in nature-deities, and when prose had usurped on poetry, that this theory was worked into a system. Euemerus, the contemporary of the Macedonian Cassander, wrote a kind of novel in which he made out that all the gods and heroes had once been men. Ennius translated this work into Latin, and the rationalising method was called Euemerism. The hold which it has retained upon the minds of succeeding ages is sufficient to show that it readily approves itself to the understanding. It seems to make everything quite smooth and easy. When, for instance, we read the revolting legend of Pasiphaë we like to fancy that after all she only fell in love

with a captain called Taurus, and that Dædalus was an artful Euemerism.
go-between. Unfortunately, however, there is no guide more
delusive than Euemerism. It destroys the true value of
mythology, considered as the expression of primitive thought
and fancy, reducing it to a mere decayed and weed-grown
ruin of prosaic fact. Plato was right when he refused to
rationalise the myths, and when, by his own use of myths, he
showed their proper nature as the vehicle for thoughts as yet
incapable of more exact expression. At the same time it
would be unphilosophical to deny that real persons and actual
events have supplied in some cases the subject-matter of
mythology. The wanderings of Odysseus, the Trojan War,
the voyage of the Argonauts, the kingdom of Minos, the
achievements of Herakles, have, all of them, the appearance
of dimly-preserved or poetised history. Yet to seek to reconstruct history from them, "to dig for a supposed basis of
truth" in them, is idle. The real thing to bear in mind is
that great men and stirring events must have been remembered
even in the mythopœic age, and that to eliminate them from
the national consciousness would have been impossible. A
nucleus of fact may, therefore, have formed the basis of
certain myths, just as a wire immersed in a solution of salts
will cause the fluid to condense in crystals round it. But, as
in the case just used by way of illustration, we do not see the
wire but the crystals after the process has been finished, so in
mythology it is not the fact but the fancy which attracts our
attention and calls for our consideration. This illustration
might be extended so as to apply to any substratum, linguistic,
solar, symbolical, or other, that may be supposed to underlie
the fancy-fabric of mythology. The truth to be looked for in
myths is psychological, not historical, æsthetic rather than
positive.

In order to make the relation of actuality to imagination Formation
of a pearl.
in the mythopœic process still more intelligible, another
illustration can be drawn from nature. Pearls are said to be

the result of a secretion effused from the pearl-oyster round a
piece of grit or thorn inserted between its flesh and the shell
in which it lives. To the production of the pearl this ex-
traneous object and the irritation which it causes, are both
necessary; yet the pearl is something in itself quite independent of the stimulating substance. Just so the myth, which
corresponds to the pearl, is a secretion of the national imagination which has been roused into activity by something
accidental and exterior.

Fetishistic theory.

It is possible to take a fifth line and to refer mythology to
fetishism. Strictly speaking, fetishism can never explain the
problem of the mythopœic faculty, except in so far as we may
assume it to have formed a necessary stage of human development anterior to polytheism. The term, moreover, is in-
adequate to describe those conditions of savage life, by studying which we come to understand best what myths really are.
Anthropology and comparative folk-lore have cast in recent
years a flood of new light upon the problem under consideration. We now perceive that, at a certain period in the
development of the human race, all nations passed through a
stage of thinking in fables and fancies. There is even a
singular similarity between the myths of peoples so remote
from one another as Aryans and Polynesians. Totemism and
Animism—the sense of kinship with beasts, of close con-
sanguinity with nature—the dim belief, derived perhaps
from dreams, of spirits surviving death on earth—explain
many mythological conceptions. Others are connected with
tribal customs and habits of life peculiar to the savage state.
Again we are enabled to interpret the origin of nature-worship,
and to account for the fact that external objects were regarded
as living sentient beings in the myths. Long before the
philosophers of Ionia conjectured that the stars are fiery
vapours, people fancied they were gods. It has been well
observed that the Greeks never speak of a god *of the* sun, or a
goddess *of the* moon. They worshipped the sun as a god in

Helios, the moon as a goddess in Selene. This direct reference of the mind to natural things as objects of adoration began with savage ways of attributing to them a will and senses, intellect and vital force, analogous to those of men.[1]

According to yet a sixth view the myths are to be considered as nothing more or less than poems. This theory is not, at first sight, very different from that which is involved in the first account given of the mythopœic faculty. It is clear that the stories of Galatea, of Pan and Pitys, of Hesperus and Hymenæus, and, in a deeper sense, perhaps, of Prometheus and Pandora, are pure poems. That is to say, the power which produced them was analogous to the power which we observe in poetic creation at the present day, and which has continued the mythopœic age into the nineteenth century. Yet we should lose a great deal in exactitude and fulness of conception if we identified mythology with poetry. Poetry is conscious of its aim; it demands a fixed form; it knows itself to be an art, and, as an art, to be different from religion and distinguished from history. Now, mythology in its origin was antecedent to all such distinctions, and to all the conscious adaptations of means to ends. Behind the oldest poetry which we possess there looms a background of mythology, substantially existing, already expressed in language, nebulous, potential, containing in itself the germs of all the several productions of the human intellect. The whole intellect is there in embryo; and behind mythology nothing is discoverable but thought and language in the same sphere. Therefore we lose rather than gain by a too strict adherence to what may be termed the poetical hypothesis, although the analogy of poetry, and of poetry alone, places us at the right point of view for comprehending the exercise of the myth-making faculty.

Before completing the circle of inquiry by a return with

Poetic theory.

[1] Mr. Andrew Lang, in his *Myth, Ritual, and Religion*, fully discusses and illustrates this method of interpreting mythology.

fuller knowledge to the point from which we started, it is
necessary to discuss a seventh way of dealing with the problem,
which professes to be alone the truly scientific method. It
may be called the Linguistic theory, since it rests upon
analysis of language, and maintains that mythology is not so
much an independent product of the human mind, expressed
in words, as a morbid phase of language, considered as a
thing apart. Max Müller, who has given currency to this
view in England, states expressly that "Mythology, which
was the bane of the ancient world, is in truth a disease of
language. A mythe means a word, but a word which, from
being a name or an attribute, has been allowed to assume a
more substantial existence;" and again, under mythology "I
include every case in which language assumes an independent
power, and reacts on the mind, instead of being, as it was
intended to be, the mere realisation and outward embodiment
of the mind." The first thing which strikes a student
accustomed to regard mythology as a necessary and important phase in the evolution of thought, when he reads
these definitions, is the assumption that $\mu\hat{v}\theta o\varsigma$ is synonymous
with what we mean by word, instead of including the wider
content of a story told in words. He is thus led to suspect a
theory which contrives to make the problem of mythology
pass for a branch of philology. Nor can he comprehend in
what sense mythology may be called "a disease of language,"
rather than a disease of the mind which uses language. Does
Max Müller mean that language suffered, or that the thinking
subject suffered through the action of the bane? He probably
means the former; but if so, language must be supposed to
live a life apart from thought, triumphing over the freedom
of the human mind, and imposing its figments on the intellect.
Such a belief might seem due partly to a too exclusive study
of language in itself, in the course of which the philologer
comes to regard it as disconnected from thought, and partly
to the neglect of the fact that it is the same human subject

which produces language and myths, that language and thought in their origin are inseparable, but that when language has once been started, it has to serve the various purposes of thought, and lend itself to myth and poem, philosophical analysis and religious dogma. Another point to criticise is the inevitable corollary that the soul of a great nation, like the Greeks, for instance, in the course of its advance to the maturity of art and freedom, passes through a period of derangement and disease, by which its civilisation is vitiated, its vitality poisoned at the root, and all its subsequent achievements tainted; and that this spiritual phthisis can be traced to a sickly state of language, at a very remote historical period, when as yet the nation was scarcely constituted. Seriously to entertain this view is tantamount to maintaining that corruption and disease may be the direct efficient causes of the highest art on which humanity can pride itself, since it is indubitable that the poems of Homer and the sculptures of Pheidias are the direct outgrowth of that "bane of the ancient world," which, to quote another pithy saying of Max Müller, converted *nomina* into *numina*. It is hardly necessary to point out the curious want of faith in the Welt-Geist (or God) which this implies; the unimaginative habit of mind we should encourage if we failed to discern the excellence of a civilisation that owed its specific character to mythology; the unphilosophical conclusions to which we might be brought if we denied that the intelligence is free while following the fixed laws of its evolution, and that the essential feature in this evolution is the advance from rudimentary to more developed thought. Language, however potent in reaction upon thought, is after all the vehicle and instrument of thought, and not its master. This leads to yet a further criticism; granting that language was "intended to be the mere realisation and outward embodiment of the mind" —though this is a wide begging of the most difficult of all questions—it does not follow that in mythology language is not pursuing its appointed function. If the mythological phase of thought is less apparent among the Semitic than among the Aryan nations, are we to say that this is so because the Semitic languages escaped the whooping-cough of mythology, or not far rather because the mind of the Aryan races had a greater aptitude for mythology, a greater aptitude for art? In the fifth place, the definition of mythology is too wide for the special purpose of the problem. Bacon long ago pointed out that one of the chief sources of error arises from our tendency to mistake words for realities. This imperfect adjustment of language to the purposes of thought is not peculiar to the mythopœic age. When we use such phrases as "vital force," we are designating the results of observation and experience by a word which ought not to be regarded as more than a sign. Yet, because "vital force" has sometimes been recognised as something positive and substantially existent, we cannot on that account call it a myth without impoverishing the resources of language, and making one word do the work of two. The truth, therefore, is, that in the mythopœic, as in every other age, words have done violence to thought, nor need it be contested that the *eidôla fori* were more potent in the infancy than in the maturity of intelligence. While concerned with this branch of our critique, it is curious to observe the satisfaction with which the advocates of the linguistic theory use it as the means of rehabilitating the moral character of the ancient Greeks, by trying to make out that the tales of Œdipus, Pelops, and Kronos owe their repulsive elements to verbal mistakes. To the student it is undoubtedly a relief to fancy that the incest of Jocasta was originally no more than a figurative way of speaking about the alternations of day and night. He derives, indeed, the same sort of contentment by this method as the rationalist who explains the legend of Pasiphaë upon Euemeristic principles. Yet it is surely a poor way of whitewashing the imagination of the ancients to have recourse to a theory

which sees in myths nothing better than a mange or distemper
breaking out in language, and tormenting the human mind
for a season.   Nor can the theory be stretched so far as to
exonerate the nation from its share of interest in these stories.
The people who made the supposed linguistic mistakes,
delighted in the grotesque and fantastic legends which were
produced.   Even if words deluded them, their wills were free
and their brains at work while under the pernicious influence.
The real way of exculpating the conscience of the Greeks,
indicated both by philosophy and common sense, is to point
out that, in the age of reflection, the tragic poets moralised
these very myths, and made them the subject-matter of the
gravest art, while the sages instituted a polemic against the
confusion of fabulous mythology with the pure notion of Godhead obtained by reflection.

The theory of development which seems to underlie the   The savage
linguistic doctrine, is that thought in its earliest stage is posi-   mind.
tive and clear and adequate.   The first savage who thinks,
sees the sun, for example, and calls it the sun ; but in talking
about the sun he begins to use figurative language, and so
converts his simple propositions into myths.   At this point,
argues the philologer, he goes wrong and becomes the victim
of delusions.   The fallacy in this view appears to lie in
attributing to the simple and sensuous apprehension of the
savage the same sort of simplicity as that which we have
gained by a process of abstraction, and consequently inferring
that the importation of fancy into the thinking process implies
a species of degeneracy.   The truth seems rather to be quite
the contrary.   If we grant, for the sake of argument, that the
first thoughts are in a certain sense simple, they have nothing
in common with the generalisations of the understanding.
Except in relation to immediate perceptions, their generality
is empty until it has been filled up with the varied matter of
the senses and the imagination.   Mythology and poetry are,
therefore, an advance upon the primitive prose of simple

apprehension. What was a mere round ball becomes a dædal world; and it is not till the full cycle of the myth-creating fancy has been exhausted, that the understanding can return upon a higher level by abstraction to intellectual simplicity. The same is true about theology. The first dim sense of the divine in nature as an unity may, possibly, have been prior to the many deities of polytheism : men may have looked upon the open sky and called that god. Yet it was not a retrogression but an advance from that first perception to the mythological fulness and variety which gave concreteness to the notion of the deity. In this way the whole content of human nature—feeling, sense, activity, and so forth—was imported into the original and hollow notion ; or, to state the process with greater accuracy, the germ of thought, by un-folding its potentiality, showed that what had seemed a barren unit was a complicated organism with a multiplicity of parts. It remained for a further stage of thought, by reflection and abstraction, to return at a higher level to the conception of intellectual unity. What we have to guard against is the temptation to attribute our own abstractedness, the definiteness of positivism, the purity of monotheism, to the first stage of thought. Ours is the triumph of the understanding in its vigour over bewildering fulness; theirs was the poverty and nakedness of a first awakening of intelligence. The same critique might be applied to the theory that language starts with universals. Here, again, all turns upon the question, what sort of universals? Unless we are cautious, we run the risk of ending in a view almost identical with the theory of primitive revelation, by following which to its conclusions we are forced to regard the history of the human race, not as a process of development, but as a series of disastrous errors and of gradual decline.

What remains the solid outcome of the linguistic theory is that in the mythopœic age when there was no criticism and no reflection possible, the *idola fori* were far more powerful than now, and consequently many legends were invented to account for words of which the true meaning had been forgotten. Accordingly philology is one of the keys by which the door of mythology may be unlocked. At the same time, considering the complex relations of thought to language, especially in their commencement, it is wrong to concentrate attention upon language. In like manner, it will be admitted that the genders of the nouns contributed their quota to the personification of female and male deities; but it would be wrong to argue that the *numina* were divided into male and female because the *nomina* were so distinguished. In order to appreciate the personifying instinct, we must go back in imagination to a point beyond the divergence of thought and language; and we shall find that if priority can be assigned to either, it will be to thought as that by which alone the human subject can be said to be. Language has sex because sex is a property of the talking being. The deities are male and female, not because their names have genders, but because the thinking being, for whom sex is all-important, thinks its own conditions into the world outside it.

True relation of language to mythology.

The linguistic theory for the interpretation of mythology is based upon comparative philology, which has proved beyond all contest that the Aryan races had not only their grammar but a certain number of their myths in common before the separation of the Hindhu, Hellenic, and Teutonic stocks. The Vedic literature exhibits the mythological material in rudiment, and its style approximates to that of poetry. Hence it has been assumed that the disease of language was less virulent in the oldest Aryan writings than it afterwards became in Hesiod and Homer. The *nomina* had not as yet been so utterly deformed and corrupted into *numina*. The inefficiency of arguments like this is that they have no value except in relation to a previously adopted view. To the opponent of the linguistic as the only scientific method for the explanation of myths, it is left to answer: What you regard as corruption of

The Aryans.

language I regard as development of thought. What interests me in Greek mythology is precisely this : that the Aryan poems have passed into complicated stories, illustrative of pure Hellenic modes of thought and feeling, which in their turn will give occasion for epics, dramas, statues, and philosophies. In the same way, the amount of similarity which comparative mythology has demonstrated in the myths of all the members of the Aryan family is, from the Greek historian's point of view, far less important than their differences. The similarity belongs to the stock as it existed in prehistoric times. The differences mark the external conditions and internal qualities of the nations as they played their part in the world's history. The "disease of language" which severally afflicted the Hindhus, the Persians, the Greeks, and the Scandinavians, turns out to be a faithful mirror of their concrete life. Any one, by way of illustration, can work out the problem of national psychology offered by the nature-worship of the sun in Ormuzd, in Phœbus, and in Balder. The pale and beautiful Balder, who must perish and whose death involves the world in wailing; the radiant and conquering Phœbus, the healing deity, the purifier, the voice of prophecy and poetry and music ; Ormuzd, the antagonist of darkness and of evil, the object of desire and adoration to the virtuous and pure ; these sun-gods answer to the races, as their geographical conditions and their spirit made them. Nor is this all. The mythology of each nation has a physiognomy and character of its own— that of the Greeks being clearness and articulation in opposition to the formlessness and misty vagueness of the Hindhus. To mistake a Greek tale of deity or hero for a Hindhu tale of deity or hero is impossible. While the student of prehistorical antiquities will, therefore, direct attention to the likeness revealed by comparative mythology, the historian of nations will rather be attracted by those differences which express themselves in mature art, literature, and religion.[1]

National character.

[1] The dissimilarity between Greek and Roman religion has often been

One of the most salient points of similarity between the several families of Aryan myths concerns those which are called solar legends. In all of these we read of children fated to slay their fathers, of strong giants condemned to obey the rule of feeble princes, of heroic young men forced to quit their first love for another woman. The heroes of these stories are marked out in their cradle by miraculous signs and wonders, or are suckled by wild beasts in the absence of their parents; in their youth they slay serpents sent to destroy them; in their manhood they shine forth as conquerors. Their death is not unfrequently caused by slight and unforeseen, though fated, occurrences—by a weapon that strikes the only vulnerable part of their body, in the case of Achilles and Siegfried; by a twig of mistletoe, in the case of Balder; by a thorn, in the case of Isfendiyar; by an envenomed mantle, in the case of Herakles. One great mythus fascinated the imagination of Norseman and Hindhu, Greek and Persian, German and Roman; interwove itself with their history; gave a form to their poetry; and assumed a prominent place in their religion. So far, it may be said that comparative philology has established something solid, which is at the same time of vast importance for the student of prehistorical antiquity. It is also not improbable that these legends referred originally to the vicissitudes of the sun in his yearly and daily journeys through the heavens. Thus much may be conceded to the solar theorists, remembering always that this primitive astronomical significance, if it existed, was forgotten by the races for whom the myths became the material of poetry and religion. But, unfortunately, the discovery has

observed, and will be touched upon below. Supposing it to be proved that the Romans can produce one relic of an Aryan myth in Romulus, we find that their most native deities—Saturnus, Ops, Bellona, Janus, Terminus, Concordia, Fides, Bonus Eventus, and so forth—are abstractions which have nothing in common with Greek or other Aryan legends. They are the characteristic product of the Roman mind, and indicate its habit of thought. In like manner it is only by a crisis amounting to confusion that Mercurius can be identified with Hermes, or Hercules with Herakles.

been strained beyond its proper limits by students who combine a solar theory with the linguistic in their interpretation of mythology. In their hands all the myths are made to refer to the sun and the moon, to dawn and evening. "The difficulty," says Max Müller, "which I myself have most keenly felt is the monotonous character of the dawn and sun legends. Is everything the dawn? is everything the sun? This question I had asked myself many times before it was addressed me by others." How consistently Professor Max Müller found himself obliged to answer this question in the affirmative is known to every student of his works, not to mention those of Mr. Cox. The handbooks of mythology which are now in vogue in England, expound this solar theory so persistently that it is probable a race is growing up who fancy that the early Greeks talked with most "damnable iteration" of nothing but the weather, and that their conversation on that fruitful topic fell sick of some disease breeding the tales of Thebes and Achilles and Pelops' line, as a child breeds measles. It is therefore necessary to subject it to criticism.

Meteorological theory.
The first point for notice is that mythology lends itself almost as well to meteorological as to solar theories. Kuhn and Schwartz, as Professor Müller himself informs us, arrived at the conclusion that "originally the sun was conceived implicitly as a mere accident in the heavenly scenery." Instead, therefore, of finding the sun and the dawn in all the myths, they are always stumbling upon clouds and winds and thunder. This differing of the doctors is, after all, no great matter. Yet it warns us to be careful in adopting so exclusively as is the present fashion either the solar or the meteorological hypothesis. A second consideration which inclines to caution is the facility of adapting the solar theory to every story, whether fabulous or historical. In this sense the famous tract which proved that Napoleon the Great only existed in the mythical imagination may be taken as a *reductio ad absurdum* of the method. A third ground for sus-

pension of judgment lies in the very elaborate manipulation
which the etymologies of such words as Erôs, Erinnys, and
the Charites have undergone before they yielded up their
solar content. But the multiplication of general objections is
not to the present purpose. It is enough to bear in mind that,
however important the sun was to the ancient Aryans, he
could not have been everything; he was, after all, but one
among many objects of interest; and what requires to be
still more remembered, is that the Greeks themselves, in dealing with the tales of Achilles, or of Kephalos and Prokris, did
not know that they were handling solar stories. It is, therefore, misleading to base handbooks which serve as introduc-
tions to Greek literature and art, upon speculation about the
solar groundwork of the myths. In the works of Homer and
Hesiod, of Æschylus and Sophocles, the myths were animated with spiritual, intellectual, and moral life. To draw
the lessons from them which those poets drew, to demonstrate
the grandeur of the imagination which could deal with those
primæval tragic tales, should be the object of the educator;
not to fill his pages with extremely doubtful matter about sun
and dawn *ad infinitum*. The true relation of the solar theory to   Herakles.
a Greek myth may be illustrated by the tale of Herakles,
whom the Greeks themselves may perhaps have recognised as
a solar deity, since Herodotus identified him with a Phœnician
god.[1] We are therefore justified in dealing with this hero as a
personification of the sun. Herakles is the child of Zeus. He
strangles in his cradle the serpents of the night. He loves
Iole, or the violet-coloured clouds of dawn. He performs
twelve labours, corresponding to the twelve months of the
solar year. He dies of a poisoned robe amid flames that
may be taken for the blood-red sunset clouds. The maiden
Iole, now evening and not morning, visits him again in death;
and he ascends from his funeral pyre of empurpled mountain
peaks to heaven. Let all this be granted. So far the solar

[1] ii. 44.

theory carries us. But is this all? In other words, is this, which the current handbooks tell us about Herakles, the pith of the matter as it appeared to the Greeks? When we turn to the *Philosophy of History* of Hegel, who worked by another than the solar method, and was more anxious to discover thoughts than etymologies, we read : " Hercules is among the Hellenes that spiritual humanity which, by native energy, attains Olympus through the twelve far-famed labours ; but the foreign idea that lies at the basis, is the sun completing its revolution through the twelve signs of the Zodiac." Here we touch the truth. The solar foundation of the mythus is wholly valueless and unimportant—in other words, is alien to its essence, when compared with the moral import it acquired among the Greeks. It is the conception of lifelong service to duty, of strength combined with patience, of glory followed at the cost of ease, of godhead achieved by manhood through arduous endeavour—it is this that is really vital in the myth of Herakles. By right of this the legend entered the sphere of religion and of art. In this spirit the sophist enlarged upon it, when he told how Herakles in his youth chose virtue with toil rather than pleasure, incorporating thus the high morality of Hesiod with the mythical element. If myths like these are in any sense diseased words about the sun, we must go further and call them immortalised words, words that have attained eternal significance by dying of the disease that afflicted them. The same remarks apply to all the solar and lunar stories—to Achilles, Endymion, Kephalos, and all the rest. As solar myths these tales had died to the Greeks. As poems, highly capable of artistic treatment, in sculpture, or in verse, pregnant with humanity, fit to form the subject of dramatic presentation or ethical debate, they retained incalculable value. The soul of the nation was in them. And that is their value for us.

To deny the important part which the sun, like the earth or the sea, played in early mythology would be absurd. To dis-

Hegel's reading of the Heraklean myth.

pute the illumination which comparative philology has thrown, not only upon the problem of the myths, but also upon the early unity of races until recently divided in our thought, would be still more ridiculous. The point at issue is simply this, that in Greek mythology there is far more than linguistic and solar theories can explain, and that *more* is precisely the Greek genius. The philologer from his point of view is justified in directing attention to the verbal husk of myths; but the student of art and literature must keep steadily in view the kernel of thought and feeling which the myths contain. It is only by so doing that the poetry and art which sprang from them can be intelligently studied. Thus the modern text-books of mythology are misleading, in so far as they draw the learner's mind away from subjects of historical importance to bare archæology.

As the result of analysis, the following propositions may Summary. be advanced. In the earliest ages the races to whom we owe languages and literature and art, possessed a faculty which may be called the mythopœic, now almost wholly extinct, or rather superseded by the exercise of other faculties which it contained in embryo. The operation of this faculty was analogous to that of the poetic; that is to say, it was guided by the imagination more than by the dry light of the understanding, and its creative energy varied in proportion to the imaginative vigour of the race which exercised it. The distinction here introduced is all-important; for only thus can we explain the very different nature of the Greek and Roman religions. The tendency to personification which distinguishes mythology was due to the instinct of uncivilised humanity to impute to external objects a consciousness similar to that by which men are governed—in other words, to regard them as living agents with wills and passions like our own. If fetishism be the rudimentary phase of this instinct, polytheism indicates an advance by which the mind has passed from the mere recognition of spiritual power in nature to the investment of that power with personal and corporeal qualities. But just as the imagination varies in degree and force in different races, so will this power of carrying the personifying instinct onward into art be found to vary. The Romans stopped short at allegories; in other words, they did not carry their personification beyond the first stage. The Greeks created divine personalities. Many myths contain moral and philosophical ideas conveyed in parables, and some of them have indubitable reference to real events and persons. But in no case of a primitive and genuine mythus are we to expect deliberate fiction or conscious symbolism; or, again, to seek for a discoverable substratum of solid fact. Entering the sphere of mythology, facts become etherealised into fancies, the actual value of which lies in the expression of the national mind, so that mythical and spiritual are in this respect synonymous. To use a metaphor, a myth is a Brocken-spectre of the thought which produced it, and owes the features by which we can distinguish it to the specific character of the people among whom it sprang into existence. The analysis of language shows that the whole Aryan family held a great number of their myths in common, that many legends are stories told to account for words and phrases which had lost their original significance, and that in these stories the alternations of night and day and the procession of the seasons played a very important part. Philology can, however, furnish no more than the prolegomena to mythology. After hearing its report, the student of Greek art and literature must take the Greek myths at a Greek valuation—must consider what they were for the Athenians, for example, and not what they had once been. Finally, it may be remembered that to hope for a complete elucidation of a problem so far removed from observation and experiment, would be vain. The conditions of the mythopœic age cannot be reconstituted; and were they to reappear through the destruction of civilisations, the reflective understanding would not be present to examine and record them.

The difficulty which besets the problem of mythology owing   Mediæval myths.
to the remote antiquity of the myth-making age, is to some
extent removed by observing the operation of the mythopœic
faculty in the historic period.   Given social circumstances
similar, if even only in a limited degree, to those of the prehistoric age ; given a defect of the critical and reflective faculty,
an absence of fixed records, and a susceptible condition of the
popular imagination, myths have always sprung up.   While it
is not, therefore, possible to find exact analogies to the conditions under which the Greek mythology originated, something
may be gained by directing attention to mediæval romance.
The legends which in Italy converted Virgil into a magician,
the epic cycles of Charles the Great and Arthur, the Lives of
the Saints, the fable of Tannhäuser and the Venusberg, the
Spanish tale of Don Juan, and the German tale of Faust, are
essentially mythical.   What is instructive about mediæval
romance for the student of mythology in general, is that here
the mythopœic imagination has been either dealing with dim
recollections of past history, or else has been constructing for
itself a story to express a doctrine.   After excluding the
hypothesis of conscious working to a prefixed end, we, therefore, find in these legends an illustration of the sense in which
the symbolical and rationalistic theories can be said to be justified.   In the case of Virgil, the poetry of Rome's greatest singer
never ceased to be studied during the darkest years of the dark
ages, and his name was familiar even to people who could not
read his verse.   He was known to have been a Pagan, and at
the same time possessed with what then seemed like superhuman knowledge.   It followed that he must have been a
wizard, and have gained his power and wisdom by compelling
fiends.   Having formed this notion of Virgil, the popular
fancy ascribed to him all the vast works of architecture and
engineering which remained at Rome and Naples, inventing
the most curious stories to explain why he had made them.
Ovid, in his native place, Sulmona, was subjected to the same

mythologising process, and many curious legends about his
magic power exist there still. When we turn to the Carlovingian cycle, we discover that the great name of the
Frankish Emperor, the memory of his wars, and the fame
of his generals have survived and been connected with the
crusading enthusiasm which pervaded Europe at a later period.
Border-warfare between France and Spain plays a prominent
part in this epic, and gradually the figure of Roland usurps
upon the more historically important personages. To "dig
for a supposed basis of truth " in the Carlovingian cycle would
be vain; yet the view is forced upon us that without some
historical basis the cycle would not have sprung into existence,
or have formed a framework for the thought and feeling
of one period of the Middle Ages. The achievements of
Arthur must be regarded as still more wholly mythological.
The more we inquire into his personality the less we find of
real historical subsistence. A Celtic hero, how created it is
impossible to say, becomes the central figure of the most
refined romance which occupied the attention of German,
French, and British poets in the Middle Ages. Round the
fictitious incidents of his biography gathers all that chivalry,
with its high sense of humanity and its profound religious
mysticism, conceived of purest and most noble ; while, at the
same time, certain dark and disagreeable details, especially the
incestuous union from which Mordred sprang, remind us of
the savage and unmoralised origin of the fable. We therefore
find in the Arthurian cycle something very much analogous to
the Tale of Troy. The dim memory of a national struggle, an
astronomical myth, perchance, and many incidents of merely
local interest have been blent together and filled with the very
spirit of the ages and the races that delighted in the story as
a story. This spiritual content gives its value to the epic.
Mediæval hagiography furnishes abundant examples of the way
in which facts transform themselves into fables, and mythological material is moulded into shape around some well-

remembered name, the religious consciousness externalising Poetry.
itself in acts which it attributes to its heroes. When we read
the *Fioretti di San Francesco*, we are well aware that the saint
lived—his life is one of the chief realities of the thirteenth
century ; but we perceive that the signs and wonders wrought
by him proceed from the imagination of disciples ascribing to
St. Francis what belongs partly to the ideal of his own character and partly to that of monastic sanctity in general. In
the fable of Tannhäuser we meet with another kind of
reminiscence. There is less of fact and more of pure invention.
The Pagan past, existent as a sort of dæmonic survival, is
localised at Hörsel. The interest, however, consists here wholly
in the parabolic meaning—whether Tannhäuser ever existed
does not signify. His legend is a poem of the Christian
knight ensnared by sin, aroused to a sense of guilt, condemned
by the supreme tribunal of the Church, and pardoned by the
grace of God. In like manner, the lust for knowledge, for
power, and for pleasure, withheld by God and nature, finds
expression in the Faust legend ; while inordinate carnal ap-
petite is treated tragically in Don Juan. These three legends
deserve to be called myths rather than poems in the stricter
sense of the word, because they appear at many points and
cannot be traced up to three definite artistic sources, while
it is clear from their wide acceptance that they embodied
thoughts which were held to be of great importance. In them,
therefore, we find illustrated the theory which explains mythology by the analogy of poetry. That the mediæval myths which
have been mentioned, never attained the importance of Greek
mythology, is immediately accounted for by the fact that they
sprang up, as it were, under the shadow of philosophy, religion,
and history. They belonged to the popular consciousness ;
and this popular consciousness had no need or opportunity of
converting its creatures into a body of beliefs, because both
science and orthodoxy existed. In the historic period mythology must always occupy this subordinate position ; and,

perhaps, this fact might be reflected back as a further argument, if such were needed, against the theories that the Greek myths, while leading onward to the Greek Pantheon and Greek art, originated as an undergrowth beneath the decaying fabric of revealed truth or firmly apprehended philosophical ideas. At all events, both the positive and negative circumstances which we observe in them, confirm the general view of mythology that has been advanced.

Greek religion.   The Homeric and Hesiodic poems were interposed between the reflective consciousness of the Greeks in the historic age and the mass of myths already existent in Hellas at the time of their composition, and thus mythology passed into the more advanced stage of art. It did not, however, cease on that account to retain some portion of its original plasticity and fluidity. It is clear from Pindar and the fragments of the minor lyric poets, from the works of the dramatists, from Plato, and from other sources, that what Herodotus reports about Homer and Hesiod having fixed the genealogies of the gods, cannot be taken too literally. Non-Homeric and non-Hesiodic versions of the same tales were current in various parts of Greece. The same deities in different places received different attributes and different forms of worship ; and the same legends were localised in widely separated spots. Each division of the Hellenic family selected its own patron deities, expressing in their cult and ritual the specific characteristics which distinguished Dorian, Æolian, and Ionian Hellas. At the same time certain headquarters of worship, like the shrine of Delphi and the temple of Olympian Zeus, were strictly Panhellenic. In this way it is clear that while Greek mythology acquired the consistence of a national religion, it retained its free poetic character in a great measure. The nation never regarded their myths as a body of fixed dogma to alter which was impious. Great liberty consequently was secured for artists ; and it may be said with truth that the Greeks arrived through sculpture at a consciousness of their gods. A new statue was, in a certain sense, a new deity, although the whole aim of the sculptor must, undoubtedly, have been to render visible the thoughts contained in myths and purified by poetry, and so to pass onward step-wise to a fuller and fuller realisation of the spiritual type. It is this unity combined with difference that makes the study of Greek sculpture fascinating in itself, and fruitful for the understanding of the Greek religion.

It lies beyond the scope of this chapter to consider how the Greek intelligence was first employed upon the articulation of its mythology, and next upon its criticism. The tradition of a Titanomachy, or contest between nature powers and deities of reason, marks the first step in the former process. The cosmogonical forces personified in the Titans gave place to the presiding deities of political life and organised society, in whom the human reason recognised itself as superior to mere nature. Olympus was reserved for gods of intellectual order, and thus the Greeks worshipped what was best and noblest in themselves. At the same time the cosmogonical divinities were not excluded from the Greek Pantheon, and so there grew up a kind of hierarchy of greater and lesser deities. Oceanus, Poseidon, Proteus, the Tritons and the Nereids, Amphitrite and Thetis, for example, are all powers of the sea. They are the sea, conceived under different aspects, its divine personality being multitudinously divided and delicately characterised in each case to accord with the changes in the element. The same kind of articulation is observable in the worship of deities under several attributes. Aphrodite Ourania and Aphrodite Pandemos are one as well as two; Erôs and Himeros and Pothos are not so much three separate Loves, as Love regarded from three different points of view. Here the hierarchy is psychological, and represents an advance made in reflection upon moral qualities; whereas in the former case it was based on the observation of external nature. To this inquiry, again, belongs the question of imported myths and foreign cults. The worship of Corinthian Aphrodite, for example, was originally

Hierarchy of deities.

Asiatic. Yet, on entering Greek thought, Mylitta ceased to be Oriental and assumed Hellenic form and character. Sensuality was recognised as pertaining to the goddess whose domain included love and beauty and the natural desires.

Art and Religion.

More than the vaguest outlines of such subjects of interest cannot be indicated here. It is enough to have pointed out that, as Greek mythology was eminently imaginative, fertile in fancy and prolific in dramatic incident, so it found its full development in poetry and art. Only through art can it be rightly comprehended; and the religion for which it supplied the groundwork was itself a kind of art. It is just this artistic quality which distinguished the Greeks from the Romans. As Mommsen well observes, "there was no formation of legend in the strict sense in Italy." The Italian gods were in their origin more matter-of-fact than Greek gods. They contained from the first a prosaic element which they never threw aside, nor did they give occasion to the growth of fable with its varied fabric of human action and passion. Thus the legal and political genius of the Latin race worshipped its own qualities in these allegorical beings.

Greek criticism of mythology.

The process hitherto described has been the passage of mythology into religion and the expression of religion by art. When the Greek intelligence became reflective in the first dawn of philosophy, it recognised that the notion of divinity, τὸ θεῖον, was independent and in some sense separable from the persons of the Pantheon in whom it inhered. This recognition led to a criticism of the myths by the standard of ideal godhead. Just as the Olympic deities, as representative of pure intellect or spirit, had superseded the bare nature forces, so now the philosophers sought to distil a refined conception of God from the myths in general. Their polemic was directed against Homer, in whom, like Herodotus, they recognised the founder of the current mythological theology. Both Pythagoras and Heraclitus are reported to have said that Homer ought to be publicly thrust from the assembly and scourged. Xeno-

phanes plainly asserted that the Greek anthropomorphism was
no better than a worship of humanity with all its vices, illustrating his critique by adding that just in the same way might lions
adore lions and horses horses.   His own conception of the
deity was monotheistic, to this extent at least that he abstracted
from the universe a notion of divine power and wisdom, and
ascribed to it the only reality.   Plato, in the *Republic*, unified
these points of view, severely criticising Homer for the immorality of his fictions, attributing to his own demiurgic deity
those qualities of Goodness, Truth, and Beauty which are the
highest ideals of the human spirit.   In connection with this
polemic against poetical theology, we have to notice the
attempts of physical philosophers to explain the universe by
natural causes, and the great saying of Anaxagoras that
reason rules the world.   Thus the speculative understanding,
following various lines of thought and adopting divers
theories, tended to react upon mythology and to corrode the
ancient fabric of Greek polytheism.   In the course of this
disintegrating process a new and higher religion was developed, which Plato expressed by saying that we ought "to
become like God, as far as this is possible ; and to become like
Him is to become holy and just and wise."   At the same time
those who felt the force of the critique, but could not place
themselves at the new scientific point of view, remained
sceptical ; and against this kind of scepticism, which implied
personal lawlessness, Aristophanes directed his satire.   Whatever may have been the attitude of philosophers in their
schools, mythology meanwhile retained its hold upon the
popular mind.   It was bound up with the political traditions,
the Gentile customs, the ritual, and the arts of the whole race.
To displace it by a reasoned system of theology, enforced by   Philo-
nothing stronger than the theories of the sages, was impossible. sophical
                                                                  theology.
The extent to which philosophy permanently affected the creed
of thinking and religious men in Greece by substituting theism
for the fabulous theology of the poets has been well expressed

in Plutarch's *Life of Pericles.* "So dispassionate a temper," he observes, "a life so pure and unblemished in authority, might well be called Olympian, in accordance with our conceptions of the divine beings to whom, as the natural authors of all good and of nothing evil, we ascribe the rule and government of the world—not as the poets represent, who, while confounding us with their ignorant fancies, are themselves confuted by their own poems and fictions, and call the place, indeed, where they say the gods make their abode 'a secure and quiet seat, untroubled with winds or clouds,' and 'equally through all time illumined with a soft serenity and a pure light,' as though such were a home most agreeable for a blessed and immortal nature ; and yet, in the meanwhile, affirm that the gods themselves are full of trouble and enmity and anger, and other passions, which no way become or belong to even men that have any understanding." It is clear that when the religious consciousness had reached this point of purified clairvoyance, the race was ready for a more spiritual theology, which philosophers like Marcus Aurelius found in natural religion, while the common folk accepted Christianity.

Greek mythology survives as poetry.

After flowing side by side for many centuries, the currents of mythological belief and of philosophical speculation reunited at Alexandria, where a final attempt was made to animate the Homeric Pantheon with the spirit of metaphysical mysticism. Homer became a priest as well as poet, and the *Iliad* was made to furnish allegories for an age grown old in intellectual subtlety. This was the last period of mythology. While Hypatia was lecturing on Homer the Christians were converting the world. To keep the gods of Greece alive was no longer possible. Regarded from the beginning as persons with a body corresponding to their spiritual substance, they had in them the certainty of dissolution. Though removed ideally beyond the sphere of human chance and change, they remained men and women with passions like our own. Pure spirit had not been realised in them ; and blind fate had from the first been held to be supreme above them. Unlike the incarnate God of Christianity, they had not passed forth from the spiritual world to abide here for a season and return to it again. Therefore they perished. During the domination of mediæval Christianity the utmost they could do was to haunt the memory like wraiths and phantoms, to linger in neglected and unholy places like malignant powers of evil. But when the force of ascetic Christianity declined, and the spirit of humane culture re-awoke in Europe, these old gods reasserted their ascendency —no longer as divinities indeed, but as poems forming an essential element of the imagination. The painters and sculptors of Italy gave once more in breathing marble and fair colour form to those immortal thoughts. The poets sang the old songs of Hellas in new language to new measures, Even the churchmen invoked God from Roman pulpits as *Summus Jupiter*, and dignified Madonna with the attributes of Artemis and Pallas.

Such is the marvellous vitality of this mythology. Such is its indissoluble connection with the art and culture which sprang from it, of which it was the first essential phase, and to which we owe so much. Long after it has died as religion, it lives on as poetry, retaining its original quality, though the theology contained in it has been for ever superseded or absorbed into more spiritual creeds.

CHAPTER III

ACHILLES

Unity of *Iliad*—Character of Achilles— Structure of the whole Poem—
Comparison with other Epics—Energy dividing into Anger and Love
—Personality of Achilles—The Quarrel with Agamemnon—Pallas
Athene—The Embassy—Achilles' Foreknowledge of his Death—The
Message of Antilochus—Interview with Thetis—The Shouting in the
Trench—The Speech of Xanthus—The Pæan over Hector's Corpse—
The Ghost of Patroclus — The Funeral Obsequies of Patroclus—
Achilles and Priam—Achilles in Hades—Achilles considered as a
Greek Ideal—Friendship among the Greeks—Heroism and Knight-
hood : Ancient and Modern Chivalry—The *Myrmidones* of Æschylus
—Achilles and Hector—Alexander the Great—The Dæmonic Nature
of Achilles.

Origin of the *Iliad*.

IT is the sign of a return to healthy criticism that scholars are
beginning to acknowledge that the *Iliad* may be one poem—
that is to say, no mere patchwork of ballads and minor epics
put together by some diaskeuast in the age of Pisistratus, but
the work of a single poet, who surveyed his creation as an
artist, and was satisfied with its unity. We are not bound to
pronounce an opinion as to whether this poet was named
Homer, whether Homer ever existed, and, if so, at what period
of the world's history he lived. We are not bound to put
forward a complete view concerning the college of Homer-
idæ, from which the poet must have arisen, if he did not
found it. Nor, again, need we deny that the *Iliad* itself
presents unmistakable signs of having been constructed in a
great measure out of material already existing in songs and

romances, dear to the Greek nation in their youth, and familiar to the poet. The æsthetic critic finds no difficulty in conceding, nay, is eager to claim, a long genealogy through antecedent, now forgotten, poems for the *Iliad*. But about this, of one thing, at any rate, he will be sure, after due experience of the tests applied by Wolf and his followers, that a great artist gave its present form to the *Iliad*, that he chose from the whole Trojan tale a central subject for development, and that all the episodes and collateral matter with which he enriched his epic were arranged by him with a view to the effect that he had calculated.

What, then, was this central subject, which gives the unity of a true work of art to the *Iliad* ? We answer, the person and the character of Achilles. It is not fanciful to say, with the old grammarians of Alexandria, that the first line of the poem sets forth the whole of its action.

The wrath of Achilles.

> " Sing, goddess, the wrath of Achilles, son of Peleus."

The wrath of Achilles and the consequences of that wrath in the misery of the Greeks, left alone to fight without their fated hero ; the death of Patroclus, caused by his sullen anger ; the energy of Achilles, reawakened by his remorse for his friend's death ; and the consequent slaughter of Hector ; form the whole of the simple structure of the *Iliad*. This seems clear enough when we analyse the conduct of the poem.

The first book describes the quarrel of Achilles with Agamemnon and his secession from the war. The next seven books and a half, from the second to the middle of the ninth, are occupied with the fortunes of the Greeks and Trojans in the field, the exploits of Diomede and Ajax, and Hector's attack upon the camp. In the middle of the ninth book Achilles reappears upon the scene. Agamemnon sends Ulysses and Phœnix to entreat him to relax his wrath and save the Greeks ; but the hero remains obdurate. He has resolved

Conduct of the poem.

that his countrymen shall pay the uttermost penalty for the offence of their King. The poet having foredetermined that Achilles shall only consent to fight in order to revenge Patroclus, is obliged to show the inefficacy of the strongest motives from without; and this he has effected by the episode of the embassy. The tenth book relates the night attack upon the camp of the Trojan allies and the theft of the horses of Rhesus. The next five books contain a further account of the warfare carried on among the ships between the Achaians and their foes. It is in the course of these events that Patroclus comes into prominence. We find him attending on the wounded Eurypylus and warning Achilles of the imminent peril of the fleet. At last, in the sixteenth book, when Hector has carried fire to the ship of Protesilaus, Achilles commands Patroclus to assume the armour of Peleus and lead his Myrmidons to war. The same book describes the repulse of Hector and the death of Patroclus, while the seventeenth is taken up with the fight for the body of Achilles' friend. But from the eighteenth onward the true hero assumes his rank as protagonist, making us feel that what has gone before has only been a preface to his action. His seclusion from the war has not only enabled the poet to vary the interest by displaying other characters, but has also proved the final intervention of Achilles to be absolutely necessary for the success of the Greek army. All the threads of interest are gathered together and converge on him. Whatever we have learned concerning the situation of the armies, the characters of the chiefs, and the jealousies of the gods, now serves to dignify his single person and to augment the terror he inspires. With his mere shout he dislodges the Trojans from the camp. The divine arms of Hephæstus are fashioned for him, and forth he goes to drive the foe like mice before him. Then he contends with Simois and Scamander, the river-gods. Lastly, he slays Hector. What follows in the twenty-third and twenty-fourth books seems to be intended as a repose from the vehement action and high-wrought passion of the preceding five. Patroclus is buried, and his funeral games are celebrated. Then, at the very end, Achilles appears before us in the interview with Priam, no longer as a petulant spoilt child or fiery barbarian chief, but as a hero, capable of sacrificing his still fierce passion for revenge to the nobler emotion of reverence for the age and sorrow of the sonless king.

The centralisation of interest in the character of Achilles, constitutes the grandeur of the *Iliad*. It is also by this that the *Iliad* is distinguished from all the narrative epics of the world. In the case of all the rest there is one main event, one deed which has to be accomplished, one series of actions with a definite beginning and ending. In none else are the passions of the hero made the main points of the movement. This may be observed at once by comparing the *Iliad* with the chief epical poems of European literature. To begin with the *Odyssey*. The restoration, after many wanderings, of Odysseus to his wife and kingdom forms the subject of this romance. When that has been accomplished, the *Odyssey* is completed. In the same way the subject of the *Æneid* is the foundation of the Trojan kingdom in Italy. Æneas is conducted from Troy to Carthage, from Carthage to Latium. He flies from Dido, because fate has decreed that his empire should not take root in Africa. He conquers Turnus because it is destined that he, and not the Latin prince, should be the ancestor of Roman kings. As soon as Turnus has been killed and Lavinia has been wedded to Æneas, the action of the poem is accomplished and the *Æneid* is completed. When we pass to modern epics, the first that meets us is the *Nibelungen Lied*. Here the action turns upon the murder of Sigfrit by Hagen, and the vengeance of his bride Chriemhilt. As soon as Chriemhilt has assembled her husband's murderers in the halls of King Etzel, and there has compassed their destruction, the subject is complete, the *Nibelungen* is at an end. The British epic of the Round Table, if we may regard Sir Thomas Mallory's *Morte d'Arthur* as a poem, centres in the life and

The Iliad *compared with other epics.*

predestined death of King Arthur. Upon the fate of Arthur hangs the whole complex series of events which compose the romance. His death is its natural climax, for with him expires the Round Table he had framed to keep the Pagans in awe. After that event nothing remains for the epic poet to relate. Next in date and importance is the *Orlando Furioso* of Ariosto. The action of this poem is bound up with the destinies of Ruggiero and Bradamante. Their separations and wanderings supply the main fabric of the plot. When these are finally ended, and their marriage has been consummated, nothing remains to be described. The theme of the *Gerusalemme Liberata*, again, is the conquest of the Holy City from the Saracens. When this has been described, there is nothing left for Tasso to tell. The *Paradise Lost*, in spite of its more stationary character, does not differ from this type. It sets forth the single event of the Fall. After Adam and Eve have disobeyed the commands of their Maker and have been expelled from Eden, the subject is exhausted, the epic is at an end.

The *Iliad* is the epic of an episode.

Thus each of these great epic poems has one principal event, on which the whole action hinges and which leaves nothing more to be narrated. But with the *Iliad* it is different. At the end of the *Iliad* we leave Achilles with his fate still unaccomplished, the Trojan war still undecided. The *Iliad* has no one great external event or series of events to narrate. It is an episode in the war of Troy, a chapter in the life of Peleus' son. But it does set forth, with the vivid and absorbing interest that attaches to true æsthetic unity, the character of its hero, selecting for that purpose the group of incidents which best display it.

The Passion of Achilles.

The *Iliad*, therefore, has for its whole subject the Passion of Achilles—that ardent energy or ΜΗΝΙΣ of the hero, which displayed itself first as anger against Agamemnon, and afterwards as love for the lost Patroclus. The truth of this was perceived by one of the greatest poets and profoundest critics of the modern world, Dante. When Dante, in the

Inferno, wished to describe Achilles, he wrote, with characteristic brevity :—

" Achille
Che per amore al fine combatteo."

" Achilles
Who at the last was brought to fight by love."

In this pregnant sentence Dante sounded the whole depth   Wrath and
                                                            love.
of the *Iliad*.[1] The wrath of Achilles against Agamemnon,
which prevented him at first from fighting; the love of
Achilles, passing the love of women, for Patroclus, which
induced him to forego his anger and to fight at last; these
are the two poles on which the *Iliad* turns. Two passions—
heroic anger and measureless love—in the breast of the chief
actor, are the motive forces of the poem. It is this simplicity
in the structure of the *Iliad* which constitutes its nobleness.
There is no double plot, no attempt to keep our interest alive
by misunderstandings, or treacheries, or thwartings of the
hero in his aims. These subtleties and resources of art the
poet, whom we will call Homer, for the sake of brevity, dis-
cards. He trusts to the magnitude of his chief actor, to the
sublime central figure of Achilles, for the whole effect of his
epic. It is hardly necessary to insist upon the highly tragic
value of this subject. The destinies of two great nations hang
trembling in the balance. Kings on the earth below, gods in
the heavens above, are moved to turn this way or that the
scale of war. Meanwhile the whole must wait upon the
passions of one man. Nowhere else, in any work of art, has
the relation of a single heroic character to the history of the
world been set forth with more of tragic pomp and splendid
incident. Across the scene on which gods and men are contending in fierce rivalry, moves the lustrous figure of Achilles,

[1] I am bound to admit that this interpretation of the line is not taken
by all commentators, and that Scartazzini reads *con amore.—Inferno*, v.
65.

ever potent, ever young, but with the ash-white aureole of coming death around his forehead. He too is in the clutch of destiny. As the price of his decisive action, he must lay his life down and retire with sorrow to the shades. It is thus that in the very dawn of civilisation the Greek poet divined the pathos and expounded the philosophy of human life, showing how the fate of nations may depend upon the passions of a man, who in his turn is but the creature of a day, a ripple on the stream of time. Nothing need be said by the æsthetic critic about the solar theory, which pretends to explain the tale of Troy. The Mythus of Achilles may possibly in very distant ages have expressed some simple astronomical idea. But for a man to think of this with the actual *Iliad* before his eyes would be about as bad as botanising on his mother's grave. Homer was not thinking of the sun when he composed the *Iliad*. He wove, as in a web, all elements of tragic pity and fear, pathos and passion and fateful energy, which constitute the dramas of nations and of men.

Grandeur of the passions.

In the two passions, anger and love, which form the prominent features of the character of Achilles, there is nothing small or mean. Anger has scarcely less right than ambition to be styled the last infirmity of noble minds. And love, when it gives the motive force to great action, is sublime. The love of Achilles had no softness or effeminacy. The wrath of Achilles never degenerated into savagery. Both of these passions, instead of weakening the hero, add force to his activity. Homer has traced the outlines of the portrait of Achilles so largely that criticism can scarcely avoid dwarfing them. In looking closely at the picture, there is a danger lest, while we examine the parts, we should fail to seize the greatness of the whole. It is better to bring together in rapid succession those passages of the *Iliad* which display the character of Achilles under the double aspect of anger and love. The first scene (i. 148-246) shows us Agamemnon surrounded by the captains of the Greek host, holding the same position among them as Charlemagne among his peers, *Achilles and Agamemnon.* or King John among the English Barons. They recognise his heaven-descended right of monarchy ; but their allegiance holds by a slight thread. They are not afraid of bearding him, browbeating him with threats, and roundly accusing him of his faults. This turbulent feudal society has been admirably sketched by Marlowe in *Edward II.*, and by Shakespeare in *Richard II.* And it must be remembered that between Agamemnon and the Hellenic βασιλεῖς (kings or chieftains), there was not even so much as a feudal bond of fealty. Calchas has just told Agamemnon that, in order to avert the plague, Chryseis must be restored to her father. The king has answered that if he is forced to relinquish her, the Greeks must indemnify him richly. Then the anger of Achilles boils over :—

"Ah, clothed upon with impudence, and greedy-souled ! How, thinkest thou, can man of the Achaians with glad heart follow at thy word to take the field or fight the foe ? Not for the quarrel of the warlike Trojans did I come unto these shores, for they had wronged me not. They never drove my cattle nor my steeds, nor ever, in rich, populous Phthia, did they waste the corn ; since far between us lie both shadowy mountains and a sounding sea : but following thee, thou shameless king, we came to gladden thee, for Menelaus and for thee, thou hound, to win you fame from Troy. Of this thou reckest not and hast no care. Yea, and behold thou threatenest even from me to wrest my guerdon with thy hands, for which I sorely strove, and which the sons of the Achaians gave to me. Never, in sooth, do I take equally with thee, when Achaians sack a well-walled Trojan town. My hands do all the work of furious war ; but when division comes, thy guerdon is far greater, and I go back with small but well-loved treasure to the ships, tired out with fighting. Now, lo ! I am again for Phthia ; for better far, I ween, it is homeward to sail with beaked ships : nor do I think that if I stay unhonoured wilt thou get much wealth and gain.

"Him, then, in answer, Agamemnon, king of men, bespake :—

"Away ! fly, if thy soul is set on flying. I beg thee not to stay for me. With me are many who will honour me, and most of all, the Counsellor Zeus. Most hateful to me of the Zeus-born kings art thou. For ever dost thou love strife, warfare, wrangling. If very stout of limb thou art, that did God give thee. Go home, then, with thy ships and friends. Go, rule the Myrmidons. I care not for thee, nor regard thy wrath, but this will I threaten—since Phœbus robs me of Chryseis, her with my ship and with my followers will I send; but I will take fair-cheeked Briseis, thy own prize, and fetch her from thy tent, that thou mayest know how far thy better I am, and that others too may dread to call themselves my equal, and to paragon themselves with me.

"So spake he. And Peleides was filled with grief; and his heart within his shaggy bosom was cut in twain with thought, whether to draw his sharp sword from his thigh, and, breaking through the heroes, kill the king, or to stay his anger and refrain his soul. While thus he raged within his heart and mind, and from its scabbard was in act to draw the mighty sword, came Athene from heaven; for Here, white-armed goddess, sent her forth, loving both heroes in her soul, and caring for them. She stood behind, and took Peleides by the yellow hair, seen by him only, but of the rest none saw her. Achilles marvelled, and turned back; and suddenly he knew Pallas Athene, and awful seemed her eyes to him; and, speaking winged words, he thus addressed her :—

"Why, daughter of ægis-bearing Zeus, art thou come hither? Say, is it to behold the violence of Agamemnon, Atreus' son? But I will tell to thee what verily I think shall be accomplished, that by his own pride he soon shall slay his soul.

"Him then the gray-eyed goddess Athene bespake :—

"I came to stay thy might, if thou wilt hear me, from Heaven; for Here, white-armed goddess, sent me forth, loving you both alike, and caring for you. But come, give up strife, nor draw thy sword! But, lo, I bid thee taunt him with sharp words, as verily shall be. For this I say to thee, and it shall be accomplished : the time shall come when thou shalt have thrice-fold as many splendid gifts, because of his violence. Only restrain thyself; obey me.

"To her, in turn, spake swift-footed Achilles :—

"Needs must I, goddess, keep thy word and hers, though sorely grieved in soul; for thus is it best. He who obeys the gods, him have they listened to in time of need.

"He spake, and on the silver handle pressed a heavy hand, and back into the scabbard thrust the mighty sword, nor swerved from Athene's counsel. But she back to Olympus fared, to the house of ægis-bearing Zeus unto the other gods.

"Then Peleides again with bitter words bespake Atrides, and not yet awhile surceased from wrath :—

"Wine-weighted, with a dog's eyes and a heart of deer! Never
hadst thou spirit to harness thee for the battle with the folk, nor
yet to join the ambush with the best of the Achaians. *This* to thee
seems certain death. Far better is it, verily, throughout the broad
camp of Achaians to filch gifts when a man stands up to speak
against thee — thou folk-consuming king, that swayest men of
nought. Lo, of a sooth, Atrides, now for the last time wilt thou
have dealt knavishly. But I declare unto thee, and will swear
thereon a mighty oath; yea, by this sceptre, which shall never put
forth leaf nor twig since that day that it left the stock upon the
mountains, nor again shall bud or bloom, for of its leafage and its
bark the iron stripped it bare; and sons of the Achaians hold it in
their palms for judgment, they who guard the laws by ordinance
of Zeus; and this shall be to thee a mighty oath. Verily, and of
a truth, the day shall be when sore desire for Achilles shall come
upon Achaians one and all. Then shalt thou, though grieved in
soul, have no power to help, while in multitudes they fall and die
at Hector's murderous hands; but thou shalt tear thy heart within
thy breast for rage, seeing thou honouredst not the best of the
Achaians aught.

"So spake Peleides; and on the earth cast down the sceptre
studded with nails of gold; and he sat down upon his seat."

What is chiefly noticeable in this passage is the grand scale
upon which the anger of Achilles is displayed. He is not
content with taunting Agamemnon, but he includes all the
princes in his scorn:

δημοβόρος βασιλεὺς, ἐπεὶ οὐτιδανοῖσιν ἀνάσσεις.

"Thou folk-consuming king, that swayest men of nought."

We may also notice the interference of Athene. The *Pallas
Athene.*
Athene of the *Iliad* is a different goddess from the Athene of
the Parthenon. In strength she is more than a match for
Ares; her cunning she subordinates to great and masculine
ends, not to the arts of beauty or to study. She is the saint
of the valiant and wary soldier. While checking Achilles,
she does not advise him to avoid strife in any meek and
gentle spirit. She simply reminds him that, if he gets to
blows with Agamemnon, he will put himself in the wrong;
whereas, by contenting himself with sharp words and with

secession from the war, he will reduce the haughty king to sue him with gifts and submission. Athene in this place acts like all the other deities in Homer when they come into direct contact with the heroes. She is exterior to Achilles, and at the same time a part of his soul. She is the expression of both thought and passion deeply seated in his nature, the force of his own character developed by circumstance, the god within his breast externalised and rendered visible to him alone. What Athene is to the son of Peleus, Ate is to Agamemnon.

The embassy to Achilles.

The next passage in which Achilles appears in the forefront of the scene is in the Ninth Book (307-429). Worn out with the losses of the war, Agamemnon has at last humbled his pride, and sent the wisest of the chiefs, silver-tongued Odysseus, and Phœnix, the old guardian of the son of Peleus, to beg Achilles to receive back Briseis, and to take great gifts if only he will relax his wrath. But Achilles remains inflexible. In order to maintain the firmness of his character, to justify the righteousness of his indignation, Homer cannot suffer him to abandon his resentment at the first entreaty. Some more potent influence must break his resolution than the mere offer to restore Briseis. Homer has the death of Patroclus in the background. He means to show the iron heart of Peleides at last softened by his sorrow and his love. Therefore, for the time, he must protract the situation in which Achilles is still haughty, still implacable toward his repentant injurer. In this interview with the ambassadors we have to observe how confident Achilles abides in the justice of his cause and in his own prowess. It is he with his valiant bands who has sacked the Trojan cities; it is he who kept Hector from the ships; and now in his absence the Achaians have had to build a wall in self-defence. And for whom has he done this? For the sons of Atreus and for Helen. And what has he received as guerdon? Nothing but dishonour. These arguments might seem to savour too much of egotism and want of feeling for the dangers of the host. But at the end come those great lines upon the vanity of gifts and possessions in comparison with life, and upon the doom which hangs above the hero :—

"You may make oxen and sheep your prey ; you may gather together tripods and the tawny mane of horses ; but none can make the soul of man return by theft or craft when once it has escaped. As for me," he resumes, " my goddess mother, silver-footed Thetis, warns me that fate lays two paths to bear me deathward. If I abide and fight before the walls of Troy, my return to Hellas is undone, but fame imperishable remains for me. If I return to my dear country then my good glory dies, but long life awaits me, nor will the term of death be hastened."

This foreknowledge of Achilles that he has to choose be- *The coming doom.*
tween a long, inglorious life, and a swift-coming, but splendid death, illuminates his ultimate action with a fateful radiance. In the passage before us it lends dignity to his obstinate and obdurate endurance. He says: I am sick at heart for the insults thrust on me. I am wounded in my pride. Toiling for others I get no reward. And behold, if I begin to act again, swift death is before me. Shall I, to please Agamemnon, hasten on my own end ?

When the moment arrives for Achilles to be aroused from *Honour and heroic fame.*
inactivity by his own noblest passion, then, and not till then, does he fling aside the thought of death, and trample on a long reposeful life. He is conscious that his glory can only be achieved by the sacrifice of ease and happiness and life itself ; but he holds honour dearer than these good things. Yet at the same time he is not eager to throw away his life for a worthless object, or to buy mere fame by an untimely end. It requires another motive, the strong pressure of sorrow and remorse, to quicken his resolution ; but when once quickened nothing can retard it. Achilles at this point might be compared to a mass of ice and snow hanging at the jagged edge of a glacier, suspended on a mountain brow. We have seen such avalanches brooding upon Monte Rosa, or the Jungfrau,

beaten by storms, loosened, perchance, by summer sun, but motionless. In a moment a lightning-flash strikes the mass, and it roars crumbling to the deep.

The death of Patroclus. This lightning-flash in the case of Achilles was the death of Patroclus (xviii. 15). Patroclus has gone forth to aid the Achaians and has fallen beneath Hector's sword. Antilochus, sent to bear the news to Achilles, finds him standing before the ships, already anxious about the long delay of his comrade. Antilochus does not break the news gently. His tears betray the import of his message, and he begins :—

"Woe is me, son of brave Peleus ! Verily thou shalt hear right sorrowful tidings : Patroclus lies slain ; round his corpse they are fighting ; stripped it lies, but plumed Hector hath his armour.

"So he spake. But a black cloud of woe covered the hero. With both hands he took the dust of ashes and flung them down upon his head, and disfigured his fair face, and on his fragrant tunic lay the black cinders. But he, huge in his hugeness, stretched upon the dust lay, and with his hands he tore and ravaged his hair."

Thus Achilles receives the first shock of grief. When his mother rises from the sea to comfort him, he refuses consolation, and cries :—

"My mother, the Olympian hath done all these things ; but of what pleasure is this to me, now that my dear friend is dead, Patroclus, whom above all my comrades I honoured, even as myself ? Him have I slain !"

This is the pith and marrow of his anguish. I slew Patroclus ; it was I who sent him forth to fight. "Now," he resumes a few lines lower down, "Now my soul bids me no longer live or be with men, save only I strike Hector first and slay him with my spear, and make him pay the fine of Patroclus."

Thetis reminds him that, if he slay Hector, his own life will be short. This only serves to turn his anguish into desperate resolve :—

"Straight let me die, seeing I might not come to the aid of my comrade when he was dying. Far from his fatherland he perished. He looked for me that I should have been his helper. But now, since never to my home shall I return, nor was I a light in trouble to Patroclus, nor to my other comrades who are slain by hundreds by the god-like Hector—while I here sit beside the ships, a useless load upon the earth—I who am such as there is none else like me among brazen-coated Achaians in the war—others may be better perchance in council—now let strife perish from among gods and men, with anger which stirs up the prudent even to fury."

Thus he foregoes his wrath, and flings resentment from him like a mantle. Then he rises ready for the fight. "If death come, let death be welcome. Death came to Herakles. In his due time he comes to me. Meanwhile I thirst to make Dardan ladies widows in the land."

When he next appears, his very form and outward semblance are transfigured. He stands alone and unarmed in the trench. A fire surrounds his head and flames upon his curls. His voice thrills the armies like the blare of a victorious trumpet. This is how Homer has described him shouting in the trench (xviii. 203):— *Achilles in the trench.*

"But Achilles, dear to Zeus, arose, and around his mighty shoulders Athene cast her tasselled ægis; and about his head the queenly goddess set a crown of golden mist, and from it she made blaze a dazzling flame. As when smoke rises to the clear sky from a town, afar from an island which foemen beleaguer, who all day long contend in grisly war, issuing from their own town; but at sundown beacons blaze in rows, and on high the glare goes up, and soars for neighbouring men to see, if haply warders off of woe may come to them with ships—so from the head of Achilles the flame went up to heaven. He stood at the trench, away from the wall, nor joined the Achaians, for he honoured his mother's wise command. There he stood and shouted; and beside him Pallas Athene cried; but among the Trojans he raised infinite tumult. As when a mighty voice, when the trumpet shrills for the murderous foemen that surround a town, so was the mighty voice of the son of Æacus. They then, when they heard the brazen cry of Æacides, in the breasts of all of them the heart was troubled; but the fair-maned horses turned the cars backward; for in their heart they knew the sorrows that were to be. And the charioteers were stricken when they saw the tireless flame terrible above the head of big-hearted Peleus' son blazing. The gray-eyed goddess Athene kindled it. Thrice above the trench shouted the godlike Achilles in his might: thrice were the Trojans and their noble allies troubled."

Achilles
hastens to
the battle.

From this moment the action of the *Iliad* advances rapidly. Achilles takes his proper place, and occupies the whole stage. The body of Patroclus is brought home to him; he mourns over it, and promises to bury it, when he shall have slain Hector, and slaughtered twelve sons of the Trojans on the pyre. Then he reconciles himself with Agamemnon, and formally renounces anger. Lastly, when he has put on the divine armour made for him by Hephæstus, he ascends his car, and hastens into the fight. But again at this point, when Achilles is at the very pitch and summit of his glory, the voice of fate is heard. It is with the promise of the tomb that he enters the battle. Turn to Book xix. 399. Achilles has just mounted his chariot :—

"Fiercely did he cheer the horses of his sire :—Xanthus and Balius, far-famed children of Podargé, take other heed, I warn ye, how to save your master, and to bring him to the Danaan host, returning of war satisfied ; nor leave him, like Patroclus, dead there on the field.

"To him then from beneath the yoke spake the fleet-footed horse Xanthus, and straightway drooped his head ; and all his mane, escaping from the collar by the yoke, fell earthward. Goddess Here, of the white arms, gave him speech :—

"Verily shall we save thee yet this time, fierce Achilles ; but close at hand is thy doom's day. Nor of this are we the cause, but great God in heaven and resistless fate. For neither was it by our sloth or sluggishness that Trojans stripped the arms from Patroclus his shoulders ; but of Gods the best, whom fair-haired Leto bare, slew him among the foremost, and gave to Hector glory of the deed. We, though we should run apace with Zephyr's breath, the fleetest, as 'tis said, yet for thee it is decreed to perish by the might of God and man.

"When he had thus spoken the Erinnyes stayed his voice ; and, high in wrath, fleet-foot Achilles answered him :—

"Xanthus! why prophesy my death? Thou hast no call. Right well know I, too, that it is my fate to perish here, far from dear sire and mother; yet for all this will I not surcease before I satiate the Trojans with war.

"He spoke, and vanward held his steeds with mighty yell."

This dialogue between Achilles and Xanthus is not without great importance. Homer is about to show the hero raging in carnage, exulting over suppliants and slain foes, terrible in his ferocity. It is consistent with the whole character of Achilles, who is fiery, of indomitable fury, that he should act thus. Stung as he is by remorse and by the sorrow for Patroclus, which does not unnerve him, but rather kindles his whole spirit to a flame, we are prepared to see him fierce even to cruelty. But when we know that in the midst of the carnage he is himself moving a dying man, when we remember that he is sending his slain foes like messengers before his face to Hades, when we keep the warning words of Thetis and of Xanthus in our minds, then the grim frenzy of Achilles becomes dignified. The world is in a manner over for him, and he appears the incarnation of disdainful anger and revengeful love, the conscious scourge of God and instrument of destiny. We need not dwell upon the details of the battle, in which Achilles drives the Trojans before him, and is only withheld by the direct interposition of the gods from carrying Ilium by assault. To borrow a simile from Dante, his foes are like frogs scurrying away from the approach of their great foe, the water-snake. Then follow the episode of Lycaon's slaughter, the fight with the river-gods, and the death of Hector. To the assembled Greeks Achilles cries (xxii. 386):—

The warning voice of Xanthus.

"By the ships, a corpse, unburied, unbewailed, lies Patroclus: but of him I will not be unmindful so long as I abide among the living and my knees have movement. Nay, should there be oblivion of the dead in Hades, yet I even there will remember my loved comrade. But rise, ye youths of Achaia, and singing Pæan, let us hasten to the ships, and take this slain man with us. Great glory have we got. Divine Hector have we slain, to whom the Trojans in their city prayed as to a god."

So the Pæan rings. But Achilles by the ships, after the hateful banquet, as he calls it in the sorrowful loathing of all comfort, has been finished, lays himself to sleep (xxiii. 59) :—

"The son of Peleus, by the shore of the roaring sea lay, heavily groaning, surrounded by his Myrmidons ; on a fair space of sand he lay, where the waves lapped the beach. Then slumber took him, loosing the cares of his heart, and mantling softly around him, for sorely wearied were his radiant limbs with driving Hector on by windy Troy. There to him came the soul of poor Patroclus, in all things like himself, in stature, and in the beauty of his eyes and voice, and on his form was raiment like his own. He stood above the hero's head, and spake to him :—

"Sleepest thou, and me hast thou forgotten, Achilles ? Not in my life wert thou neglectful of me, but in death. Bury me soon, that I may pass the gates of Hades. Far off the souls, the shadows of the dead, repel me, nor suffer me to join them on the river bank ; but, as it is, thus I roam around the wide-doored house of Hades. But stretch to me thy hand, I entreat ; for never again shall I return from Hades when once ye shall have given me the meed of funeral fire. Nay, never shall we sit in life apart from our dear comrades, and take counsel together. But me hath hateful fate enveloped—fate that was mine at the moment of my birth. And for thyself, divine Achilles, it is doomed to die beneath the noble Trojans' wall. Another thing I will say to thee, and bid thee do it if thou wilt obey me :—Lay not my bones apart from thine, Achilles, but lay them together ; for we were brought up together in your house, when Menœtius brought me, a child, from Opus to your house, because of woful bloodshed on the day in which I slew the son of Amphidamas, myself a child, not willing it, but in anger at our games. Then did the horseman, Peleus, take me, and rear me in his house, and caused me to be called thy squire. So then let one grave also hide the bones of both of us, the golden urn thy goddess-mother gave to thee.

"Him answered swift-footed Achilles :—

"Why, dearest and most honoured, hast thou hither come, to lay on me this thy behest ? All things most certainly will I perform, and bow to what thou biddest. But stand thou near : even for one moment let us throw our arms upon each other's neck, and take our fill of sorrowful wailing.

"So spake he, and with his outstretched hands he clasped, but could not seize. The spirit, earthward, like smoke, vanished with a shriek. Then all astonished arose Achilles, and beat his palms together, and spoke a piteous word :—

"Heavens ! is there then, among the dead, soul and the shade of life, but thought is theirs no more at all ? For through the night the soul of poor Patroclus stood above my head, wailing and sorrowing loud, and bade me do his will: it was the very semblance of himself.

"So spake he, and in the hearts of all of them he raised desire of lamentation ; and while they were yet mourning, to them appeared rose-fingered dawn about the piteous corpse."

There is surely nothing more thrilling in its pathos through- *The funeral pyre of Patroclus.* out the whole range of poetry than this scene, in which the iron-hearted conqueror of Hector holds ineffectual communing in dreams with his dear, lost, never-to-be-forgotten friend. But now the pyre is ready to be heaped, and the obsequies of Patroclus are on the point of being celebrated. Thereupon Achilles cuts his tawny curls, which he wore clustering for Spercheius, and places them in the hand of dead Patroclus. At the sight of this token that Achilles will return no more to Hellas, but that he must die and lie beside his friend, all the people fall to lamentation. Agamemnon has to arouse them to prepare the pyre. A hundred feet each way is it built up ; oxen and sheep are slaughtered and placed upon the wood, with jars of honey and olive oil. Horses, too, and dogs are slain to serve the dead man on his journey ; and twelve sons of the great-souled Trojans are sacrificed to the disconsolate ghost. Then Achilles cast fire upon the wood, and wailed, and called on his loved friend by name :—

"Hail, Patroclus ! I greet thee even in the tomb : for now I am performing all that erst I promised. Twelve valiant sons of the great-souled Trojans with thee the fire devours ; but Hector, son of Priam, I will give to no fire to feed on, but to dogs."

Meanwhile the pyre of Patroclus refused to burn, and *The burning of the body.* Achilles summoned the two winds, Boreas and Zephyrus, to help him. They at this time were feasting in the house of Zephyrus, and Iris had to fetch them from their cups. They rose and drove the clouds before them, and furrowed up the

sea, and passed to fertile Troy, and fell upon the pyre, and the
great flame crackled, hugely blazing :—

"All night they around the pyre together cast a flame, blowing
with shrill breath, and all night swift Achilles, from a golden bowl,
holding a double goblet, drew wine, and poured it on the ground,
and soaked the earth, calling upon the soul of poor Patroclus. As
when a father wails who burns the bones of his son unwed, so
wailed Achilles, burning his friend's bones, pacing slowly round the
fire, and uttering groan on groan.

"But when the star of dawn came to herald light upon the
earth, whom following morn, with saffron robe, spread across the
sea, then the pyre languished and the flame was stayed.

"The winds again went homeward, back across the Thracian
deep. It groaned beneath them, raging with the billow's swell.
But the son of Peleus turned from the pyre, and lay down weary,
and sweet sleep came upon him."

The funeral
games.

After this manner was the burning of Patroclus. And here
the action of the *Iliad* may be said to end. What follows in
the last two books is, however, of the greatest importance in
adding dignity to the character of Achilles, and in producing
that sense of repose, that pacification of the more violent emotions, which we require in the highest works of tragic art. First
come the games around the barrow of Patroclus. Presiding
over them is Achilles, who opens his treasure-house to the
combatants with royal generosity, for ever mindful that in
honouring them, he is paying honour to the great sad ghost
of his dead friend. The bitterness of his sorrow is past; his
thirst for vengeance is assuaged. Radiant and tranquil he
appears among the chiefs of the Achaians; and to Agamemnon
he displays marked courtesy.

Priam's visit
to Achilles.

But it is not enough to show us Achilles serene in the
accomplishment of his last service to Patroclus. As the
crowning scene in the whole *Iliad*, Homer has contrived to
make us feel that, after all, Achilles is a man. The wrathful
and revengeful hero, who bearded Agamemnon on his throne,
and who slew the unarmed suppliant Lycaon, relents in pity
at a father's prayer. Priam, in the tent of Achilles, presents

one of the most touching pictures to be found in poetry. We know the leonine fierceness of Achilles; we know how he has cherished the thought of insult to dead Hector as a final tribute to his friend: even now he is brooding in his lair over the Trojan corpse. Into this lion's den the old king ventures. Instead of springing on him, as we might have feared, Achilles is found sublime in generosity of soul. Begging Patroclus to forgive him for robbing his ghost of this last satisfaction, he relinquishes to Priam the body of his son. Yet herein there is nothing sentimental. Achilles is still the same—swift to anger and haughty—but human withal, and tender-hearted to the tears of an enemy at his mercy.

This is the last mention made of Achilles in the *Iliad*. The hero, whom we have seen so noble in his interview with Priam, was destined within a few days to die before the walls of Troy, slain by the arrow of Paris.[1] His ashes were mingled with those of Patroclus. In their death they were not divided.

Once again in the Homeric poems does Achilles appear. But this time he is a ghost among the pale shadows of Elysium (*Od.* xi. 466):— *Achilles in Hades.*

"Thereupon came the soul of Achilles, son of Peleus, and of Patroclus, and of brave Antilochus, and of Ajax, who was first in form and stature among the Achaians after great Peleides. The soul of fleet Æacides knew me, and wailing, he thus spake:—

"Zeus-born son of Laertes, wily Ulysses, why in thy heart, unhappy man, dost thou design a deed too great for mortals? How darest thou descend to Hades, where dwell the thoughtless dead, the phantoms of men whose life is done?

"So he spake; but I in turn addressed him:—

"Achilles, son of Peleus, greatest by far of Achaians, I am come to learn of Teiresias concerning my return to Ithaca. But none of men in elder days or of those to be, is more blessed than thou art, Achilles; for in life the Argives honoured thee like a god, and now again in thy greatness thou rulest the dead here where thou art. Therefore be not grieved at death, Achilles.

---

[1] That the poet of the *Iliad* in its present form had this legend before him is clear from Books xxi. 297 xxii. 355-360.

"So spake I, and he straightway made answer :—

"Console not me in death, noble Odysseus ! Would rather that I were a bondsman of the glebe, the servant of a master, of some poor man, whose living were but scanty, than thus to be the king of all the nations of the dead."

Achilles viewed as a Greek ideal.   Some apology may be needed for these numerous quotations from a poem which is hardly less widely known and read than Shakespeare or the Bible.   By no other method, however, would it have been possible to bring out into prominence the chief features of the hero whom Homer thought sufficient for the subject of the greatest epic of the world. For us Achilles has yet another interest.   He, more than any character of fiction, reflects the qualities of the Greek race in its heroic age.   His vices of passion and ungovernable pride, his virtue of splendid human heroism, his free individuality asserted in the scorn of fate, are representative of that Hellas which afterwards, at Marathon and Salamis, was destined to inaugurate a new era of spiritual freedom for mankind.   It is impossible for us to sympathise with him wholly, or to admire him otherwise than as we admire a supreme work of art ; so far is he removed from our so-called proprieties of moral taste and feeling.   But we can study in him the type of a bygone, infinitely valuable period of the world's life, of that age in which the human spirit was emerging from the confused passions and sordid needs of barbarism into the higher emotions and more refined aspirations of civilisation.   Of this dawn, this boyhood of humanity, Achilles is the fierce and fiery hero.   He is the ideal of a race not essentially moral or political, of a nation which subordinated morals to art, and politics to personality ; and even of that race he idealises the youth rather than the manhood.   In some respects Odysseus is a truer representative of the delicate and subtle spirit which survived all changes in the Greeks. But Achilles, far more than Odysseus, is an impersonation of the Hellenic genius, superb in its youthfulness, doomed

to immature decay, yet brilliant at every stage of its brief
career.

To exaggerate the importance of Achilles in the education
of the Greeks, who used the *Iliad* as their Bible, and were
keenly sensitive to all artistic influences, would be difficult.
He was the incarnation of their chivalry, the fountain of
their sense of honour. The full development of this subject
would require more space than I can here give to it. It will
be enough to touch upon the friendship of Achilles for
Patroclus as the central point of Hellenic chivalry ; and to
advert to the reappearance of his type of character in Alexander at the very moment when the force of Hellas seemed to
be exhausted.

Achilles, the type of Hellenic chivalry.

Nearly all the historians of Greece have failed to insist
upon the fact that fraternity in arms played for the Greek
race the same part as the idealisation of women for the knighthood of feudal Europe. Greek mythology and history are
full of tales of friendship, which can only be paralleled by the
story of David and Jonathan in our Bible. The legends of
Herakles and Hylas, of Theseus and Peirithous, of Apollo and
Hyacinth, of Orestes and Pylades, occur immediately to the
mind. Among the noblest patriots, tyrannicides, lawgivers,
and self-devoted heroes in the early times of Greece, we
always find the names of friends and comrades recorded with
peculiar honour. Harmodius and Aristogeiton, who slew the
despot Hipparchus at Athens ; Diocles and Philolaus, who
gave laws to Thebes ; Chariton and Melanippus, who resisted
the sway of Phalaris in Sicily ; Cratinus and Aristodemus,
who devoted their lives to propitiate offended deities when a
plague had fallen upon Athens ; these comrades, staunch to
each other in their love, and elevated by friendship to the
pitch of noblest enthusiasm, were among the favourite saints
of Greek legendary history. In a word, the chivalry of
Hellas found its motive force in friendship rather than in the
love of women ; and the motive force of all chivalry is a

Fraternity in arms and comrade-ship.

generous, soul-exalting, unselfish passion. The fruit which friendship bore among the Greeks was courage in the face of danger, indifference to life when honour was at stake, patriotic ardour, the love of liberty, and lion-hearted rivalry in battle. "Tyrants," said Plato, "stand in awe of friends."

Love and arms.

It may seem at first sight paradoxical to speak at all of Greek chivalry, since this word, by its very etymology, is appropriated to a mediæval institution. Yet when we inquire what chivalry means, we find that it implies a permanent state of personal emotion, which raises human life above the realities of everyday experience, and inspires men with unselfish impulses. Furthermore, this passionate condition of the soul in chivalry. is connected with a powerful military enthusiasm, severing the knight from all vile things, impelling him to the achievement of great deeds, and breeding in his soul a self-regardless temper. Both the ancient and the mediæval forms of chivalry included love and arms. The heroes and the knights alike were lovers and warriors. The passion, which Plato called Mania in the *Phædrus*, and which the Provençal Troubadours knew by the name of *Joie*, was excited in the heroes by their friends, and in the knights by their ladies. But the emotion was substantially the same ; nor, with the tale of Patroclus and with the whole of Greek history before us, can we allow our modern inaptitude for devoted friendship to blind us to the seriousness of this

Patriotism and religion.

passion among the Greeks. Beside war and love, chivalry implies a third enthusiasm. In the case of the Greek heroes this was patriotic. In the case of the mediæval knights it was religious. Thus, antique chivalry may be described as a compound of military, amatory, and patriotic passions meeting in one enthusiastic habit of the soul; mediæval chivalry as a compound of military, amatory, and religious passions meeting in a similar enthusiastic habit of soul. It is hardly necessary to point out the differences between Hellenic heroism and Teutonic knighthood, or to show how far the former failed to

influence society as favourably as the latter.   The Christian
chivalry of mercy, forgiveness, gentleness, and long-suffering,
which claims the title of charity in armour, was a post-Hellenic
ideal.   Greeks could not have comprehended the oath which
Arthur imposed upon his knights, and which ran in the
following words : " He charged them never to do outrage nor
murder, and alway to flee treason, also by no means to be
cruel, but to give mercy unto him that asked mercy, and
alway to do ladies, damosels, and gentlewomen succour upon
pain of death."   The murder of Lycaon by Achilles, the
butchery of Dolon by Diomedes, and the treachery practised
upon Philoctetes by Odysseus are sufficiently at variance with
the spirit of this oath ; nor do any of the heroic legends tell
a tale of courtesy towards women.   Thus much about the **Greek heroism.**
unchivalrous aspects of Greek heroism I have thought it right
to say, before returning to the view which I first stated, that
military friendship among the Greeks played for Hellenic
civilisation a part not wholly dissimilar to that of chivalrous
love among the nations of mediæval Europe.   Regarded as
an institution, with ethics of its own, and with peculiar social
and political regulations, this Greek chivalry was specially
Dorian.[1]   Yet it spread through all the states of Hellas.
In Athens it allied itself with philosophy, as afterwards at
Florence did the chivalry of knighthood ; and in Thebes,
during the last struggle for Hellenic freedom, it blazed forth
in the heroism of the Three Hundred, who fell together face-
forward to the Macedonian lances at Chæronea.[2]   Meanwhile,
Achilles remained for all Greece the eponym of passionate
friendship ; and even in the later periods of Greek poetry
the most appropriate title for a pair of noble comrades was
" Achilleian."   Concerning the abuse and debasement of such

---

[1] See Müller's *Dorians*, vol. ii. pp. 306-313.

[2] Sections 18 and 19 of Plutarch's *Life of Pelopidas* contain the best
account of the Sacred Band, and place the Greek chivalrous sentiment in
the clearest light.

passion among the historic Greeks this is not the place to speak. Achilles and Patroclus cannot be charged with having sanctioned by example any vice, however much posterity may have read its own moods of thought and feeling into Homer.

Æschylean and Sopho-clean tragedies.

Æschylus wrote a tragedy entitled the *Myrmidones*, in commemoration of the love of Achilles; and, perhaps, few things among the lost treasures of Greek literature are so much to be regretted as this play, which would have cast clear light upon the most romantic of Greek legends. It may also be mentioned in passing that we possess fragments of a play of Sophocles which bears the name Ἀχιλλέως ἔρασται, or *Lovers of Achilles;* but what its subject was, and whether the drama was Satyric, as seems probable, or not, we do not know. The beautiful passage in which love is compared to a piece of glittering ice held in the hand of children, has been preserved from it by Stobæus.

The *Myr-midones.*

Enough, fortunately, has survived the ruin of time to enable us to conjecture how Æschylus, in the *Myrmidones*, handled the materials afforded him by Homer. The play, as was frequent, took its name from the Chorus, who represented the contingent of Thessalian warriors led by Peleus' son against Troy. It opened, if we may trust the scholiast to the *Frogs* of Aristophanes, with a reproach uttered by the Chorus against Achilles for his inactivity :—

> τάδε μὲν λεύσσεις, φαίδιμ᾽ Ἀχιλλεῦ,
> δοριλυμάντους Δαναῶν μόχθους
> οὓς * * εἴσω κλισίας.

"Seest thou these things, glorious Achilles—the sufferings of the Danaans beneath victorious spears? Whom thou within thy tent——" here the fragment breaks off; but enough has been said to strike the keynote of the tragedy. The next fragment, according to Dindorf's arrangement, formed, prob-ably, part of Achilles' defence.[1] It is written in iambics and

---

[1] It may be questioned whether this fragment ought not to be referred to the scene with the embassy later on in the play.

contains the famous simile of the eagle stricken to death by
an arrow fledged with his own feather. Like that eagle,
argues the hero, have we Greeks been smitten by our own ill-
counsel. After the drama has thus been opened, the first
great incident seems to have been the arrival of the embassy
of Phœnix at Achilles' tent. One corrupt, but precious fragment, put by Aristophanes as a quotation into the mouth of
Euripides in the *Frogs*, indicates the line of argument taken
by the ambassadors :—

> Φθιῶτ᾽ Ἀχιλεῦ, τί ποτ᾽ ἀνδροδάϊκτον ἀκούων
> ἰήκοπον οὐ πελάθεις ἐπ᾽ ἀρωγάν;

Though the Greek as it stands is untranslatable, the meaning is pretty clearly this : Achilles of Phthia, how can you
bear to hear of these woes nor lend a helping hand ? The
next fragment must be received with caution. It occurs in
the *Frogs* as a quotation :—

> Βέβληκ᾽ Ἀχιλλεὺς δύο κύβω καὶ τέτταρα.

> " Achilles has cast two dice, and four : "

On which the scholiast makes the following remark : " This is
from the *Myrmidones ;* for the poet feigned them playing dice ;
and it is the custom of gamesters to cry thus : two, four,
three, five. Dionysus says this to show that Æschylus has
won." Another scholiast puts it in doubt whether the verse
be taken from the *Telephus* of Euripides or some other source.
The foundation is, therefore, too slender to build upon securely ;
else we might imagine that, after the departure of the ambassadors, and perhaps after the equipment of Patroclus for
the war, Achilles was represented by Æschylus as whiling away
the time with his companions at a game of hazard. Then
enters Antilochus, the messenger of bad news. He recites
the death of Patroclus, and lifts up his voice in lamentation.
Our next fragment brings the whole scene vividly before us :—

> Ἀντίλοχ᾽, ἀποίμωξόν με τοῦ τεθνηκότος
> τὸν ζῶντα μᾶλλον.

Achilles and
the corpse
of Patroclus.

The words are spoken undoubtedly by Achilles : "Anti-lochus, wail thou for me rather than for the dead—for me who live." It is again from a comedy of Aristophanes, the *Ecclesiazusæ*, that this exclamation comes ; and in passing we may remark, that such frequent citations from this single play of Æschylus by a comic poet prove its popularity at Athens. Between the narration of Antilochus and the bringing in of the dead body of Patroclus there must have been a solemn pause in the dramatic action, which Æschylus, no doubt, filled up with one of his great choric passages. Then followed the crowning scene in the tragedy. Achilles, front to front with the corpse of his friend, uttered a lamentation, which the ancients seem to have regarded as the very ecstasy of grief and love and passionate remembrance. Lucian, quoting one of the lines of this lament, introduces it with words that prove the strong impression it produced :—"Achilles, when he be-moaned Patroclus' death, in his unhusbanded passion burst forth into the very truth." It would be impossible to quote and comment upon the three lines which have been preserved from this unique Threnos without violating modern taste. To understand them at all is difficult, and to recompose from them the hero's speech is beyond our power. The value of the meagre and conflicting citations given by Plutarch, Athenæus, and Lucian, lies in the impression they convey of the deep effect wrought upon Greek sympathy by the passion of the soliloquy. When we call to mind the lamentation uttered by Teucer over the corpse of Ajax in the tragedy of Sophocles, we may imagine how the genius of Æschylus rose to the height of this occasion in his *Myrmidones*. In what way the drama ended is not known. We may, however, hazard a con-jecture that the poet did not leave the hero without some out-look into the future, and that the solemn note of reconciliation upon which the tragedy closed responded to the first querulous interrogation of the Chorus at its commencement. The situa-tion was a grand one for working out that purification of the

passions which Greek tragedy required.   The sullen and selfish
wrath of Achilles had brought its bitter consequence of suffering and sorrow for the hero, as well as of disaster for the host.
Out of that deadly suffering of Achilles—out of the paroxysm
of grief beside the body of his friend—has grown a nobler
form of anger, which will bring salvation to his country at the
certain loss of his own life.   Can we doubt that Æschylus
availed himself of this so solemn and sublime a cadence?   The
dead march and the funeral lamentations for Patroclus mingle
with the neighing of war-horses and the braying of the
trumpets that shall lead the Myrmidons to war.   And over
and above all sounds of the grief that is past and of the
triumph that is to follow, is heard the voice of fate pro-
nouncing the death-doom of the hero, on whose ἁμαρτία
(fault, proceeding from some quality of character) the tragic
movement has depended.

Thus, in the prime of Athens, the poet-warrior of Marathon,
the prophet of the highest Hellenic inspiration, handled a
legend which was dear to his people, and which to them spoke
more, perhaps, than it can do to us.   Plato, discussing the
Myrmidones of Æschylus, remarks in the *Symposium* that the
tragic poet was wrong to make Achilles the lover of Patroclus,
seeing that Patroclus was the elder of the two, and that
Achilles was the youngest and most beautiful of all the Greeks.
The fact, however, is that Homer himself raises no question in
our minds about the relations of lover and beloved.   Achilles
and Patroclus are comrades.   Their friendship is equal.   It
was only the reflective activity of the Greek mind, working
upon the Homeric legend by the light of subsequent custom,
which introduced these distinctions.   The humanity of Homer
was purer, larger, and more sane than that of his posterity
among the Hellenes.   Still, it may be worth while suggesting
that Homer, perhaps, intended in Hector and Achilles to contrast domestic love with the love of comrades.   The tenderness of Hector for Andromache, side by side with the fierce

passion of Achilles, seems to account, at least in some measure,
for the preference felt for Hector in the Middle Ages.
Achilles controlled the Greek imagination. Hector attracted
the sympathies of mediæval chivalry, and took his place upon
the list of knightly worthies.[1] Masculine love was Hellenic.
The love of idealised womanhood was romantic. Homer, the
sovereign poet, understood both passions of the human heart,
delineating the one in Achilles without effeminacy, the other
in Hector without sickly sentiment. At the same time,
Hector's connection with the destinies of Rome and his
appearance in the *Æneid*, if only as a ghost, must not be
forgotten when we estimate the reasons why he eclipsed
Achilles in the Middle Ages.

It is not till we reach Alexander the Great that we find
how truly Achilles was the type of the Greek people, and to
what extent he had controlled their growth. Alexander expressed in real life that ideal which in Homer's poetry had
been displayed by Achilles. Alexander set himself to imitate
Achilles. His tutor, Lysimachus, found favour in the eyes of
the royal family of Macedon, by comparing Philip to Peleus,
his son to Achilles, and himself to Phœnix. On all his ex-
peditions Alexander carried with him a copy of the *Iliad*,
calling it "a perfect portable treasure of military virtue." It
was in the spirit of the Homeric age that he went forth to
conquer Asia. And when he reached the plain of Troy, it
was to the tomb of Achilles that he paid special homage.
There he poured libations to the mighty ghost, anointed his
grave, and, as Plutarch says, "ran naked about his tomb, and
crowned it with garlands, declaring how happy he esteemed
him in having, while he lived, so faithful a friend, and, when
he was dead, so famous a poet to proclaim his actions." We
have seen that the two chief passions of Achilles were his
anger and his love. In both of these Alexander followed him.
The passage just quoted from Plutarch hints at the envy with

---

[1] See Caxton's Preface to the *Morte d'Arthur*.

which Alexander regarded the friendship of Achilles and Hephæs-
Patroclus. In his own life he entertained for Hephæstion a tion.
like passion. When Hephæstion died of fever at Ecbatana,
Alexander exaggerated the fury and the anguish of the son of
Peleus. He went forth and slew a whole tribe—the Cosseans
—as a sacrifice to the soul of his comrade. He threw down
the battlements of neighbouring cities, and forbade all signs
of merry-making in his camp. Meanwhile he refused food
and comfort, till an oracle from Ammon ordained that divine
honours should be paid Hephæstion. Then Alexander raised
a pyre, like that of Patroclus in the *Iliad*, except that the
pyre of Hephæstion cost 10,000 talents, and was adorned with
all the splendour of Greek art in its prime. Here the Homeric
ceremonies were performed. Games and races took place;
then, like Achilles, having paid this homage to his friend, of
bloodshed, costly gifts, and obsequies, Alexander at last rested
from his grief. In this extravagance of love for a friend we
see the direct working of the *Iliad* on the mind of the Macedonian king. But the realities of life fall far short of the
poet's dream. Neither the love nor the sorrow of Alexander
for Hephæstion is so touching as the love and sorrow of
Achilles for Patroclus.

In his wrath, again, Alexander imitated and went beyond Clitus.
his model. When he slew Clitus in a drunken brawl, there
was no Athene at his side to stay his arm and put the sword
back in the scabbard. Yet his remorse was some atonement
for his violence. "All that night," says Plutarch, "and the
next day he wept bitterly, till, being quite spent with lamenting and exclaiming, he lay, as it were, speechless, only fetching
deep sighs." It is noticeable that Alexander, here also like
Achilles, conqueror and hero though he was, scorned not to
show his tears, and to grovel on the ground in anguish. His
fiery temper added indomitable energy to all he did or felt.
In a few years he swept Asia, destroying kingdoms, and
founding cities that still bear his name; and though his rage

betrayed him now and then into insane acts, he, like Achilles,
was not wholly without the guidance of Athene.   In both we
have the spectacle of a gigantic nature moved by passions ;
yet both are controlled by reason, not so much by the reflective understanding, as by an innate sense of what is great
and noble.   Alexander was Aristotle's pupil.   In his best
moments, in his fairest and most solid actions, the spirit of
Aristotle's teaching ruled him and attended him, as Achilles
was ruled and attended by Pallas.   Again, in generosity,
Alexander recalls Achilles.   His treatment of the wife and
daughters of Darius reminds us of the reception of Priam by
the son of Peleus.   Grote, indeed, points out that good policy
prompted him to spare the life of the Persian queen.   That
may be true ; but it would have been quite consistent with
the Greek standard of honour to treat her with indignity
while he preserved her life.   This Alexander refrained from
doing.   His entertainment of Stateira was not unworthy of
a queen ; and if he did not exhibit the refined courtesy of the
Black Prince, he came as near to this ideal of modern chivalry
as a Greek could do.   In the last place Alexander, like
Achilles, was always young.   Like Achilles, he died young,
and exists for us as an immortal youth.   This youthfulness is
one of the peculiar attributes of a Greek hero, one of the
distinguishing features of Greek sculpture—in a word, the
special mark of the Greek race.   " O Solon ! Solon ! " said
the priest of Egypt, " you Greeks are always boys ! "   Achilles
and Alexander, as Hegel has most eloquently demonstrated,
are for ever adolescent.   Yet, after all is said, Alexander fell
far below his prototype in beauty and sublimity.   He was
nothing more than a heroic man.   Achilles was the creature
of a poet's brain, of a nation's mythology.   The one was the
ideal in its freshness and its freedom.   The other was the
real, dragged in the mire of the world, and enthralled by the
necessities of human life.

It is very difficult, by any process of criticism, to define the impression of greatness and of glory which the character of Achilles leaves upon the mind.   There is in him a kind of magnetic fascination, something incommensurable and indescribable, a quality like that which Goethe defined as dæmonic. They are not always the most noble or the most admirable natures which exert this influence over their fellow-creatures. The Emperor Napoleon and our own Byron had each, perhaps, a portion of this Achilleian personality.   Men of their stamp sway the soul by their prestige, by their personal beauty and grandeur, by the concentrated intensity of their character, and by the fatality which seems to follow them.   To Achilles, to Alexander, to Napoleon, we cannot apply the rules of our morality.   It is, therefore, impossible for us, who must aim first at being good citizens, careful in our generation, and subordinate to the laws of society around us, to admire them without a reservation.   Yet, after all is said, a great and terrible glory does rest upon their heads; and though our sentiments of propriety may be offended by some of their actions, our sense of what is awful and sublime is satisfied by the contemplation of them.   No one should delude us into thinking that true culture does not come from the impassioned study of everything, however eccentric and at variance with our own mode of life, that is truly great.   Greatness, of whatever species it may be, is always elevating and spirit-stirring. When we listen to the Eroica Symphony, and remember that that master-work of music was produced by the genius of Beethoven, brooding over the thoughts of Achilles in the *Iliad*, and of Napoleon upon the battlefields of Lombardy, we may feel how abyss cries to abyss, and how all forms of human majesty meet and sustain each other.

The splendour and sublimity of Achilles.

CHAPTER IV

THE WOMEN OF HOMER

Helen of Troy—Her Eternal Youth—Variety of Legends connected with her—Stesichorus—Helen in the *Iliad*—Helen in the *Odyssey*—The Treatment of Helen by Æschylus—Euripidean Handling of her Romance—Helen in Greek Art—Quintus Smyrnæus—Apollonius of Tyana and the Ghost of Achilles—Helen in the Faust Legend — Marlowe and Goethe — Penelope — Her Home - love—Calypso and the Isle of Ogygia—Circe—The Homeric and the Modern Circe—Nausicaa—Her Perfect Girlishness—Briseis and Andromache—The Sense of Proportion and of Relative Distance in Homer's Pictures—Andromache and Astyanax—The Cult of Heroes and Heroines in Greece—Artistic Presentation of Homeric Persons—Philostratus.

> "For first of all the spherèd signs whereby
>   Love severs light from darkness, and most high
>   In the white front of January there glows
>   The rose-red sign of Helen like a rose."
>   Prelude to *Tristram and Iseult*, lines 91-94.

HELEN OF TROY is one of those ideal creatures of the fancy over which time, space, and circumstance, and moral probability, exert no sway. It would be impossible to conceive of her except as inviolably beautiful and young, in spite of all her wanderings and all she suffered at the hands of Aphrodite and of men. She moves through Greek heroic legend as the desired of all men and the possessed of many. Theseus bore her away while yet a girl from Sparta. Her brethren, Castor and Polydeukes, recovered her from Athens by force, and gave to her Æthra, the mother of Theseus, for The legend
of Helen. bondwoman. Then all the youths of Hellas wooed her in the young world's prime. She was at last assigned in wedlock to Menelaus, by whom she conceived her only earthly child, Hermione. Paris, by aid of Aphrodite, won her love and fled with her to Egypt and to Troy. In Troy she abode more than twenty years, and was the mate of Deiphobus after the death of Paris. When the strife raised for her sake was ended, Menelaus restored her with honour to his home in Lacedæmon. There she received Telemachus and saw her daughter mated to Neoptolemus. But even after death she rested not from the service of love. The great Achilles, who in life had loved her by hearsay, but had never seen her, clasped her among the shades upon the island Leuké and begat Euphorion. Through all these adventures Helen maintains an ideal freshness, a mysterious virginity of soul. She is not touched by the passion she inspires, or by the wreck of empires ruined in her cause. Fate deflowers her not, nor do years impair the magic of her charm. Like beauty, she belongs alike to all and none. She is not judged as wives or mothers are, though she is both ; to her belong soul-wounding blossoms of inexorable love, as well as pain-healing poppy-heads of oblivion ; all eyes are blinded by the adorable, incomparable grace which Aphrodite sheds around her form.[1]

Whether Helen was the slave or the beloved of Aphrodite, Helen and
Aphrodite. or whether, as Herodotus hinted, she was herself a kind of Aphrodite, we are hardly told. At one time she appears the willing servant of the goddess ; at another she groans beneath her bondage. But always and on all occasions she owes everything to the Cyprian queen. Her very body-gear preserved the powerful charm with which she was invested at her birth.

[1] I take this occasion of calling attention to the essay on Helen considered as an allegory of Greek Beauty, by Paul de St. Victor in his *Hommes et Dieux*.

When the Phocians robbed the Delphian treasure-house, the wife of one of their captains took and wore Helen's necklace, whereupon she doted on a young Epirot soldier and eloped with him.

Helen, the phantom of romance. Whose daughter was Helen? The oldest legend calls her the child of Leda and of Zeus. We have all read the tale of the swan who was her father amid the rushes of Eurotas— the tale which Leonardo and Sodoma and Buonarroti and Correggio thought worthy of their loveliest illustration. Another story gives her for the offspring of Oceanus and Tethys, as though, in fact, she were an Aphrodite risen from the waves. In yet a third, Zeus is her sire and Nemesis her mother : and thus the lesson of the tale of Troy was allegorised in Helen's pedigree. She is always god-begotten and divinely fair. Was it possible that anything so exquisite should have endured rough ravishment and borne the travail of the siege of Troy? This doubt possessed the later poets of the legend- ary age. They spun a myth according to which Helen reached the shore of Egypt on the ship of Paris; but Paris had to leave her there in cedar-scented chambers by the stream of Nile, when he went forth to plough the foam, uncomforted save by her phantom. And for a phantom the Greeks strove with the Trojans on the windy plains of Ilium. For a phantom's sake brave Hector died, and the leonine swiftness of Achilles was tamed, and Zeus bewailed Sarpedon, and Priam's towers were levelled with the ground. Helen, meanwhile—the beautiful, the inviolable—sat all day long among the palm-groves, twining lotus-flowers for her hair, and learning how to weave rare Eastern patterns in the loom. This legend hides a delicate satire upon human strife. For what do men disquiet themselves in warfare to the death, and tossing on sea-waves? Even for a phantom—for the shadow of their desire, the which remains secluded in some un- approachable, far, sacred land. A wide application may thus be given to Augustine's passionate outcry : "Quo vobis adhuc et adhuc ambulare vias difficiles et laboriosas? Non Helen, the sacrosanct. est requies ubi quæritis eam. Quærite quod quæritis; sed ibi non est ubi quæritis. Beatam vitam quæritis in regione mortis; non est illic." [1] Those who spake ill of Helen suffered. Stesichorus ventured in the Ἰλίου Πέρσις (Fall of Troy) to lay upon her shoulders all the guilt and suffering of Hellas and of Troy. Whereupon he was smitten with blindness, nor could he recover his sight till he had written the palinode which begins—

οὐκ ἔστ᾽ ἔτυμος λόγος οὗτος,
οὐδ᾽ ἔβας ἐν ναυσὶν ἐυσέλμοις,
οὐδ᾽ ἵκεο πέργαμα Τροίας.[2]

Even Homer, as Plato hints, knew not that blindness had fallen on him for like reason. To assail Helen with reproach was not less dangerous than to touch the Ark of the Covenant, for with the Greeks beauty was a holy thing. How perfectly beautiful she was, we know from the legend of the cups modelled upon her breasts suspended in the shrine of Aphrodite. When Troy was taken, and the hungry soldiers of Odysseus roamed through the burning palaces of Priam and his sons, their sword-points dropped before the vision of her loveliness. She had wrought all the ruin; yet Menelaus could not clasp her, when she sailed forth, swanlike, fluttering white raiment, with the imperturbable sweet smile of a goddess on her lips. It remained for a Roman poet, Virgil, to describe her vile and shrinking—

" Illa sibi infestos eversa ob Pergama Teucros,
Et pœnas Danaûm et deserti conjugis iras

---

[1] "To what end do ye travel hither and thither upon paths of toil and difficulty ? There is no repose where you are seeking it. Seek what you are seeking, but know it is not there where you are seeking it. A life of blessedness you look for in the realm of death. It is not there."

[2] "Not true is that tale ; nor didst thou journey in benched ships, or come to towers of Troy."

Permetuens, Troiæ et patriæ communis Erinnys,
Abdiderat sese atque aris invisa sedebat." [1]

The morality of these lines belongs to a later age of reflection
upon Greek romance. In Homer we discover no such epigrams. Between the Helen of the *Iliad*, reverenced by the
elders in the Scæan gate, and the Helen of the *Odyssey*, queenlike among her Spartan maidens, there has passed no agony
of fear. The shame which she has truly felt has been
tempered to a silent sorrow, and she has poured her grief
forth beside Andromache over the corpse of Hector. [2]

Helen in the
Iliad.

If we would fain see the ideal beauty of the early Greek
imagination in a form of flesh-and-blood reality, we must
follow Helen through the Homeric poems. She first appears
when Iris summons her to watch the duel of Paris and Menelaus. Husband and lover are to fight beneath the walls of Troy.
She, meanwhile, is weaving a purple peplus with the deeds of
war done and the woes endured for her sake far and wide :—

"She in a moment round her shoulders flings
Robe of white lawn, and from the threshold springs,
Yearning and pale, with many a tender tear.
Also two women in her train she brings,
The larged-eyed Clymené and Æthra fair,
And at the western gates right speedily they were." [3]

English eyes know in some slight measure how Helen looked
when she left her chamber and hastened to the gate ; for has
not Leighton painted her with just so much of far-off sorrow

[1] "She, shrinking from the Trojans' hate,
Made frantic by their city's fate,
Nor dreading less the Danaan sword,
The vengeance of her injured lord :
She, Troy's and Argos' common fiend,
Sat cowering, by the altar screened."—*Conington.*

[2] We may add that Virgil's treatment of Helen was necessitated by the
Roman's point of view. She had brought disaster upon Troy, and had
driven forth Æneas, the progenitor of Roman kings, into exile.

[3] Worsley's *Iliad*, iii. 17. The other quotations are from the same
version.

in her gaze as may become a daughter of the gods? In the gate sat Priam and his elders; and as they looked at Helen no angry curses rose to their lips, but reverential admiration filled them, together with an awful sense of the dread fate attending her :—

> " These, seeing Helen at the tower arrive,
>   One to another wingèd words addressed :
> ' Well may the Trojans and Achæans strive,
>   And a long time bear sorrow and unrest,
>   For such a woman, in her cause and quest,
> Who like immortal goddesses in face
>   Appeareth ; yet 'twere even thus far best
>   In ships to send her back to her own place,
> Lest a long curse she leave to us and all our race.' "

It is thus simply, and by no mythological suggestion of Aphrodite's influence, that Homer describes the spirit of beauty which protected Helen among the people she had brought to such sore straits.

Priam accosts her tenderly ; not hers the blame that high gods scourge him in his hoary age with war. Then he bids her sit beside him and name the Greek heroes while they march beneath. She obeys, and points out Agamemnon, Odysseus, and Ajax, describing each as she knew them of old. But for her twin brothers she looks in vain ; and the thought of them touches her with the sorrow of her isolation and dishonour. In the same book, after Paris has been withdrawn, not without discredit, from the duel by Aphrodite, Helen is summoned by her liege-mistress to his bed. Helen was standing on the walls, and the goddess, disguised as an old spinning-woman, took her by the skirt, bidding her hie back to her lover, whom she would find in his bedchamber, not as one arrayed for war, but as a fair youth resting haply from the dance. Homer gives no hint that Aphrodite is here the personified wish of Helen's own heart going forth to Paris. On the contrary, the Cyprian queen appears in the interests

[marginal note: Helen in the bedroom of Paris.]

of the Phrygian youth, whom she would fain see comforted. Under her disguise Helen recognised Aphrodite, the terrible queen, whose bondwoman she was forced to be. For a moment she struggled against her fate. "Art thou come again," she cried, "to bear me to some son of earth beloved of thee, that I may serve his pleasure to my own shame? Nay, rather, put off divinity, and be thyself his odalisque."

> "With *him* remain,
> *Him* sit with, and from heaven thy feet refrain ;
> Weep, till his wife he make thee, or fond slave.
> I go to him no more, to win new stain,
> And scorn of Trojan women again outbrave,
> Whelmed even now with grief's illimitable wave."

But go she must. Aphrodite is a hard taskmistress, and the mysterious bond of beauty which chains Helen to her service cannot be broken. It is in vain, too, that Helen taunts Paris : he reminds her of the first fruition of their love in the island Cranaë; and at the last she has to lay her down at his side, not uncomplying, conquered as it were by the reflex of the passion she herself excites. It is in the chamber of Paris that Hector finds her. She has vainly striven to send Paris forth to battle; and the sense of her own degradation, condemned to love a man love-worthy only for the beauty of his limbs, overcomes her when she sees the noble Hector clothed in panoply for war. Her passionate outbreak of self-pity and self-reproach is, perhaps, the strongest indication given in the *Iliad* of a moral estimate of Helen's crime. The most consummate art is shown by the poet in thus quickening the conscience of Helen by contact with the nobility of Hector. Like Guinevere, she for a moment seems to say : "Thou art the highest, and most human too !" casting from her as worthless the allurements of the baser love for whose sake she had left her home. In like manner, it was not without the most exquisite artistic intention that Homer made the parting scene between Andromache and Hector follow immediately upon

Helen and
Hector.

this meeting. For Andromache in the future there remained
only sorrow and servitude. Helen was destined to be tossed
from man to man, always desirable and always delicate, like
the sea-foam that floats upon the crests of waves. But there
is no woman who, reading the *Iliad*, would not choose to weep
with Andromache in Hector's arms, rather than to smile like
Helen in the laps of lovers for whom she little cared. Helen
and Andromache meet together before Hector's corpse, and it
is here that we learn to love best what is womanly in Leda's
daughter. The mother and the wife have bewailed him in
high thrilling threni. Then Helen advances to the bier and
cries :— *(Helen at Hector's funeral.)*

> " Hector, of brethren dearest to my heart,
>   For I in sooth am Alexander's bride,
>   Who brought me hither : would I first had died !
>   For 'tis the twentieth year of doom deferred
>   Since Troyward from my fatherland I hied ;
>   Yet never in those years mine ear hath heard
>   From thy most gracious lips one sharp accusing word ;
>   Nay, if by other I haply were reviled,
>   Brother, or sister fair, or brother's bride,
>   Or mother (for the king was alway mild),
>   Thou with kind words the same hast pacified,
>   With gentle words, and mien like summer-tide.
>   Wherefore I mourn for thee and mine own ill,
>   Grieving at heart : for in Troy town so wide
>   Friend have I none, nor harbourer of goodwill,
>   But from my touch all shrink with deadly shuddering chill."

It would have been impossible to enhance more worthily
than thus the spirit of courtesy and knightly kindness which
was in Hector—qualities, in truth, which, together with his
loyalty to Andromache, endeared the champion of the Trojans
to chivalry, and placed Hector, not Achilles, upon the list of
worthies beside King Arthur and Godfrey of Boulogue.[1]

---

[1] Hector was reckoned among the worthies because he belonged to the
race which founded the Roman empire. He was a link in that long chain
of causation summed up in Virgil's line :

> "Tantae molis erat Romanam condere gentem."

The character of Helen loses much of its charm and becomes
more conventional in the *Odyssey*. It is difficult to believe
that the poet who put into her lips the last lines of that
threnos could have ventured to display the same woman calm
and innocent and queenlike in the home of Menelaus :—

> " While in his mind he sat revolving this,
>   Forth from her fragrant bower came Helen fair,
>   Bright as the golden-spindled Artemis.
>   Adraste set the couch ; Alcippe there
>   The fine-spun carpet spread ; and Phylo bare
>   The silver basket which Alcandra gave,
>   Consort of Polybus, who dwelt whilere
>   In Thebes of Egypt, whose great houses save
>   Wealth in their walls, large store, and pomp of treasure brave."

Helen shows her prudence and insight by at once declaring
the stranger guest to be Telemachus ; busy with housewifely
kindness, she prepares for him a comfortable couch at night ;
nor does she shrink from telling again the tales of Troy, and
the craft which helped Odysseus in the Wooden Horse. The
blame of her elopement with Paris she throws on Aphrodite,
who had carried her across the sea :—

> " Leaving my child an orphan far away,
>   And couch, and husband who had known no peer,
>   First in all grace of soul and beauty shining clear."

Such words, no doubt, fell with honey-sweet flattery from
the lips of Helen on the ears of Menelaus. Yet how could he
forget the grief of his bereavement, the taunts of Achilles and
Thersites, and the ten years' toil at Troy endured for her ?
Perhaps he remembered the promise of Proteus, who had said,
" Thee will the immortals send to the Elysian plains and
furthest verge of earth ; where dwells yellow-haired Rhadamanthus, and where the ways of life are easiest for men ;
snow falls not there, nor storm, nor any rain, but Ocean ever
breathes forth delicate zephyr breezes to gladden men ; since

thou hast Helen for thine own, and art the son-in-law of Zeus." Helen's
nepenthé.
Such future was full recompense for sorrow in the past.
Besides, Helen, as Homer tells, had charms to soothe the soul
and drown the memory of the saddest things. Even at this
time, when thought is troublesome, she mixes Egyptian
nepenthé with the wine—nepenthé "which, whoso drinks
thereof when it is mingled in the bowl, begets for him oblivion
of all woe; through a whole day he drops no tear adown his
cheek, not even should his sire or mother die, nay, should
they slay his brother or dear son before his face, and he behold
it with his eyes. Such virtuous juices had the child of Zeus,
of potent charm, which Polydamna, wife of Thon, gave to her,
the Egyptian woman, where earth yields many medicines,
some of weal and some of bane." This nepenthé—the material
drug that lulls the soul in dreams, used by the spiritual power
of beauty which snares souls through the eyes—was Helen's
secret. In the fifteenth book of the *Odyssey* we have yet
another glimpse of Helen in the palace of Menelaus. She
interprets an omen in favour of Odysseus, which had puzzled
Menelaus, and gives to Telemachus a costly mantle, star-bright,
the weft of her own loom, produced from the very bottom of
the chest in which she stored her treasures. The only shadow
cast upon Helen in the *Odyssey* is to be found lurking in the
ominous name of Megapenthes, Menelaus' son by a slave-
woman, who was destined after his sire's death to expel her
from fair Lacedæmon. We may remember that it was on the
occasion of the spousal of this son to Alector's daughter, and
of the sending of Hermione to be the bride of Neoptolemus,
that Telemachus first appeared before the eyes of Helen.

The charm of Helen in the Homeric poems is due in a Helen in
Æschylus.
great measure to the divine limpidity of the poet's art. The
situations in which she appears are never strained, nor is the
ethical feeling, though indicated, suffered to disturb the calm
influence of her beauty. This is not the case with Æschylus.
Already, as before hinted, Stesichorus in his lyric interludes

had ventured to assail the character of Helen, applying to her
conduct the moral standard which Homer kept carefully out
of sight. Æschylus goes further. His object was to use
Hellenic romance as the subject-matter for a series of dramatic
studies which should set forth his conception of the divine
government of the world. A genius for tragedy which has
never been surpassed, was subordinated by him to a sublime
philosophy of human life. It was no longer possible for
Helen to escape judgment. Her very name supplied the keynote of reproach. Rightly was she called Helen—ἑλέναυς,
ἑλανδρος, ἑλέπτολις—"a hell of ships, hell of men, hell of
cities," she sailed forth to Troy, and the heedless Trojans sang
marriage songs in her praise, which soon were turned to songs
of mourning for her sake. She, whom they welcomed as "a
spirit of unruffled calm, a gentle ornament of wealth, a darter
of soft glances, a soul-wounding love-blossom," was found to
be no less a source of mischief than is a young lion nurtured
in the palace for the ruin of its heirs. Soon had the Trojans
reason to revile her as a "Fury bringing woe on wives."
The choruses of the *Agamemnon* are weighted with the burden
of her sin. "Ah, ah! misguided Helen!" it breaks forth:
"thine is the blood-guilt of those many many souls slain
beneath Troy walls!" She is incarnate Até, the soul-seducing,
crime-engendering, woe-begetting curse of two great nations.
Zeus, through her sin, wrought ruin for the house of Priam,
wanton in its wealth. In the dark came blinded Paris and
stole her forth, and she went lightly through her husband's
doors, and dared a hateful deed. Menelaus, meanwhile,
gazed on the desecrated marriage-bed, and seemed to see her
floating through his halls; and the sight of beauteous statues
grew distasteful to his eyes, and he yearned for her across
the sea in dreams. Nought was left, when morning came, but
vain forth-stretchings of eager hands after the shapes that
follow on the paths of sleep. Then war awoke, and Ares,
who barters the bodies of men for gold, kept sending home to

Hellas from Troy a little white dust stored in brazen urns.
It is thus that Æschylus places in the foreground, not the
witchery of Helen and the charms of Aphrodite, but her
lightness and her sin, the woe it wrought for her husband,
and the heavy griefs that through her fell on Troy and Hellas.
It would be impossible to accentuate the consequences of the
woman's crime with sterner emphasis.

Unfortunately we have no means of stating how Sophocles   Helen in
dealt with the romance of Helen.   Judging by analogy, how-   Euripides.
ever, we may feel sure that in this, as in other instances, he
advanced beyond the ethical standpoint of Æschylus, by
treating the child of Leda, no longer as an incarnation of
dæmonic Até, but as a woman whose character deserved the
most profound analysis.   Euripides, as usual, went a step
farther.   The bloom of unconscious innocence had been
brushed by Æschylus from the flower of Greek romance.
Subsequent dramatists were compelled in some way or another
to moralise the character of Helen.   The way selected by
Euripides was to bring her down to the level of common life.
The scene in the *Troades* in which Helen stands up to plead
for her life against Hecuba before the angry Menelaus is one
of the most complete instances of the Euripidean sophistry.
The tragic circumstances of Troy in ruins and of injured
husband face to face with guilty wife are all forgotten, while
Helen develops a very clever defence of her conduct in a long
rhetorical oration.   The theatre is turned into a law-court,
and forensic eloquence is substituted for dramatic poetry.
Hecuba replies with an elaborate description of the lewdness,
vanity, and guile of Helen, which we may take to be a fair
statement of the poet's own conception of her character, since
in the *Orestes* he puts similar charges into the mouth of
Agamemnon's daughter.   There is no doubt that Hecuba has
the best of the argument.   She paints the beauty of her son
Paris and the barbaric pomp which he displayed at Sparta.
Then turning to Helen—

ὁ σὸς δ' ἰδών νιν νοῦς ἐποιήθη κύπρις·
τὰ μῶρα γὰρ πάντ' ἐστὶν Ἀφροδίτη βροτοῖς,
καὶ τοὔνομ' ὀρθῶς ἀφροσύνης ἄρχει θεᾶς.[1]

The Troades. Sentencious epigrams like this, by which the myths were philosophised to suit the occasions of daily life, exactly suited the temper of the Athenian audience in the age of Euripides. But Hecuba proceeds : " You played your husband off against your lover, and your lover against your husband, hoping always to keep the one or the other by your artifice ; and when Troy fell, no one found you tying the halter or sharpening the knife against your own throat, as any decent woman in your position would have done." At the end of her speech she seems to have convinced Menelaus, who orders the attendants to carry off Helen to the ships in order that she may be taken to Argos and killed there. Hecuba begs him not to embark her on the same boat with himself. "Why ?" he asks. "Is she heavier than she used to be?" The answer is significant :—

οὐκ ἔστ' ἐραστὴς ὅστις οὐκ ἀεὶ φιλεῖ.

The Orestes. "Once a lover, always a lover." And so it turns out ; for, at the opening of the *Orestes,* Helen arrives in comfort at the side of Menelaus. He now is afraid lest she should be seized and stoned by the Argives, whose children had been slain for her sake in Troy. Nor is the fear vain. Orestes and Pylades lay hold of her, and already the knife is at her throat, when Phœbus descends and declares that Helen has been caught up to heaven to reign with her brothers Castor and Polydeukes. A more unethical termination to her adventures can hardly be imagined ; for Euripides, following hitherto upon the lines of the Homeric story, has been at great pains to analyse her legend into a common tale of adultery and female fascination. He now suddenly shifts his ground and deifies the woman he

[1] "Thy own soul, gazing at him, became Kupris : for Aphrodite, as her name denotes, is all the folly of mortals."

has sedulously vilified before. His true feeling about Helen
is expressed in the lines spoken by Electra to Clytemnestra
(*Electra*, 1062) :—

> τὸ μὲν γὰρ εἶδος αἶνον ἄξιον φέρει
> Ἐλένης τε καὶ σοῦ, δύο δ᾽ ἔφυτε συγγόνω,
> ἄμφω ματαίω Κάστορός τ᾽ οὐκ ἀξίω.
> ἡ μὲν γὰρ ἁρπασθεῖσ᾽ ἑκοῦσ᾽ ἀπώλετο,
> σὺ δ᾽ ἄνδρ᾽ ἄριστον Ἑλλάδος διώλεσας.

"You and your sister are a proper pair, and your beauty has
brought you the credit you deserve ; both are light women
and unworthy of Castor ; for Helen allowed herself to be
ravished and undone, while you killed the best man in
Greece." Further illustrations of the Euripidean conception
of Helen as a worthless woman, who had the art to reconquer
a weak husband's affection, might be drawn from the tirade
of Peleus against Menelaus in the *Andromache* (590, etc.)[1]

This Euripidean reading of the character of Helen was
natural to a sceptical and sophistical age, when the dimly
moralised myths of ancient Hellas had become the raw
material for a poet's casuistry. Yet, in the heart of the
Greek people, Homer had still a deeper, firmer place than
even Euripides ; and the thought of Helen, ever beautiful
and ever young, survived the rude analysis of the Athenian
drama. Her romance recovered from the prosaic rationalism
to which it had been subjected—thanks, no doubt, to the
many sculptors and painters who immortalised her beauty,
without suggesting the woes that she had brought upon the
world. Those very woes, perhaps, may have added pathos
to her charm : for had not she too suffered in the strife of
men ? How the artists dealt with the myth of Helen, we only

[1] Quite another view of Helen's character is developed in the *Helena*,
where Euripides has followed the Stesichorean version of her legend with
singular disregard for consistency. Much might be said on this point
about the licence in handling mythical material the Attic dramatists
allowed themselves.

In plastic art.

know by scattered hints and fragments. One bas-relief, engraved by Millingen, reveals her standing calm beneath the sword of Menelaus. That sword is lifted, but it will not fall. Beauty, breathed around her like a spell, creates a magic atmosphere through which no steel can pierce. In another bas-relief, from the Campana Museum, she is entering Sparta on a chariot, side by side with Menelaus, not like a captive, but with head erect and haughty mien, and proud hand placed upon the horse's reins. Philostratus, in his *Lives of the Sophists*, describes an exceedingly beautiful young philosopher, whose mother bore a close resemblance to the picture of Helen by Eumelus. If the lineaments of the mother were repeated in the youth, the eyes of Helen in her picture must have been large and voluptuous, her hair curled in clusters, and her teeth of dazzling whiteness. It is probable that the later artists, in their illustrations of the romance of Helen, used the poems of Lesches and Arctinus, now lost, but of which the *Posthomerica* of Quintus Smyrnæus preserve to us a feeble reflection. This poet of the fourth century after Christ does all in his power to rehabilitate the character of Helen by laying the fault of her crime on Paris, and by describing at length the charm which Venus shed around her sacred person. It was only by thus insisting upon the dæmonic influence which controlled the fate of Helen, that the conclusions reached by the rationalising process of the dramatists could be avoided. The Cyclic poems thus preserved the heroic character of Helen and her husband at the expense of Aphrodite, while Euripides had said plainly : " What you call Aphrodite is your own lust." Menelaus, in the *Posthomerica*, finds Helen hidden in the palace of Deiphobus ; astonishment takes possession of his soul before the shining of her beauty, so that he stands immovable, like a dead tree, which neither north nor south wind shakes. When the Greek heroes leave Troy town, Agamemnon leads Cassandra captive, Neoptolemus is followed by Andromache, and Hecuba weeps

In Quintus Smyrnæus.

torrents of tears in the strong grasp of Odysseus. A crowd of Trojan women fill the air with shrill laments, tearing their tresses and strewing dust upon their heads. Meanwhile, Helen is delayed by no desire to wail or weep; but a comely shame sits on her black eyes and glowing cheeks. Her heart leaps, and her whole form is as lovely as Aphrodite was when the gods discovered her with Ares in the net of Hephæstus. Down to the ships she comes with Menelaus hand in hand; and the people, "gazing on the glory and the winning grace of the faultless woman, were astonished; nor could they dare by whispers or aloud to humble her with insults; but gladly they saw in her a goddess, for she seemed to all what each desired." This is the apotheosis of Helen; and this reading of her romance is far more true to the general current of Greek feeling than that suggested by Euripides. Theocritus, in his exquisite marriage-song of Helen, has not a word to say by hint or innuendo that she will bring a curse upon her husband. Like dawn is the beauty of her face; like the moon in the heaven of night, or the spring when winter is ended, or like a cypress in the meadow, so is Helen among Spartan maids. When Apollonius of Tyana, the most famous *medium* of antiquity, evoked the spirit of Achilles by the pillar on his barrow in the Troad, the great ghost consented to answer five questions. One of these concerned Helen: Did she really go to Troy? Achilles indignantly repudiated the notion. She remained in Egypt; and this the heroes of Achaia soon knew well; "but we fought for fame and Priam's wealth." *In Theocritus and Apollonius.*

It is curious at the point of transition in the Roman world from Paganism to Christianity to find the name of Helen prominent. Helena, the mother of Constantine, was famous with the early Church as a pilgrim to Jerusalem, where she discovered the true cross, and destroyed the Temple of Venus. For one Helen, East and West had warred together on the plains of Troy. Following the steps of another Helen, West *Saint Helena.*

and East now disputed the possession of the Holy Sepulchre.
Such historical parallels are, however, little better than puns.
It is far more to the purpose to notice how the romance of
Helen of Troy, after lying dormant during the Middle Ages,
shone forth again in the pregnant myth of Faustus.   The
final achievement of Faust's magic was to evoke Helen from
the dead and hold her as his paramour.   To the beauty of
Greek art the mediæval spirit stretched forth with yearning
and begot the modern world.   Marlowe, than whom no poet
of the North throbbed more mightily with the passion of the
Renaissance, makes his Faust exclaim :—

Helen in the
Faust legend
—Marlowe.

> " Was this the face that launched a thousand ships
> And burnt the topless towers of Ilium ?
> Sweet Helen, make me immortal with a kiss !
> Her lips suck forth my soul : see where it flies !
> Come, Helen, come, give me my soul again.
> Here will I dwell, for heaven is in these lips,
> And all is dross that is not Helena.
> I will be Paris, and, for love of thee,
> Instead of Troy shall Wertenberg be sacked ;
> And I will combat with weak Menelaus,
> And wear thy colours on my plumèd crest ;
> Yea, I will wound Achilles in the heel,
> And then return to Helen for a kiss.
> Oh, thou art fairer than the evening air
> Clad in the beauty of a thousand stars ;
> Brighter art thou than flaming Jupiter
> When he appeared to hapless Semele ;
> More lovely than the monarch of the sky
> In wanton Arethusa's azured arms ;
> And none but thou shalt be my paramour."

Marlowe, as was natural, contented himself with an external
handling of the Faust legend.   Goethe allegorised the whole,
and turned the episode of Helen into a parable of modern
poetry.   When Lynkeus, the warder, is reprimanded for not
having duly asked Helen into the feudal castle, he defends
himself thus :—

In Goethe's
Faust.

" Harrend auf des Morgens Wonne,
    Oestlich spähend ihren Lauf,
    Ging auf einmal mir die Sonne
    Wunderbar im Süden auf.

" Zog den Blick nach jener Seite,
    Statt der Schluchten, statt der Höh'n,
    Statt der Erd und Himmelsweite,
    Sie, die Einzige, zu spähn." [1]

The new light that rose upon the Middle Ages came not from the East, but from the South; no longer from Galilee, but from Greece.   The fruit of her union with Faust is Euphorion, the genius of romantic art.

Thus, after living her long life in Hellas as the ideal of beauty, unqualified by moral attributes, Helen passed into modern mythology as the ideal of the beauty of the Pagan world.   True to her old character, she arrives to us across the waters of oblivion with the cestus of the goddess round her waist, and the divine smile upon her lips.   Age has not impaired her charm, nor has she learned the lesson of the Fall. Ever virginal and ever fair, she is still the slave of Aphrodite.   In Helen we welcome the indestructible Hellenic spirit.

The ideal of beauty.

PENELOPE is the exact opposite to Helen.   The central point in her character is intense love of her home, an almost cat-like attachment to the house where she first enjoyed her husband's love, and which is still full of all the things that make her life worth having.   Therefore, when at last she

Penelope, the faithful wife.

[1] " Eastward was my glance directed,
        Watching for the sun's first rays ;
        In the south—oh, sight of wonder !
        Rose the bright orb's sudden blaze.

    " Thither was my eye attracted ;
        Vanished bay and mountain height,
        Earth an   heaven unseen and all things,
        All but that enchanted light."—*Anster*.

thinks that she will have to yield to the suitors and leave it, these words are always on her lips :—

$$\delta\hat{\omega}\mu\alpha$$
$$\kappa o \upsilon \rho \acute{\iota} \delta \iota o \nu\; \mu \acute{\alpha} \lambda \alpha\; \kappa \alpha \lambda \grave{o} \nu\; \acute{\epsilon} \nu \acute{\iota} \pi \lambda \epsilon \iota o \nu\; \beta \iota \acute{o} \tau o \iota o,$$
$$\tau o \hat{\upsilon}\; \pi o \tau \epsilon\; \mu \epsilon \mu \nu \acute{\eta} \sigma \epsilon \sigma \theta \alpha \iota\; \acute{o} \acute{\iota} o \mu \alpha \iota\; \acute{\epsilon} \nu \pi \epsilon \rho\; \grave{o} \nu \epsilon \acute{\iota} \rho \psi.[1]$$

Home and husband.

We can scarcely think of Penelope except in the palace of Ithaca, so firmly has this home-loving instinct been embedded in her by her maker. Were it not that the passion for her home is controlled and determined by a higher and more sacred feeling, this Haushälterischness of Penelope would be prosaic. Not only, however, has Homer made it evident in the *Odyssey* that the love of Ithaca is subordinate in her soul to the love of Odysseus; but a beautiful Greek legend teaches how in girlhood she sacrificed the dearest ties that can bind a woman to her love for the hero who had wooed and won her. Pausanias says that when Odysseus was carrying her upon his chariot forth to his own land, her father Icarius followed in their path and besought her to stay with him. The young man was ready, busked for the long journey. The old man pointed to the hearth she had known from childhood. Penelope between them answered not a word, but covered her face with her veil; this action Odysseus interpreted rightly, and led his bride away, willing to go where he would go, yet unwilling to abandon what she dearly loved. No second Odysseus could cross the woman's path. Among the suitors there was not one like him. Therefore she clung to her house-tree in Ithaca, the olive round which Odysseus had built the nuptial chamber; and none, till he appeared, by force or guile might win her thence. It is precisely this tenacity in the character of Penelope which distinguishes her from Helen, the daughter of adventure and the child of change, to whom migration was no less natural than to the swan that gave her life. Another characteristic of Penelope is her prudence. Having to deal

---

[1] "The home of my wedded years, exceeding fair, filled with all the goods of life, which even in dreams methinks I shall remember."

with the uproarious suitors camped in her son's halls, she
deceives them with fair words, and promises to choose a
husband from their number when she has woven a winding-
sheet for Laertes. Three years pass, and the work is still not
finished. At last a maiden tells the suitors that every night
Penelope undoes by lamplight what she had woven in the
daytime. This ruse of the defenceless woman has passed into
a proverb, and has become so familiar that we forget, perhaps,
how true a parable it is of those who in their weakness do
and undo daily what they would fain never do at all, trifling
and procrastinating with tyrannous passions which they are
unable to expel from the palace of their souls. The prudence
of Penelope sometimes assumes a form which reminds us of
the heroines of Hebrew story; as when, for example, she
spoils the suitors of rich gifts by subtle promises and engage-
ments carefully guarded. Odysseus, seated in disguise near
the hall-door, watches her success and secretly approves. The
same quality of mind makes her cautious in the reception of
the husband she has waited for in widowhood through twenty
years. The dog Argus has no doubt. He sees his master
through the beggar's rags, and dies of joy. The handmaid
Eurycleia is convinced as soon as she has touched the wound
upon the hero's foot and felt the well-remembered scar. Not
so Penelope. Though the great bow has been bent and the
suitors have been slain, and though Eurycleia comes to tell
her the whole truth, the queen has yet the heart to seat
herself opposite Odysseus by the fire, and to prove him with
cunningly-devised tests. There is something provocative of
anger against Penelope in this cross-questioning. But our
anger is dissolved in tears, when at last, feeling sure that her
husband and none other is there verily before her eyes, she
flings her arms around him in that long and close embrace.
Homer even in this supreme moment has sustained her
character by a trait, which, however delicate, can hardly
escape notice. Her lord is weary, and would fain seek the

(marginal notes)
Penelope and the suitors.

Meeting of Penelope and Odysseus.

solace of his couch. But he has dropped a hint that still more labours are in store for him. Then Penelope replies that his couch is ready at all times and whensoever he may need; no hurry about that; meanwhile she would like to hear the prophecy of Teiresias. Helen, the bondwoman of Dame Aphrodite, would not have waited thus upon the verge of love's delight, long looked for with strained widow's eyes. Yet it would be unfair to Penelope to dwell only on this prudent and somewhat frigid aspect of her character. She is, perhaps, most amiable when she descends among the suitors and prays Phemius to cease from singing of the heroes who returned from Troy. It is more than she can bear to sit weaving in the silent chamber mid her damsels, listening to the shrill sound of the lyre and hearing how other men have reached their homes, while on the waves Odysseus still wanders, and none knows whether he be alive or dead. It may be noticed that just as Helen is a mate meet for easily-persuaded Menelaus and luxurious Paris, so Penelope matches the temper of the astute, enduring, persevering Odysseus. As a creature of the fancy she is far less fascinating than Helen; and this the poet seems to have felt, for side by side with Penelope in the *Odyssey* he has placed the attractive forms of Circe, Calypso, and Nausicaa. The gain is double; not only are the hearers of the romance gladdened by the contrast of these graceful women with the somewhat elegiac figure of Penelope, but the character of Odysseus for constancy is greatly enhanced. How fervent must the love of home have been in the man who could quit Calypso, after seven years' sojourn, for the sake of a wife grown gray with twenty widowed years! Odysseus tells Calypso to her face that she is far fairer than his wife : [1]—

Calypso.

οἶδα καὶ αὐτὸς
πάντα μάλ', οὕνεκα σεῖο περίφρων Πηνελόπεια
εἶδος ἀκιδνοτέρη, μέγεθός τ', εἰς ὄμμα ἰδέσθαι.

---

[1] "I know well that Penelope is inferior to thee, in form and stature, to the eyes of men."

"As far as looks go, Penelope is nothing beside thee." But what Odysseus leaves unsaid—the grace of the first woman who possessed his soul—constrains him with a deeper, tenderer power than any of Calypso's charms. Penelope, meanwhile, is pleading that her beauty in the absence of her lord has perished : [1]—

> ξεῖν᾽ ἤτοι μὲν ἐμὴν ἀρετὴν εἶδός τε δέμας τε
> ὤλεσαν ἀθάνατοι ὅτε Ἴλιον εἰσανέβαινον
> Ἀργεῖοι.

These two meet at last together, he after his long wanderings, and she having suffered the insistance of the suitors in her palace ; and this is the pathos of the *Odyssey*. The woman, in spite of her withered youth and tearful years of widowhood, is still expectant of her lord. He, unconquered by the pleasures cast across his path, unterrified by all the dangers he endures, clings in thought to the bride whom he led forth, a blushing maiden, from her father's halls. O just, subtle, and mighty Homer ! There is nothing of Greek here more than of Hebrew, or of Latin, or of German. It is pure humanity.

Calypso is not a woman, but a goddess. She feeds upon ambrosia and nectar, while her maidens spread before Odysseus the food of mortals. Between her and Hermes there is recognition at first sight ; for god knows god, however far apart their paths may lie. Yet the love that Calypso bears Odysseus brings this daughter of Atlas down to earth ; and we may reckon her among the women of Homer. How mysterious, as the Greek genius apprehended mystery, is her cavern, hidden far away in the isle Ogygia, with the grove of forest-trees before it and the thick vine flourishing around its mouth. Meadows of snowflake and close-flowering selinus gird it round ; and on the branches brood all kinds of birds. It is an island such as the Italian painters bring before us in their rarest moments of artistic divination, where the blue-

---

[1] "Of a truth my goodliness and beauty of person the gods destroyed what time the Argives went up into Troy town."

green of the twilight mingles with the green-blue sea, and the overarching verdure of deep empurpled forest-shade. Under those trees, gazing across the ocean, in the still light of the evening star, Odysseus wept for his far-distant home. Then, heavy at heart, he gathered up his raiment, and clomb into Calypso's bed at night : [1]—

> ἐπεὶ οὐκέτι ἥνδανε νύμφη.
> ἀλλ' ἦτοι νύκτας μὲν ἰαύεσκεν καὶ ἀνάγκῃ
> ἐν σπέσσι γλαφυροῖσι παρ' οὐκ ἐθέλων ἐθελούσῃ.

To him the message of Hermes recalling him to labour on the waves was joy. But to the nymph herself it brought mere bitterness: "Hard are ye, gods, and envious above all, who grudge that goddesses should couch thus openly with mortal men, if one should make a dear bedfellow for herself. For so the rosy-fingered morning chose Orion, till ye gods that lead an easy life grew jealous, and in Ogygia him the golden-throned maid Artemis slew with her kind arrows." This wail of the immortal nymph Calypso for her roving spouse of seven short years has a strange pathos in it. It seems to pass across the sea like a sigh of winds awakened, none knows how, in summer midnight, that swells and dies far off upon moon-silvered waves. The clear human activity of Odysseus cuts the everlasting calm of Calypso like a knife, shredding the veil that hides her from the eyes of mortals; then he fares onward to resume the toils of real existence in a land whereof she nothing knows. There is a fragment of his last speech to Penelope, which sounds like an echo of Calypso's lamentation. "Death," he says, "shall some day rise for me, tranquil from the tranquil deep, and I shall die in delicate old age." We seem to feel that in his last trance Odysseus might have heard the far-off divine sweet voice of Calypso, like the voice of waves and waters, calling him and have hastened to her cry.

---

[1] "For the nymph pleased him no longer. Nathless, as need was, he slept the night in hollow caverns, beside her loving him who loved her not."

Circe is by no means so mysterious as Calypso. Yet she Circe and
her island. belongs to one of the most interesting families in Greek romance : her mother was Perse, daughter of Oceanus ; her father was Helios ; she is own sister, therefore, to the Colchian Æetes, and aunt of the redoubtable Medea. She lives in the isle of Æææa, not, like Calypso, deep embowered in groves, but in a fair open valley sweeping downward to the sea, whence her hearth-smoke may be clearly descried. Nor is her home an ivy-curtained cavern of the rocks, but a house well built of polished stone, protected from the sea-winds by oak-woods. Here she dwells in grand style, with nymphs of the streams and forests to attend upon her, and herds of wild beasts, human-hearted, roaming through her park. Odysseus always speaks of her with respect as πότνια Κίρκη . . . . δῖα θεάων . . . . Κίρκη ἐϋπλόκαμος δεινὴ θεὸς αὐδήεσσα (august Circe . . . . divine among goddesses . . . . Circe of the fair tresses, dread goddess, using the speech of mortals). Like Calypso, she has a fair shrill voice that goes across the waters, and as her fingers ply the shuttle, she keeps singing through the summer air. By virtue of her birthright, as a daughter of the sun, she under-stands the properties of plant and drug. Poppy and henbane and mandragora, all herbs of subtle juice that draw soul-quelling poison from the fat earth and the burning sun, are hers to use as she thinks fit. And the use she makes of them is malicious ; for, fairy-like and wanton, she will have the men who visit her across the seas, submit their reason to her lure. Therefore she turns them to swine ; and the lions and wolves of the mountain she tames in like manner, so that they fawn and curl their long tails and have no heart to ravin any more. This is how she treats the comrades of Odysseus : " She drew them in and set them on benches and on chairs, and put before them cheese and meal and yellow honey, mixing there-with Pramnian wine ; but with the food she mingled baleful drugs, to make them quite forget their fatherland. But when

Her park of
human
beasts.
she had given them thereof and they had drunk, straightway
she smote them with a rod and shut them up in styes. Of
swine they had the head, the voice, the form, the bristles; but
their mind stayed firm as it had been before. So they then
were penned up, weeping bitter tears; but Circe threw before
them acorns of the oak and ilex and cornel-berries, food that
the forest-ranging swine are wont to eat." What is admirable
in this description is its gravity. Circe is not made out particularly wicked or malignant. She is acting only, after her
kind, like some beautiful but baleful plant—a wreath, for
instance, of red briony berries, whereof if children eat, they
perish. Nor, again, is there a touch of the burlesque in the
narration. Therefore, in the charming picture which Rivière
has painted of Circe, we trace a vein of modern feeling.
Clasping her knees with girlish glee, she sits upon the ground
beneath a tangle of wild vine, and watches the clumsy hogs
that tumble with half-comic, half-pathetic humanity expressed
in their pink eyes and grunting snouts before her. So, too,
the solemn picture by Burne-Jones, a masterpiece of colouring,
adds something mediæval to the Homeric Circe. The tall
sunflowers that remind us of her father, the cringing panthers,
black and lithe, the bending figure of the saffron-vested witch,
the jars of potent juices, and the distant glimpse of sea and
shore, suggest more of malignant intention than belongs to
the πότνια Κίρκη (august Circe), the Κίρκη πολυφάρ-
μακος (Circe of many charmful drugs) of Homer's tale. It
was inevitable that modern art should infuse a deeper meaning into the allegory. The world has lived long and suffered
much and grown greatly since the age of Homer. We cannot
be so limpid and so childlike any longer. Yet the true charm
of Circe in the *Odyssey*, the spirit that distinguishes her
from Tannhäuser's Venus and Orlando's Fata Morgana and
Ruggiero's Alcina and Tancred's Armida, lies just in this,
that the poet has passed lightly over all the dark and perilous
places of his subject. This delicacy of touch can never be

regained by art. It belonged to the conditions of the first
Hellenic bloom of fancy, to suggest without insistance and to
realise without emphasis. Impatient readers may complain of
want of depth and character; they would fain see the Circe
of the *Odyssey* as strongly moralised as the Medea of Euripides.
But in Homer only what is human attains to real intensity.
The marvellous falls off and shades away into soft air-tints and
delightful dreams. Still, it requires the interposition of the
gods to save Odysseus from the charms of the malicious maid.
As Hermes came to Priam on the path between Troy town The visit of
and the Achaian ships, so now he meets the hero : [1]—
Hermes.

νεηνίῃ ἀνδρὶ ἐοικὼς
πρῶτον ὑπηνήτῃ· τοῦπερ χαριεστάτη ἥβη.

A plant of moly is in his hand; and this will be the anti-
dote to Circe's philtre. Odysseus' sword and strong will must
do the rest. When Circe has once found her match, we are
astonished at the *bonhomie* which she displays. The game is
over : there remains nothing but graceful hospitality on her
part—elegant banquets, delicious baths, soft beds, the restoration of the ship's crew to their proper shape, and a store of
useful advice for the future. "There all the days, for a whole
year, we sat feasting and drinking honeyed wine; but when
the year was full, and the seasons had gone round, moon
waning after moon, and the long days were finished, my dear
comrades called on me by name, and spake once more of
home."

One more female figure from the *Odyssey* remains as yet Nausicaa.
untouched; and this is the most beautiful of all. Nausicaa
has no legendary charm; she is neither mystic goddess nor
weird woman, nor is hers the dignity of wifehood. She is

[1] " Like to a young man when his beard has just begun to grow, whose
bloom is then most full of charm." This beautiful description of Hermes,
which occurs twice over in the Homeric poems, has received a perfect
plastic illustration in the statue recently discovered at Olympia.

simply the most perfect maiden, the purest, freshest, lightest-hearted girl of Greek romance. Odysseus passes straight from the solitary island of Ogygia, where elm and poplar and cypress overshadow Calypso's cavern, into the company of this real woman. It is like coming from a land of dreams into a dewy garden when the sun has risen; the waves through which he has fared upon his raft have wrought for him, as it were, a rough re-incarnation into the realities of human life. For the sea-brine is the source of vigour; and into the deep he has cast, together with Calypso's raiment, all memory of her.

Nausicaa's dream.

Nausicaa was asleep in her Phæacian chamber when Athene, mindful of Odysseus' need, came down and warned her in a dream that she should bestir herself, and wash her clothes against her marriage day. When the damsel woke, she went straight to her father, Alcinous, and begged him to provide a horse and mules. Like a prudent girl, she said nothing of her marriage, but spoke of the cares of the household. Her five brothers, she said, the two wedded and the other three in the bloom of youth, want shining raiment for the dance, and her duty it is to see that the clothes are always ready. Alcinous knew in his heart what she really meant, but he answered her with no unseemly jest. Only he promised a cart and a pair of mules; and her mother gave her food to eat, and wine in a skin, and a golden cruse of oil, that she and her maidens might spend a pleasant morning by the sea-beach, and bathe and anoint themselves when their clothes-washing was finished.

Meeting of Odysseus and Nausicaa.

A prettier picture cannot be conceived than that drawn by Homer of Nausicaa, with her handmaidens thronging together in the cart, which jogs downward through the olive-gardens to the sea. The princess holds the whip and drives; and when she reaches the stream's mouth by the beach, she loosens the mules from the shafts, and turns them out to graze in the deep meadow. Then the clothes are washed, and the luncheon is taken from the basket, and the game of

ball begins.   How the ball flew aside and fell into the water,
and how the shrill cries of the damsels woke Odysseus from
his sleep, every one remembers.   The girls are fluttered by
the sight of the great naked man, rugged with brine and
bruised with shipwreck.   Nausicaa alone, as becomes a
princess, stands her ground and questions him.   The simple
delicacy with which this situation is treated, makes the
whole episode one of the most charming in Homer.   Very
natural and not less noble is the change from pity to admiration, expressed by the damsel, when Odysseus has bathed in
running water and rubbed himself with oil and put on goodly
raiment given him by the girls.   Pallas sheds treble grace
upon his form, and makes his hair to fall in clusters like
hyacinth-blossoms, so that an artist who moulds figures of
gilt silver could not shape a comelier statue.   The princess,
with yesternight's dream still in her soul, wishes he would
stay and be her husband.   The girlish simplicity of Nausicaa
is all the more attractive because the Phæacians are the most
luxurious race described by Homer.   The palace in which The palace
she dwells with her father is all of bronze and silver and $_{of\ Alcinous.}$
gold; it shines like the sun, and a blue line marks the brazen
cornice of the walls.   Dogs of silver and gold, Hephæstus'
work, which never can grow old through length of days,
protect the entrance.   Richly-woven robes are cast upon the
couches in the hall, and light is shed upon the banquet-tables
from blazing torches in the hands of golden boys.   Outside
the palace grows the garden, with well-divided orchard-rows,
where pears and figs and pomegranates and burnished apples
and olives flourish all year long.   The seasons change not in
Phæacian land for winter or for summer.   The west wind is
always blowing.   Pear follows after pear, and apple after
apple, and grape bunch after grape bunch, in a never-ending
autumn dance.   Vintage, too, is there; and there are the
trim flower-beds; and through the garden flow two fountains.
The whole pleasure-ground seems to have been laid out with

The life of
the Phæa-
cians.

geometrical Greek taste. It is a Paradise of neatness, sun-
bright, clear to take in at a glance. In this delightful palace
dwells Alcinous, a kind old man, among his sons; and much
delight they take in dance and song and games of strength.
The young men, whose beards are but just growing, leap in
rhythmic movement to the flute; the elder and more muscular
run or wrestle, and much contempt do these goodly fellows,
like English lads, reserve for men who are not athletes.
Odysseus has to rebuke one of them, Euryalus, by reminding
him that faultlessly fair bodies are not always the temples of
a godlike soul. Zeus gives not all of his good gifts to all;
for some men owe grace and favour to eloquence, others to
beauty, and a man may be like to the immortals in face and
form, and yet a fool. Alcinous well describes the temper of
his people when he says: "We are not faultless boxers, nor
yet wrestlers; but with our feet we race swiftly, and none
can beat us in rowing; and we aye love the banquet, and the
lyre, and dancing, and gay raiment, and warm baths, and
joys of love." It is therefore not without propriety that
Demodocus, their blind bard, "whom the Muse loved much,
and gave him good and evil; for she reft him of his sight and
gave him honeyed song," sings of Aphrodite tangled with
Ares in the net of Hephæstus. From this soft, luxurious,
comely, pleasure-loving folk Nausicaa springs up like a pure
blossom—anemone or lily of the mountains. She has all the
sweetness of temper which distinguishes Alcinous; but the
voluptuous living of his people cannot spoil her. The
maidenly reserve which she displays in her first reception of
Odysseus, her prudent avoidance of being seen with him in
the streets of the town while he is yet a stranger, and the
care she takes that he shall suffer nothing by not coming
with her to the palace, complete the portrait of a girl who
is as free from coquetry as she is from prudishness. Perhaps
she strikes our fancy with most clearness when, after bathing
and dressing, Odysseus passes her on his way through the

hall to the banquet. She leaned against the pillar of the roof and gazed upon Odysseus, and said : "Hail, guest, and be thou mindful of me when perchance thou art in thine own land again, for to me the first thou dost owe the price of life." This is the last word spoken by Nausicaa in the *Odyssey*. She is not mentioned among the Phæacians who took leave of the hero the day he passed to Ithaca.

Before quitting the women of Homer, we must return to the *Iliad ;* for without Briseis and Andromache their company would be incomplete. As the figures in a bas-relief are variously wrought, some projecting like independent statues in sharp light and shadow, while others are but half detached, and a third sort offer mere outlined profiles scarcely embossed upon the marble background ; even so the poet has obeyed a law of relative proportion in his treatment of character. The subordinate heroes, for example, in the *Iliad* fall away from the central figure of Achilles into more or less of slightness. This does not mean that we can trace the least indecision in Homer's touch, or that he has slurred his work by haste or incapacity. On the contrary, there is no poet from whom deeper lessons in the art of subordinating accessories to the main subject without impairing their real value can be learned. A sculptor like Pheidias knows how to give significance to the least indication of a form which he has placed upon the second plane in his bas-relief. Just so Homer inspires his minor characters with personality. To detach this personality in each case is the task of the critic ; yet his labour is no light one ; for the Homeric characters draw their life from incidents, motives, action. To the singer's fancy they appeared, not as products of the self-conscious imagination, but as living creatures ; and to separate them from their environment of circumstance is almost to destroy them. This is the specific beauty of the art of Homer. In its origin it must have been the outcome, not of reflection, but of inspired instinct ; for in the Homeric age psychological analysis was

Minor characters in Homer.

unknown, and the very nomenclature of criticism had yet to be invented. We can draw inexhaustible lessons in practical wisdom from the Homeric poems; but we cannot with impunity subject those delicate creations to the critical crucible. They delight both intellect and senses with a many-toned harmony of exquisitely modulated parts; but the instant we begin to dissect and theorise, we run a risk of attributing far more method and deliberation than was natural to a poet in the early age of Hellas. It is almost impossible to set forth the persons of Homer except in his own way, and in close connection with the incidents through which they are revealed; whereas the characters of a more self-conscious artist —the Medea, for example, or the Phædra of Euripides—can be described without much repetition of their speeches or reconstruction of the dramas in which they play their parts.

Andro-
mache.

Andromache offers a not inapt illustration to these remarks. She is beautiful, as all heroic women are; and Homer tells us she is "white-armed." We know no more about her person than this; and her character is exhibited only in the famous parting scene and in the two lamentations which she pours forth for her husband. Yet who has read the *Iliad* without carrying away a distinct conception of this, the most lovable among the women of Homer? She owes her character far less to what she does and what she says, than to how she looks in that ideal picture painted on our memory by Homer's verse. The affection of Hector for his wife, no less distinguished than the passion of Achilles for his friend, has made the Trojan prince rather than his Greek rival the hero of modern romance. When he leaves Ilion to enter on the long combat which ends in the death of Patroclus, the last thought of Hector is for Andromache. He finds her, not in their home, but on the wall, attended by her nurse, who carries in her arms his only son: [1]—

’Εκτορίδην ἀγαπητὸν ἀλίγκιον ἀστέρι καλῷ.

------

[1] "Hector's only son, like unto a fair star."

Her first words, after she has wept and clasped him, are : Parting from Hector. "Love, thy stout heart will be thy death ; nor hast thou pity of thy child or me, who soon shall be a widow. My father and my mother and my brothers are all slain : but, Hector, thou art father to me and mother and brother, and thou too art the husband of my youth. Have pity, then, and stay here in the tower, lest thy son be orphaned and thy wife a widow." The answer is worthy of the hero. "Full well," he says, "know I that Troy will fall, and I foresee the sorrow of my brethren and the king : but for these I grieve not : to think of thee, a slave in Argos, unmans me almost : yet even so I will not flinch or shirk the fight. My duty calls, and I must away." He stretches out his mailed arms to Astyanax ; but the child is frightened by his nodding plumes. So he lays aside his helmet, and takes the baby to his breast, and prays for him. Andromache smiles through her tears, and down the clanging causeway strides the prince. Poor Andromache has nothing left to do but to return home and raise the dirge for a husband as good as dead. When we see her again in the 22nd *Iliad*, she is weaving, and her damsels are heating a bath against Hector's return from the fight. Then suddenly the cry of Hecuba's anguish thrills her ears. Shuttle and thread drop from her hands ; she gathers up her skirts, and like a Mænad flies forth to the wall. She arrives in time to see her husband's body dragged through dust at Achilles' chariot-wheels away from Troy. She faints, and when she Lamentation for Astyanax and Hector. wakes, it is to utter the most piteous lament in Homer—not, however, for Hector so much, or for herself, as for Astyanax. He who was reared upon a father's knees and fed with marrow and the fat of lambs, and when play tired him, slept in soft beds among nursing-women, will now roam, an orphan, wronged and unbefriended, hunted from the company of happier men, or fed by charity with scanty scraps. The picture of an orphan's misery among cold friends and hard oppressors is wrought with the pathos of exquisite simplicity. And to the

same theme Andromache returns in the coronach which she
pours forth over the body of Hector.[1] "I shall be a widow
and a slave, and Astyanax will either be slaughtered by Greek
soldiers or set to base service in like bondage." Then the
sight of the corpse reminds her that the last words of her
sorrow must be paid to Hector himself. What touches her
most deeply is the thought of death in battle : [2]—

> οὐ γάρ μοι θνῄσκων λεχέων ἐκ χεῖρας ὄρεξας·
> οὐδέ τί μοι εἶπες πυκινὸν ἔπος, οὗτέ κεν αἰεὶ
> μεμνῄμην νύκτας τε καὶ ἤματα δακρυχέουσα.

Briseis. As far as studied delineation of character goes, Briseis is still
more a silhouette than Andromache. We know her as the
fair-cheeked damsel who was fain to stay with Achilles, and
who loved Patroclus because he kept for her a soothing word.
In her threnos for Patroclus she exclaims, " How one woe
after another takes me ! I saw my husband slain before our
city, and my three brethren ; but you, Patroclus, then comforted me, and said I should be Achilles' wife : you were ever
gentle." This is really all we know about her. Yet Briseis
lives in our memory by virtue of the great passions gathered
round her, and the weighty actions in which she plays her
part.

The cult of heroes. In course of years the heroes of the Homeric romances came
to be worshipped, not exactly like gods with θυσίαι (sacrifices),
but like the more than mortal dead with ἐναγίσματα (offerings). They had their chapels and their hearths, distinct
from the temples and the altars of the deities. These were
generally raised upon the supposed spot of their sepulture, or
in places which owed them special reverence as œkists or as

[1] What the Greeks called a *threnos,* exactly corresponds to the Celtic
coronach and Corsican *vocero ;* a funeral wail improvised by women over
the corpse of a dead relative or friend.

[2] " For, dying, thou didst not reach to me thy hand from the bed, nor
say to me words of wisdom, the which I might have aye remembered
night and day with tears."

ancestors. In the case of Œdipus, the translation of the hero
to the company of gods secured for him a cultus in Colonos.
It was supposed that heroes exercised a kindly influence over
the people among whom they dwelt ; haunting the neighbourhood in semi-corporeal visitations, conferring benefits upon
the folk, and exhibiting signs of anger when neglected. Thus
Philostratus remarks that Protesilaus had a fane in Thessaly,
"and many humane and favourable dealings doth he show the
men of Thessaly ; yea, and angerly also if he be neglected."[1]
The same Philostratus, whose works are a treasure-house of
information respecting the latest forms of Hellenic Paganism,
reports the actual form of prayer used by Apollonius of
Tyana at the tomb of Palamedes,[2] and makes the ghost of
Achilles complain : "The Thessalians for a long time have
remitted my offerings ; still I am not yet minded to display
my wrath against them." Achilles, who has been evoked
above his tomb in the Troad by the prayers of Apollonius,
proceeds to remark that even the Trojans revere him more
than his own people, but that he cannot restore the town of
Troy to its old prosperity. He hints, however, pretty broadly,
that if the Thessalians do not pay him more attention, he will
reduce them to the same state of misery as the Trojans. The
dæmon, it may be said in passing, vanishes, like a mediæval
ghost, at cockcrow.[3]

This cultus of the Homeric heroes was, of course, insepar- The heroes
able from a corresponding growth of artistic associations ; and art.
here it is not a little curious to compare our own indefinite
conceptions of the outward form of the heroic personages
with the very concrete incarnation they received from Greek
sculptors and painters. The first memorable attempt to express the heroes of Homer in marble was upon the pediment
at Ægina ; the first elaborate pictorial representation was
that of Polygnotus on the walls of the *Lesche* at Delphi. A
Greek *Lesche* was not unlike an Italian or Oriental café, ex-

[1] Ἡρωϊκός, 680.   [2] *Life of Apollonius*, 150.   [3] *Ibid*. 153, 154.

tended to suffice for the requirements of a whole city. What
has been discovered at Pompeii, in addition to the full
description of the Delphian *Lesche* by Pausanias, inclines us
to believe that the walls of these public places of resort were
not unfrequently decorated with Homeric pictures. The
beautiful frescoes of Achilles among the daughters of Lyco-
medes, of Achilles bathed by Thetis in the Styx, of Briseis
led forth by Patroclus into the company of the Achaian chiefs,
and of Penelope questioning the disguised Odysseus about
her husband, which have been unearthed in various parts of
Pompeii, sufficiently illustrate to modern minds the style of
this wall-painting. The treatise surnamed Εἰκόνες, or Images,
by Philostratus is an elaborate critical catalogue of a picture-
gallery of this sort ; and from many indications contained in
it we learn how thoroughly the heroes of Homer had acquired
a fixed corporeal personality. In describing, for example, a
picture of the lamentation for Antilochus, he says : "These
things are Homer's paintings, but the painter's action." Then
he goes on to point out the chief persons : "You can distinguish Odysseus at once by his severe and wideawake
appearance, Menelaus by his gentleness, Agamemnon by his
inspired look ; while Tydeus is indicated by his freedom, the
Telamonian Ajax by his grimness, and the Locrian by his
activity." [1] In another place he tells us that Patroclus was of
a honey-pale complexion (μελίχλωρος), with black eyes and
rather thick eyebrows ; his head was erect upon the neck,
like that of a man who excels in athletic exercises, his nose
straight, with wide nostrils, like an eager horse. These
descriptions occur in the *Heroic Dialogue.* They are supposed
to have been communicated by the dæmon, Protesilaus, to a
vine-dresser who frequented his tomb. Achilles, on the other
hand, had abundant hair, more pleasant to the sight in hue
than gold, with a nose inclining to the aquiline, angry brows,
and eyes so bright and lively that the soul seemed leaping

---

[1] Εἰκόνες, 820. (By Kayser, Zurich, 2nd ed.)

from them in fire.   Hector, again, had a terrible look about
him, and scorned to dress his hair ; and his ears were crushed,
not indeed by wrestling, for barbarians do not wrestle, but by
the habit of struggling for mastery with wild bulls.[1]

Some of the women of Homeric story, Helen for example, Cult of
and Iphigenia, received divine honours, together with suitable heroines.
artistic personification.   But women were not closely connected with the genealogical and gentile foundations of the
Greek cultus ; only a few, therefore, were thus distinguished.
What has here been said about the superstition that gave form
and distinctness to the creatures of Homeric fancy, may be
taken as applying in general to the attitude assumed by ancient
art.   The persons of a poem or a mythus were not subjected
to critical analysis as we dissect the characters of Hamlet or
of Faust.   But they were not on that account the less vividly
apprehended.   They tended more and more to become external
realities—beings with a definite form and a fixed character.   In
a word, through sculpture, painting, and superstition, they
underwent the same personifying process as the saints of
mediæval Italy.   To what extent the Attic drama exercised a
disturbing influence and interrupted this process has been
touched upon with reference to the Euripidean Helen.

[1] Ἡρωϊκός, 736, 733, 722.   For the curious detail about Hector's ears,
compare Theocr. 22, 45, where athletes are described τεθλαγμένοι οὔατα
πυγμαῖς (crushed about the ears by fisticuffs).   Statues of Hercules show
this.

CHAPTER V

HESIOD

The Difference between the Homeric and the Hesiodic Spirit—The Personality of Hesiod more Distinct than that of Homer—What we know about his Life—Perses—The Hesiodic Rhapsodes—*Theogony* and *Works and Days*—Didactic Poetry—The Story of Prometheus —Greek and Hebrew Myths of the Fall—The Allegorical Element in the Promethean Legend—The Titans—The Canto of the Four Ages—Hesiodic Ethics—The Golden Age—Flaxman's Illustrations —Justice and Virtue—Labour—Bourgeois Tone of Hesiod—Marriage and Women—The Gnomic Importance of Hesiod for the Early Greeks.

Transition
from Homer
to Hesiod.

HESIOD, though he belongs to the first age of Greek literature, and ranks among the earliest of Hellenic poets, marks the transition from the Heroic period to that of the Despots, when ethical inquiry began in Greece. Like Homer, Hesiod is inspired by the Muses; alone, upon Mount Helicon, he received from them the gift of inspiration. But the message which he communicates to men does not concern the deeds of demigods and warriors. It offers no material for tragedies upon the theme of

> " Thebes or Pelops' line,
> Or the tale of Troy divine."

On the contrary, Hesiod introduces us to the domestic life of shepherds, husbandmen, and merchants. Homely precepts for the conduct of affairs and proverbs on the utility of virtue replace the glittering pictures of human passions and heroic strife which the Homeric poems present. A new element is introduced into literature, the element of man reflecting on himself, questioning the divine laws under which he is obliged to live, and determining the balance of good and evil which the days of youth and age bring with them in his earthly course. The individual is now occupied with his own cares and sorrows and brief joys. Living in the present, and perforce accommodating his imagination to the prose of human existence, he has forgotten to dream any longer of the past, or to reconstruct in fancy the poetic charm of visionary heroism. It was just this difference between Homer and Hesiod which led the aristocratic Greeks of a later age to despise the poet of Ascra. Cleomenes, the king of Sparta, chief of that proud military oligarchy which had controlled the destinies of decaying Hellas, is reported by Plutarch to have said that, while Homer was the bard of warriors and noble men, Hesiod was the singer of the Helots. In this saying the contempt of the martial class for the peaceable workers of the world is forcibly expressed. It is an epigram which endears Hesiod to democratic critics of the modern age. They can trace in its brief utterance the contempt which has been felt in all periods—especially among the historic Greeks, who regarded labour as ignoble, and among the feudal races, with whom martial prowess was the mainstay of society—for the unrecorded and unhonoured earners of the bread whereby the brilliant and the well-born live. *The poet of common life.*

Hesiod, therefore, may be taken as the type and first expression of a spirit in Greek literature alien from that which Homer represents. The wrath and love of Achilles, the charm of Helen and the constancy of Penelope, the councils of the gods, the pathos of the death of Hector, the sorrows of King Priam and the labours of Odysseus, are exchanged for dim and doleful ponderings upon the destiny of man, for the shadowy mythus of Prometheus and the vision of the ages ever growing worse as they advance in time. All the rich and *Doom and troubles of life.*

manifold arras-work of suffering and action which the *Odyssey*
and the *Iliad* display, yield to such sombre meditation as a
sad soul in the childhood of the world may pour forth, brooding on its own wrongs and on the woes of men around.   The
climax of the whole, after the justice of God has been
querulously arraigned, and the violence of princes has been
appealed against with pitiful vain iteration, is a series of
practical rules for daily conduct, and a calendar of simple
ethics.

Hesiod's
personality.

Very little is known about Hesiod himself; nor can the
date at which the poems ascribed to him were composed be
fixed with any certainty.   Something of the same semi-
mythical obscurity which surrounds Homer envelops Hesiod.
Just as Homer was the eponymous hero of the school of epic
poets in Asia Minor and the islands, so Hesiod may be regarded as the titular president of a rival school of poets
localised near Mount Helicon in Bœotia.   That is to say, it is
probable that the Hesiodic, like the Homeric, poems did not
emanate from their supposed author, as we read them now;
but we may assume that they underwent changes and received
additions from followers who imbibed his spirit and attempted
to preserve his style.   And, further, the poems ascribed to
Hesiod became, as years went by, a receptacle for gnomic
verses dear to the Greeks.   Like the elegies of Theognis, the
ethical hexameters of Hesiod were, practically, an anthology
of anonymous compositions.   Still Hesiod has a more distinct
historic personality than Homer.   In the first place, the
majority of ancient critics regarded him as later in date and
more removed from the heroic age.   Then again, he speaks in
his own person, recording many details of his life, and mentioning his father and his brother.   Homer remains for ever
lost, like Shakespeare, in the creatures of his own imagination.
Instead of the man Homer, we have the Achilles and Odysseus
whom he made immortal.   Hesiod tells us much about himself.
A vein of personal reflection, a certain tone of peevish melan-

choly peculiar to the individual, runs through his poems. He is far less the mouthpiece of the heavenly Muse than a man like ourselves, touching his lyre at times with a divine grace, and then again sweeping the chords with a fretfulness that draws some jarring notes.

We learn from the hexameters of Hesiod that he was born at Ascra in Bœotia (*Works and Days*, 640). His father was an emigrant from Æolian Kumé, whence he came to Ascra in search of better fortune, "forsaking not plenty nor yet wealth and happiness, but evil poverty which Zeus gives to men : near Helicon he dwelt in a sorry village, Ascra, bad in winter, rigorous in summer heat, at no time genial." From the exordium of the *Theogony* (line 23) it appears that Hesiod kept sheep upon the slopes of Helicon ; for it was there that the Muse descended to visit him, and, after rebuking the shepherds for their idleness and grossness, gave him her sacred laurel-branch and taught him song. On this spot, as he tells us in the *Works and Days* (line 656), he offered the first prize of victory which he obtained at Chalkis. It would seem clear from these passages that poetry had been recognised as an inspiration, cultivated as an art, and encouraged by public contests, long before the date of Hesiod.

Husbandry was despised in Bœotia, and the pastoral poet led a monotonous and depressing life. The great event which changed its even tenor was a lawsuit between himself and his brother Perses concerning the division of their inheritance.[1] Perses, who was an idle fellow, after spending his own patrimony, tried to get that of Hesiod into his hands, and took his cause before judges whom he bribed. Hesiod was forced to relinquish his property, whereupon he retired from Ascra to Orchomenos. At Orchomenos he probably passed the remainder of his days. This incident explains why Hesiod dwelt so much upon the subject of justice in his poem of the *Works and Days*, addressed to Perses. Μέγα νήπιε Πέρση

Hesiod's life.

Agricultural pursuits.

---

[1] *Works and Days*, 219, 261, 637.

(most foolish Perses) he always calls this brother, as though,
while heaping the coals of good counsel upon his head, he
wished to humble his oppressor by the parade of moral and
intellectual superiority.   Some of Hesiod's finest passages, his
most intense and passionate utterances, are wrung from him
by the injustice he had suffered; so true is the famous saying
that poets

> " Learn in suffering what they teach in song."

One parable will for the moment serve as a specimen of the
poetry which the wrong-dealing of Perses drew from him.
" Thus spake the hawk to the nightingale of changeful throat,
as he bore her far aloft among the clouds, the prey of his
talons : she, poor wretch, wailed piteously in the grip of his
crooked claws; but he insultingly addressed her : 'Wretch,
why criest thou ?   Thou art now the prey of one that is the
stronger : and thou shalt go whither I choose to take thee,
song-bird as thou art.   Yea, if I see fit, I will make my supper
of thee, or else let thee go.   A fool is he who kicks against
his betters : of victory is he robbed, and suffers injury as well
as insult.' "   Hesiod himself is, of course, meant by the nightingale, and the hawk stands for violence triumphing over justice.

In verse and dialect the Hesiodic poems are not dissimilar
from the Homeric, which, supposing their date to have been
later, proves that the *Iliad* had determined the style and
standard of Epic composition, or, supposing a contemporary
origin, would show that the Greeks of the so-called heroic age
had agreed upon a common literary language.   We may refer
the *Theogony* and the *Works and Days*, after the deduction of
numerous interpolations, to Hesiod, but only in the same
sense and with the same reservation as we assign the *Iliad* and
the *Odyssey* to Homer.[1]   Unlike the heroic epos, they were

---

[1] There are probably few scholars who would now venture to maintain
confidently that the *Iliad* and the *Odyssey* were composed by one and the
same poet.   The name of Homer must be used like the *x* of algebra for an
unknown power.

recited, not to the accompaniment of the cithara, but by the poet standing with a laurel staff, called ῥάβδος or σκῆπτρον (rod or sceptre), in his hand. Hesiod, at the opening of the *Theogony*, tells us how he had received a staff of this kind from the Muse upon Mount Helicon. Either, then, the laurel rod had already been recognised in that part of Greece as the symbol of the poet's office, or else, from the respect which the followers of Hesiod paid to the details of his poem, they adopted it as their badge.

Of the two poems ascribed to Hesiod, the *Theogony* and the *Works and Days*, the former—though its genuineness as a Hesiodic production seems to have been disputed from a very early period—was perhaps, on the whole, of greater value than the latter to the Greeks. It contained an authorised version of the genealogy of their gods and heroes, an inspired dictionary of mythology, from which to deviate was hazardous. Just as families in England try to prove their Norman descent by an appeal to the Roll of Battle Abbey, so the canon of the *Theogony* decided the claims of god or demigod to rank among celestials. In this sense, Herodotus should be interpreted, when he says that Hesiod joined with Homer in making their Theogonia for the Greeks. But though this poem had thus an unique value for the ancients, it is hardly so interesting in the light of modern criticism as the *Works and Days*. The *Works and Days*, while for all practical purposes we may regard it as contemporaneous with the *Iliad*, marks the transition from the heroic epic to the moral poetry of the succeeding age, and forms the basis of direct ethical philosophy in Hellas. Hesiod is thus not only the mouthpiece of obscure handworkers in the earliest centuries of Greek history, the poet of their daily labours, sufferings, and wrongs, the singer of their doubts and infantine reflections on the world in which they had to toil ; he is also the immediate parent of gnomic verse, and the ancestor of those deep thinkers who speculated in the Attic age upon the mysteries of human life.

The Theogony.

The Works and Days.

The first ten verses of the *Works and Days* are spurious—
borrowed, probably, from some Orphic hymn to Zeus, and recognised as not the work of Hesiod by critics as ancient as
Pausanias. The poem begins with these words : "Not, as I
thought, is there only one kind of strife ; but on the earth
there are two, the one praiseworthy, the other to be blamed."
It has been conjectured that Hesiod is referring to that passage
of the *Theogony*[1] in which Eris, daughter of Night, is said to
have had no sister. We are, therefore, justified in assuming
that much of his mythology is consciously etymological ; and
this should be borne in mind while dealing with the legend of
Prometheus. The nobler strife whereof he speaks in his exordium is what we should now call competition. It rouses the
idle man to labour ; it stirs up envy in the heart of the poor
man, making him eager to possess the advantages of wealth ; it
sets neighbour against neighbour, craftsman against craftsman,
in commendable emulation. Very different, says the poet, is
this sort of strife from that which sways the law-courts ; and at
this point he begins to address his brother Perses, who had
litigiously deprived him of his heritage. The form of didactic
poetry, as it has since been practised by the followers of
Hesiod, was fixed by the appeal to Perses. Empedocles, it
will be remembered, addressed his poem on Nature to the
physician Pausanias ; Lucretius invoked the attention of
Memmius, and Virgil that of Mæcenas ; the gnomes of Theognis
were uttered to the Megarian Cyrnus ; Poliziano dedicated his
Silva to Lorenzo de' Medici, Vida his *Poetics* to the Dauphin,
Fracastorio his medical poem to Bembo, and Pope the *Essay
on Man* to Bolingbroke. After this preface on competition
as the inducement to labour, and on strife as the basis of
injustice, the poet proceeds to the mythus of Prometheus, which
is so artificially introduced as to justify the opinion that it may
be an interpolation by some later craftsman of the Hesiodic
school. Work, he says, is necessary for men, because Zeus

---

[1] Line 225.

has concealed and hidden far away our means of livelihood; so
that we are forced to toil and suffer in the search for sustenance. This grudge Zeus owed mankind because of the sin of
Prometheus. In the *Works and Days* the account given of
the trick played upon Zeus is brief : Hesiod only says, "seeing
that Prometheus of crooked counsel deceived him." We may,
however, supplement the story from the *Theogony*.[1] In old
days the human race had fire, and offered burned sacrifice to
heaven; but Prometheus by his craft deceived the gods of
their just portion of the victims, making Zeus take the bones
and fat for his share. Whereupon Zeus deprived men of the
use of fire. Prometheus then stole fire from heaven, and gave
it back to men. "Then," says Hesiod, "was cloud-gathering
Zeus full wroth of heart, and he devised a great woe for all
mankind." He determined to punish the whole race by giving
them Pandora. He bade Hephæstus mix earth and water, and
infuse into the plastic form a human voice and human powers,
and liken it in all points to a heavenly goddess. Athene was
told to teach the woman, thus made, household work and skill in
weaving. Aphrodite poured upon her head the charm of beauty,
with terrible desire, and flesh-consuming thoughts of love. But
Zeus commanded Hermes to give to her the mind of a dog
and wily temper. After this fashion was the making of
Pandora. And when she had been shaped, Athene girded and
adorned her ; the Graces and divine Persuasion hung golden
chains about her flesh, and the Hours crowned her with spring
blossoms. Zeus called her Pandora, because each dweller on
Olympus had bestowed on her a gift. Then Pandora was
sent under the charge of Hermes to Epimetheus, who remembered not his brother's words, how he had said : "Receive no
gift from Zeus, but send it back again, lest evil should befall
the race of men." But as soon as Epimetheus had housed
her, he recognised his error. Before this time men had lived
upon the earth apart from evils, apart from painful toil, and

[1] Line 535.

wearful diseases which bring death on mortals. The woman with her hands lifted the lid of the great jar where all these bad things were shut up, and let them loose into the air. Hope alone remained behind—for the lot of humanity is hopeless; but a hundred thousand woes abode at large to plague the race of men. Earth is full of them; the sea is full; and sickness roams abroad by night and day, where it listeth, bearing ills to mortals in silence, for Zeus in his deep craft took away its voice that men might have no warning. Thus not in any way is it possible to avoid the will of God.

Hebrew and Greek conceptions of the Fall of Man.

Such is the mythus of the Fall, as imagined by the early Greeks. Man in rebellion against heaven, pitted in his weakness at a game of mutual deception against almighty force, is beaten and is punished. Woman, the instrument of his chastisement, is thrust upon him by offended and malignant deity; the folly of man receives her, and repents too late. Both his wisdom and his foolishness conspire to man's undoing —wisdom which he cannot use aright, and foolishness which makes him fall into the trap prepared for him. We are irresistibly led to compare this legend with the Hebrew tradition of the Fall. In both there is an act of transgression on the part of man. Woman in both brings woe into the world. That is to say, the conscience of the Greeks and Jews, intent on solving the mystery of pain and death, convicted them alike of sin; while the social prejudices of both races made them throw the blame upon the weaker but more fascinating sex, by whom they felt their sterner nature softened and their passions quickened to work foolishness. So far the two myths have strong points of agreement. But in that of the Greeks there is no Manicheism. The sin of Prometheus is not, like the sin of Adam, the error of weak human beings tempted by the machinations of an evil spirit to trangress the law of good. It is rather a knavish trick played off upon the sire of gods and men by a wild gamester;

and herein it seems to symbolise that tendency to overreach,
which formed a marked characteristic of the Hellenes in all
ages. The Greek of Hesiod's time conceived of the relations
between man and god as involving mutual mistrust and guile ;
his ideal of intellectual superiority both in Prometheus and in
Zeus implied capacity for getting the upper hand by craft.
Again, the Greek god takes a diabolical revenge, punishing
the whole human race, with laughter on his lips and self-
congratulation for superior cunning in his heart. We lack
the solemn moment when God calls Adam at the close of
day, and tells him of the curse, but also promises a Saviour.
The legend of Prometheus has, for its part also, the prophecy
of a redeemer ; but the redeemer of men from the anger of
God does not proceed from the mercy of the deity himself,
who has been wronged, but from the iron will of Fate, who
stands above both god and man, and from the invincible Æschylean
fortitude of the soul which first had sinned, now stiffening develop-
                                                              ment of the
itself against the might of Zeus, refusing his promises, reject- legend of
                                                              Prometheus.
ing his offers of reconciliation, biding in pain and patience till
Herakles appears and cuts the Gordian knot. This is the
spectacle presented by Æschylus in his *Prometheus Bound*.
To deny its grandeur would be ridiculous ; to contend that it
offers some features of sublimity superior to anything contained in the Hebrew legend, would be no difficult task. In
the person of Prometheus, chained on Caucasus, pierced by
fiery arrows in the noonday and by frosty arrows in the night,
humanity wavers not, but endures with scorn and patience
and stoical acceptance. Unfortunately the outlines of this
great tragic allegory have been blurred by time and travestied
by feeble copyists. What we know about the tale of
Prometheus is but a faint echo of the mythus apprehended
by the Greeks anterior to Hesiod, and handled afterwards by
Æschylus. Enough, however, remains to make it certain that
it was the creation of a race profoundly convinced of present
injustice in the divine government of the world. If the soul

of man is raised by the attribution of stern heroism, God is lowered to the infamy of a tyrant. But neither is the Hebrew legend on its side theologically flawless. Greek and Jew fail alike to offer a satisfactory solution of the origin of evil. While in the Greek mythus Zeus plays with mankind like a cat with a mouse, the Hebrew story does not explain the justice of that omnipotent Being who created man with capacity for error, and exposed him to temptation. The true critique of the second and third chapters of Genesis has been admirably expressed by Omar Khayyam in the following stanzas :—

> " O Thou, who didst with pitfall and with gin
> Beset the road I was to wander in,
>   Thou wilt not with predestination round
> Enmesh me, and impute my fall to sin ?

> " O Thou, who man of baser earth didst make,
> And who with Eden didst devise the snake,
>   For all the sin wherewith the face of man
> Is blackened, man's forgiveness give—and take ! "

Both tales are but crude and early attempts to set forth the primitive mystery of conscience, and to account for the prevalence of pain and death. The æsthetic superiority of the Hebrew conception lies in its idealisation of the deity at all costs. God is at least grand and consistent, justified by His own august counsels ; and at the very moment of punishing His creatures, He promises deliverance through their own seed. Moreover, a vast antagonistic agency of evil is brought into the field to account for the fall of man ; and we are not precluded from even extending our compassion to the deity, who has been thwarted in His schemes for good.

Relation of Prometheus to humanity.

Before quitting the discussion of this ancient tale of human suffering and sin, it would be well to notice that Hesiod identifies Prometheus with the human race. His hero is the son of the Titan Iapetus by Clymene, daughter of the Titan Oceanus ; and his brethren are Atlas, Menoitios,

and Epimetheus. These names are significant. Just as
Prometheus signifies the forecasting reason of humanity,[1] so
Epimetheus indicates the overhasty judgment foredoomed to
be wise too late. These are intellectual qualities. Atlas, in
like manner, typifies the endurance of man, who bears all to
the very end, and holds upon his back the bulk of heaven.
In Menoitios is shadowed forth the insolence and rebellious
spirit for which a penalty of pain and death is meted. These,
then, are moral qualities. In the children of Iapetus and
Clymene we consequently trace the first rude attempt at
psychological analysis. The scientific import of the mythus
was never wholly forgotten by the Greeks. Pindar calls
Prophasis, or excuse, the daughter of Epimetheus, or back-
thought as opposed to forethought. Plato makes the folly
of Epimetheus to have consisted in his giving away the
natural powers of self-preservation to the beasts; whereupon
Prometheus was driven to supplement with fire the unprotected
impotence of man. Lucian, again, says of Epimetheus that
repentance is his business; while Synesius adds that he
provides not for the future, but deplores the past. The
Titans, it should further be remarked, are demiurgic powers
—elemental forces of air, fire, earth, water—conditions of
existence implied by space and time—distributors of darkness
and of light—parents, lastly, of the human race. Though
some later Greek authors identified Prometheus with the
Titans, and made him the benefactor of humanity, this was
not the conception of Hesiod. Prometheus is stated, both in
the *Theogony* and the *Works and Days*, to have been the son
of Titans, the protagonist of men, who strove in vain to cope
with Zeus. Zeus himself belongs in like manner to a
secondary order of existences. Begotten by the Titan Cronos,
he seems to typify the reason as distinguished from the brute
powers of the universe, mind emergent from matter, and over-

*Ethical im-
port of the
legend.*

---

[1] That Prometheus was *Pramanthas*, the fire-lighting stick, has been
assumed by modern philology, but was not known by Hesiod.

coming it by contest. Prometheus is connected, by his
parentage, with the old material order of the world; but he
represents that portion of it which is human, and which, *quâ*
human, has affinity to Zeus. Herein we trace the mystery of
the divine in man, though man has been placed in antagonism
to the deity. The same notion is further symbolised by the
theft of fire, and by the fiction of Prometheus breathing a
particle of the divine spirit into the clay figures whereof he
made men. In the decaying age of Greek mythology this
aspect of the legend absorbed attention to the exclusion of
the elder Hesiodic romance, as students of Horace will
remember, and as appears abundantly from Græco -Roman
bas-reliefs. To reconcile man and Zeus, cognate in their
origin, yet hostile owing to their ancient feud, it was needful
that a deliverer, Herakles, should be born of god and woman,
of Zeus and Alcmene, who sets free the elementary principle
of humanity typified in Prometheus, and for the first time
establishes a harmony between the children of earth and the
dwellers on Olympus. So far I have remained within the
limits of the Hesiodic legend, only hinting at such divergences
as were adopted by the later handlers of the tale. The new
aspect given to the whole myth by Æschylus deserves
separate consideration in connection with the tragedy of
Prometheus. It is to be regretted that we only possess so
important a relique of Greek religious speculation in fragments ;
and these fragments are so tantalisingly incomplete that it is
impossible to say exactly how much may be the *débris* of
original tradition, or where the free fancy of later poets has
been remoulding and recasting the material of the antique
myth to suit more modern allegory.

The four ages.

The tale of Prometheus may be called the first canto of
the *Works and Days.* The second consists of the vision of the
four ages of man. Hesiod, in common with all early poets,
imagined a state of primæval bliss, which he called the Age of
Gold. Then Cronos reigned upon the earth, and men lived

without care or pain or old age. Their death was like the coming on of sleep, and the soil bore them fruits untilled. When this race came to an end, Zeus made them genii of goodwill, haunting the world and protecting mortals. Theirs it is to watch the decrees of justice, and to mark wrong-doing, wrapped around with mist, going up and down upon the earth, the givers of wealth; such is the royal honour which is theirs. The next age he calls the silver, for it was inferior to the first; and Zeus speedily swept it away, seeing that the men of this generation waxed insolent, and paid no honour to the gods. The third age is the brazen. A terrible and mighty brood of men possessed the land, who delighted in nought but violence and warfare. They first ate flesh. Their houses and their armour and their mattocks were of brass. In strife they slew themselves, and perished without a name. After them came the heroes of romance, whom Zeus made most just and worthy. They fell fighting before seven-gated Thebes and Troy; but after death Father Zeus transferred them to the utmost limits of the world, where they live without care in islands of the blest, by ocean waves, blest heroes, for whom thrice yearly the soil bears blooming fruit-age honey-sweet. Then cries Hesiod, and the cry is wrenched The iron age. from him with agony, Would that I had never been born in the fifth generation of men, but rather that I had died before or had lived afterwards; for now the age is of iron! On the face of the world there is nought but violence and wrong; division is set between father and son, brother and brother, friend and friend; there is no fear of God, no sense of justice, no fidelity, no truth; the better man is subject to the worse, and jealousy corrupts the world. Soon, very soon, will wing their way to heaven again—leaving the earth with her broad ways, robed in white raiment, joining the immortal choir, deserting men—both modest shame and righteous indignation. But dismal woes will stay and harbour here, and against evil there shall be no aid. This ends the second canto of the

Works and Days, and brings us down to the two hundredth line of the poem. The remainder consists for the most part of precepts adapted to the doleful state in which mortals of the present have to suffer.

Justice.

What may be called the third canto is occupied with justice, the advantages of which, from a purely utilitarian point of view, as well as æsthetically conceived, are urged in verse. It begins with the apologue of the hawk and nightingale already quoted. Then the condition of a city where justice is honoured, where the people multiply in peace, and there is fulness and prosperity, where pestilence and calamity keep far away, is contrasted with the plagues, wars, famines, wasting away of population, and perpetual discomforts that beset the unjust nation. For the innocent and righteous folk, says the poet, the earth bears plenty, and in the mountains the oak-tree at the top yields acorns, and in the middle bees, and the woolly sheep are weighed down with their fleeces. The women give birth to children like their fathers. With blessings do men always flourish, nor need they tempt the sea in ships, but earth abundantly supplies their wants.

The age of gold.

It is worth while to pause for a moment and contemplate the pastoral ideal of perfect happiness and pure simplicity which, first set forth by Hesiod in these passages, found afterwards an echo in Plato, in Empedocles, in Lucretius, in Virgil, in Poliziano, and in Tasso ; all of whom have lingered lovingly upon the *bell' età dell' oro*. The Hesiodic conception of felicity is neither stirring nor heroic. Like the early Christian notion of heaven, expressed by the pathetic iteration of *in pace* on the sepulchral tablets of the Catacombs, it owes its beauty to a sense of contrast between tranquillity imagined and woe and warfare actually experienced. We comprehend why the Spartan king called Hesiod the poet of the Helots, when, in the age that idealised Achilles and Odysseus, the all-daring, all-affronting heroes of a radiant romance, we find that his sole aspiration was to live in peace, decorously fulfilling social duties, and growing old in the routine of moderate labour. It is a commonplace, and what the French would call a *bourgeois*, aspiration. Just this lot in life Achilles rejected with disdain, in exchange for the dazzling prospect of victory and death, that fascinated the noblest of the Greeks, and produced their Alexander. Still we must remember that Hesiod was not, like Homer, singing in the halls of fiery and high-fed chieftains, who stood above the laws. His plaintive note was uttered to the watchers of the seasons and the tillers of the soil, whose very livelihood depended on the will and pleasure of δωροφάγοι βασιλεῖς (gift-devouring chieftains). In the semi-barbarous state of society which Homer and Hesiod represent from different points of view, when violence prevails, and when life and property alike are insecure, justice may well be selected as the prime of virtues, and peace be idealised as heaven on earth. In one sense, as the Greek philosophers argued, justice does include all the excellences of a social being. The man who is perfectly just will be unimpeachable in all his conduct ; and the simpler the state of society, the more outrageous the wrongs inflicted by one man on another, the more apparent will this be.

Putting aside, however, for further consideration, the ethical aspect of Hesiod's ideal, we find in it an exquisite and permanently attractive æsthetic beauty. Compared with the fierce heroism of Achilles, the calm happiness of Hesiod's pastoral folk soothes our fancy, like the rising of the moon in twilight above harvest sheaves at the end of a long intolerable day. Therefore great poets and artists, through all the resonant and gorgeous ages of the world, have turned their eyes with sympathy and yearning to these lines ; and the best that either Virgil or Poliziano could achieve, was to catch an echo of Hesiod's melody, to reproduce a portion of his charm. Perhaps the most complete homage to the poetry of Hesiod on this point has been rendered by Flaxman. Nature, so prodigal to the English race in men of genius untutored, singular, and

Æsthetic charm of Hesiod's pastoral ideal.

solitary, has given us but few seers who, in the quality of
prolific invention, can be compared with Flaxman.   For pure
conceptive faculty, controlled by unerring sense of beauty, we
have to think of Pheidias or Raphael before we find his equal.
His powers were often employed on uncongenial subjects; nor
had he, perhaps, a true notion of the limitations of his art;
else he would not have attempted to give sculpturesque form
even in outline to many scenes from the *Divine Comedy*.   The
conditions, again, of modern life were adverse to his working
out his thought in marble, and precluded him from gaining a
complete mastery over the material of sculpture.   It may also
be conceded that, to a large extent, his imagination, like a
parasite flower, was obliged to bloom upon the branches of
Greek art.   What Flaxman would have been without the bas-
reliefs, the vases, and the hand-mirrors of the ancients, it is
difficult to conceive.   Herein, however, he did no more than
obey the law which has constrained the greatest modern minds
by indissoluble bondage to the service of the Greek spirit.
Allowing for all this, the fact remains that within a certain
circle, the radius of which exceeds the farthest reach of many
far more frequently belauded artists, Flaxman was supreme.
Whatever could be expressed according to the laws of bas-
relief, embossed in metal, or hewn out of stone, or indicated in
pure outline, he conveyed with a truth to nature, a grace of
feeling, and an originality of conception, absolutely incomparable.   Moreover, in this kind his genius was inexhaustible.
Nowhere are the fruits of this creative skill so charming as in
the illustrations of the *Works and Days*.   The ninth plate, in
which the Age of Gold is symbolised by a mother stretching
out her infant to receive his father's kiss, might be selected as
a perfect idyll, conveyed within the strictest and severest
bounds of sculptural relief.   The man and his girl-wife are
beautiful and young: age, we feel, will never touch them by
whitening her forehead or spoiling his smooth chin with hair.
Both are naked, seated on the ground; their outstretched

Flaxman's
Hesiod.

arms enfold as in a living cradle the robust and laughing boy. On one side shoots a heavy sheaf of barley; on the other stands an altar, smoking with bloodless offerings to heaven; above, the strong vine hangs its clusters and its wealth of lusty leaves. More elaborate, but scarcely more beautiful—like a double rose beside a wilding blossom from the hedge of June—is the seventeenth plate, which sets forth the felicity of god-fearing folk who honour justice. These, too, are seated on the ground, young men and girls, with comely children. pledges of their joy : one child is suckled at her mother's breast; another lies folded in his father's arms; a girl and boy are kissing on their parents' knees ; while a beardless youth pipes ditties on the double reed. Above the group vine-branches flourish, and the veiled Hours, givers of all goodly things, weave choric dance with song, scattering from their immortal fingers flowers upon the men beneath. In order to com- Flaxman prehend the purity of Flaxman's inspiration, the deep and and Ingres. inborn sympathy that made him in this nineteenth century a Greek, we ought to compare these illustrations with the picture of the Golden Age by Ingres. For perfection of scientific drawing from the nude, this masterpiece of the great French painter has never been excelled. It is a treasure-house of varied attitude and rhythmically studied line. Yet the whole resembles a theatrical *tableau vivant*, which an enlightened choreograph, in combination with an enterprising manager, might design to represent the Garden of Eden on a grand scale. The power displayed by Flaxman is of a very different order. There is no effort, no *mise en scène*, no parade of science, no suggestion of voluptuousness. His outlines are as simple and as pure as Hesiod's verse. We see that, whereas Ingres is using the old vision as a schema for the exhibition of his skill, Flaxman has felt its poetry and given form to its imagination. This is not the occasion to linger over these illustrations ; yet, before closing the volume that contains them, I cannot forbear from turning a page, and pointing to the

pictures of the Pleiads. Seven beautiful interwoven female
shapes are rising in the one plate, like a wreath of light or
vapour moulded into human form, above the reapers ; in the
other are descending, with equal grace of now inverted movement, over the ploughman at his toil. By no other artist's
hand have the constellations elsewhere been converted, with so
much feeling for their form, into the melodies of rhythmically
moving human shapes. Flaxman's outlines of the Pleiads
might be described as a new celestial imagery, a hitherto
unapprehended astronomical mythology.

Address to
the judges of
the people.

Continuing what I have called the third canto of the *Works
and Days*, Hesiod addresses himself in the next place to the
Basileis, or judges of the people : " Kings in judgment, do ye
also ponder this divine justice ; for the immortals, dwelling near
and among men, behold who waste their fellows by wrong
judgment, scorning the wrath of God. Verily, upon earth
are thrice ten thousand immortals of the host of Zeus, guardians
of mortal man. They watch both justice and injustice, robed
in mist, roaming abroad upon the earth." Again he reminds
them that Justice, virgin child of Zeus, is ever ready with ear
open to observe the injury to right and fair dealing done
against her honour. She complains of the wrongful judge ;
but it is the people who suffer for his sin. Therefore let the
princes so greedy of bribes take heed, forego their crooked
sentences, and bear in mind that the man who works evil
for another, works it for himself, that bad intentions harm
those who have conceived them, and that Zeus sees all and
knows all. This period is concluded with a bitterly ironical
repudiation of the poet's own precepts—May neither I nor my
son be just ; for now the wrongful man has by far the
best of it upon the earth ! It will be observed that Zeus
throughout this tirade on justice is a different being from the
Zeus in the mythus of Prometheus. The dramatic personage
of the legend, whose guile inflicts so much misery on men, has
been supplanted by a moral idea personified. It is not that a

new mythology has been superinduced upon the old one, or that we are now in the track of esoteric religious teaching; the poet is only expressing his internal certainty that, though fraud and violence prevail on earth, yet somewhere in the eternal and ideal world justice still abides. It is not a little singular, considering his querulous and hopeless tone in other passages, that Hesiod should here assert the cognisance which Zeus takes of unfair dealing, and the continued action of protective and retributive dæmons. We could scarcely find stronger faith in the superiority of justice among the moral writings of the Jews. Furthermore, Hesiod reminds Perses that justice is human, violence bestial, and that in the long run honesty will be found to be the best policy. Then follows the sublimest passage of the whole poem—one of great celebrity among the Greeks, who quoted it, and worked it up in poems, parables, and essays : "Behold, thou mayest choose badness easily, even in heaps; for the path is plain, and she dwells very near. But before excellence the immortal gods have placed toil and labour : afar and steep is the road that leads to her, and rough it is at first; but when you reach the height, then truly is it easy, though so hard before." [1]

The subject of Justice being now exhausted, Hesiod passes, in the fourth canto of the *Works and Days*, to the eulogy of labour, regarded as the source of all good. The unheroic nature of his life-philosophy is very apparent in this section. He thinks and speaks like a peasant, whose one idea it is to add pence to pence, and to cut a good figure in his parish. A man must work, in order to avoid hunger and grow rich : gods and men hate the idle, who are like drones in the hive : if you work, you will get flocks and herds, and folk will envy you : to grow rich from dishonest gains brings no profit, for they are unlucky : the great aim for a good man is to live a respectable life, to work soberly, to fulfil righteousness, to be punctual in paying homage to the gods—to go to church, in

Praise of industry.

---

[1] *Works and Days*, 286.

fact—with this end in view, that he may buy the estates of
his neighbour, instead of having to sell his own. Such is the
bathos of Hesiod's ethical ideal : Do right and abstain from
wrong, in order that you may be richer than the tenant of the
adjacent farm. Many other precepts of like tenor might be
quoted : Call your friend to your banquet, and leave your
enemy alone ; invite him most who lives nearest, for he will
be most useful in time of need ; love him who loves you,
and cleave to him who cleaves to you ; give to him who gives,
and give not to him who gives not, for to a giver gifts are
given, but to him who gives not no man hath given. Of such
sort are the Hesiodic rules of conduct. They reveal the spirit
of a prudent clown, the practical and calculating selfishness
which the doleful conditions of the early age of Hellenic civilisation intensified. The social life of great political centres,
and the patriotism of the Persian war, helped at a later period to
raise the Greeks above these low and sordid aims in life. It
was only in a century when justice could be bought, and
penury meant starving, unheeded or derided, by the roadside,
that a poet of Hesiod's temper could write,[1] Money is a man's
soul :—

$$\chi\rho\dot{\eta}\mu\alpha\tau\alpha \ \gamma\grave{\alpha}\rho \ \psi\upsilon\chi\grave{\eta} \ \pi\acute{\epsilon}\lambda\epsilon\tau\alpha\iota \ \delta\epsilon\acute{\iota}\lambda o\iota\sigma\iota \ \beta\rho\acute{o}\tau o\iota\sigma\iota.$$

" For money is the soul of miserable mortals."

In criticising the Solonian reforms at Athens, we should never
forget the dismal picture of Hellenic misery revealed to us by
Hesiod.

The farmer's Calendar.　　Thus ends the first part of the *Works and Days*. The
second half of the poem consists of rules for husbandry.
Hesiod goes through the seasons of the year, detailing the
operations of the several months, and adorning his homely
subject with sober but graceful poetry. It is an elegant

───────

[1] *Works and Days*, 686. It must here again be repeated that, though
it is convenient to talk of Hesiod as a poet and a person, the miscellaneous
ethical precepts of the *Works and Days* are derived from a variety of
sources.

farmer's calendar, upon which Virgil founded his *Georgics*, translating into Augustan Latin the rude phrases of the bard of Ascra, and turning all he touched to gold. Scattered among precepts relating to the proper seasons and successions of agricultural labour, are descriptive passages and moral reflections. One picture of winter is so long and elaborate as to justify the notion that it is a separate interpolated poem. The episode upon procrastination (line 408), and the rules for the choice of a wife (line 693), might be selected as offering special topics for comment. The latter passage deserves particular attention; since, if the condition of the working man was wretched in this early age of Greece, far more miserable, may we argue, was that of his helpmate. A man, according to *Marriage and women.* Hesiod, ought to be about thirty when he marries, and his wife about nineteen. He should be very careful, in choosing her, to insure that she will not bring him into contempt among his neighbours; and he must remember that if a good wife be a prize, it is not possible to get a worse plague than a bad one. What his general notion about women was, we gather from the long invective against the female sex in the *Theogony*.[1] Pandora was the greatest curse imaginable to the human race, for from her sprang women; and now, if a man refrains from marriage, he must endure a wretched old age, and leave his money to indifferent kindred; or if he marries and gets a good wife, curses and blessings are mingled in his lot; if his wife be of the bad sort, his whole life is ruined. So utterly impossible is it to avoid the misery devised for the human race by Zeus.

The whole argument of Hesiod in this passage, taken in *Greek regard for the female sex.* connection with his few lines on the choice of a wife in the *Works and Days*, and with his grim silence upon the subject of women as the companions of men, proves that he regarded them as a necessary deduction from the happiness of life— the rift within the lute that spoils its music—the plague

[1] *Theogony*, 587-612.

invented by the malice of an all-wise god in vengeance for a man's deceit. This appreciation of women is substantially consistent with the curious poem by Simonides of Amorgos; with the treatment of the female sex at Athens; with the opinion of Pindar and Plato that to be a woman-lover as compared with a boy-lover was sensual and vile; with the disdainful silence of Thucydides; with the caricatures of society presented by the comic poets; with the famous epigram of Pericles; with the portrait of Xanthippe; and with the remarkable description of female habits in Lucian's *Amores*. Thus, running through the whole literature of the Greeks, we can trace a vein of contempt for women, which may fairly be indicated as the greatest social blot upon their brilliant but imperfect civilisation. Exceptions can, of course, be found. In the age of the despots women rose into far more importance than they afterwards enjoyed in democratic Athens. At Sparta their right to engross property (severely criticised by Aristotle) gave them a social status which they had in no other Greek state. At Lesbos, during the brief blooming period of Æolian culture, in freedom of action and in mental training they were at least the equals of the male sex. The fact, however, remains that in Athens, the real centre of Hellenic life, women occupied a distinctly inferior rank. It is significant that in the *Lives of Plutarch*, whereas we read of many noble Lacedæmonian ladies, comparatively little account is taken of the wives or mothers of Athenian worthies.

Gnomic precepts.

Some scattered proverbs about the conduct of the tongue and the choice of friends, followed by an enumeration of lucky and unlucky days, and by a list of truly rustic rules of personal behaviour, conclude the poem of the *Works and Days*. How far these saws and maxims belong to the original work of Hesiod it is quite impossible to say. The book became popular in education, and consequently suffered, like the gnomes of Theognis and Phocylides, from frequent interpolations at a later period. As it stands, the whole is chiefly valuable for the concrete picture which it offers of early peasant life in Hellas. As the Epics of Homer present us with the ideal toward which the princes and great nobles raised their souls amid the plenty and the splendour of their palaces, so, in the lines of Hesiod, we learn how the Thetes, whom Achilles envied in Elysium, toiled and suffered in their struggle for their only source of comfort, gold.

CHAPTER VI

PARMENIDES

Greek Philosophical Poetry—The Emergence of Philosophy from Mytho-
logy—The Ionian Sages—The Pythagoreans—Anaxagoras—Demo-
critus—The Eleatics—Heraclitus—Xenophanes of Colophon—His
Critique of the Myths—Assertion of Monotheism—Fragments of his
Poem on Nature—Parmenides of Elea—His Political Importance—
Parmenides in the Dialogues of Plato—His Metaphysic of Being—
His Natural Philosophy—The Logic deduced from him by Zeno
and Melissus—Translation of the Fragments of his Poem—The
Dualism of Truth and Opinion—Impossibility of obtaining Absolute
Knowledge.

Metaphysi-
cal poets. IT might well be questioned whether the founders of the
Eleatic School deserve to rank among Greek poets ; for though
they wrote hexameters, composing what the Greeks call ἔπη,
yet it is clear that they did this with no artistic impulse, but
only because in the dawn of thought it was easier, or perhaps
more consistent with traditional custom, to use verse than
prose for fixed and meditated exposition. The moment in
the development of human thought when abstractions were
being wrung for the first time with toil from language, and
when as yet the vehicle of rhythmic utterance seemed indispensable, is so interesting that a point in favour of Xenophanes and Parmenides may be fairly stretched, and a place
may be given them between Hesiod, the creator of didactic
poetry, and Empedocles, the inspired predecessor of Lucretius.

The problem which lay before the earliest philosophers of
Greece, was how to emerge from mythological conceptions

concerning the origin and nature of the world into a region of exact and abstract thought. They had their list of demiurgic agencies, Titans and deities, some of them dramatically personified in the poems of Homer and the legends of Olympus, others but vaguely indicated by the names of Earth and Ocean, Heaven and Time. The polytheistic and mythologising instincts of the race at large tended to individualise these primal powers with more and more distinctness, collecting legends around the popular among them, and attributing moral sympathies and passions to those who were supposed to have relations with humanity. But there remained a background of dimly-descried and cloudy forces upon which the mythopœic imagination had taken little hold ; and these supplied a starting-point for scientific speculation. It was in this field that the logical faculty of the Greek mind, no less powerful and active than its poetic fancy, came first into play. Thus we find Thales brooding in thought upon the mythus of Oceanus, and arriving at the conception of water as the elementary principle of the universe ; while Gaia, or earth, in like manner is said to have stimulated Pherecydes. Anaximenes is reported to have chosen air as the groundwork of his cosmogony, and Heraclitus developed the material world from fire.

Passage from mythology through poetry to philosophy.

It must not be supposed that any of these early speculators invented a complete hypothesis for deducing phenomena from earth, air, fire, or water, as apprehended by the senses. Their elements or ἀρχαί are rather to be regarded in the light of symbols—metaphors adopted from experience for shadowing forth an extremely subtle and pervasive substance, a material of supersensible fluidity and elasticity, capable of infinite modification by rarefaction and condensation. At the same time they were seeking after intellectual abstractions ; but the problems of philosophy as yet presented themselves in crude and concrete form to their intellects.

Primordial elements.

A further step in the direction of the abstract was taken by

Anaximander, the Milesian astronomer, who is reported to have made a sun-dial, to have calculated the recurrence of the equinoxes and the solstices, and to have projected geographical charts for the first time in Greece. This practical mathematician derived the universe from the unlimited (τὸ ἄπειρον) hurling thought thus at a venture, as it were, into the realm of metaphysical conceptions. It would appear from the dim and hazy tradition which we have received about Anaximander, that he instituted a polemic against the so-called physicists, arguing that to the elements of fire or water there can be attributed a beginning and an ending, but that the abstract indefinite, as uncreate and indestructible, takes precedence of all else. His thought, however, though fruitful of future consequences, was in itself barren; nor have we any reason to conclude that by the *unlimited* he meant more than a primordial substance, or *Grund*, without quality and without limitation—a void and hollow form containing in itself potentialities of all things. It is characteristic of this early age of Greek speculation that Simplicius found it necessary to criticise even Anaximander for using poetic phraseology (ποιητικω-τέροις ὀνόμασιν). In his polemic, however, he started one of the great puzzles, the contrast between birth and death, and the difficulty of discovering an element subject to neither, which agitated the schools of Greece throughout their long activity.

While the thinkers of Ionia were endeavouring to discover terms of infinite subtlety, through which to symbolise the uniform and unchangeable substance underlying the multiplicity of phenomena, the Pythagoreans in Italy turned their attention to the abstract relations of which numbers are the simplest expression. Numbers, they saw, are both thoughts and also at the same time universally applicable to things of sense. There is nothing tangible which can escape the formulæ of arithmetic. Mistaking a power of the mind for a power inherent in the universe, they imagined that the figures of the

multiplication table were the essential realities of things, the
authentic inner essence of the sensible world ; and to number
they attributed a mystic potency. Speculation was still so
immature that they failed to observe the sterility of the conception.   This much, however, they effected :—by resting
upon the essentially mental conception of quantity, and by
apprehending the universe as number, they took the first
important step in the direction of pure metaphysic.   They
initiated the study of things in their relation to one another
and to the cosmic whole by suggesting the possibility of a
common term of measurement.

Anaxagoras of Clazomenæ, following another path, pronounced that the really efficient agency in the universe is
Mind.   For this utterance he has been justly eulogised by
the metaphysicians of all succeeding centuries.   It was, in
fact, the starting-point of what in German phraseology is called
Begriffsphilosophie.   Anaxagoras insisted on a point which
had been neglected by his contemporaries—the form-giving
activity of mind, as known to us immediately in the human
reason—and asserted the impossibility of leaving this out of
the account of the universe.   But, as Socrates complained, he
stopped here, and diverged into material explanations, talking
about attraction and repulsion and homogeneous particles, without attempting to connect them with the action of his Nous.

Anaxagoras and the philosophy of mind.

Democritus of Abdera, a little later in time than the thinkers
who have hitherto been mentioned, was so attracted by the
indefinite divisibility of matter that he explained the universe
by the theory of a Void in which an infinity of Atoms moved
and met in varied combination.   It is well known that this
hypothesis, the parent of the Epicurean and the Lucretian
systems, has been the mainstay of materialism in all ages, and
that something like it has lately been received into favour by
the most advanced physicists.   Yet it must not be imagined
that the Atomism of Democritus was in any true sense scientific
according to our acceptation of the term.   Like the Infinite

Democritus and Atom- ism.

of Anaximander, the Mind of Anaxagoras, the Numbers of Pythagoras, the fire of Heraclitus, his Plenum and Vacuum was a conjectural hypothesis founded upon no experiment or observation properly so called. All these early systems were freaks of fancy, shrewd guesses, poetic thoughts, in which abstractions from language, elementary refinements upon mythology, together with crude speculations about natural objects, were made the groundwork of dogmatism. At the same time thought at this period was both active and creative ; nearly all the permanent problems which occur to human ignorance—the antitheses of a beginning and an ending, of being and not being, of rest and motion, of the continuous and the discrete, of the one and the many—the criterion of knowledge and opinion, the antagonism of the senses and the reason, the relation of the vital principle to inanimate existence —were posed in the course of animated controversy. Logic had not been formulated as a method. Philosophical termin- ology had not as yet been settled. But the logical faculty was working in full vigour, and language was being made to express general ideas hitherto unapprehended.

Eleatic philosophy of being.

This brief survey of the origin of Greek philosophy will enable us to understand the position of the Eleatics. Re- garded collectively, and as a school developing a body of doctrine, they advanced in abstraction beyond any of their predecessors or contemporaries. Whereas other philosophers had sought for the abstract in phenomenal elements, the Eleatics went straight through language to the notion of pure being ; even the numbers of Pythagoras were not sufficient for the exigencies of their logic. The unity of being, as the one reality, and the absolute impossibility of not-being, revealed by the consciousness and demonstrated by language in the copula ἐστί ("is"), forms the groundwork of their dog- matism.[1] How important was the principle thus introduced

[1] The word ἐστί is the third person singular of the present tense of the verb "to be." It predicates, by the force inherent in its simple affirma-

into the fabric of European thought, is evident to every student of the history of philosophy. It is enough in this place to point out to what extent it has influenced our language through such words as entity, existence, essence. The Eleatics may claim as their own coinage the title of all metaphysics—Ontology, or the Science of Being.

In order to make the attitude of these earliest Greek thinkers still more clear, we must return for a moment to Heraclitus, who instituted a polemic against the Eleatic doctrine of Being. He asserted that Being is no more than not-Being. Regarded in itself as an abstraction, a void and hollow concept, sublimated from language and robbed of the phenomena which give it reality to our percipient intellect, Being turns out to be identical with nothing. The relation of Being to not-Being in Becoming formed the central point of his metaphysic, and was enunciated in the axiom, All is flowing, πάντα ῥεῖ. In other words, Heraclitus fixed his mind upon the universe considered as a process, upon the biological and dynamical changes of the natural world, rejecting bare ontology as a sterile ground for speculation. He had in him the stuff of Bruno and of Hegel. Though the Heraclitean polemic was directed against the school at large, it would be in the last degree inaccurate to treat the Eleatic doctrine, as maintained by Xenophanes, Parmenides, Zeno, and Melissus, from the point of view of one consistent system. By so doing not only would the truth of history be violated, but one of the most valuable examples of the growth of thought in Greece would be lost.

Heraclitus and his philosophy of becoming.

Xenophanes, who is regarded as the founder of the school, was a native of Colophon. He left his fatherland, and spent the greater portion of his life in Sicily and Magna Græcia.

Xenophanes.

tion, the existence and objective actuality of those things to which we apply it. The mind, by continually using this term, is continually asserting to itself a belief in reality.

We hear of him first at Messana, then at Catana; and there is good reason to believe that he visited the Phocæan colony of Elea (afterwards Velia) on the western coast of Calabria, a little to the south of Pæstum. At all events, antiquity spoke of him as the father of philosophy at Elea, and Diogenes Laertius mentions a poem of two thousand hexameters which he composed in joint praise of this city and Colophon. Xenophanes lived to a great age. In a couplet preserved from one of his elegies he speaks of having wandered, absorbed in thought and contemplation, for sixty-seven years through Hellas, and fixes twenty-five years as the age at which he began his travels. He was celebrated, like his fellow-countryman, Mimnermus, for his elegiac poetry, some fragments of which are among the most valuable relics we possess of that species of composition. About 538 B.C. is the date usually assigned to him.

Critique of Polytheism.   The starting-point of philosophy for Xenophanes was found in theology. "Looking up to universal heaven," says Aristotle, "he proclaimed that unity is God." The largest fragment of his metaphysical poem consists of a polemic against Polytheism, both as regards the anthropomorphic conception of deity prevalent in Greece, and also as regards the immorality attributed by Homer and Hesiod to the gods. His own God is a sublime abstraction of mind, one and indivisible, without motion, without beginning or ending, in no way like to man. To the divine unity he attributed senses, thought, and volition; but he does not appear to have attempted to connect God with the universe. Like the other speculators of his age and nation, he theoretically deduced the world from simple elements, choosing earth and water, as we gather from some fragments of his poem, for the primordial constituents. At the same time he held a doctrine which afterwards became the central point of Eleatic science. This was a disbelief in the evidence of the senses, a despair of empirical knowledge, which contrasts singularly with his own

vehement dogmatism upon the nature of the Divine Being. The unity of the Divine Being.
Thus the originality of Xenophanes consisted in his pronoun-
cing, without proof, that the universe must be regarded as an
unity, and that this unity is the Divine Existence, all human
mythology being but dreams and delusions. Of his philosophical poem only inconsiderable portions have been preserved. These, however, are sufficient to make clear the line
he took, both in his assertion of monotheism and his polemic
against the anthropomorphic theology of the Greeks. Such
as they are, I have translated them as follows : [1]—

"One god there is, among gods and men the greatest, neither in
body like to mortals, nor in mind.

"With the whole of him he sees, with the whole of him he
thinks, with the whole of him he hears.

"Without exertion, by energy of mind he sways the universe
of things.

"That he abides for ever in the same state, without movement,
or change from place to place, is evident.

"But mortals fancy that gods come into being like themselves,
and have their senses, voice, and body. But, of a truth, if oxen or
lions had hands, and could draw with their hands, and make what
men make, then horses like unto horses, and oxen like unto oxen,
would both paint the images of gods, and shape their bodies also
after the similitude of their own limbs.

"Homer and Hesiod attributed to gods everything that is dis-
graceful and blameworthy among men, and very many lawless
deeds of gods they recorded—theft, adultery, and mutual deceit."

Another set of scattered fragments, small in number and Natural philosophy.
meagre in their information, from the poem by Xenophanes
on φύσις (or the natural scheme of things), show that he held

---

[1] In my translations of the fragments of Xenophanes and Parmenides
I have followed the text of their most recent editor, W. A. Mullach, not
without reference, however, to that of Karsten, some of whose emendations
seem almost necessary to the sense. The meaning of many Parmenidean
sentences may, however, be fairly said to be now irrecoverable, owing to
the uncertainty of readings and the lack of context.

the views afterwards developed by Parmenides concerning
the uncertainty of human opinion, and that the elemental
substances which he favoured in his cosmogonical theory
were earth and water.   These also I have translated :—

"For all of us from earth and water sprang.

"Earth and water are all things that come into being and have
birth.

"The spring of water is the sea.

"This upper surface of the earth beneath our feet is open to
the sight, and borders on the air ; but the lower parts reach down
into infinity.

"What we call Iris, that also is a cloud, purple-dark, scarlet-
bright, yellow-pale to look upon.

"The very truth itself no man who hath been or will be can
know concerning gods and all whereof I speak ; for though he
publish the most absolute, yet even so he does not know : opinion
is supreme o'er all things.

"These things are matters of opinion, shadows of the truth.

"Not from the beginning did gods reveal all things to mortals ;
but in course of time by seeking they make progress in discovery."

Dualism in
the Eleatic
system.

The essential weakness of the Eleatic way of thinking was
not glaringly apparent, though implicit, in the utterance of
Xenophanes.   This consisted in the unreconciled antithesis
between the world of unity, of true being, of rational thought,
and the world of multiplicity, of phenomenal appearance, of
opinion.   By pushing the tenets of his master to their logical
conclusions, and by exchanging theological for metaphysical
phraseology, Parmenides, the greatest teacher of the school,
exposed the fatal insufficiency of Eleatic dualism.   At the
same time he achieved an ever-memorable triumph in
philosophy by forcing the problem of essential reality upon
the earliest Greek speculators, and by defining the battle-
ground of future ontological controversy.

Parmenides, a native of Elea, who flourished about the
year 503, enjoyed a reputation in his native city scarcely
inferior to that of Pythagoras at Crotona, of Empedocles at

Acragas, or of Solon at Athens. Speusippus, quoted by Diogenes Laertius, asserts that the magistrates of Elea were yearly sworn to observe the laws enacted by Parmenides. Cebes talks about a "Pythagorean or Parmenidean mode of life," as if the austere ascesis of the Samian philosopher had been adopted or imitated by the Eleatic. Indeed, there is good reason to suppose that Parmenides held intercourse with members of the Pythagorean sect, his neighbours in the south of Italy. Diogenes Laertius relates that he was united in the bonds of closest friendship to Ameinias and Diochætes, two Pythagoreans. Of these the latter was a poor man, but excellent in breeding and in character; Parmenides so loved him and respected him that, when he died, he dedicated a hero's chapel to his memory. The philosophers of this period in Greece, as might be proved abundantly, were no mere students, but men of action and political importance. Their reputation for superior wisdom caused them to be consulted in affairs of state, and to be deferred to in matters of constitutional legislation. Some of them, like Thales, Anaximander, and Empedocles, were employed on works of public utility. Others, like Pythagoras, remodelled the society of cities, or, like Anaxagoras, through their influence with public men and rulers, raised the tone of politics around them. All of them devoted a large portion of their time and attention to the study of public questions. It was this kind of prestige, we may conjecture, which, in the next phase of Greek thought, threw so much power into the hands of sophists, and which finally encouraged Plato in his theory that those states would be best governed where the sages were the rulers.

Of Parmenides himself some precious notices have been preserved by Plato. It appears that the great Eleatic teacher visited Athens in his old age. Socrates was a young man at the period of this visit; and Plato, whether inventing an occasion for their meeting or relying on actual tradition, brings them into conversation. In the prelude to the dialogue *Parmenides* we read : [1]—

> " He told us that Pythodorus had described to him the appearance of Parmenides and Zeno ; they came to Athens, he said, at the great Panathenæa ; the former was, at the time of his visit, about sixty-five years old, very white with age, but well favoured. Zeno was nearly forty years of age, of a noble figure and fair aspect ; and in the days of his youth he was reported to have been beloved of Parmenides. He said that they lodged with Pythodorus in the Ceramicus, outside the wall, whither Socrates and others came to see them ; they wanted to hear some writings of Zeno, which had been brought to Athens by them for the first time. He said that Socrates was then very young, and that Zeno read them to him in the absence of Parmenides, and had nearly finished when Pythodorus entered, and with him Parmenides and Aristoteles, who was afterwards one of the Thirty ; there was not much more to hear, and Pythodorus had heard Zeno repeat them before."

The *Theætetus* contains another allusion to Parmenides, which proves in what reverence the old philosopher was held by Socrates :—

> " My reason is that I have a kind of reverence, not so much for Melissus and the others, who say that 'all is one and at rest,' as for the great leader himself, Parmenides, venerable and awful, as in Homeric language he may be called—him I should be ashamed to approach in a spirit unworthy of him. I met him when he was an old man and I was a mere youth, and he appeared to me to have a glorious depth of mind. And I am afraid that we may not understand his language, and may fall short even more of his meaning."

Finally, in the *Sophistes* a passing allusion to the same event is put into the mouth of Socrates : " I remember hearing Parmenides use the latter of the two methods, when I was a young man, and he was far advanced in years, in a very noble discussion." These notices of the Eleatic sage, we feel, are not in any sense accidental. Plato has introduced them

---

[1] This and the two following translations from Plato are Professor Jowett's.

in important moments of his three most studied dialogues upon those very points which occupied the mind of Parmenides, and by the elaboration of which he made his greatest contribution to philosophy. The problems of knowledge and of the relation of the phenomenal universe to real existence were for the first time methodically treated in the school of Elea. Their solution in the theory of Ideas was the main object of Plato's philosophical activity.

The unity asserted by Xenophanes gave its motto to the Eleatic school; ἓν τὰ πάντα (one is the whole complex of things) became their watchword. Parmenides, however, abstracted from this unity all theological attributes. Plain existence, obtained apparently by divesting thought of all qualifications derived from sensation and imagination, and regarding it in primitive and abstract nakedness or nothingness, was the only positive condition which he left to the principle of Being; and though he seems to have identified this Being with Thought, we must be careful not to be misled by modern analogies into fancying that his ἀρχή involved a purely intellectual idealism. Nor, again, can we regard it as the totality of things presented to the senses; the most earnest polemic of the philosopher is directed against this view. The Unity, the Being, of Parmenides, was in truth the barest metaphysical abstraction, deduced, we are tempted to believe, in the first instance from a simple observation of language, and yet, when formed, not wholly purged from corporeity. Being is proved by the word ἐστί. The singular number indicates the unity of the subject; the present tense proves its eternity, for it neither asserts a *has been* nor a *will be*, but an everlasting *is*. Its antithesis Not-Being is impossible and inconceivable; οὐκ ἐστί (it is *not*). Completing his conception of Being as the sole reality, and carrying out the arguments attributed by Aristotle to his master,[1] Parmenides shows that the eternal One is indivisible, immovable,

The Unity of Being.

---

[1] See the treatise, *De Xenophane, Zenone, et Gorgia.*

Qualities of Being.

continuous, homogeneous, absolutely self-identical, beyond the reach of birth, or change, or dissolution. Furthermore it is finite and spheroid. In rounding and completing his notion of the Unity of Being, Parmenides seems at this point to have passed into the region of geometrical abstractions. The sphere of mathematics requires to be circumscribed by a superficies equidistant at all points from the centre. These conditions of perfection Parmenides attributed to Being, forgetting that the finite sphere thus conceived by him implied, by a necessity of human thought, a beyond against which it should be defined. At the same time, this geometrical analogy prevents us from assuming that the further identification of Being with Thought excluded a concrete and almost material conception of the Ens.

Phenomenal existence.

As opposed to this unique ἀρχή (principle or element), the sole and universal reality, which can only be apprehended by the reason, and which is eternally and continuously One, Parmenides places the totality of phenomena, multiplex, diverse, subject to birth, change, division, dissolution, motion. These, he asserts, are non-existent, the illusions of the senses, mere names, the vague and unreal dream-world of impotent mortals. Not having advanced in his analysis of thought beyond the first category of Being, he felt obliged to abandon the multiplicity of things as hopeless and unthinkable. Yet he cannot deny their phenomenal existence; there they are, deceiving the sage and the simple man alike: experience asserts them; language and the opinion of humanity take them for granted as realities. Parmenides feels bound to offer an explanation of this cosmos of illusion, this many-formed and many-coloured mirage. His teaching consequently contains a paradox deeply embedded in its very substance. Having first expounded the law of absolute truth, he proceeds to render a grave and meditated account of error. Having demonstrated the sole existence of abstract Being, he turns a page and begins to discourse like any physicist of his age in Greece, concerning Light and Night, Hot and Cold, Fire and Earth, Active and Passive, Male and Female, Rare and Dense. By a singular irony of fate it was precisely for this portion of his teaching that he received the praise of Bacon in the *Novum Organum*. To connect the doctrine of Being, τὰ πρὸς ἀλήθειαν (things that tend toward truth, the philosophy of truth), and the doctrine of Appearance, τὰ πρὸς δόξαν (things that lead toward opinion, the philosophy of opinion), was beyond his power. It was what Plato afterwards attempted in his theory of ideas, and Aristotle in the theory of forms and matter (εἴδη and ὕλη). Parmenides himself seems to have regarded man as a part of the cosmos, subject to its phantasmagoric changes and illusions, yet capable of comprehending that, while the substratum of Being is alone immutable, real, and one, all else is shifting, non-existent, and many. Neglect, he says, the object of sense, the plurality of things obedient to change, and you will arrive at the object of reason, the unity that alters not and can be only apprehended by thought. Yet, while on the one hand he did not disdain to theorise the universe of sense, so, on the other hand, as already hinted, he had not arrived at the point of abstracting corporeity from Being. To do this from his point of view was indeed impossible. Having posited pure being as the sole reality, he was obliged to form a figurative presentation of it to his mind. A new stage had to be accomplished by human thought before the intellect could fairly grapple with the problems nakedly and paradoxically propounded by the sage of Elea.

From the immense importance attached by Parmenides to the verb ἐστί, and from his assertion that men deal with names and not with realities, it followed that to his metaphysical teaching a logical set of corollaries had to be appended. To construct these was the task of Zeno, his beloved pupil and authorised successor. Zeno undertook to maintain the Parmenidean Unity, both against the vulgar

Relation of Nature to real Being.

Zeno's logic.

evidence of the senses and also against philosophers who, like Heraclitus, directed their attention to the flux and multiplicity of things. His method was, not to prove the necessity of unity at rest, but to demonstrate the contradictions involved in the ideas of plurality and motion. The intellectual diffi- culties implied in the divisibility of time and space and matter were developed by Zeno with a force and subtlety that justified Aristotle in calling him the founder of dialectic. His logic, however, was but the expansion of positions implicit in Xenophanes and clearly indicated by Parmenides. How the Eleatic arguments, as further handled by Melissus, helped the Sophists, and influenced the school of Megara, who went so far as to refuse any but identical propositions, are matters that belong to another chapter of Greek history. So, too, is Plato's attempt to resolve the antinomies revealed in human thought by the polemic of his predecessors. Enough has now been said to serve as preface to the follow- ing version of the fragments of Parmenides.

Induction to
Parmenides'
poem.

His poem—for, strange as it must always seem, Parmenides committed the exposition of his austerely abstract and argu- mentative doctrine to hexameters — begins with an epical allegory. He feigns to have been drawn by horses on a chariot to the house of Truth : the horses may, perhaps, be taken, as in Plato's vision of the *Phædrus*, to symbolise faculties of the soul; and the gates of Truth open upon two roads—one called the way of night, or error; the other of light, or real knowledge. The goddess who dwells there, divine Sophia, instructs him equally in the lore of truth and of opinion and makes no attempt, as will be seen from her own words, to conceal the futility of the second part of her discourse. From a literary point of view the poem has no merit. Even the exordium is stiff and tame. It begins thus:—

"The steeds which bear me, and have brought me to the bounds of my desire, since they drew and carried me into the way renowned of Her who leads the wise man to all knowledge—on that road I journeyed, on that road they bore me, those steeds of thought that whirl the car along. But maidens showed the way, sun-born maids, who left the halls of gloom and brought us to the light, withdrawing with their fingers from their brows the veils. And the axle in the socket made a whistling sound, glowing as by two round wheels on either side it ran, while the steeds drove the car swiftly on. There are the gates which open on the paths of Night and Day. A lintel shuts them in above, and a floor of stone beneath ; but the airy space they close is fastened with huge doors, which Justice the avenger locks or unlocks by the key she holds. Her did the maidens sue with gentle words, and wisely won her to draw for them the bolted barrier from the gates. The gates flew open, and the doors yawned wide, back rolling in the sockets their brazen hinges wrought with clasps and nails. Straight through the portal drove the maidens car and horses on the broad highway. And me the goddess graciously received ; she took my right hand in her hand, and spoke these words, addressing me : 'Child of man, companion of immortal charioteers, that comest drawn by horses to our home, welcome ! for thee no evil fate sent forth to travel on this path—far from the track of men indeed it lies—but Right and Justice were thy guides. Thy lot it is all things to learn ; both the sure heart of truth that wins assent, and the vain fancies of mortals which have no real ground of faith. Yet these, too, shalt thou learn, since it behoves thee to know all opinions, testing them, and travelling every field of thought.' "

Here the exordium, as we possess it, ends, and we start upon the fragments of the lecture addressed by divine Sophia to the mortal sage. The order and the connection of these fragments are more than doubtful. So much, however, is clear, that they fall into two sections—the first treating of scientific truth, the second of popular opinion. The instrument of knowledge in the one case is the reason; in the other the senses bear confused and untrustworthy witness to phenomena.

Doctrine of Being and Not-Being— truth and opinion.

"Come now, for I will tell, and do thou hear and keep my words, what are the only ways of inquiry that lead to knowledge. The one which certifies that being is, and that not-being is not, is the pathway of persuasion, for truth follows it. The other which declares that being is not, and that not-being must be, that I affirm is wholly unpersuasive ; for neither couldst thou know not-being, since it cannot be got at, nor couldst thou utter it in words, seeing that thought and being are the same.

"To me it is indifferent where I begin, for again to the same point I shall return. It must be that speech and thought are being, for being is, and that not-being is nothing : which things I bid thee ponder. First, keep thy mind from that path of inquiry, then, too, from that on which mortals who know nothing wander in doubt ; helplessness sways in their breasts the erring mind ; hither and thither are they borne, deaf, yea and blind, in wonderment, confused crowds who fancy being and not-being are the same and not the same ; the way of all of them leads backwards."

Some light is thrown upon these fragments by a passage in the *Sophistes* of Plato, where the Eleatic stranger is made to say : " In the days when I was a boy, the great Parmenides protested against this (*i.e.* against asserting the existence of not-being), and to the end of his life he continued to inculcate the same lesson—always repeating, both in verse and out of verse, *Keep your mind from this way of inquiry, for never will you show that not-being is.*" The fragment which immediately follows, if we are right in assuming the continuity and order of its verses, forms the longest portion of the poem extant.

Exposition of the nature of Being.

"Never do thou learn to fancy that things that are not, are ; but keep thy mind from this path of inquiry ; nor let custom force thee to pursue that beaten way, to use blind eyes and sounding ear and tongue, but judge by reason the knotty argument which I declare. One only way of reasoning is left—that being is. Wherein are many signs that it is uncreate and indestructible, whole in itself, unique in kind, immovable and everlasting. It never was, nor will be, since it exists as a simultaneous present, a continuous unity. What origin shall we seek of it ? Where and how did it grow ? That it arose from not-being I will not suffer thee to say or think, for it cannot be thought or said that being is not. Then, too, what necessity could have forced it to the birth at an earlier or later moment ? for neither birth nor beginning belongs to being. Wherefore either to be or not to be, is the unconditioned alternative. Nor will the might of proof allow us to believe that anything can spring from being but itself. Therefore the law of truth permits no birth or dissolution in it, no remission of its chains, but holds it firm. This, then, is the point for decision : it is, or it is not. Now we have settled, as necessity obliged, to leave the one path, inconceivable, unnamed, for it is not the true way ; but to affirm, as sure, that being is. How then could being have a future or a past ? If it began to be, or if it is going to be, then it is not : wherefore birth and death are alike put aside as inconceivable. Nor is it divisible, since it is all homogeneous, in no part more itself than in another, which would prevent its coherence, nor in any part less ; but all is full of being. Wherefore it is one continuous whole, for being draws to being. Immovable within the bounds of its great chains it is, without beginning, without end, since birth and dissolution have moved far away, whom certainty repelled. Eternally the same, in the same state, for and by itself, it abides ; thus fixed and firm it stays, for strong necessity holds it in the chains of limit and clenches it around. Wherefore being cannot be infinite, seeing it lacks nothing ; and if it were, it would lack all.

" Look now at things which, though absent, are present to the mind. For never shall being from being be sundered so as to lose its continuity by dispersion or recombination.

" Thought and the object of thought are the same, for without being, in which is affirmation, thou wilt not find thought. For nothing is or will be besides being, since fate hath bound it to remain alone and unmoved, which is named the universe—all things that mortal men held fixed, believing in their truth—birth, and death, to be and not to be, change of place, and variety of colour.

" Now since the extreme limit of being is defined, the whole is like a well-rounded sphere, of equal radius in all directions, for it may not be less or greater in one part or another. For neither is there not-being to prevent its attaining to equality, nor is it possible that being should in one place be more and in another less than being, since all is inviolably one. For this is certain, that it abides, an equal whole all round, within its limits.

" Here then I conclude my true discourse and meditation upon Truth. Turn now and learn the opinions of men, listening to the deceptive order of my words."

The divine Sophia calls the speech which she is about to utter   Phenomena. deceptive ($\grave{a}\pi\alpha\tau\eta\lambda\acute{o}\nu$), because it has to do no longer with the immutable and imperturbable laws of entity, but only with the delusions to which the human mind is exposed by the evidence of the senses. If Parmenides had been in any true sense of the word a poet, he would not have subjected Sophia to the ridicule of condemning her own observations, when he might have invented some other machinery for the conveyance of his physical hypothesis. Nothing, in fact, can be more artistically monstrous than to put lies into the mouth of Truth personified. The fragments of this portion of his poem may, in spite of their scientific worthlessness, be translated, if only for the sake of completeness. We must suppose, therefore, that Wisdom has resumed her parable, and is speaking as follows :—

Natural philosophy.

"Two forms have they determined by their minds to name, for those are wrong who take but one of these. Corporeally and by signs they have distinguished them, setting on the one side fire, ethereal, gentle, very subtle, everywhere identical, but different from the other element. That, too, is self-identical, diverse from fire, dark night, a thick and weighty body. Of these I will reveal to you the whole disposition, as it appears, so that no thought of mortals may ever elude you.

"Now, seeing that all things are called by the name of light and night, and the qualities that severally pertain to them, the universe is full of light and murky night, rivals equally balanced, since neither partakes of the other.

"For the narrower spheres have been fashioned of impure fire ; those next of night, interpenetrated by a portion of flame ; and in the midst of all is the goddess who controls the whole. For everywhere she is the cause of dire parturition and procreation, making female mix with male, and male with female."

At this point in the murky exposition there shines forth a single line, which, seized upon by poets and poetic souls in after years, traverses the dismal waste of false physics and imperfect metaphysics like a streak of inspiration—"fair as a star when only one is shining in the sky."

"Love, first of all the gods, she formed."
"Thou, too, shalt know the nature of ether, and in ether all the signs, and the hidden acts of the bright sun's pure lamp, and

whence they sprang ; and thou shalt learn the revolutions of the
round-eyed moon, and whence she is ; and thou shalt understand
the all-surrounding heaven, whence it arose, and how fate ruling it
bound it to keep the limits of the stars.

"How earth and sun and moon and ether shared by all, and
the galaxy and farthest Olympus, and the hot might of stars sprang
into being.

"Another light that shines in revolution round the earth by
night.

"For ever gazing at the radiant sun.

"For as the elements are mixed in the jointed framework of
our limbs, so are the minds of men made up. For the nature of
the members is the same as that which thinks in the case of all and
each ; it is mind that rules.

"From the right side boys, from the left girls.

"Thus, according to opinion, were born and now are these
things : and afterwards, when they have grown to the full, will
perish : whereto men have affixed, unto each, a name."

It is only by a complete translation of the extant fragments   *Reason and
of Parmenides that any notion can be formed of the hiatus   the senses.*
between what he chose to call truth, and what he termed
opinion. As a thinker, he revealed both the weakness of his
metaphysical system and the sincerity of his intention by pro-
claiming this abrupt division between the realm of the pure
reason and the field of the senses, without attempting a
synthesis. No other speculator has betrayed the vanity of
dogmatism about the Absolute more conclusively by the
simultaneous presentation of lame guesses in the region of the
Relative. The impartial student of his verse is forced to the
conclusion that the titles (τὰ πρὸς ἀλήθειαν and τὰ πρὸς
δόξαν) which have been given to the two departments of his
exposition, are both arbitrary ; for what warrant have we that
his intuitions into the nature of pure Being are more certain
than his guesses about the conditions of phenomenal existence ?
Parmenides might indeed be selected as a parable of the human
mind pretending to a knowledge of the unconditioned truth,
and after all arriving at nothing more cogent than opinion.
The innumerable ontological assertions, which in the pride of

the speculative reason have been made by men, are δόξαι (opinions), and the epigram pointed by Parmenides against the common folk, is equally applicable to his own sect—

Κωφοὶ ὁμῶς τυφλοί τε, τεθηπότες, ἄκριτα φῦλα.

"Deaf, yea and blind, in wonderment, confused tribes."

As soon as men begin to dogmatise, whether the supposed truth to which they pin their faith be the barest metaphysical abstraction, or some assumed intuition into the Divine nature, they create a schism between the multiplicity of the universe and the unity which they proclaim. In other words, they distinguish, like Parmenides, between what they arbitrarily denote as truth and what they cannot account for as phenomena. To quit the sphere of our own mind is impossible; and therefore nothing can be discovered which is not some mode of the mind. The utmost the metaphysician can do is to describe the operations of the human intellect without explaining its existence, and all systematised knowledge is but a classification of the categories of consciousness. Thus the sophistic position that man is for man the measure of all things is irrefutable. But when he attempts to hypostasise his own thoughts as realities, to argue outward from his conceptions to the universe, this is the same as taking a leap in the dark across an undefined abyss from the only ascertained standing-ground to a hypothetical beyond.

During the two-and-twenty centuries which have elapsed since the days of Parmenides, the philosophers have learned wisdom. They are now too wary to parade the distinction between two kinds of opinion, and to construct one system of truth, another of illusion. They either content themselves with omitting what they regard as the insoluble; or they endeavour to invent an all-embracing schema, which shall supersede the cruder distinctions between subject and object, mind and nature, ego and non-ego. Yet nothing in the realm

of absolute knowledge has been gained in all this space of
time.

The owl of Minerva, to quote one of Hegel's most luminous
epigrams, still starts upon its flight when the evening twilight,
succeeding the day of work, has fallen. Metaphysic goes on
shaping from the human consciousness a fabric which it calls
reality. Science has magnified and multiplied phenomena
until, instead of one, we have in every case a million problems
to employ intelligence. Social conditions grow more complex,
and more and more is ascertained about the inner life of man.
But the fact remains that, while theologian, logician, physicist,
and moralist, each from his own standing-point, may cry
"Eureka !" we can know nothing in itself. The most complicated system, created by the Aristotle of the modern world,
involves at the outset an assumption. From reflection on the
laws of human thought, on the varied acquisitions of the human
mind, and on the successive phases of human history, it carries
over the synthetic statement of its conclusions to the account
of the universe. In other words, it postulates the identity of
the human and the Divine mind, and ends by asserting that
thought is the only reality. Does not a fallacy lie in this, that
while the mind possesses the faculty of reflecting upon itself,
everything which it knows is of necessity expressed in terms
of itself, and therefore in pretending to give an account of the
universe it is only giving an account of its own operations ?
The philosophy of the *Idea* is thus a way of looking at things ;
to explain them or deduce them is beyond its reach. How,
for example, except by exercise of faith, by dogmatism and
initial begging of the question, can we be assured that an intelligence differently constituted from the human mind should
not cognise a different κόσμος νοητός or intelligible world,
and be equally justified in claiming to have arrived at Truth ?
It is comparatively easy to acquire encyclopædic knowledge,
to construct a system, to call the keystone of the system the
Idea, and to assert that the *Idea* is God. But is all this of any

Impossi-
bility of
absolute
knowledge.

value except as a machine for arranging and formulating thoughts and opinions? At the end of philosophies one feels tempted to exclaim :—

" I heard what was said of the universe,
   Heard it and heard it of several thousand years :
   It is middling well as far as it goes,—But is that all ? "

CHAPTER VII

EMPEDOCLES

THE figure of Empedocles of Agrigentum, when seen across *Sublime personality of Empedocles.* the twenty-three centuries which separate us from him, presents perhaps a more romantic appearance than that of any
other Greek philosopher. This is owing in great measure
to the fables which invest his life and death with mystery, to
his reputation for magical power, and to the wild sublimity
of his poetic utterances. Yet, even in his lifetime, and among
contemporary Greeks, he swept the stage of the world like a
great tragic actor, and left to posterity the fame of genius as
poet, physician, patriot, and sage. The well-known verses of
Lucretius suffice to prove that the glory of Empedocles increased with age, and bore the test of time. Reading them,
we cannot but regret that poems which so stirred the reverent
enthusiasm of Rome's loftiest singer have been scattered to
the winds, and that what we now possess of their remains
affords but a poor sample of their unimpaired magnificence.

Nothing is more remarkable about Empedocles than his
versatility and comprehensiveness. Other men of his age
were as nobly born, as great in philosophic power, as distin-

His versatility and many-sidedness.

guished for the part they bore in politics, as celebrated for poetic genius, as versed in mystic lore, in medicine, and in magic arts. But Parmenides, Pythagoras, Pausanias, and Epimenides could claim honour in but one, or two at most, of these departments. Empedocles united all, and that too, if we may judge by the temper of his genius and the few legends handed down to us about his life, in no ordinary degree. He seems to have possessed a warmth and richness of nature which inclined him to mysticism and poetry, and gave a tone of peculiar solemnity to everything he did, or thought, or said. At the same time, he was attracted by the acuteness of his intellect to the metaphysical inquiries which were agitating the western colonies of Greece, while his rare powers of observation enabled him to make discoveries in the then almost unexplored region of natural science. The age in which he lived had not yet thrown off the form of poetry in philosophical composition. Even Parmenides committed his austere theories to hexameter verse. Therefore, the

Poet, philosopher, priest, purifier.

sage of Agrigentum was easily led to concentrate his splendid powers on the production of one great work, and made himself a poet among philosophers, and a philosopher among poets, without thereby impairing his claims to rank highly both as a poet and also as a thinker among the most distinguished men of Greece. But Empedocles had not only deeply studied metaphysics, nature, and the arts of verse; whatever was mysterious in the world around him, in the guesses of past ages, and in the forebodings of his own heart, possessed a powerful attraction for the man who thought himself inspired of God. Having embraced the Pythagorean theories, he maintained the fallen state of men, and implored his fellow-creatures to purge away the guilt by which they had been disinherited and exiled from the joys of heaven. Thus he appeared before his countrymen not only as a poet and philosopher, but also as a priest and purifier. Born of a wealthy and illustrious house, he did not expend his substance

merely on horse-racing and chariots, by which means of display his ancestors had gained a princely fame in Sicily ; but,
not less proud than they had been, he shod himself with
golden sandals, set the laurel crown upon his head, and, trailing
robes of Tyrian purple through the streets of Agrigentum, went
attended by a crowd of serving-men and reverent admirers.
He claimed to be a favourite of Phœbus, and rose at length to Claim to
divinity.
the pretension of divinity. His own words show this, gravely
spoken, with no vain assumption, but with a certainty of
honour well deserved :—

" Friends who dwell in the great city hard by the yellow stream
of Acragas, who live on the Acropolis, intent on honourable cares,
harbours revered of strangers, ignorant of what is vile ; welcome :
but I appear before you an immortal god, having overpassed the
limits of mortality, and walk with honour among all, as is my due,
crowned with long fillets and luxuriant garlands. No sooner do
I enter their proud prosperous cities than men and women pay
me reverence, who follow me in thousands, asking the way to
profit, some desiring oracles, and others racked by long and cruel
torments, hanging on my lips to hear the spells that pacify disease of
every kind."

We can hardly wonder that some of the fellow-citizens of
Empedocles were jealous of his pretensions, and regarded him
with suspicious envy and dislike, when we read such lines of
lofty self-exaltation.   Indeed, it is difficult for men of the nineteenth century to understand how a great and wise philosopher
could lay claim to divine honours in his own lifetime. This
arrogance we have been accustomed to associate with the
names of a Caligula and a Claudius. Yet when we consider
the circumstances in which Empedocles was placed, and the
nature of his theories, our astonishment diminishes. The line of
demarcation between this world and the supernatural was then
but vague and undetermined. Popular theology abounded in
legends of gods who had held familiar intercourse with men,
and of men who had been raised by prowess or wisdom to
divinity. The pedigrees of all distinguished families ended in

a god at no great distance.   Nor was it then a mere figure of speech when bards and priests claimed special revelations from Apollo, or physicians styled themselves the children of Asclepius.   Heaven lay around the first Greeks in their infancy of art and science ; it was long before the vision died away and faded into the sober daylight of Aristotelian philosophy.   Thus when Empedocles proclaimed himself a god, he only stretched beyond the usual limit a most common pretension of all men learned in arts and sciences.   His own speculations gave him further warrant for the assumption of the style of deity.   For he held the belief that all living souls had once been demons or divine spirits, who had lost their heavenly birthright for some crime of impurity or violence, and yet were able to restore themselves to pristine splendour by the rigorous exercise of abstinence and expiatory rites.   These rites he thought he had discovered ; he had prayed and fasted ; he had held communion with Phœbus the purifier, and received the special favour of that god, by being made a master in the arts of song, and magic, and healing, and priestcraft.   Was he not therefore justified in saying that he had won again his rights divine, and transformed himself into a god on earth ?   His own words tell the history of his fall :—

Metempsychosis.

" Woe to me that I did not fall a prey to death before I took the cursed food within my lips ! . . . From what glory, from what immeasurable bliss, have I now sunk to roam with mortals on this earth ? "

Again, he says—

" For I have been in bygone times a youth, a maiden, and a flowering shrub, a bird, yea, and a fish that swims in silence the deep sea."

From this degraded state the spirit gradually emerges.   Of the noblest souls he says :—

" Among beasts they become lions dwelling in caverns of the earth upon the hills, and laurels among leafy trees, . . . and at last prophets, and bards, and physicians, and chiefs among the men of earth, from whence they rise to be gods supreme in honour, . . . sitting at banquets with immortal comrades, in their feasts unvisited by human cares, beyond the reach of fate and wearing age."

Empedocles, by dint of pondering on nature, by long pen- *Mysticism.* ance, by the illumination of his intellect and the coercion of his senses, had been raised before the natural term of life to that high honour, and been made the fellow of immortal gods. His language upon this topic is one of the points in which we can trace an indistinct resemblance between him and some of the Indian mystics. There is, however, no reason to suppose that Asiatic thought had any marked or direct influence on Greek philosophy. It is better to refer such similarities to the working of the same tendencies in the Greek and Hindu minds.

To those who disbelieved his words he showed the mighty *Miracles.* works which he had wrought. Empedocles, during his lifetime, was known to have achieved marvels, such as only supernatural powers could compass. More than common sagacity and in-genuity in the treatment of natural diseases, or in the removal of obstacles to national prosperity, were easily regarded by the simple people of those times as the evidence of divine authority. Empedocles had devised means for protecting the citizens of Agrigentum from the fury of destructive winds. What these means were, we do not know; but he received in consequence the title of κωλυσανέμας, or "warder-off of winds." Again, he resuscitated, from the very jaws of death, a woman who lay senseless and unable to breathe, long after all physicians had despaired of curing her. This entitled him to be regarded as a master of the keys of life and death ; nor did he fail to attribute his own power to the virtue of super-natural spells. But the greatest of his achievements was the deliverance which he wrought for the people of Selinus from a grievous pestilence. It seems that some exhalations from a marsh having caused this plague, Empedocles, at his own cost, cut a channel for two rivers through the fen, and purged away the fetid vapours. A short time after the cessation of the sickness, Empedocles, attired in tragic state, appeared before the Selinuntians at a banquet. His tall and stately figure wore the priestly robe ; his brazen sandals rang upon the marble as he slowly moved with front benign and solemn eyes ; beneath the sacrificial chaplet flowed his long Phœbean locks, and in his hand he bore a branch of bay. The nobles of Selinus rose ; the banquet ceased ; all did him reverence, and hailed him as a god, deliverer of their city, friend of Phœbus, intercessor between angry Heaven and suffering men.

Magic rites and incantations

Closely connected with his claim to divinity was the position which Empedocles assumed as an enchanter. Gorgias, his pupil, asserts that he often saw him at the magic rites. Nor are we to suppose that this wizardry was a popular misinterpretation of his real power as a physician and philosopher. It is far more probable that Empedocles himself believed in the potency of incantations, and delighted in the ceremonies and mysterious songs by which the dead were recalled from Hades, and secrets of the other world wrung from unwilling fate. We can form to ourselves a picture of this stately and magnificent enchanter, convinced of his own supernatural ascendency, and animated by the wild enthusiasm of his ardent nature, alone among the mountains of Girgenti, or by the seashore, invoking the elemental deities to aid his conjurations, and ascribing the forebodings of his own poetic spirit to external inspiration or the voice of gods. In solitary meditations he had wrought out a theory of the world, and had conceived the notion of a spiritual God, one and unseen, pure intellect, an everlasting omnipresent power, to whom might be referred those natural remedies that stopped the plague, or cured the sick, or found new channels for the streams. The early Greek philosophers were fond of attributing to some "common wisdom" of the world, some animating soul or universal intellect, the arts and intuitions to which they had themselves attained.   Therefore, with this belief predominating in his mind, it is not strange that he should have trusted to the divine efficacy of his own spells, and have regarded the results of observation as a kind of supernatural wisdom.   To his friend Pausanias the physician he makes these lofty promises, " Thou shalt learn every kind of medicines that avert diseases and the evils of old age. Thou too shalt curb the fury of untiring winds, and when it pleases thee thou shalt reverse thy charms and loose avenging storms.   Thou shalt replace black rain-clouds with the timely drought that men desire, and when the summer's arid heat prevails, thou shalt refresh the trees with showers that rustle in the thirsty corn.   And thou shalt bring again from Hades the life of a departed man." Like the Pytha-goreans whom he followed, he seems to have employed the fascination of music in effecting cures; it is recorded of him that he once arrested the hand of a young man about to slay his father, by chanting to the lyre a solemn soul-subduing strain.   The strong belief in himself which Empedocles pos-   Personal sessed, inspired him with immense personal influence, so that   influence. his looks, and words, and tones, went farther than the force of other men.   He compelled them to follow and confide in him, like Orpheus, or like those lofty natures which in every age have had the power of leading and controlling others by innate supremacy.   That Empedocles tried to exhibit this superiority, and to heighten its effect by gorgeous raiment and profuse expenditure, by public ceremonies and mysterious modes of life, we need not doubt.   There was much of the spirit of Paracelsus in Empedocles, and vanity impaired the simple grandeur of his genius.   In every age of the world's history there have been some such men—men in whom the highest intellectual gifts are blent with weakness inclining them to superstitious juggleries.   Not content with their philosophical pretensions, or with poetical renown, they seek a more mysterious fame, and mix the pure gold of their reason with the dross of idle fancy. Their very weakness adds a glow of colour, which we miss in the whiter light of more purely scientific intellects. They are men in whom two natures cross—the poet and the philosopher, the mountebank and the seer, the divine and the fortune-teller, the rigorous analyst and the retailer of old wives' tales. But none have equalled Empedocles, in whose capacious idiosyncrasy the most opposite qualities found ample room for coexistence, who sincerely claimed the supernatural faculties which Paracelsus must have only half believed, and who lived at a time when poetry and fact were indistinguishably mingled, and when the world was still absorbed in dreams of a past golden age, and in rich foreshadowings of a boundless future.

Legends relating to his death. We are not, therefore, surprised to read the fantastic legends which involve his death in a mystery. Whatever ground of fact they may possess, they are wholly consistent with the picture we have formed to ourselves of the philosopher, and prove at least the superstition which had gathered round his name. One of these legends has served all ages as a moral for the futility of human designs, and for the just reward of inordinate vanity. Every one who knows the name of Empedocles has heard that, having jumped into Etna in order to conceal the time and manner of his death, and thus to establish his divinity, fate frustrated his schemes by casting up his brazen slippers on the crater's edge. According to another legend, which resembles that of the death of Romulus, of Œdipus, and other divinised heroes, Empedocles is related to have formed one of a party of eighty men who assembled to celebrate by sacrifice his restoration of the dying woman. After their banquet they retired to sleep. But Empedocles remained in his seat at table. When morning broke, Empedocles was nowhere to be found. In reply to the question of his friends, some one asserted that he had heard a loud voice

calling on Empedocles at midnight, and that, starting up, he
saw a light from heaven and burning torches. Pausanias, who
was present at the sacrificial feast, sent far and wide to inquire
for his friend, wishing to test the truth of this report. But
piety restrained his search, and he was secretly informed by
heavenly messengers that Empedocles had won what he had
sought, and that divine honours should be paid to him. This
story rests on the authority of Heraclides Ponticus, who professed to have obtained it from Pausanias. The one legend we
may regard as the coinage of his foes, the other as a myth
created by the superstitious admiration of his friends.

We have hitherto regarded Empedocles more in his private *Political*
and priestly character than as a citizen. Yet it was not to be *career.*
expected that a man so nobly born, and so remarkable for
intellectual power, should play no public part in his native
state. A Greek could hardly avoid meddling with politics,
even if he wished to do so, and Empedocles was not one to
hide his genius in the comparative obscurity of private life.
While he was still a young man, Theron, the wise tyrant of
Agrigentum, died, and a powerful aristocracy endeavoured
to enslave the state. Empedocles manfully resisted them,
supporting the liberal cause with vehemence, and winning so
much popular applause that he is even reported to have
received and refused the offer of the kingly power. By these
means he made himself many foes among the nobility of Agrigentum; it is also probable that suspicion attached to him for
trying to establish in his native city the Pythagorean commonwealth, which had been extirpated in South Italy. That he
loved spiritual dominion we have seen; and this he might
have hoped to acquire more easily by taking the intellectual
lead among citizens of equal rights, than by throwing in his
lot with the aristocratic party, or by exposing himself to the
dangers and absorbing cares of a Greek tyrant. At any rate,
it is recorded that he impeached and procured the execution
of the leaders of the aristocracy; thus rescuing the liberty of

his nation at the expense of his own security. After a visit to Peloponnesus Empedocles returned to Agrigentum, but was soon obliged to quit his home again by the animosity of his political enemies. Where he spent the last years of his life, and died, remains uncertain.

Various poetical compositions.   It remains to estimate the poetical and philosophical renown of Empedocles. That his genius was highly valued among the ancients appears manifest from the panegyric of Lucretius. Nor did he fail to exhibit the versatility of his powers in every branch of poetical composition. Diogenes Laertius affirms that forty-three tragedies bearing his name were known to Hieronymus, from whom he drew materials for the life of Empedocles. Whether these tragedies were really written by the philosopher, or by another Sicilian of the same name, admits of doubt. But there is no reason why an author, possessed of such varied and distinguished talents as Empedocles, should not have tried this species of composition. Xenophanes is said to have composed tragedies; and Plato's youthful efforts would, we fondly imagine, have afforded the world fresh proofs of his commanding genius, had they escaped the flames to which they were condemned by his maturer judgment. No fragments of the tragedies of Empedocles survive; they probably belonged to the class of semi-dithyrambic compositions, which prevailed at Athens before the days of Æschylus, and which continued to be cultivated in Sicily. Some of the lyrical plays of the Italians—such, for instance, as the *Orfeo* of Poliziano—may enable us to form an idea of these simple dramas. After the tragedies, Diogenes makes mention of political poems. These may be referred to the period of the early manhood of Empedocles, when he was engaged in combat with the domineering aristocracy, and when he might have sought to spread his liberal principles through the medium of gnomic elegies, like those of Solon or Theognis. The fragments of the καθαρμοί, or poem on lustral rites, sufficiently display his style of earnest and

imperious exhortation to make us believe that at a time of
political contention he would not spare this powerful instrument of persuasion and attack. In the next place, we hear of
an epic poem on the invasion of Greece by Xerxes, which Epic on the
Persian war.
Empedocles is said to have left unfinished, and which his sister
or his daughter burned with other papers at his death. The
great defeat of the Medes took place while Empedocles was
still a youth. All Hellas had hung with breathless expectation
on the event of Marathon and Salamis. The fall of Xerxes
brought freedom and relief from terrible anxiety, not only to
the towns of Attica and the Peloponnesus, but also to the
shores of Sicily and Italy. It is not, therefore, unlikely that
the triumph which excited Simonides and Æschylus to the
production of masterpieces, may have stirred the spirit of the
youthful patriot of Agrigentum. Another composition of
Empedocles which perished under his sister's hands, was a
Proemium to Apollo. The loss of this poem is deeply to be
regretted. Empedocles regarded himself as specially protected
by the god of song and medicine and prophetic insight. His
genius would therefore naturally take its highest flight in
singing praises to this mighty patron. The hymn to Zeus,
which has been ascribed to Cleanthes, and some of the pseudo-
Orphic declamations, may give us an idea of the gravity and
enthusiasm which Empedocles would have displayed in treating so stirring a theme. Of his remaining works we possess
fragments. The great poem on Nature, the Lustral Precepts,
and the Discourse on Medicine, were all celebrated among the
ancients. Fortunately, the inductions to the first and second
of these have been preserved, and some lines addressed to
Pausanias may be regarded as forming the commencement of
the third. It is from these fragments, amounting in all to
about 470 lines, that we must form our judgment of Empedocles, the poet and the sage.

That Empedocles was a poet of the didactic order is clear Didactic
poetry.
from the nature of his subjects. Even as early as the time

of Aristotle, critics disputed as to whether poems written for
the purpose of scientific instruction deserved the name of
poetry. In the *Poetics*, Aristotle says,—οὐδὲν δὲ κοινόν
ἐστιν Ὁμήρῳ καὶ Ἐμπεδοκλεῖ πλὴν τὸ μέτρον· διὸ τὸν
μὲν ποιητὴν δίκαιον καλεῖν, τὸν δὲ φυσιόλογον μᾶλλον
ἢ ποιητήν.[1] The title φυσιόλογος, or philosopher of
nature, was of course generic, and might have been claimed
by Heraclitus, on the strength of his prose writings, no less
than by Empedocles. Lucretius, in the exordium to his
poem, argues for the utility of disguising scientific precepts
under the more attractive form of art; as we sweeten the lips
of the vessel that contains bitter medicine, in order to induce
the child to take it readily. And not only had Empedocles
this reason in his favour for the use of verse, but also, at the
age in which he lived, it was still a novelty to write prose at
all; nor would it have been consistent with his theories of
inspiration, and with the mysticism he professed, to abandon
the poetic form of utterance. He therefore thought and
wrote hexameters as naturally as the scientific men of the
present day think and write their sentences and paragraphs,
until the discourse is formed into a perfect whole. Allowing,
then, for the subject of his poem, Empedocles was regarded
by antiquity as first among the Greek didactic singers, though
he competed with Parmenides for this distinction, and was
placed upon a level with Lucretius. Lactantius mentions
them both together, in his definition of this kind of poetry.
And Aristotle, in another treatise, now lost, but quoted by
Diogenes, praises the artistic genius of the philosopher in
these words: Καὶ Ὁμηρικὸς ὁ Ἐμπεδοκλῆς καὶ δεινὸς
περὶ τὴν φράσιν γέγονε μεταφορικός τε ὢν καὶ τοῖς
ἄλλοις περὶ τὴν ποιητικὴν ἐπιτεύγμασι χρώμενος.[2] The

Philosophical hexameters.

[1] "Between Homer and Empedocles there is nothing in common except
their metre: therefore it is right to call the former a poet, the latter a
natural philosopher rather than a poet."

[2] "Empedocles again was Homeric in style, and clever in his use of

epithet Ὁμηρικὸς is very just; for not only is it clear that
Empedocles had studied the poems of Homer with care, and
had imbibed their phraseology, but he also possessed a genius
akin to that of Homer in love of simplicity, in fidelity to
nature, in unimpeded onward flow of energetic verse.

The simile of the girl playing with a water-clock, whereby
Empedocles illustrates his theory of respiration, and that of
the lantern, which serves to explain his notion of the
structure of the eye, are both of them Homeric in their
unadorned simplicity and vigour.   Again, such epithets as
these, πολυαίματον (full‑blooded) for the liver, ἱλάειρα
(gentle) for the moon, ὀξυβελὴς (quick-darting) for the sun,
πολυστέφανος (crowned) for majesty, θεμερῶπις (grave-
visaged) for harmony, and the constant repetition of θεοὶ
δολιχαίωνες τιμῆσι φέριστοι (the long-aged gods in honour
foremost), have the true Homeric ring.   Like Homer, he
often chooses an epithet specific of the object which he wishes
to describe, but not especially suited to the matter of his
argument.   Thus πολυκλαύτων γυναίκων (women given
to tears) occurs when there is no particular reason to fix the
mind upon the tearfulness of women.   But the poetic value
of the passage is increased by the mind being thus carried
away from the logical order of ideas to a generality on which
it can repose.   At other times, when this is necessary, the
epithets are as accurately descriptive as those of a botanist
or zoologist: ἐν κόγχαισι θαλασσονόμοις βαρυνώτοις (in
whelks that inhabit the sea with heavy backs) . . . λιθορ-
ρίνων τε χελωνῶν (stony‑coated tortoises), for example.
Again, Empedocles gives rein to his imagination by creating
bold metaphors; he calls the flesh σαρκῶν χιτών (a robe of
flesh), and birds πτεροβάμονας κύμβας (boats that move
with wings).   Referring to his four elements, he thus per-
sonifies their attributes: "Fiery Zeus, and Herè, source of

Homeric phraseology.

phrase, for he inclined to metaphor, and employed the other admirable
instruments of the poetic art."

vital breath, and Aidoneus, and Nestis, with her tears." At
another time he speaks of "earth, and ocean with his countless waves, and liquid air, the sun-god and ether girdling
round the universe in its embrace."

Misery of
mortal life.

The passage, too, in which he describes the misery of
earth rises to a sublime height. It may well have served
as the original of Virgil's celebrated lines in the sixth
Æneid :—

"I lifted up my voice, I wept and wailed, when I beheld the
unfamiliar shore. A hideous shore, on which dwell murder, envy,
and the troop of baleful destinies, wasting corruption, and disease.
Through Ate's meadow they go wandering up and down in gloom.
There was the queen of darkness, and Heliope with her far-searching
eyes, and bloody strife, and mild-eyed peace, beauty and ugliness,
swiftness and sloth, and lovely truth, and insincerity with darkling
brows. Birth too and death, slumber and wakefulness, motion and
immobility, crowned majesty and squalid filth, discordant clamour
and the voice of gods."

Qualities of
his poetic
style.

We can understand by these passages how Empedocles
not only was compared with Homer by Aristotle, but also
with Thucydides and Æschylus by Dionysius of Halicarnassus,
who speaks of his "austere harmony" (αὐστηρὰν ἁρμονίαν).
The conciseness of his argumentative passages, the breadth of
his treatment, and the dryness of his colouring, to quote the
terms of painting, resemble the style of Thucydides, while his
bold figures and gloomy grandeur are like those of Æschylus.
Plutarch, in the treatise on the genius of Socrates, speaks of
the style of Empedocles at large, both as regards his poems and
his theories, as "inspired with dithyrambic ecstasy" (μάλα
βεβακχευμένη). This seems a contradiction to the "austere
harmony" of Dionysius. But there are passages which justify
the title. This exordium, for instance, savours of prophetic
fury :—

"It stands decreed by fate, an ancient ordinance of the immortal
gods, established from everlasting, ratified by ample oaths, that,
when a spirit of that race, which has inherited the length of years

divine, sinfully stains his limbs with blood, he must go forth to wander thrice ten thousand years from heaven, passing from birth to birth through every form of mortal mutability, changing the toilsome paths of life without repose, even as I now roam, exiled from God, an outcast on this world, the bondman of insensate strife.

"Alas, ill-fated race of mortals, thrice accursed! from what dire struggles and what groans have ye been born! The air in its anger drives them to the sea, and ocean spues them forth upon the solid land, earth tosses them into the flames of the untiring sun, he flings them back again into the whirlwinds of the air; from one to the other are they cast, and all abhor them."

And the following adjuration has a frantic energy, to modern readers almost laughable but for its indubitable gravity :— *Metempsychosis and its corollaries.*

"Wretches, thrice wretches, keep your hands from beans!"

or, again, with reference to the abomination of animal food :—

"The father drags along his dear son changed in form, and slays him, pouring prayers upon his head. But the son goes begging mercy from his maniac sire. The father heeds him not, but goads him on, and, having slaughtered him, prepares a cursed meal. In like manner sons take their fathers, and children their mothers, and tearing out the life devour the kindred flesh. Will ye not put an end to this accursed slaughter? Will ye not see that ye consume each other in blind ignorance of soul?"

It is not strange that the poems of Empedocles were pilfered by oracle-mongers in after-ages.

Besides these passages, there are some of a milder beauty which deserve high praise for their admirable power of suggesting the picture that the poet wishes to convey. The following lines describe the golden age of old, — to which Empedocles looked back with melancholy longing :— *The golden age.*

"There every animal was tame and familiar with men, both beasts and birds, and mutual love prevailed. Trees flourished with perpetual leaves and fruits, and ample crops adorned their boughs through all the year. Nor had these happy people any

Ares or mad Uproar for their god ; nor was their monarch Zeus, or Cronos, or Poseidon, but Queen Cypris. Her favour they besought with pious symbols and with images, and fragrant essences, and censers of pure myrrh, and frankincense, and with brown honey poured upon the ground. The altars did not reek with bullocks' gore."

It may sound ridiculous to say so, yet Empedocles resembles Shelley in the quality of his imagination and in many of his utterances. The lines just quoted, the belief in a beneficent universal soul of nature, the hatred of animal food, the love of all things moving or growing on the face of earth, the sense of ancient misery and present evil, are all, allowing for the difference of centuries, and race, and education, points by which the Greek and the English poets meet in a community of nature. Two more passages illustrative of the poetical genius of Empedocles may be quoted. In the first he describes the nature of God, invisible and omnipresent. In the second he asserts the existence of an universal law. They both are remarkable for simplicity and force, and elevation of style :—

God and universal law.

" Blessed is the man who hath obtained the riches of the wisdom of God ; wretched is he who hath a false opinion about things divine.

" He (God) may not be approached, nor can we reach him with our eyes or touch him with our hands. No human head is placed upon his limbs, nor branching arms ; he has no feet to carry him apace, nor other parts of man ; but he is all pure mind, holy, and infinite, darting with swift thought through the universe from end to end."

" This law binds all alike, and none are free from it ; the common ordinance which all obey prevails through the vast spaces of wide-ruling air and the illimitable fields of light in endless continuity."

Pythagorean tone of this philosophy.

The quotations which have served to illustrate the poetical genius of Empedocles have also exhibited one aspect of his philosophy—that wherein he was connected with the Pythagoreans. It is quite consistent with the whole temper of his

intellect that he should have been attracted to the semi-
Oriental mysticism which then was widely spread through
Grecian Italy and Sicily.   After the dissolution of the monastic commonwealth founded by Pythagoras, it is probable
that refugees imbued with his social and political theories
scattered themselves over the adjacent cities; and from some
of these men Empedocles may have imbibed in early youth
the dream-like doctrines of an antenatal life, of future immortality, of past transgression and the need of expiation,
of abstinence, and of the bond of fellowship which bound man
to his kindred sufferers upon the earth.   It is even asserted
in one legend that the philosopher of Agrigentum belonged to
the Pythagorean Society, and was expelled from it for having
been the first to divulge its secrets.   In later life these theories
were developed by Empedocles after his own fashion, and
received a peculiar glow of poetic colouring from his genius.
There is no need to suppose that he visited the East and
learned the secrets of Gymnosophists.   A few Pythagorean
seeds sown in his fruitful soil sprang up and bore a hundred-
fold.   Referring to the exordium of his poem on Nature, and
to the lines in which he describes the unapproachable Deity,
we find that Empedocles believed in a pristine state of happiness, when the " Dæmons," or "gods, long of life, supreme in
honour," dwelt together, enjoying a society of bliss.   Yet this
state was not perfect, for some of these immortals stained
their hands with blood, and some spoke perjury, and so sin
entered in and tainted heaven.   After such offence the erring
spirit, by the fateful, irrevocable, and perennial law of the
divine commonwealth, had to relinquish his heavenly throne
and wander "thirty thousand seasons" apart from his comrades.   In this period of exile he passed through all the
changes of metempsychosis.   According to the rigorous and
gloomy conception of Empedocles, this change was caused by
the hatred of the elements; earth, air, fire, and water refusing
to retain the criminal, and tossing him about from one to the

Theory of the fall from pristine bliss.

other without intermission. Thus, he might be a plant, a
bird, a fish, a beast, or a human being in succession. But the
transmigration did not depend upon mere chance. If the
tortured spirit, environed, as he was, by the conflicting shapes
and contradictory principles and baleful destinies which
crowded earth—"the over-vaulted cave," the "gloomy meadow
of discord," as Empedocles in his despair described our globe—
could yet discover some faint glimmering of the truth, seize
and hold fast some portion of the heavenly clue, then he might
hope to reascend to bliss. Instead of abiding among birds,
and unclean beasts, and common plants, his soul passed into
the bodies of noble lions, and mystic bay-trees, or became a
bard, a prophet, a ruler among men, and lastly rose again to
the enjoyment of undying bliss. Throughout these wanderings death was impossible. Empedocles laughed at the notion
of birth and death; he seems to have believed in a fixed
number of immortal souls, capable of any transformation, but
incapable of perishing. Therefore, when his spirits, falling
earthward, howled at the doleful aspect of the hideous land,
the very poignancy of their grief consisted in that bitter
thought of Dante's, "questi non hanno speranza di morte"—
in that thought which makes the Buddhist welcome annihila-
tion. It has been already hinted, that although the soul by
its forced exile lost not only happiness but also knowledge,
yet the one might be in part retrieved, and the other toilsomely
built up again in some degree by patient observation, prayer,
and magic rites. On this point hinges the philosophy of
Empedocles. It is here that his mysticism and his science
are united into one system. In like manner, Plato's philosophy
rests upon the doctrine of Anamnesis, and is connected with
the vision of a past beatitude, the tradition of a miserable fall,
and the prospect of a possible restoration. Empedocles, like
Parmenides and Xenophanes in their disquisitions on the
eternal Being, like Plato in his references to the Supreme
Idea, seems to have imagined that the final Essence of the

universe was unapproachable, and to have drawn a broad
distinction between the rational and sensual orders, between
the world as cognisable by pure intellect, and the world as
known through the medium of human sense. The lines of
Empedocles upon God, which have been already quoted, are
similar to those of Xenophanes : both philosophers assert the
existence of an unknown Deity pavilioned in dense inscruta-
bility, yet not the less to be regarded as supreme and omnipresent and omnipotent—as God of gods, as life of life. How
to connect this intuition with the physical speculations of
Empedocles is difficult. The best way seems to be to refrain
from identifying his eloquent description of the unknown God
with the Sphærus of his scientific theories, and to believe that
he regarded the same universe from different points of view
at different times, as if in moments of high exaltation he
obtained a glimpse of the illimitable Being by a process of
ecstatic illumination, while in more ordinary hours of meditation his understanding and his senses helped him to obtain a
knowledge of the actual phenomena of this terrestrial globe.
His own language confirms this view of the case :—

God and the universe.

"Weak and narrow," he says, "are the powers implanted in
the limbs of men ; many the woes that fall on them and blunt the
edge of thought ; short is the measure of the life in death through
which they toil ; then are they borne away, like smoke they vanish
into air, and what they dream they know is but the little each
hath stumbled on in wandering about the world ; yet boast they
all that they have learned the whole—vain fools ! for what *that* is,
no eye hath seen, no ear hath heard, nor can it be conceived by
mind of man. Thou, then, since thou hast fallen to this place,
shalt know no more than human wisdom may attain.

"But, O ye gods, avert the madness of those babblers from my
tongue, and cause the stream of holy words to issue from my
hallowed lips. And thou, great Muse of Memory, maiden with
the milk-white arms, I pray to thee to teach me things that
creatures of a day may hear. Come from the House of Holiness,
and bring to me her harnessed car."

Here we see plainly set forth the impossibility of mortal,

fallen intellects attaining to a perfect knowledge of the Universe, the impiety of seeking such knowledge, or pretending to have found it; and, at the same time, the limitations under which true science remains within the reach of human beings. How this science may be reached, he tells us in some memorable lines, probably supposed to issue from the lips of the Muse whom he invokes :—"But come, search diligently, and discover what is clear in every realm of sense, . . . check the conviction of thy senses, and judge by reason what is evident in every case."

Theory of knowledge.

Thus the senses, although feeble and erring guides, are, after all, the gates to knowledge; and their reports, when tested by the light of reason, form the data for human speculation. The senses, resident in the limbs, are composed in certain proportions of the four elements, which also constitute the earth. Therefore, between the frame of man and the world outside him, there is a community of substance, whereby he is enabled to know. Ὅμοια ὁμοίοις γιγνώσκεται (likes are known by likes) is the foundation of our philosopher's theory of knowledge. The rational soul, being that immortal part of man whereon depends his personal identity, whether he take the shape of plant or animal, receives and judges the results of sensation. This theory, it will be observed, has a kind of general similarity to that of Parmenides. Empedocles draws a marked difference between the province of the senses and of the reason, and inveighs against the impotence of the former. Again, he speaks of the real being of the world as pure and perfect intellect; and at the same time elaborately describes the universe as it appears to human sense and understanding. But here the likeness ends. Parmenides has no mysticism, and indulges in no theology. He believes in the actual truth of his rational ontology, and sneers at the senses. "Thy fate it is," he says, "all mysteries to learn, both the unswerving mind of truth that wins a sure assent, and the vain thoughts of men, in which no certainty abides. But, baseless as they are, these also shalt thou learn; since thou must traverse every field of knowledge, and discern the fabric of the dreams of men." His ontology is just as elaborate as his physics, and he evidently considers its barren propositions of more value than any observations on astronomy or physiology. Empedocles, on the other hand, despaired of ontology, and gave all his mind to explanations of the physical universe—how it came to be, and what laws governed its alternations,—believing all along that there was a higher region of pure intellect beyond the reach of his degraded soul. "Here we see in a glass darkly, but then face to face." In this respect he resembled Xenophanes more than Parmenides. Xenophanes had said, "No man hath been, nor will ever be, who knows for certain all about the gods, and everything of which I speak; for should one publish the most sure and settled truth, yet even he cannot be said to *know;* opinion is supreme in all things." Empedocles belonged more to the age behind him than to that which followed; and his extensive knowledge of nature was a part of his artistic rather than his scientific temperament.

Yet, allowing for the march of human progress during twenty-three centuries, we are bound to hold much the same language as Empedocles regarding the limitations of knowledge. We have, indeed, infinitely extended our observation of phenomena; we have gained fuller conceptions of the Deity and of the destinies of man. But the plummet which he threw into the bottomless abyss of science has as yet found no bottom, and the circle which it made by striking on the surface of the illimitable ocean has grown and grown, but yet has touched no shore on any side. Like him, we still speak of an unapproachable God, utterly beyond the reach of human sense and intellect; like him, we still content ourselves with receiving the reports of our senses, comparing and combining them by means of our understanding, and thus obtaining some conception of the universe in which we live. If we reject the light of Christianity, the guesses which we form about a future world are less vague than those of Empedocles, but founded on no surer scientific basis; the God we worship still remains enveloped in symbols; we still ascribe to Him, if not a human form, at least the reason, partialities, and passions of mankind. Indeed, in this respect, the sage of Agrigentum stood unconsciously upon the platform which only our profoundest thinkers have attained. He felt the awe of the Unseen—he believed in the infinite Being,—but he refused to dogmatise about His attributes, confining his own reason to the phenomenal universe which he strove in every way to understand, and to employ for the good of his race. Empedocles was greater than most of his contemporaries, for he neither believed it possible to explain the whole mystery of the world, nor did he yet reject the notion of there being a profound mystery. He steered clear between the Parmenides and Democritus of his own day—between the Spinoza and the materialist of modern speculation. Herein the union of philosophy and poetry, of thought and feeling, in his nature, gave the tone to all his theories. We must not, however, in our praise forget that all these problems appeared in a far more simple form to the Greeks of that age than to ourselves, and were therefore more hastily and lightly answered. Between the ontology of Parmenides and that of Hegel what a step there is! What meagre associations gather round the one; what many-sided knowledge gives substance to the other!

Physical theories.

Remembering, therefore, in what light Empedocles regarded his own physical speculations, we may proceed to discuss them more in detail. We shall find that he deserved a large portion of that praise which Bacon rather whimsically lavished on the pre-Socratic philosophers, to the disadvantage of the mightier names of Plato and Aristotle.

The poem on Nature is addressed to Pausanias the physician, who was a son of Anchitus of Agrigentum, and a special friend of Empedocles. To Pausanias, the philosopher begins his instruction with these words:—"First learn what are the four chief roots of everything that is : fiery Zeus, and Herè, source The four
elements. of vital breath, and Aidoneus, and Nestis with her tears, who is the fount of moisture in the world." Thus Empedocles, after the fashion of the Pythagoreans, allegorised his four elements. In other passages he calls them "fire, water, earth, and air's immeasurable height ; " or "earth, and ocean with his countless waves, and liquid air, the sun-god, and ether girdling the universe in its embrace ; " or again, "Hephæstus, rain, and radiant ether ; " or lastly, "light, earth, heaven, and ocean." It will be seen that he designated his elements sometimes by mythological titles, sometimes by abstract terms, and sometimes by selecting one or other natural object—such as the sun, the air, the ocean—in which they were most manifest. It is well known that Empedocles was the first philosopher to adopt the four elements, which, since his day, continued to rule supreme over natural science, until modern analysis revealed far simpler and broader bases. Other speculators of the Ionian sect had maintained each of these four elements,—Thales the water, Anaximenes the air, Heraclitus the fire, and perhaps (but this rests on no sure evidence), Pherecydes the earth. Xenophanes had said, "Of earth and water are all things that come into existence." Parmenides had spoken of dark and light, thick and subtle, substances. Each of these fundamental principles is probably to be regarded not as pure fire, or pure water, or pure air, but as an universal element differing in rarity, and typified according to the analogical necessities of language, by means of some familiar object. The four elements of Empedocles appear to have been suggested to him, partly by his familiarity with contemporary speculation, and partly by his observation of Nature. They held their ground so long in scientific theory, because they answered so exactly to a superficial view of the world. Earth with everything of a solid quality, water including every kind of fluid, fire that burns or emits light, air that can be breathed, appear to constitute an exhaustive division of the universe. Of the eternity of these four primal substances, according to the Empedoclean theory, there is no doubt. The philosopher frequently re-iterates his belief in the impossibility of an absolute beginning or ending, though he acquiesces in the popular use of these terms to express the scientific conceptions of dissolution and recombination.

Love and discord.

These elements, then, were the material part of the world according to Empedocles. But inherent in them, as a tendency is inherent in an organism, and yet separable in thought from them as the soul is separable from the body, were two con-flicting principles of equal power, love and discord. Love and discord by their operation wrought infinite changes in the universe : for it was the purpose of love to bind the elements together into a compact, smooth, motionless globe ; and of discord to separate them one from another, and to keep them distinct in a state of mutual hostility. When, therefore, either love or discord got the upper hand, the phenomenal universe could not be said to exist, but in the intermediate state was a perpetual order of growth and decay, composition and dis-solution, whereby the world, as we behold it, came into exist-

Being and Becoming.

ence. This intermediate state, *das Werdende*, τὸ γιγνόμενον καὶ ἀπολλύμενον (the Becoming, that which comes into existence and passes out of it again by dissolution), was φύσις, or Nature. The conflicting energies of love and dis-cord formed the pulses of its mighty heart, the systole and diastole of its being, the one power tending to life, the other power to death, the one pushing all the elements forward to a perfect unity of composition, the other rending them apart. To the universe when governed by love in supremacy Em-pedocles gave the name of σφαῖρος (perfect globe), which he also called a god. This σφαῖρος answered to the Eleatic ἓν (one, or unity), while the disjointed elements subservient to the force of strife corresponded to the Eleatic πολλά (the many, or multiplicity). Thus the old Greek antagonism of Good and Evil, One and Many, Love and Hatred, Being and

Not-Being, were interpreted by Empedocles. He looked on all that is, *das Werdende*, as transitory between two opposite and contradictory existences.

Again, according to his system, the alternate reigns of love Nature. and discord succeeded one another at fixed intervals of time ; so that, from one point of view, the world was ceaselessly shifting, and from another point of view, was governed by eternal and unalterable Law. Thus he reconciled the Hera- clitean flux and the Parmenidean immobility by a middle term. Each of the elements possessed a separate province, had separate functions, and was capable of standing by itself. To fire it would seem that the philosopher assigned a more active influence than to any of the other elements ; therefore a kind of dualism may be recognised in his Universe between this ruling principle and the more passive ingredients of air, earth, and water. The influence of love and harmony kept them joined and interpenetrated, and so mingled as to bring the different objects which we see around us into being. Empedocles professed to understand the proportions of these mixtures, and measured them by Pythagorean rules of arith- metic. Thus everything subsists by means of transformation and mixture ; absolute beginning and ending are impossible.

Such, briefly stated, is the theory of Empedocles. The fol- Formation of the lowing passage may be quoted to show how the phenomenal Universe. Universe comes into being under the influence of love :—

" When strife has reached the very bottom of the seething mass, and love assumes her station in the centre of the ball, then everything begins to come together, and to form one whole—not instantaneously, but different substances come forth, according to a steady process of development. Now, when these elements are mingling, countless kinds of things issue from their union. Much, however, remains unmixed, in opposition to the mingling elements, and these malig- nant strife still holds within his grasp. For he has not yet with- drawn himself altogether to the extremities of the globe ; but part of his limbs still remain within its bounds, and part have passed beyond. As strife, however, step by step, retreats, mild and inno- cent love pursues him with her force divine ; things which had been immortal instantly assume mortality; the simple elements become confused by interchange of influence. When these are mingled, then the countless kinds of mortal beings issue forth, furnished with every sort of form—a sight of wonder."

The Sphærus.

In another passage this development is compared to the operation of a painter mixing his colours, and forming with them a picture of various objects. Discord is said to have made the elements immortal, because he kept them apart, and would willingly have preserved their separate qualities; whereas love mixes them together, breaks up their continuity, and confuses their kinds. What Empedocles exactly meant by Sphærus is hard to understand; nor do we know how far he intended Chance to operate in the formation of the Universe. He often uses such expressions as these, "So they chanced to come together," and describes the amorphous condition of the first organisms in a way that makes one think he fancied a perfectly chaotic origin. Yet "the art of Aphrodite," "so Cypris ordained their form," are assertions of designing intelligence. In fact, we may well believe that Empedocles, in the infancy of speculation, was led astray by his double nomenclature. When talking of Aphrodite, he naturally thought of a person ruling creation; when using the term "Love," he naturally conceived an innate tendency, which might have been the sport of chance in a great measure. It also appears probable that, when Empedocles spoke of "Chance" and "Necessity," he referred to some inherent quality in the elements themselves, whereby they grew together under certain laws, and that the harmony and discord which ruled them in turn, were regarded by him as forces aiding and preventing their union.

To understand the order of creation, we may begin by imagining the sphere, which, in the words of Empedocles, " by the hidden bond of harmony is stablished, and rejoices in unbroken rest . . . in perfect equipoise, of infinite extent, it stays a full-orbed sphere rejoicing in unbroken rest." Love

now is omnipotent; she has knit all the elements into one Evolution
whole; Discord has retreated, and abides beyond the globe. of the
But soon his turn begins: he enters the sphere, and "all the world.
limbs of the god begin to tremble." Now the elements are
divided one from the other—ether first, then fire, then earth,
then water from the earth. Still the elements are chaotic;
but wandering about the spaces of the world, and "permeating
each the other's realm," they form alliances and tend to union.
Love is busy no less than Discord. The various tribes of
plants and animals appear at first in a rudimentary and
monstrous condition: "many heads sprouted up without
necks, and naked arms went wandering forlorn of shoulders,
and solitary eyes were straying destitute of foreheads." Still
the process of seething and intermingling continued; "when
element with element more fully mixed, these members fell
together by haphazard . . . many came forth with double
faces and two breasts, some shaped like oxen with a human
front, others, again, of human race with a bull's head; and
some were mixed of male and female parts." Unfortunately,
the lines in which he describes the further progress of development have been lost, and we do not know how the interval
between chaos and order was bridged over in his system.
Only with reference to human beings he asserts that in the
earliest stage they were produced in amorphous masses, containing the essence, as it were, of both male and female; and
that after the separation of these masses into two parts, each
part yearned to join its tally. And therefrom sprang the
passion of desire in human hearts. This theory has been
worked out by Plato artistically in the *Symposium*. Also with
reference to the accretion of the phenomenal universe, he says
that earth formed the basis of all hard and solid substances,
preponderating in the shells of fish, and so on. Bones were
wrought of earth, and fire, and water, "marvellously jointed
by the bonds of Harmony." It is needless to follow Empedocles through all his scattered fancies, to show that he knew

that the night was caused by the earth intercepting the sun's rays, or that he thought the sun reflected heaven's fire like a mirror, or that he placed the intellect in the blood, and explained respiration by a theory of pores, and the eyesight by imagining a fire shut up within the pupil. The fragments we possess are too scanty to allow of our obtaining a perfect view of his physical theory ; all we gather from them is that Empedocles possessed more acquired and original knowledge than any of his contemporaries.

Eclecticism of Empedocles.

It may appear from what has been said about his system that Empedocles was at best a great Eclectic. But this is not entirely the case. If he deserves the name of Eclectic, he deserves it in the same sense as Plato, though it need not be said how infinitely inferior, as an original thinker, he is to Plato. Empedocles was deeply versed in all the theories, metaphysical, cosmogonical, mystical, and physiological, of his age. He viewed from a high station all the problems, intellectual, social, and moral, which then vexed Greece. But he did not pass his days in a study or a lecture-room, nor did he content himself with expounding or developing the theories of any one master. He went abroad, examined nature for himself, cured the sick, thought his own thoughts, and left an impress on the constitution of his native state. In his comprehensive mind all the learning he had acquired from men, from books, from the world, and from reflection, was consolidated into one system, to which his double interest for mysticism and physics gave a double aspect. He was the first in Greece to reconcile Eleatic and Heraclitean speculations, the puzzle of plurality and unity, the antagonism of good and evil, in one theory, and to connect it with another which revealed a solemn view of human obligations and destinies, and required a life of social purity and self-restraint. The misfortune of Empedocles as a philosopher consisted in this—that he succeeded only in resuming the results of contemporary speculation, and of individual research, in a philosophy of indisputable originality, without anticipating the new direction which was about to be given to human thought by Socrates and Plato. He closed one period,—the period of poetry and physical theories and mysticism. The period of prose, of logic, and of ethics, was about to begin. He was the last of the great colonial sages of Greece. The Hellenic intellect was destined henceforth to centre itself at Athens.

CHAPTER VIII

THE GNOMIC POETS

Ethical and elegiac verse. THE term Gnomic, when applied to a certain number of Greek
poets, is arbitrary. There is no definite principle for rejecting
some and including others in the class. It has, however, been
usual to apply this name to Solon, Phocylides, Theognis, and
Simonides of Ceos. Yet there seems no reason to exclude some
portions of Callinus, Tyrtæus, Mimnermus, and Xenophanes.
These poets, it will be observed, are all writers of the elegy.
Some of the lyric poets, however, and iambographers, such as
Simonides of Amorgos and Archilochus, have strong claims for
admission into the list. For, as the derivation of the name
implies, gnomic poets are simply those who embody γνῶμαι,
or sententious maxims on life and morals, in their verse; and
though we find that the most celebrated masters of this style
composed elegies, we yet may trace the thread of gnomic
thought in almost all the writers of their time. Conversely,
the most genuine authors of elegiac gnomes trespassed upon
the domain of lyric poetry, and sang of love and wine and per-

sonal experience no less than of morality. In fact, the gnomic
poets represent a period of Greek literature during which the
old and simple forms of narrative poetry were giving way to
lyrical composition on the one hand, and to meditative writing
on the other; when the epical impulse had become extinct,
and when the Greeks were beginning to think definitely. The
elegy, which seems to have originated in Asia Minor, and to
have been used almost exclusively by poets of the Ionian race
for the expression of emotional and reflective sentiments, lent
itself to this movement in the development of the Greek genius,
and formed a sort of midway stage between the impassioned
epic of the Homeric age and the no less impassioned poetry
and prose of the Athenian age of gold.

Viewed in this light, the gnomic poets mark a transition from
Homer and Hesiod to the dramatists and moralists of Attica.
The ethical precepts inherent in the epos received from them
a more direct and proverbial treatment; while they in turn
prepared for the sophists, the orators, and Socrates.

Transitional period in poetry.

This transitional period in the history of Greek literature,
corresponding, as it does, to similar transitions in politics, religion, and morality, offers many points of interest. Before
Homer, poetry had no historical past, but after the age of the
Epic a long time elapsed before the vehicle of verse was exchanged for that of prose. Xenophanes, Parmenides, and
Empedocles wrote poems upon nature in hexameters. Solon
and Theognis committed their state-craft and ethics to elegiac
couplets. Yet at the same time Heraclitus and the seven sages
were developing the germs of prose, and preparing the way for
Attic historians and philosophers.

Again, whereas Homer introduces us to a Hellas small in its
extent, and scarcely separated from surrounding tribes, we find
in the transitional period that the strength and splendour of
the Greek race are dissipated over distant colonies, Hellenic
civilisation standing out in definite relief against adjacent
barbarism. The first lyrical and elegiac poets come from the

Age of the colonies.

islands of the Archipelago, or from the shores of Asia Minor. The first dramatists of note are Sicilian. Italy and Sicily afford a home to the metaphysical poets, while the philosophers of the Ionian sect flourish at Ephesus and Miletus.

Age of the despots.

Corresponding to this change in the distribution of the race, a change was taking place in the governments of the States. The hereditary monarchies of Homer's age have disappeared, and, after passing through a period of oligarchical supremacy, have given place to tyrannies. The tyrants of Miletus and of Agrigentum, rising from the aristocracy itself; those of Corinth, Athens, and Megara, owing their power to popular favour; others, like Cylon, flourishing a while by force of mere audacity and skill; others, again, like Pittacus of Mitylene, using the rights of their dictatorship for the public benefit,—had this one point in common: it was the interest of all of them to destroy the traditional prejudices of the race, to gather a powerful and splendid court around them, to patronise art, to cultivate diplomacy, and to attach men of ability to their persons. As the barons of feudalism encouraged the romances of the Nibelungen, Carlovingian, and Arthurian cycles, so the hereditary monarchies had caused the cyclical epos to flourish. It was not for the interest of the tyrants to revive Homeric legends, but rather to banish from the State all traces of the chivalrous past. With this view Cleisthenes of Sicyon put down the worship of Adrastus, and parodied the heroic names of the three tribes. Poetry, thus separated from the fabulous past, sought its subjects in the present,—in personal experience, in pleasure, in politics, in questions of diplomacy, in epigrammatic morality.

Such, then, was the period during which the gnomic poets flourished,—a period of courts and tyrannies, of colonial prosperity, of political animation, of social intrigue, of intellectual development, of religious transformation, of change and uncertainty in every department. Behind them lay primitive Homeric Hellas; before them, at no great distance, was the time when the Greek genius would find its home in Athens. Gnomic poetry. Poetry and Science were then to be distinguished; the philosophers, historians, and orators were to make a subtle and splendid instrument of Greek prose; the dramatists were to raise the choric and dialectic beauty of the Greek language to its highest possible perfection; tyrannies were to be abolished, and the political energies of Hellas to be absorbed in the one great struggle between the Dorian and the Ionian families. But in the age of gnomic poetry these changes were still future; and though the mutations of Greek history were accomplished with unparalleled rapidity, we yet may draw certain lines, and say—Here was a breathing-time of indecision and suspense; this period was the eve before a mighty revolution. I propose, therefore, to consider the gnomic poets as the representatives to some extent of such an age, and as exponents of the rudimentary, social, and political philosophy of Greece before Socrates.

Three periods may be marked in the development of the The elegy. early Greek elegiac poetry—the Martial, the Erotic, and the Gnomic. Callinus and Tyrtæus are the two great names by which the first is distinguished. Mimnermus gave a new direction to this style of composition, fitting the couplet, which had formerly been used for military and patriotic purposes, to amatory and convivial strains.[1] In after years it never lost the impress of his genius; so that Ovid, Tibullus, and Propertius may be regarded as the lineal descendants of the Colophonian bard. Solon at a later date applied the elegiac measure to severer subjects. He was the first perhaps to use it for purely gnomic purposes, maintaining, however, the martial spirit in his Salaminian verses, and imitating the example of Mimnermus in his lighter compositions. Phocylides, to judge

[1] This seems to have been recognised by the ancients, as is proved by the lines quoted from Hermesianax in Athenæus, xiii. 597, where the epithet μαλαχός (effeminate), assigned to his pentameter, is meant to be emphatic. Mimnermus gave it a luxurious and tender quality.

by the scanty fragments which we possess of his poems, was almost wholly gnomic in his character. But Theognis, who is the latest and most important of the elegiac writers of this period, combined the political, didactic, and erotic qualities to a remarkable degree. As a poet, Simonides was greater than any of those whom I have named; but his claims to rank among the sententious philosophers rest more upon the fragments of his lyrics than upon the elegiac epitaphs for which he was so justly famed.

Educational and rhetorical value of gnomic verse.

These are the poets of whom I intend to speak in detail. Taken together with Homer and Hesiod, their works formed the body of a Greek youth's education at the time when Gorgias and Hippias were lecturing at Athens. From them the contemporaries of Pericles, when boys, had learned the rules of good society, of gentlemanly breeding, of practical morality, of worldly wisdom. Their saws and precepts were on the lips of the learned and the vulgar; wise men used them as the theses for subtle arguments or the texts for oratorical discourses. Public speakers quoted them as Scripture might be quoted in a synod of the clergy. They pointed remarks in after-dinner conversation or upon the market-place. Polemarchus, for instance, in Plato's *Republic*, starts the dialogue on Justice by a maxim of Simonides. Isocrates, the Rhetor, alludes to them as being "the best counsellors in respect of human affairs," and Xenophon terms the gnomes of Theognis "a comprehensive treatise concerning men." Having been used so commonly and largely by the instructors of youth, and by men of all conditions, it was natural that these elegies should be collected into one compendious form, and that passages of a gnomic tendency should be extracted from larger poems on different subjects. In this way a body of sententious poetry grew up and received the traditional authority of Solon, Phocylides, Simonides, and Theognis. But in the process of compilation confusions and mistakes of all kinds occurred, so that the same couplets were often attributed to several authors. To bear this in mind at the outset is a matter of some moment; for at this distance of time it is no longer possible to decide the canon of the several elegists with accuracy. In dealing with them, we must, therefore, not forget that we are handling masses of heterogeneous materials roughly assigned to a few great names.

The earliest elegiac poet was Callinus, a native of Ephesus, Callinus. between the years 730 and 678 B.C. His poems consist almost exclusively of exhortations to bravery in battle. "How long will ye lie idle?" he exclaims; "put on your valour; up to the fight, for war is in the land!" He discourses in a bold and manly strain upon the certainty of death, and the glory of facing it in defence of home and country, winding up with this noble sentiment:—"The whole people mourns and sorrows for the death of a brave-hearted man; and while he lives he is the peer of demigods." The lines of Tyrtæus, whose prominent part during the second Messenian war is the subject of a well-known legend, embody the same martial and patriotic sentiments in even more masculine verse.

It would be alien from my purpose to dwell long upon Tyrtæus. these military poems, since the only gnomic character which they display is the encouragement of a heightened honour, unselfishness, indifference to gain, devotion to the State, and love of public fame. Yet the moment in the history of Hellas represented by Tyrtæus, the leader whose voice in the battlefield was like a clarion to his manly Spartans, and in the council-chamber was a whisper of Athene quelling strife, is so interesting that I cannot omit him in this place. "Never," to use the words of Müller, "was the duty and the honour of bravery impressed on the youth of a nation with so much beauty and force of language, by such natural and touching motives." If of a truth it be, as Milton says, the function of the poet "to inbreed and cherish in a great people the seeds of virtue and public civility," then Tyrtæus, less by his specific maxims than by the spirit that his verses breathe,

deserves an honoured place among the bards whom Aristotle
would have classed as ἠθικώτατοι, most serviceable for the
formation of a virile and powerful temperament, most suited
for the education of Greek youth. The following translation
stands as Thomas Campbell made it from a martial elegy
ascribed to the bard of Lacedæmon : [1]—

"How glorious fall the valiant, sword in hand,
    In front of battle for their native land !
But oh ! what ills await the wretch that yields,
    A recreant outcast from his country's fields !
The mother whom he loves shall quit her home,
    An aged father at his side shall roam ;
His little ones shall weeping with him go,
    And a young wife participate his woe ;
While scorned and scowled upon by every face,
    They pine for food, and beg from place to place.

"Stain of his breed ! dishonouring manhood's form,
    All ills shall cleave to him : affliction's storm
Shall blind him wandering in the vale of years,
    Till, lost to all but ignominious fears,
He shall not blush to leave a recreant's name,
    And children, like himself, inured to shame.

"But we will combat for our fathers' land,
    And we will drain the life-blood where we stand,
To save our children :—fight ye side by side,
    And serried close, ye men of youthful pride,
Disdaining fear, and deeming light the cost
    Of life itself in glorious battle lost.

"Leave not our sires to stem the unequal fight,
    Whose limbs are nerved no more with buoyant might ;
Nor, lagging backward, let the younger breast
    Permit the man of age (a sight unblessed)
To welter in the combat's foremost thrust,
    His hoary head dishevell'd in the dust,

---

[1] Without attempting to discuss the vexed question whether Tyrtæus
was a native Spartan, or, according to the ancient tale, an Athenian
naturalised in Sparta, his self-identification with the people he inspired
justifies the phrase that I have used above.

And venerable bosom bleeding bare.
But youth's fair form, though fallen, is ever fair,
And beautiful in death the boy appears,
The hero boy, that dies in blooming years :
In man's regret he lives, and woman's tears ;
More sacred than in life, and lovelier far,
For having perished in the front of war." [1]

Strangely different are the elegies of Mimnermus, the poet Mimnermus.
of Colophon, who flourished toward the end of the seventh
century B.C.[2] His name has passed into a proverb for luxurious
verse, saddened by reflections on the fleeting joys of youth,
and on the sure and steady progress of old age and death.
Tyrtæus, though a native of Attica, wrote for Spartans at war
with a strong nation ; Mimnermus was born and lived among
Ionian Greeks emasculated by barbarian control and by contact with the soft Lydians. It was of these Colophonians
that Xenophanes, a native poet, said, "Instructed in vain
luxury by the Lydians, they trailed their robes of purple
through the streets, with haughty looks, proud of their flowing
locks bedewed with curious essences and oils." For such a

[1] The sentiment of these last lines is not only ethically spirited, but
it is also singularly, exquisitely Greek. The æsthetic tact of the Greek
race felt the plastic charm of a youth's form dead upon the battlefield.
Like a statue marbled by the frost of death he lies, the perfection of
life-moulded clay ; and his red wounds are the lips of everlasting praise.
Not so the elder man. Nakedness and mutilation bring no honour to
him ; he has no loveliness of shape to be revealed and heightened by the
injuries of war ; for him the flowing beard and the robes of reverend eld
are a majestic covering, to be withdrawn by no hand seeking to unveil
secluded beauties. His lot is cast no longer in those fields intense and
passionate of art and love, where death, cropping the bloom unset, confers
a crown of immortality. Cf. *Iliad*, xxii. 71. An echo of this Greek
feeling for the beautiful young dead may be traced in David's picture of
the drummer-boy at Avignon, in Walt Whitman, and in Lord Albemarle's
Recollections of Waterloo.

[2] The birthplace of Mimnermus is not very certain. Fragment 9 in
Bergk's *Collection* would seem to justify the opinion that he was a native
of Smyrna colonised from Colophon.

people the exquisitely soft and musical verses of Mimnermus, pervaded by a tone of lingering regret, were exactly suited. They breathe the air of sunny gardens and cool banquet-rooms, in which we picture to ourselves the poet lingering out a pensive life, endeavouring to crowd his hours with pleasures of all kinds, yet ever haunted and made fretful among his roses by the thought of wrinkles and death. "When your youth is gone," he says, "however beautiful you may have been, you lose the reverence of your children and the regard of your friends." "More hideous is old age than death. It reduces the handsome and the plain man to one level—cares attend it—the senses and the intellects get deadened—a man is forgotten and put out of the way." The Greek sentiment of hatred for old age is well expressed in one epithet which Mimnermus employs—ἄμορφον, *formless*. The Greeks detested the ugliness and loss of grace which declining years bring with them, almost more than weakened powers or the approach of death. Nay, "when the flower of youth is past," says Mimnermus, "it is best to die at once." Men are like herbs, which flourish for a while in sunshine—then comes the winter of old age, with poverty or disease, or lack of children. His feeling for the charm of youth was intense; he expressed it in language that reminds us of the fervency of Sappho —"Down my flesh the sweat runs in rivers, and I tremble when I see the flower of my equals in age gladsome and beautiful."

Horror of old age and death.

This tender and regretful strain is repeated by Mimnermus with a monotonous, almost pathetic persistency, as if the one thought of inevitable age oppressed him like a nightmare day and night. His delight in the goodliness of youth and man-hood is so acute, and his enjoyment of existence is so ex-quisite, that he shrinks with loathing from the doom imposed on all things mortal to decline and wither. " May I complete my life without disease or cares, and may death strike me at my sixtieth year !" Such is the prayer he utters, feeling,

probably, that up to sixty the senses may still afford him
some enjoyment, and that, after they are blunted, there is
nothing left for man worth living for. In all this Mimnermus
was true to one type of the Greek character. I shall have
occasion further on to revert to this subject, and to dwell
again upon the fascination which the flower of youth possessed
for the Greeks, and the horror with which the ugliness of age
inspired them.[1] That some escaped this kind of despair,
which to us appears unmanly, may be gathered from the
beautiful discourse upon old age with which the *Republic*
of Plato opens. Mimnermus, however, belonged to a class of
men different from Cephalus : nowhere in the whole range
of literature can be found a more perfect specimen of unmitigated *ennui*.[2] In his verse we trace the prostrate tone
of the Oriental, combined with Greek delicacy of intellect
and artistic expression. The following passage may be cited
as at once illustrative of his peculiar lamentation, and also
of his poetical merits :—

> " What's life or pleasure wanting Aphrodite ?
>   When to the gold-haired goddess cold am I,
> When love and love's soft gifts no more delight me,
>   Nor stolen dalliance, then I fain would die !
> Ah ! fair and lovely bloom the flowers of youth ;
>   On men and maids they beautifully smile :
> But soon comes doleful eld, who, void of ruth,
>   Indifferently afflicts the fair and vile :
> Then cares wear out the heart ; old eyes forlorn
>   Scarce reck the very sunshine to behold—

---

[1] Notice particularly the couplets of Theognis beginning ὤμοι ἐγὼν
ἤβης and ἄφρονες ἄνθρωποι, Bergk, vol. ii. pp. 420, 550.

[2] Fragment 9 in Bergk's *Collection* might seem to express a manlier
spirit, if we could suppose that it referred to personal exploits of the poet.
It forms, however, part of a description of the early colonisation of
Smyrna from Pylos ; when Mimnermus alludes to martial deeds, he does
so with a tone of regret, as one who has no share in them, and lives his
own life in political stagnation.

Unloved by youths, of every maid the scorn,—
So hard a lot God lays upon the old." [1]

We are not surprised to hear that the fragments of Mimnermus belonged to a series of elegies addressed to a fluteplayer called Nanno.[2] They are worthy of such a subject. Nanno, according to one account, did not return the passion of the poet.

The Hedonism of Mimnermus.

In Mimnermus, however luxurious he may have been, we yet observe a vein of meditation upon life and destiny, which prepares us for the more distinctly gnomic poets. Considered in the light of Greek philosophy, Mimnermus anticipates the ethical teaching of the Hedonists and Epicureans. In other words, he represents a genuine view of life adopted by the Greeks. Horace refers to him as an authority in these wellknown lines :—

"Si, Mimnermus uti censet, sine amore jocisque
Nil est jucundum, vivas in amore jocisque ;" [3]

on which the scholiast observed that the elegiac poet "agreed with the sect of the Epicureans."

Solon.

Next to Mimnermus in point of time is Solon. Perhaps the verses of this great man were among his least important productions. Yet their value, in illustrating the history of Athens, would have been inestimable, had they been preserved to us in a more perfect state. "There is hardly anything," says Grote, "more to be deplored, amidst the lost treasures of the Grecian mind, than the poems of Solon; for we see by the remaining fragments that they contained notices of the public and social phenomena before him, which he was

[1] *Miscellanies*, by the late John Addington Symonds, M.D. (Macmillan & Co., 1871), p. 410.

[2] Strabo quotes "the Nanno" as Athenæus quotes "the Leontion" of Hermesianax, another Colophonian amourist.

[3] *Epistles*, bk. i. 6. Translated thus by Conington : "If, as Mimnermus tells you, life is flat With nought to love, devote yourself to that."

compelled attentively to study, blended with the touching
expression of his own personal feelings, in the post, alike
honourable and difficult, to which the confidence of his
countrymen had exalted him." The interest of Solon as a
gnomic poet is derived chiefly from the fact that he was
reckoned one of the seven wise men of Greece, that he was
one of the two most distinguished Nomothetæ of Hellas, that
he is said to have conversed familiarly with the great Lydian
monarch, and that he endeavoured at Athens to resist the
growing tyranny of Pisistratus.   Thus Solon bore a prominent
part in all the most important affairs of the period to which
the gnomic poetry belongs.   Its politics, diplomacy, and social
theories, its constitutional systems and philosophy, were
perfectly familiar to him, and received a strong impress
from his vigorous mind.   It is thought that his poems belong
to an early period of his life; yet they embody the same
sentiments as those which Herodotus refers to his old age,
and express in the looser form of elegiac verse the gist of
apophthegms ascribed to him as one of the seven sages.

Literature and politics were cultivated together at this
period among the Greeks; philosophy was gained in actual
life and by commerce with men of all descriptions.   The part
which Tyrtæus, Alcæus, Pythagoras, Parmenides, Empedocles,
and Archilochus played in the history of their States need
not be more than alluded to.   Simonides of Amorgos founded
a colony; Theognis represented a large and important party.
But Solon, in a truer sense than any of these men, combined
decisive action in public life with letters.   Nor is it, perhaps,
necessary to agree with Grote in depreciating the poetical
value of his verses.   Some of them are very fine and forcible.
The description, for example, of the storm which sweeps away
the clouds, and leaves a sunny sky (Frag. 13, ed. Bergk), is
full of noble imagery.

Poetry and politics.

The first three fragments of Solon's elegies form part of
the ode recited by him in the market-place of Athens, when

he braved the penalty of death, and urged his fellow-citizens "to rise and fight for the sweet isle of Salamis." These lines are followed by a considerable fragment of great importance, describing the misery of ill-governed and seditious Athens. Among the sayings attributed to Solon (Diog. Laer., i. 63) is one that gives the keynote to this poem. When asked what made an orderly and well-constituted state, he answered, "When the people obey the rulers, and the rulers obey the laws." The paraphrase which I subjoin exhibits in strong contrast the difference between Dysnomia and Eunomia, as conceived by the Athenian law-giver. Demosthenes, who used the name of Solon on all occasions with imposing rhetorical effect, quotes these lines in a celebrated passage of the speech *De Fals. Leg.*, 254 :—"The citizens seek to overthrow the State by love of money, by following indulgent and self-seeking demagogues, who neglect religion and pervert the riches of the temples. Yet justice, silent but all-seeing, will in time bring vengeance on them for these things. War, want, civil discord, slavery, are at our gates ; and all these evils threaten Athens because of her lawlessness. Whereas good laws and government set all the State in order, chain the hands of evil-doers, make rough places plain, subdue insolence, and blast the budding flowers of Até, set straight the crooked ways of tortuous law, root out sedition, quell the rage of strife ; under their good influence all things are fair and wise with men." Thus early and emphatically was the notion of just balance enunciated among the Greeks. It formed the ruling principle of their philosophy as well as of their politics ; for the μηδὲν ἄγαν (nothing over-much) of Solon corresponded to the μέτρον (measure) of the Ionic speculators, and contained within itself the germ of Aristotle's ethical system, no less than of the political philosophy of Plato's *Republic*.

In the fifth and sixth fragments Solon describes the amount of power he would wish to see intrusted to the Athenian

Demos; in the ninth, he prophesies the advent of a despot: "From storm-clouds descend furious snow and hail, and thunder is born of bright lightning; so great men produce the overthrow of States, and into the bondage of a despot's power the people fall unwittingly. Easy it is to raise the storm, but hard to curb the whirlwind; yet must we now take thought of all these things." Fragment the second contains a further warning on the subject of impending tyranny. The power of Pisistratus was growing to a head, and Solon told the Athenians that if he proved despotic, they would have no one but themselves to blame for it.

The remaining fragments of Solonian poetry are more purely meditative. "Bright daughters of Memory and Olympian Zeus," he begins, "Pierian Muses! hear my prayer. Grant me wealth from the blessed gods, and from all men a good name. May I be sweet to my friend and bitter to my foe; revered by the one and dreaded by the other. Money I desire, but no ill-gotten gain: for the wealth that the gods give lasts, and fleets not away; but the fruits of insolence and crime bring vengeance—sure, though slow. Zeus seeth all things, and like a wind scattering the clouds, which shakes the deep places of the sea and rages over the corn-land, and comes at last to heaven, the seat of gods, and makes a clear sky to be seen, whereupon the sun breaks out in glory, and the clouds are gone—so is the vengeance of Zeus. He may seem to forget, but sooner or later he strikes; perchance the guilty man escapes, yet his blameless children or remote posterity pay the penalty." Two points are noticeable in this passage; first, the dread of ill-gotten gain; and secondly, the conception of implacable justice. There was nothing which the Greeks more dreaded and detested than wealth procured by fraud. They were so sensitive upon this point that even Plato and Aristotle regarded usury as criminal, unnatural, and sure to bring calamity upon the money-lender. Thus Chilon, the Lacedæmonian sage, is reported to have said, "Choose loss rather than dishonourable gain: for the one will hurt you for the moment, the other will never cease to be a curse." There are few of the seven sages who have not at least one maxim bearing on this point. It would seem as if the conscience of humanity were touched at a very early period by superstitious scruples of this kind. The Jewish law contains warnings similar to those of Solon; and among our own people it has been commonly believed that wealth unlawfully acquired, money taken from the devil, or property wrested from the Church, is disastrous to its owner, and incapable of being long retained in the possession of his family. Theognis expresses nearly the same sentiments as Solon in the following verses:—"He who gets wealth from Zeus by just means, and with hands unstained, will not lose it; but if he acquire it wrongfully, covetously, or by false swearing, though it may seem at first to bring him gain, at last it turns to calamity, and the mind of Heaven prevails. But these things deceive men, for the blessed gods do not always take vengeance on crime at the moment of its being committed; but one man in his person pays for a bad deed, another leaves disaster hanging over his own children, a third avoids justice by death."

Crime revenged upon posterity.

Both Solon and Theognis, it will be observed, express emphatically their belief in a vengeance of Heaven falling upon the children, and the children's children of offenders. This conception of doom received its most splendid illustration at the hands of the tragic poets, and led philosophers like Empedocles to devise systems of expiation and purification, by means of which ancestral guilt might be purged away, and the soul be restored to its pristine blamelessness. Theognis in another fragment (731-752) discusses the doctrine, and calls in question its justice. He takes it for granted, as a thing too obvious to be disputed, that children suffer for their father's sin, and argues with Zeus about the abstract right and policy of this law, suggesting that its severity is enough to make men with-

draw their allegiance from such unjust governors. The inequality of the divine rule had appeared in the same light to
Hesiod and Homer (see *Iliad*, xiii. 631; Hesiod, *Op. et Dies*,
270). But it is in the gnomic poets that we first discover a
tendency to return and reason upon such questions : the wedge
of philosophical scepticism was being inserted into the old
beliefs of the Greek race. In some respects these gnomic
poets present even a more gloomy view of human destinies
than the epic poets. Solon says, "It is fate that bringeth
good and bad to men ; nor can the gifts of the immortals be
refused;" and in Theognis we find, "No man is either
wealthy or poor, mean or noble, without the help of the
gods." . . . "Pray to the gods; nought happens to man of
good or ill without the gods." . . . "No one, Cyrnus, is himself the cause of loss and gain; but of both these the gods
are givers."[1] It would be easy to multiply passages, where
the same conception of the divine government as that for
which Plato (*Rep.*, p. 379) blamed Homer is set forth; but
the gnomic poets go beyond this simple view. They seem to
regard Heaven as a jealous power, and superstitiously believe
all changes of fortune to be produced by the operation of a
god anxious to delude human expectations. This theology
lies at the base of the Solonian maxim, that you ought not to
judge of a man's happiness until his death : "for," in the
language of Herodotus, "there are many to whom God has
first displayed good fortune, and whom He afterwards has
rooted up and overthrown."

Thus Solon moralises in his elegies upon the vicissitudes of
life :—"Danger lies everywhere, nor can a man say where he
will end when he begins; for he who thinks to do well, without

Uncertainty
of fortune.

---

[1] The well-known passage in the *Iliad* (xxiv. 527), which describes the
two casks at the threshold of the house of Zeus, contains the germ of this
belief. But after Homer there arose a darker sense of the jealousy of the
gods, accompanied in speculative minds by a tendency to call the principles
of the divine rule in question.

forethought, comes to grief; and often when a man is doing
ill, Heaven sends him good luck, and he ends prosperously."
It must however be observed that Solon in no passage of his
elegiac poems alludes distinctly to the intervention of a jealous
or malicious destiny. He is rather deeply impressed with the
uncertainty of human affairs—an uncertainty which the events
of his own life amply illustrated, and which he saw displayed
in every town about him. Simonides repeats the same strain
of despondency, dwelling (Frag. 2, ed. Gaisford) upon the
mutabilities of life, and exclaiming with a kind of horror:
"One hideous Charybdis swallows all things—wealth and
mighty virtue."

Pessimism
of the
gnomic
poets.
At this period in Greece the old simplicity of life was
passing away, and philosophy had not yet revealed her broader
horizons, her loftier aims, and her rational sources of content.
We have seen how Mimnermus bemoaned the woes of old
age. Solon, whose manliness contrasts in every other respect
with the effeminacy and languor of the Colophonian poet, gave
way to the same kind of melancholy when he cried, "No
mortal man is truly blessed; but all are wretched whom the
sun beholds." What can be more despairing than the lamentations of Simonides?—"Few and evil are our days of life;
but everlasting is the sleep which we must sleep beneath the
earth." . . . "Small is the strength of man, and invincible are
his sorrows; grief treads upon the heels of grief through his
short life; and death, which no man shuns, hangs over him at
last: to this bourne come the good and bad alike." In the
midst of this uncertainty and gloom Theognis cannot find a
rule of right conduct. "Nothing," he says, "is defined by
Heaven for mortals, nor any way by which a man may walk
and please immortal powers." Nor can we point to any more
profoundly wretched expression of misery than the following
elegy of the same poet: "It is best of all things for the sons of
earth not to be born, nor to see the bright rays of the sun, or
else after birth to pass as soon as possible the gates of death,

and to lie deep down beneath a weight of earth." This sentiment is repeated by Bacchylides, and every student of Greek
tragedy knows what splendid use has been made of it by
Sophocles in one of the choruses of *Œdipus Coloneus*. Afterwards it passed into a commonplace. Two Euripidean fragments
embody it in words not very different from those of Theognis,
and Cicero is said to have translated it. When we consider
the uneasy and uncertain view of human life expressed in these
passages, it seems wonderful that men, conscious of utter
ignorance, and believing themselves, like Herodotus, to be
the sport of almost malignant deities, could have grown so
nobly and maintained so high a moral standard as that of the
Greek race.[1]

The remaining fragments of Solon contain the celebrated
lines upon the Life of Man, which he divided into ten periods
of seven years. He rebuked Mimnermus for wishing to make
sixty the term of human life, and bade him add another de-
cade. We also possess some amorous verses of questionable
character, supposed to have been written in his early youth.
The prudes of antiquity were scandalised at Solon, a lawgiver
and sage, for having penned these couplets. The libertines
rejoiced to place so respectable a name upon their list of
worthies. To the student of history they afford, in a compact
form, some insight into the pursuits and objects of an Athenian
man of pleasure. Plato quotes one couplet in the *Lysis*, and
the author of the dialogue περὶ ἐρώτων (On Loves), attributed to Lucian, makes use of the same verses to prove that
Solon was not exempt from the passion for which he is apolo-
gising. Apuleius mentions another as "lascivissimus ille
versus." It hould be added that the most considerable of
these elegies has also been ascribed to Theognis. The doubt

Solon's erotic poems.

---

[1] This subject will be resumed in the introduction to my chapter
on Euripides, where I attempt to show how the Herodotean notion of
divine jealousy was moralised at the time of the Persian war into the idea
of Nemesis.

of authorship which hangs over all the gnomic fragments
warns us, therefore, to be cautious in ascribing them to Solon.
At the same time there is no strong external or internal argument against their authenticity. Solon displays no asceticism
in his poetry, or in anything that is recorded of his life or
sayings.[1] It is probable that he lived as a Greek among
Greeks, and was not ashamed of any of their social customs.

Phocylides.   Passing from Solon to Phocylides we find a somewhat
different tone of social philosophy. Phocylides was a native
of Miletus, who lived between 550 and 490 B.C. If Mimnermus represents the effeminacy of the Asiatic Greeks,
Phocylides displays a kind of prosaic worldly wisdom, for
which the Ionians were celebrated. He is thoroughly *bourgeois*, to use a modern phrase ; contented with material felicity,
shrewd, safe in his opinions, and gifted with great common
sense. Here are some of his maxims :—"First get your
living, and then think of getting virtue." . . . "What is the
advantage of noble birth, if favour follow not the speech and
counsel of a man ?" . . . "The middle classes are in many
ways best off; I wish to be of middle rank in the State."
Aristotle (*Pol.*, iv. 9, 7) quotes the last of these sayings with
approbation. It is a thoroughly Ionian sentiment. Two of
his genuine fragments contain the germ of Greek ideas afterwards destined to be widely developed and applied by the
greatest thinkers of Greece. One of these describes the
Greek conception of a perfect State :—"A small city, set
upon a rock, and well governed, is better than all foolish
Nineveh." We here recognise the practical wisdom and
thorough solidity of Greek good sense. Wealth, size, and
splendour they regarded as stumbling-blocks and sources of
weakness. To be compact and well governed expressed their
ideal of social felicity. Plato in the *Republic*, and Aristotle in
the *Politics*, carry the thought expressed in this couplet of

[1] See the passage quoted from Philemon by Athenæus, xiii. 569, wheie
the institution of public *lupanaria* is ascribed to Solon.

Phocylides to its utmost logical consequences. Again he says, "In justice the whole of virtue exists entire." This verse, which has also been incorporated into the elegies of Theognis, was probably the common property of many early moralists. Aristotle quotes it in the fifth book of the *Ethics* with the preface : Διὸ καὶ παροιμιαζόμενοί φαμεν (wherefore in a proverb too we say). It might be placed as a motto on the first page of Plato's *Republic*, for justice is the architectonic virtue which maintains the health and safety of the State.

Phocylides enjoyed a high reputation among the ancients. Though few genuine fragments of his sayings have been handed down to us, there is a long and obviously spurious poem which bears his name. Some moralist of the Christian period has endeavoured to claim for his half-Jewish precepts the sanction of a great and antique authority. The greater number of those which we may with safety accept as genuine are prefaced by the words καὶ τόγε Φωκυλίδεω (and this too of Phocylides), forming an integral part of a hexameter. Phocylides was author of an epigram in imitation of one ascribed to Demodocus, which is chiefly interesting as having furnished Porson with the model of his well-known lines on Hermann. He also composed an epigrammatic satire on women, in which he compares them to four animals, a dog, a bee, a pig, and a horse, in the style of the poem by Simonides of Amorgos. *Doubtful and miscellaneous verses.*

Xenophanes, a native of Colophon, and the founder of the Eleatic school of philosophy, has left some elegies of a gnomic character, which illustrate another point in the Ionian intellect. While Phocylides celebrated the superiority of comfort and the solid goods of life, Xenophanes endeavoured to break down the prejudice in favour of mere physical advantages, and to assert the absolute pre-eminence of intellectual power. In his second fragment (ed. Bergk) he says, "You give all kinds of honours—precedence at festivals, pensions, and public maintenance — to runners, boxers, pentathletes, wrestlers, *Xenophanes* pancratists, and charioteers, who bear away the prize at Olympia; yet these men are not so worthy of reward as I am; for better than the strength of men or horses is our wisdom. What is the use of all this muscular development? It will not improve the constitution of the State or increase the revenue." [1] In this paraphrase, I have, for the sake of brevity, modernised the language of Xenophanes, while seeking to preserve the meaning of an elegy which admirably illustrates the principles of the Ionian race, and of Athens in particular, as contrasted with those of the Dorians. Plato, Aristotle, and all the political moralists of Greece, blamed Sparta and Thebes for training mere soldiers and gymnasts, to the exclusion of intellectual culture; thus retarding the growth of their constitutions and forcing them to depend in all emergencies upon brute force. Had all Ionians been like Solon and Xenophanes, had there been nothing of Mimnermus or Phocylides in their character, then the Athenians might have avoided the contrary charge of effeminacy and ignobility of purpose and merely æsthetical superiority, with which they have been taxed.

Theognis. Contemporary with Phocylides was Theognis, a poet of whose gnomic elegies nearly fourteen hundred lines are still extant. Some of these are identical with verses of Solon, and of other writers; yet we need not suppose that Theognis was himself an imitator. It is far more probable that all the gnomic poets borrowed from the same sources, or embodied in their couplets maxims of common and proverbial wisdom. That Aristotle so regarded one of their most important aphorisms on the architectonic supremacy of justice, we have already seen. Besides, it is not certain on what principle the elegies which bear the names of different poets, were assigned to them. Theognis covers more ground than any of his pre-

---

[1] We may compare with this fragment a passage preserved from the *Autolycus* of Euripides, translated by me in the second volume of these Studies.

decessors, and embraces a greater variety of subjects. It has never been imagined that the fragments we possess formed part of an elaborate and continuous poem. They rather seem to have been written as occasion served, in order to express the thoughts of the moment; while not a few included in the canon of Theognis belong probably to other poets. Many of them contain maxims of political wisdom, and rules for private conduct in the choice of friends; others seem to have been composed for the lyre, in praise of good society, or wine, or beauty; again we find discussions of moral questions, and prayers to the gods, mixed up with lamentations on the miseries of exile and poverty; a few throw light upon the personal history of Theognis; in all cases the majority are addressed to one person, called Cyrnus.[1]

Theognis was a noble, born at Megara about the middle of the sixth century B.C. His city, though traditionally subject to the yoke of Corinth, had under the influence of its aristocracy acquired independence. In course of time Theagenes, a demagogue, gained for himself despotical supremacy, and exiled the members of the old nobility from Megara. He, too, succumbed to popular force, and for many years a struggle was maintained between the democratic party, whom Theognis persistently styles κακοί and δειλοί (bad and cowardly), and

Political career of Theognis.

---

[1] A very ingenious attempt was made by Mr. Hookham Frere to reconstruct the life of Theognis from his elegies. It would be too much to assert that his conjectures are always successful. Indeed he often introduces foreign matter and modern sentiment, while he neglects the peculiarly Greek relations of the poet to his friend. Those who are curious about such works of hypercriticism would do well to study his *Theognis Restitutus* (Frere's Works, vol. ii.) In doing so, they must, however, bear in mind, as already observed above, that a great many of the couplets and short poems ascribed to Theognis by the later Greeks were not really his own. Theognis, like Hesiod, Solon, and Phocylides, was credited with more proverbial wisdom than he can be held responsible for. Contradictory utterances are therefore not unfrequent in his elegies, and this fact renders a trustworthy restoration of his biography and body of opinion almost impossible.

the aristocracy, whom he calls ἀγαθοὶ and ἐσθλοί (good and stanch). Theognis himself, as far as we can gather from the fragments, spent a long portion of his life in exile from Megara; but before the period of his banishment he occupied the position of friend and counsellor to Cyrnus, who, though clearly younger than himself, seems to have been in some sense leader of the Megarian aristocracy. A large number of the maxims of Theognis on State-government are specially addressed to him.

Friendship for Cyrnus.

Before proceeding to examine these elegies in detail, we may touch upon the subject of the friendship of Theognis for Cyrnus, which has been much misunderstood. It must be remembered that Theognis was the only Doric poet of the gnomic class—all those who have been hitherto mentioned belonging without exception to the Ionian family of the Greek race. We are not, therefore, surprised to find some purely Dorian qualities in the poetry of Theognis. Such, for instance, are the invocations to Phœbus and Artemis, with which our collection of fragments opens; but such, in a far more characteristic sense, is the whole relation of the poet to his friend. From time immemorial it had been the custom among the Dorian tribes for men distinguished in war or statecraft to select among the youths one comrade, who stood to them in the light of pupil and squire. In Crete this process of election was attended with rites of peculiar solemnity, and at Sparta the names of εἰσπνήλης and ἀΐτης, or "inbreather" and "listener," were given to the pair. They grew up together, the elder teaching the younger all he knew, and expecting to receive from him in return obedience and affection. In manhood they were not separated, but fought and sat in the assembly side by side, and were regarded in all points as each other's representatives. Thus a kind of chivalry was formed, which, like the modern chivalry of love and arms, as long as it remained within due limits, gave birth to nothing but honourable deeds and noble friendships, but which in more degenerate days became a cause of reproach

to Hellas.   There is every reason to believe that Theognis was
united to Cyrnus in the purest bonds of Doric chivalry ; and
it is interesting to observe the kind of education which he gives
his friend (see 1049-1054, Theogn., ed. Bergk).   Boys in the
Doric States were so soon separated from their home, and from
the training of the family, that some substitute for the parental
discipline and care was requisite.   This the institution to which
I have briefly alluded seems to have to some extent supplied.
A Spartan or Cretan settlement resembled a large public school,
in which the elder boys choose their fags, and teach them and
protect them, in return for duty, service and companionship.

Lines 87-100 describe the sincere and perfect affection, the *Its noble*
truthfulness and forbearance, which the poet requires from *and impassioned*
Cyrnus.   In another passage (1259-1270) he complains of the *character.*
changeable character of the youth, and compares him to a
skittish horse.   One of his longest, and, in point of poetry,
most beautiful elegies, celebrates the immortality which his
songs will confer on Cyrnus (237-254).   He tells his friend
that he has given him wings to fly with over land and sea, that
fair young men at festivals will sing of him to sweetly-sounding
pipes, and that even Hades shall not prevent him from wandering on wings of fame about the isles and land of Hellas so long
as earth and sun endure.   The lofty enthusiasm and confidence
of these promises remind us of Shakespeare's most pompous
sonnets.   I have endeavoured to preserve some portion of the
spirit of the original in the following verses :—

> " Lo, I have given thee plumes wherewith to skim
>   The unfathomed deep, and lightly hover around
>   Earth's huge circumference.   Thou shalt be found
>   At banquets on the breath of pæan and hymn :
> To shrill-voiced pipes with lips of seraphim
>   Lovely young men thy rapturous fame shall sound :
>   Yea, when thou liest lapped in the noiseless ground,
>   Thy name shall live, nor shall oblivion dim
> Thy dawn of splendour.   For these lands, these isles,
>   These multitudinous waves of refluent seas,

> Shall be thy pleasure-ground wherethrough to roam,
> Borne by no steed, but wafted by the smiles
>   Of Muses violet-crowned, whose melodies,
> While earth endures, shall make all earth thy home."

Again, he bewails the difficulties and dangers of this kind of friendship (1353 and 1369), or entreats Cyrnus not to let malicious slanders interrupt their intimacy. In some cases we cannot acquit Theognis any more than Solon of licentiousness in the expression of his love. But the general tone of his language addressed to Cyrnus is so dignified and sober that we are inclined to think his looser verses may refer to another and more scandalous attachment.

Invective against democratic innovations.

The first elegy of great importance (43-69) describes the state of Megara when under the control of a democracy. It expresses the bitter hatred and contempt which the Greek nobles in a Dorian State felt for the Periœci, or farmers of the neighbouring country, whom they strove to keep beneath them, and to exclude from all political rights :—"Cyrnus, this city is still a city, but the people are all changed, who some time since knew neither law nor justice, but wore goatskins, and dwelt like deer beyond the walls. Now they are noble, son of Polypas; and the brave of heretofore are base. Who can endure to look upon these things?" Again he says (1109-1114), "The nobles of old days are now made base, and the base are noble, . . . a man of birth takes his bride from a low man's house." In another place he complains that the rabble rule the State with monstrous laws, that the sense of shame has perished, and that impudence and insolence lord it over the land (289-292). In these perilous times he compares the State to a ship managed by incompetent and unruly mariners : the waves are breaking over her, but the sailors prevent the good pilot from guiding her helm, while they make pillage of the common good (667-682). This simile bears a striking resemblance to the passage of the *Republic* in which Plato compares a State possessed by demagogues and the mob to an

ill-governed ship.   Lastly, says Theognis, "Porters rule, and
the nobles are subject to the base."   In this state of disorder
the very principles of Dorian society are neglected.   Money is
regarded as the charter of nobility, and no attempts are made
to maintain a generous breed of citizens.   "We are careful,"
he says (183-196), "to select the best race of horses and the
like, but a noble man doubts not about marrying a mean
woman if she bring him money ; nor does a woman reject the
suit of a mean man if he be rich.   Wealth is honoured ; wealth
has confused our blood."   This passage has great interest, both
as showing the old prejudices of the Dorian aristocracy, and
also as proving that a new order of things was beginning in
Greece.   Even the Dorian States could not resist the progress
of commerce and republican institutions ; and little Megara,
situated between mercantile Corinth and democratic Athens,
had but small strength to stem the tide.   But the party of
Theognis were not always out of power.   When Cyrnus and   Advice
his friends held sway in Megara, he gives them this advice   to the
aristocracy.
(847-850) : "Trample on the empty-headed rabble ;   strike
them with the stinging goad ; and put a galling yoke upon
their neck ; for never shall you find so despot-loving a Demos
in the whole earth."   That he had frequent cause to apprehend
the rising of some tyrant from the body of the people may be
noticed in the fragments.   Among the earliest of these in our
arrangement (39-42) occurs this elegy :—"Cyrnus, this city is
pregnant ; but I fear that it will bring forth a man to chastise
our evil violence."   He then proceeds to lay down the axioms
of the oligarchical State theory : the nobility, he says, never
ruined a city ; it is only when base leaders get the upper hand,
and wrest justice in order to indulge the populace and make
their own gain, that civil dissension and ruin ensue.   Tyrants   Hatred of
despotism.
were as hateful to the true oligarchs as a democracy, and
Theognis in one place actually advises tyrannicide : "To lay
low a despot who consumes the people is no sin, and will not
be punished by the gods" (1181).   This sentiment corresponds

with the couplet of Simonides on Harmodius and Aristogeiton, and with the apophthegms of several of the sages.[1]

Theognis, seeing Cyrnus environed with political difficulties, thought fit to furnish him with rules of conduct. He was very particular about the choice of proper friends. One elegy (31-38), in which he discourses on the desirability of consorting with none but the best company, and of avoiding the contagion of low comrades, attained a wide celebrity among the Greeks. So much of their life was spent in public, and so much of their education depended on society, that the question of social intercourse was one of paramount importance. Plato in the *Meno*, Xenophon in his *Memorabilia*, and Aristotle in the ninth book of the *Ethics*, all make use of these verses :— "Come not into the company of bad men, but cling always to the good; eat and drink with them; sit with them, and seek to please those who have great power. For from the noble you will learn what is noble; but if you mix with base men you will lose the wits you have." It must always be borne in mind that by ἐσθλοὶ and ἀγαθοὶ Theognis meant the men of his own party. The "good" and "noble" were men of birth, wealth, breeding, and power, on whom, by prejudice and habit, he conferred these moral titles. In course of time, however, as the words acquired a more ethical significance, the philosophers were able to appropriate maxims of worldly prudence to their own more elevated purposes; nor were they even in the times of Theognis other than ambiguous, for the identification of aristocratic position and moral worth was so conventionally complete, that words which were intended to be taken in the one sense had an equal application in the other. In another elegy (305-308) Theognis repeats this advice, when he observes that no one is born utterly bad by nature, but that he contracts habits of depravity from his associates. Here it is obvious how much of ethical

[1] "Truly a great light dawned on the Athenians when Aristogeiton with Harmodius slew Hipparchus."

meaning the words "good" and "bad" involved, even in the
times of the Megarian poet, and how vastly important he
considered the society of well-bred companions to be in the
formation of character.   A different view of moral habits
seems to be taken in another fragment (429-438), where
Theognis attributes more influence to nature than to training : Futility of
education.
—"To beget and rear a child," he says, "is easier than to
instil good principles.   No one ever devised means for making
fools wise, or bad men good.   If Heaven had given to the
sons of Æsculapius the gift of healing wickedness and folly,
great fees would they have earned.   If you could fashion or
insert what minds you liked, good men would never have
bad sons.   But no amount of teaching will make a bad man
good."   These verses are quoted both by Plato and Aristotle,
with whose inquiries into the subject of Education *versus*
Nature (of τρόφη as opposed to φύσις) they had, of course,
considerable correspondence.

In connection with this subject of moral habits and com- Behaviour
in public.
panionship, Theognis thought fit to give his pupil advice about
his deportment at the public dinners of the Dorians.   At these
social meetings there was ample scope for political intrigue ;
and hence it followed that a public man was forced to be particular about his associates.   The poet devotes a series of
couplets (61-82) to this point, recommending Cyrnus to be
reticent, and not to communicate the whole of his plans even
to his friends.   He warns him how difficult it is to get a faithful
friend.   You could not find, he says (83-86), one shipload of
really trustworthy and incorruptible men upon the face of the
world.   Moreover, nothing requires more skill than to discover
the insincerity of a hypocrite (117-128).   You may test gold
and silver, but there are no means of getting at the thoughts
of men.   This sentiment, together with the metaphor of pinch-
beck metal, is used by Euripides in *Medea* (line 515).   Aristotle also quotes the passage in his Eudemian *Ethics* (vii. 2).
Time, however, says Theognis (963-970), and experience,

and calamity, are the true tests of friendship. If a man will bear misfortune with you, or will help you in a serious undertaking, you may then, but not till then, rely upon his expressions of attachment. This suspicious temper re-

Machiavel-
lian rules
for conduct.
calls the social philosophy of Machiavelli; indeed, Greek politics in no respect resembled those of modern Italy more closely than in the diplomatic footing upon which all the relations of society were placed. There are two very curious passages (213-218 and 1071-1074) in which Theognis bids his friend be as much as possible all things to all men. "Turn a different side of your character," he says, "to different men, and mix part of their temper with your own. Get the nature of the cuttlefish, which looks exactly like the rock it clings to: be versatile, and show a variety of complexions." Again, he boasts that "among madmen I am exceeding mad; but among the just no man is more just than I am." Nor is this subtlety to be confined to friendly relations merely. In one most Jesuitical couplet (363) Theognis urges his friend "to beguile his foe with fair words; but when he has him in his power, to take full vengeance and to spare not." As to the actual events of the life of Cyrnus, we know nothing except what is told us in one of the elegies (805-810), that he went as a Theorus to the shrine of Delphi. We may gather from some expressions of the poet that he was of a rash and haughty and unconciliatory temper.

Poverty and
exile.
Passing now to the personal history of Theognis, we are struck with his frequent lamentations over poverty and the wretchedness of exile. "Miserable poverty!" he cries, "go elsewhere; prithee stay not with a host that hates thee." "Poverty breaks the spirit of a noble man more than anything, more even than age or ague. The poor man is gagged and bound; he cannot speak or act. . . . Poverty comes not to the market or the lawsuits; everywhere she is laughed and scoffed at, and hated by all men . . . mother she is of help-lessness: she breaks the spirit of a man within his breast, so

that he suffers shame and wrong in silence, and learns to lie and cheat and do the sin his soul abhors. . . . Wretched want, why, seated on my shoulders, dost thou debase body and mind alike?" (267, 351, 385, 173-182, 649). Wealth, on the other hand, he cries with bitterness, is omnipotent (1117): "O wealth! of gods the fairest and most full of charm! with thy help, though I am a mean man, I am made noble." "Every one honours a rich man and slights a poor man: the whole world agrees upon this point." But the finest and most satirical of all his poems on this subject is one (699-718) in which he says: "Most men have but one virtue, and that is wealth; it would do you no good if you had the self-control of Rhadamanthus himself, or if you knew more wiles than Sisyphus, or if you could turn falsehood into truth with the tongue of a Nestor, or if you were more fleet of foot than the children of Boreas. You must fix your mind on wealth—wealth alone. Wealth is almighty." It was poverty that gave its bitterness to exile. My friends, he says, pass me by; "no one is the friend or faithful comrade of an exile. This is the sting of exile." "I have suffered what is as bad as death, and worse than anything besides. My friends have refused me the assistance which they owed, and I am forced to try my foes" (811-814). Hope, which has always been the food and sustenance of exiles, alone remained to him. There is one beautiful elegy (1135-1150) in which he imitates Hesiod, singing how faith and temperance and the graces have left the earth, how oaths are broken and religion is neglected, how holiness hath passed away; yet, if a pious man remain, let him wait on Hope, to Hope pray always, to Hope sacrifice first and last.

Verses 825-830 and 1197-1202 describe his condition while living as a poor man, stripped of his paternal farms, in Megara. The voice of the harvest-bird brings him sorrow, for he knows that other men will reap his fields. How can he pipe or sing, when from the market-place he sees his own land made the prey of revellers? The same sense of the *res angusta*

Tyranny of wealth.

Hope.

Personal sufferings.

domi is expressed in the welcome to Clearistus. We gather from another elegy (261-266) that Theognis had lost not only his land, but also a girl to whom he was betrothed. Her parents gave her in marriage to a man less noble and less worthy than himself. Nor do we fail to get some insight into his domestic circumstances. Mr. Frère explains one fragment (271-278), full of Lear's indignation, by conjecturing that Theognis had left a wife and children behind him at Megara during his wanderings, and had returned to find them estranged and thankless. He translates the fragment thus :—

Frere's
attempt at a
biography.

> " One single evil, more severe and rude
> Than age or sickness or decrepitude,
> Is dealt unequally, for him that rears
> A thankless offspring ; in his latter years,
> Ungratefully requited for his pains,
> A parsimonious life and thrifty gains,
> With toil and care acquired for their behoof ;
> And no return ! but insolent reproof ;
> Such as might scare a beggar from the gate,
> A wretch unknown, poor and importunate !
> To be reviled, avoided, hated, curst ;
> This is the last of evils, and the worst ! "

The same kind of ingenious conjecture supplies us with a plausible explanation of some obscure couplets (1211-1216), in which it appears that Theognis, having been taunted by a female slave, replied by making most sarcastic remarks on the servile physiognomy, and by boasting that among all his miseries he had remained a free man and a noble-minded gentleman. He often bids his soul be strong and bear bad fortune, like Ulysses when he cried, τέτλαθι δὴ κραδίη καὶ κύντερον ἄλλο ποτ' ἔτλης.[1] Nor does he fail to ease his heart by praying for vengeance, and indulging the hope that he may live to drink the blood of his foes (349), and to divide their property among his friends (562). That he was kindly

---

[1] " Be stout, O heart of mine : ere now thou hast endured even more grimly grief than this."

entertained in the various States he visited, he tells us; and
it is thought that he received the citizenship of Hyblæan
Megara. Sicily, Eubœa, and Sparta (783-788) are specially
mentioned by him as his homes in exile. Wherever he went
he carried with him fame, and found a welcome. "Yet," says
the poet, "no joy of those fair lands entered my soul, so far
was anything from seeming dearer than my native land."

Among the elegies of general interest attributed to *Hymn to the Muses and Graces.*
Theognis, none is more beautiful than the following hymn to
the goddesses of Song and Beauty, which has been very
elegantly rendered into English verse :—

> "Muses and Graces ! daughters of high Jove,
>   When erst you left your glorious seats above
>   To bless the bridal of that wondrous pair,
>   Cadmus and Harmonia fair,
>   Ye chanted forth a divine air :
>   'What is good and fair
>   Shall ever be our care.'
>   Thus the burden of it rang :
>   'That shall never be our care
>   Which is neither good nor fair.'
>   Such were the words your lips immortal sang." [1]

The very essence of the Greek feeling for the beautiful
is expressed in these simple lines. Beauty, goodness, and
truth were to the Greeks almost convertible terms; and the
nearest approach which Plato made to the conception of a
metaphysical deity was called by him the $\iota\delta\epsilon\alpha\ \tau o\hat{v}\ \kappa\alpha\lambda o\hat{v}$
(Idea of the Beautiful). Not less Greek is the sentiment *Virtue or excellence*
expressed in the following lines (1027) :—"Easy among men
is the practice of wickedness, but hard, friend Cyrnus, is the
method of goodness." Theognis here expresses very prosaically
what Hesiod and Simonides have both enunciated in noble
verse (*Op. et Dies*, 285-290, and Simonides, Frag. 15, ed.
Gaisford). It is noticeable that in his couplet $\tau o\ \grave{a}\gamma\alpha\theta o\nu$
(the good) is used instead of $\grave{a}\rho\epsilon\tau\eta$ (virtue or excellence).

[1] *Miscellanies*, by the late John Addington Symonds, M.D., p. 411.

The thought, however, is the same; nor does it differ widely
from that which is contained in the Aristotelian " Hymn to
Virtue," where we see that what the Greeks meant by this
word, included not only moral rectitude, but also the labour
of a Hercules, and all noble or patriotic deeds which implied
self-devotion to a great cause.

Dorian
clubs.

The occasions for which the elegies of this class were
composed by Theognis seem to have been chiefly banquets
and drinking parties. In the Dorian States of Greece it was
customary for men to form select clubs, which met together
after the public meals for the purpose of drinking, conversing, and enjoying music. These friendly societies formed an
appendix to the national φειδίτια, or public tables. Great
care was taken in the selection of members, who were admitted
by ballot ; and in time the clubs acquired political importance.
Periander is said (Ar. Pol., v. 9, 2) to have abolished them in
Corinth because they proved favourable to aristocracy—no
doubt by keeping up the old Doric traditions which he took
pains to break down. In the verses of Theognis we are introduced to many members of his club by name—Onomacritus,
Clearistus, Demonax, Democles, Timagoras, and doubtless
Cyrnus. Of course these customs were not confined to Doric
cities; on the contrary, the Symposia and Erani of the
Athenians are more celebrated for their wit and humour,
while readers of Thucydides remember how large a part the
clubs played in the history of the Eighth Book. But the
custom was systematised, like everything else, with greater
rigour among Dorians. It appears that, after having eaten,
the cups were filled and libations were made to the Doric
patron Phœbus (cf. Theogn., Frag. 1); then came the Comus
or drinking-bout : flute-players entered the room, and some of
the guests sang to the lyre, or addressed an elegy to the
company at large, or to some particular person. These facts
may be gathered from different fragments of Theognis (997,
757); but if we wish to gain a complete picture of one of

these parties, we may seek it in an elegy of Xenophanes, A Greek merry-making.
which is so fresh and pretty that I feel inclined to paraphrase
it at length :—

"Now the floor is cleanly swept ; the hands of all the guests
are washed ; the cups shine brightly on the board. Woven
wreaths and fragrant myrrh are carried round by the attendants,
and in the middle stands a bowl full of that which maketh glad
the heart of man. Wine too is ready in reserve, wine inexhaustible,
honey-sweet in jars, smelling of flowers. Frankincense breathes
forth its perfume among the revellers, and cold water, sweet and
pure, waits at their side. Loaves, fresh and golden, stand upon
the table, which groans with cheese and rich honey. In the midst
is an altar hung about with flowers, and singing and merriment
resound throughout the house. First must merry-making men
address the gods with holy songs and pure words ; libations must
they pour, and pray for strength to act justly ; then may they
drink as much as a man can carry home without a guide—unless
he be far gone in years. This also is right, to speak of noble deeds
and virtue over our cups ; not to tell tales of giants or Titans or
the Centaurs, mere fictions of our grandfathers, and foolish fables."

It was customary at these banquets to sing the praises of Songs of youth and death.
youth and to lament old age, ringing endless changes on the
refrain "Vivamus atque amemus," which antiquity was never
weary of repeating. Very sad and pathetic is the tone of
these old songs, wherein the pæan mingles with the dirge ; for
youth and the grave are named in the same breath, and while
we smell the roses we are reminded that they will wither.
Then comes the end—the cold and solitary tomb, eternal frost
and everlasting darkness, to which old age, the winter and
night of life, is but a melancholy portal. *Gaudeamus igitur,
juvenes cum sumus* (Let us take our pleasure then, while we
are young).

> "To pleasure, in life's bloom, yield we our powers,
>   While yet to be and to enjoy are ours ;
>   For swift as thought our glorious youth goes by,
>   Swift as the coursers that to battle fly,
>   Bearing the chief with quivering spear in hand,
>   Madly careering o'er the rich corn-land,"—

so sings Theognis (977), and with even more of pathos he exclaims—

> "Ah me ! my youth ! alas for eld's dark day :
> This comes apace, while that fleets fast away."

The same idea is repeated in many other elegies, always with the same sad cadence : "No man, as soon as the earth covers him, and he goes down to Erebus, the home of Persephone, takes any pleasure in the sound of the lyre, or the voice of the flute-player, or in the sweet gifts of Dionysus" (973-976). At another time he reckons up the ills of life : "When I am drinking I take no heed of soul-consuming poverty or of enemies who speak ill of me ; but I lament delightful youth which is forsaking me, and wail for grim old age who cometh on apace" (1129-1132). Their tone reminds us of Mimnermus, who said the utmost when he cried—

> "Zeus to Tithonus gave a grievous ill—
> Undying age, than death more horrible !"

The fragility of human life.

To multiply more elegies of this description would be useless. We may, however, allude to a poem of Simonides (Frag. 100, ed. Gaisford), which combines the sweetness of Mimnermus and the energy of Theognis :—"Nothing human endures for aye. Well said the bard of Chios, that like the leaves so is the race of men : yet few who hear this keep it in their mind ; for hope is strong within the breast of youth. When the flower of youth lasts, and the heart of a man is light, he nurses idle thoughts, hoping he never will grow old or die ; nor does he think of sickness in good health. Fools are they who dream thus, nor know how short are the days of youth and life. But learn thou this, and live thy life out, cheering thy soul with good things." The tone of these elegies pervades a great many monuments of Greek sculpture. Standing before the Genius of Eternal Repose, or the so-called Genius of the Vatican, we are moved almost to tears by the dumb sadness with which their perfect beauty has been chastened.

Like the shade of young Marcellus in Virgil, they seem to carry round them a cloud of gloom, impalpable, yet overshadowing their youth with warnings and anticipations of the tomb.

With Theognis the list of gnomic poets, strictly so called, may be said to close. Simonides, from whom I have adduced some passages in illustration of the elder elegiac writers, survived the bard of Megara, and attained a far greater reputation than he enjoyed, at the Syracusan and Athenian courts. How highly his maxims were valued by the moralists of the succeeding age, is known by every reader of the *Protagoras* and *Republic* of Plato. But a more detailed analysis of his verses would be out of place, when we consider that his chief fame rests upon epitaphs, patriotic epigrams, and lyrical fragments—none of them strictly gnomic in their character. *Simonides of Ceos.*

To modern readers the philosophy of the poets whom we have considered will perhaps seem trite, their inspiration tame, their style pedestrian. But their contemporaries were far from arriving at this criticism. To obtain concise and abstract maxims upon the ethics of society, politics, and education, was to them a new and inestimable privilege. In the gnomic poets the morality which had been merely implicit in Homer and Hesiod, received separate treatment and distinct expression. The wisdom which had been gradually collecting for centuries in the Greek mind, was tersely and lucidly condensed into a few pregnant sentences. These sentences formed the data for new syntheses and higher generalisations, the topics for enlarged investigation, the "middle axioms" between the scattered facts of life and the unity of philosophical system. *We* may regard the gnomic poets with interest, partly on account of the real, if rare, beauty of some of their fragments ; partly on account of their historical and illustrative value ; partly because all efforts of the human mind in its struggle for emancipation, and all stages in its develop- *Importance of the gnomic poets.*

ment, are worthy of attentive study. To the sophists, to the orators, to Socrates and his friends, to the tragic writers, to educated men at large in Hellas, they were authorities on moral questions ; and their maxims, which the progress of the centuries has rendered commonplace, appeared the sentences of weightiest wisdom, oracles almost, and precepts inspired by more than human prudence.

CHAPTER IX

THE SATIRISTS

Invention of the Iambic Metre—Archilochus—His Parentage and Life—
His Fame among the Ancients—Ancient and Modern Modes of Judging
Artists—The Originality of Archilochus as a Poet—Simonides of
Amorgos—His Satire on Women—The Ionian Contempt for Women—
Hipponax—Limping Iambics—Differences between the Satire of the
Greeks and Romans.

THE Greeks displayed their æsthetic instinct in nothing more Birth of
Iambic
verse.
remarkably than in their exact adaptation of the forms of art
to the nature of the subjects which they undertook to treat.
The Hexameter had sufficed for the needs of the Epic. The
Elegiac had fulfilled the requirements of pathetic or contem-
plative meditation. But with the development of the national
genius a separate vehicle for satire was demanded. Archilochus of Paros created a new style, and presented in the Iambic
metre a new instrument to the poets of his race. The circumstances of the birth and parentage of Archilochus are significant. He was the son of Telesicles, a noble Ionian, and of
Enipo, a slave-woman. Thus from the very first there were
inequalities in his circumstances which may have sufficed to
sour his temper. His birth, which may be fixed about 729 B.C.,
was predicted, according to old tradition, by the oracle at
Delphi. The same oracle busied itself at a later period with
his death, by cursing the Naxian soldier Calondas, who had
killed him in battle, because he had "slain the servant of the
Muses." As the fragments we possess of Archilochus render

it difficult to understand the very high estimation in which he was held by the Greeks, and which these stories indicate, it may be well to preface this account of him with some quotations from the ancient critics. Longinus,[1] to begin with, explains the incongruities of his poetry by saying that he "dragged disorderly elements into his verse under the impulse of divine inspiration." Plato[2] calls him ὁ σοφώτατος Ἀρχίλοχος, "the prince of sages," which, in the mouth of a philosopher, is the highest panegyric. The Alexandrian critic Aristophanes, when asked which of the poems of Archilochus he liked best, answered with laconic brevity, "the longest." Hadrian,[3] in an epigram, says that the Muses turned the attention of Archilochus to mad Iambics, in order that their darling Homer might not have so dangerous a rival in the field of the Epic. All antiquity agreed in naming him second only to Homer: "Maximus poeta aut certe summo proximus," "a poet of the highest order, or surely next unto the greatest," says Valerius Maximus. The birthdays of Homer and Archilochus were celebrated on the same day; their busts were joined in Janus fashion—two faces and one head: Hippodromus the Sophist[4] called Homer the Voice, Archilochus the Breath or Soul, of the students of wisdom. The epithet κάλλιστος (most beautiful) was ascribed to him because of his perfect style, though the subjects of his poetry were anything but beautiful. Of this style Quintilian[5] says that it excelled in "powerful as well as short and quivering sentences," that it contained "the greatest possible amount of blood and sinews." The highest praise which Gorgias could pronounce on Plato when he published his dialogues upon the Sophists, was to say that Athens had produced a new Archilochus. To multiply these panegyrics would be easy. But enough has been adduced to prove that the ancients looked on Archilochus as a worthy rival of Homer, as a poet supreme

---

[1] *On the Sublime*, xxxiii. 5.   [2] *Rep.* 365, c.   [3] *Anth. Pal.* vii. 674.
[4] Philostr. *Bioi Soph.* 620.   [5] x. l. 60.

in his own department, as the creator of a new kingdom in
poetry, as the sire of a long line of mighty artists.

What remains of the verse of Archilochus and what we
know of his life are curiously at variance with this enthusiasm.
Nothing proves the difference between ancient and modern
views of art more strongly than the fact that all antiquity
concurred in regarding as a divinely inspired benefactor of
the human race, a man who in the present day would have
been hunted from society with execrations. This son of the
slave-woman, born in an Ionian island, where license was more
tolerated than in a Dorian state, devoted himself to satire,
making his genius the instrument of private hate, and turning
the golden gifts of the Muses to the service of his selfish spite.
A greater contrast cannot be conceived than that which exists
between Homer, the priest of Gods and Heroes, the poet of
high actions and lofty passions, whose own life is buried in
sacred and sublime mystery, and this satirist who saw the
world with jaundiced eyes, prying about for subjects of his
wrath and bitterness and scorn, whose themes were the
passions of his own heart, the sordid misadventures of his
personality. It was this contrast between Archilochus and
Homer that gave the former a right in the estimation of the
Greeks to take equal rank with the Father of the Epos. He,
the greatest poet next in date to Homer, by virtue of a divine
originality of genius, exercised his art in exactly the opposite
field to that which Homer ruled as his demesne. Clearer sign
than this of inspiration could not be demanded; and how
should posterity withhold its gratitude from the poet who had
unlocked a new chamber of the treasure-house of art? This
was how the ancients reasoned, instead of measuring their
poets, as the moderns try to do, by moral standards and
conventional conceptions of propriety.

The facts of the life of Archilochus are briefly these. He
was engaged to be married to Neobulé, daughter of Lycambes.
Her father retracted his consent to the marriage, having

The maker of personal satire.

Facts of his life

possibly discovered that the temper of his proposed son-in-law was a mixture of gall, wormwood, vinegar, verjuice, vitriol, and nitric acid. Thereupon, as Horace says :—

"Archilochum proprio rabies armavit iambo." [1]

Invectives against Lycambes and his daughters. He made the Iambic metre his own, and sharpened it into a terrible weapon of attack. Each verse he wrote was polished and pointed like an arrow-head. Each line was steeped in the poison of hideous charges against his sweetheart, her sisters, and her father. The set of poems which he produced, and, as it would appear, recited publicly at the festival of Demeter, were so charged with wit and fire, that the country rang with them. The daughters of Lycambes, tradition avers, went straightway and hanged themselves—unable to endure the flight of fiery serpents that had fallen on them : for, to quote the words of Browning, Archilochus had the art of writing verse that "bit into the live man's flesh like parchment," that sent him wandering, branded and for ever shamed, about his native streets and fields. After this murderous exhibition of his power Archilochus left Paros. [2]

"Away with Paros ! her figs and fishy life !"

Wanderings of Archilochus. He removed to Thasos, where the Parians founded a colony. But Thasos was worse than Paros : [3] "Like the backbone of an ass it stood bristling with wild wood ; for, in sooth it is not a fair land, or pleasant, or delightful, like that which spreads by Siris' stream." It was here he threw his shield away in a battle with the Thracians, and gave Horace and Alcæus a precedent by writing a poem on his want of prowess. The remainder of his life was spent in wandering. He visited Sparta, where, however, he was not suffered to remain an hour. The Ephors judged rightly that this runaway soldier and foul-mouthed Ionian satirist might corrupt the Spartan

---

[1] "It was rage that armed Archilochus with his own Iambic."
[2] Bergk, *Poetæ Lyrici*, p. 696.   [3] *Ib.* p. 689.

youth, or sow dissension in the State. The publication of his
works was forbidden in this, the most conservative of all
Greek States. Finally Archilochus returned to Paros, and
was killed in battle by a native of Naxos. A more unhappy
existence, wretched in itself and the cause of wretchedness to
others, can scarcely be imagined, if the tale of the life of
Archilochus be true. Dishonoured by the inequality of his
parentage, slighted in the matter of his marriage, discontented
at home, restless and rejected abroad, he seems to have been
formed by the facts of his biography for the creation of Satire.
And this is his greatest title to fame.

It is possible that the Iambic metre existed before the date
of Archilochus. An old myth connects it with the festivals
of Demeter. Demeter, it is said, could not be made to laugh
after her daughter's loss, until a nymph, Iambé, by her jests
and sarcasms, raised a smile upon her lips. This legend
proves that the Greeks referred the origin of the Iambic to
those jokes and gibes which were common in the feasts of
Demeter, and from the licentious mirth of which the satiric
element of Comedy was developed. The Iambic is nearest in
cadence to the language of common life ; it is therefore the
fit vehicle for dialogue, and for all poetry that deals with
common and domestic topics. Again, it is essentially rapid
in movement : Horace speaks of *celeres Iambi* (swift Iambi) ;
Hadrian calls them λυσσῶντες ἴαμβοι (raging Iambi) : this
rapidity fitted them for sharp attack and swift satiric
pungency. Admitting then that the metre may have been
employed in early attempts at colloquial satire, Archilochus,
perceiving its capacities, fashioned it to suit the purpose of
his own consummate art. He was celebrated among the
ancients for having perfected the metres belonging to what
they called the διπλάσιον γένος, as distinguished from the
ἴσον γένος—that is to say, the Iambic and Trochaic rhythms,
in which either the arsis or the thesis has twice the time of
the other. In a trochee the first syllable equals two of the

Demeter and
the nymph
Iambé.

same time as the second ; in an iamb this order is reversed ;
whereas the dactyl and the spondee, on which the hexameter
and elegiac metres are based, are feet, each member of
which has the same time, the two shorts of the dactyl being
equivalent to the second long of the spondee.   Archilochus,
if not absolutely the inventor, was the creator of these two
metres, the Iambic and Trochaic, as truly as Homer was the
creator of the heroic measure.   No proof of the power of his
genius can be greater than the fact that, whatever changes
may have been subsequently wrought in the Iambic and
Trochaic metres, they remained substantially the same as
those which Archilochus employed, whether afterwards
adapted to Satire, Tragedy, or Comedy.   While speaking
of Archilochus as a technical artist, it ought to be mentioned
that he gave further proof of his originality by elaborating
the metrical systems which the Greeks called Asynartêtes, or
unconnected.   These consisted of a mixture of dactylic and
anapæstic with trochaic feet.   The Ithyphallic, which was
marked by a succession of three trochees at the end of the
line, was the most distinguished.

To translate Archilochus is almost impossible.   His merit
is the perfection of style, which will admit of no transplanta-
tion.   His language is the language of common life, exquisitely chosen, and kept within the most exact limits, with
a view to the production of a carefully studied effect.   It is
hopeless to render such fragments as we possess without
making them seem coarse or prosy, the poet's supremacy
having been achieved by his artistic handling of vernacular
Greek.   When we compare its pithy terseness with the flowing grandeur of the Epic—a grandeur which had already
become conventional in Greece, a fluency which poetasters
abused—it is easy to understand that the racy epigrams of
Archilochus, in which the subject was set forth with exquisite
point and without circumlocution, must have been an accept-
able novelty to his audience.   Greek sculpture is not more

pure in outline than the following fragment,[1] which sets
before our eyes the figure of a girl embossed on marble or
engraved in chalcedony :—

> ἔχουσα θαλλὸν μυρσίνης ἐτέρπετο
> ῥοδῆς τε καλὸν ἄνθος, ἡ δέ οἱ κόμη
> ὤμους κατεσκίαζε καὶ μετάφρενα.

Archilochus flourished between 714 and 676 B.C. The
date of the next Iambic poet, Simonides of Amorgos, is 660
B.C. It is noticeable that both of these satirists are Ionian.
The relaxation of Ionian life and the freedom of Ionian
manners, as concerned the artist and the public, rendered
the development of satire in Ionia more natural than it could
ever have been in a Dorian state. Simonides owes his
celebrity to a poem upon women, a very ungallant production of 119 lines, which presents one of the most curious
examples upon record of a perfectly smooth and yet crushing
satire. The Iambic lines flow quietly and swiftly off the
poet's lips, in mild and polished phraseology, with none of
the concentrated fury of Archilochus. Yet Simonides aims
at no less than destroying the character of a whole sex. In
a sort of gentle, well-mannered, lazy way he is successful, not
so much by persuading us through examples, after the method
of Juvenal, that his satire is justified, as by the imperturbable
expression of a profound conviction. The interest of this
poem is very great, as marking a departure from the personalities of Archilochus and an attempt to introduce generalities
into the region of satiric delineation. In this respect it is in
Greek literature almost unique, if we except Sicilian, Megarian,
and Attic Comedy, whereof this is not the place to speak.
The rhetorical treatment of a problem of social ethics from

Simonides of Amorgos.

---

[1] Bergk, p. 691 :—
> "Holding a myrtle-rod she blithely moved,
> And a fair blossoming rose ; the flowing tresses
> Shadowed her shoulders, falling to her girdle."

the point of view of satire was, as we shall see hereafter, alien to Greek literature.

This is the plan of the poem. Simonides describes the nature of the different sorts of women by comparing them successively to a hog, a fox, a dog, mud, sea-water, an ass, a weasel, a mare, an ape, a bee. Thus there are ten kinds, and only one respectable or industrious. He rushes at once *in medias res:* "God made the mind of women in the beginning of different qualities : for one he fashioned of a bristly hog ; in whose house everything tumbles about in disorder, be-spattered with mud, and rolls upon the ground : she, dirty, with unwashed clothes, sits and grows fat in a dung-heap." The woman like mud is thus hit off : "This woman is ignorant of everything both good and bad ; her only accomplishment is eating : cold though the winter be, she is too stupid to draw near the fire." Here is the woman who takes after the sea : " She has two minds ; when she laughs and is glad, the stranger seeing her at home will give her praise— there is not a better woman than this on the earth, no, nor a fairer ; but another day she is unbearable, not to be looked at or approached, but she is right mad. To friend and foe she is alike implacable and odious. Thus as the sea often is calm and innocent, a great delight to sailors in summer-time, and oftentimes again is frantic, tearing along with roaring billows ; so is this woman in her temper." The woman who resembles a mare offers other disagreeable qualities. She is "delicate and long-haired, unfit for drudgery or toil : *she* would not touch the mill or lift the sieve or clean the house out ! She bathes twice or thrice a day, and smears herself with myrrh ; then she wears her hair combed out, long and wavy, decked with flowers. It follows that this woman is a rare sight to one's guests, but to her husband she's a curse, unless he be a tyrant who prides himself on such expensive luxuries." The ape-like wife is treated even worse. But at last we reach the bee : "The man who gets her is lucky ; to her alone belongs no blame : his property thrives and increases under her; and loving with a loving helpmate she grows old, the mother of a fair and famous race. Such wives are the best and wisest Zeus grants to men." Yet even after this pretty picture Simonides winds up with a comprehensive condemnation of the female sex : "Zeus made this supreme evil—women: even though they seem to be of good, when one has got one, she becomes a plague."

The spirit of this invective is derived in a great measure *The virtuous wife.* from Hesiod, whose myth of Pandora marked his estimate of women, and whose precepts concerning the choice of a wife must have depressed the Bœotian bachelors with the certainty that nine women out of ten would prove a curse. This is precisely the proportion of bad to good that Simonides establishes. His tenth and virtuous wife is praised because she is industrious and quiet, and the mother of many children. We here get the primitive ideal of the helpmeet for man. Modern theorists would condemn it as the model of a slave. And it is certain that, as Greek civilisation advanced, without a corresponding elevation of the conception of wifehood, the chivalrous sentiment of the Greeks sought other channels than that of sexual love, exalting a form of passionate friendship between men as the real source of heroic action and inspiring thought.[1] The outline traced by Simonides was filled in by subsequent satirists. Susarion, the Comic Poet, makes this grandiloquent proclamation : "Hear, O ye people ! These

---

[1] The inferiority of women was undoubtedly the source of many of the worst faults of the Greek race. Yet it is easy to overestimate the importance of such satires as that of Simonides ; nor would it be fair to take them as expressing the deliberate opinion of the nation. The Jews, who gave a nobler place in social life to women, ascribed the fall of man to Eve. Modern literature again, in spite of Christianity and chivalry, is not wanting in epigrams like the following, ascribed to Leo Battista Alberti : "Levity and inconstancy were given to women as a counterbalance to their perfidy and badness ; for, could woman stick to her purpose, she would destroy all the fair works of man."

are the words of Susarion of Tripodiscus, Philinus' son, of
Megara: Woman is a curse!" Aristophanes in his plays, the
Lysistrata, the *Thesmophoriazusæ*, and the *Ecclesiazusæ*, gives
to the Athenian women all the attributes of the hog, the ape,
the clay, the sea, and the fox; in the *Clouds* he draws the
picture of one who is like the blood-mare; but he does not
hint, even by way of parody, that there existed any bees.
The Greeks never learned the art of making women their
companions in the noblest sense. It must, however, be borne
in mind that the Ionians were less civilised in this respect
than the Dorians, who had a higher regard for the excellences
of women, and allowed them greater liberty.[1] Simonides is
expressing Ionian rather than Dorian sentiments, and at the
same time may be reasonably supposed to be overstraining
them for the sake of a burlesque effect.

Next in date to Simonides among the Iambographers ranks
Hipponax of Ephesus, who flourished about 540 B.C. He too
was an Ionian. The satire which Archilochus had directed
against private enemies was extended, as we have seen, by
Simonides to a whole sex; and thus its purely selfish
character had been considerably modified. But Hipponax
restored it to its primitive function. He used the Iambic as
a weapon of personal attack: and as Archilochus had shot
his arrows against Lycambes and his daughters, so Hipponax
found a butt in Bupalus and Athenis, sculptors of Chios.
These two artists had begun by ridiculing the poet, who was
short and thin and ugly. They seem to have made caricatures
of him, piquing themselves no doubt upon the durability of
the marble in which they worked. But they found more
than their match in Hipponax, whose biting verses are said
to have driven Bupalus to hang himself. Whether this is a
mere echo of the tale of Lycambes remains doubtful; but at
any rate the statues of the sculptor have perished, while the

---

[1] Plutarch's *Life of Cleomenes* contains two historical pictures of heroic
wifehood.

poet's Iambics exist in sufficient force to justify his reputation
among the ancients for having been the most caustic, crabbed,
and sour of satirists. They called him ὁ πικρός (the
pungent), and in their epigrams, made merry over his
traditional bad temper. Leonidas of Tarentum, for instance,
warns travellers not to touch his tomb, lest they should rouse
the sleeping wasp; and Alcæus of Messene says that no ivy,
vine, or rose, should adorn his grave, but only thorns and
thistles.

In order apparently to bring the metre still more within
the sphere of prose and common speech, Hipponax ended his
Iambics with a spondee or a trochee instead of an iambus,
doing thus the utmost violence to the rhythmical structure.
These deformed and mutilated verses were called χωλίαμβοι
or ἴαμβοι σκάζοντες (lame or limping Iambics). They communicate a curious crustiness to the style. The Choliambi
are in poetry what the dwarf or cripple is in human nature.
Here again, by their acceptance of this halting metre, the
Greeks displayed their acute æsthetic sense of propriety,
recognising the harmony which subsists between crabbed
verses and the distorted subjects with which they dealt—the
vices and perversions of humanity—as well as their agreement with the snarling spirit of the satirist. Deformed verse
was suited to deformed morality. Meanwhile it is but just
to Hipponax to record that he appears to have been a sincere
castigator of crime, extravagance, and folly. Without the
sublime perfection and fervid energy of Archilochus, he does
not seem to have shared the unamiable personal qualities of
the greater poet. Two of his lines give a sufficient notion of
his style :—

> δύ' ἡμέραι γυναικός εἰσιν ἥδισται,
> ὅταν γαμῇ τις κἀκφέρῃ τεθνηκυῖαν.

"A woman gives two days of happiness to man, in her bridal
and her burial."

The limping
Iambic
measure.

Greek and
Roman
satire.   The satire which these three Ionians, Archilochus, Simonides, and Hipponax, inaugurated in Greece, was continued by the Attic comic poets. Satire in the Roman and the modern sense of the term never flourished among the Greeks. The life of the Agora, the Ecclesia, and the Theatre, was too complete and free to need the supplement of rhetorical invective intended either for reading or for recitation. Of satirical comments upon individuals and of pasquinades of every kind the Greeks had plenty. We hear, for example, that Alcæus exercised his poetical talent in satirising Pittacus, and one of the most considerable fragments of Anacreon contains a very ludicrous caricature of Artemon, his rival for the affections of a certain yellow-haired Eurypyle. But their satire did not incline to the form which the earlier writers of Iambics had invented. It found its true sphere in the Dorian Comedy of Epicharmus and the Athenian Comedy of Aristophanes, who combined the personalities of Archilochus and the generalities of Simonides in his own consummate work of dramatic art. Among the lost treasures of Greek literature we have to regret few things more Epicharmus. than the plays of the Syracusan Epicharmus, from whom we might have learned directly what now we can only infer—that the Dorians, when uncontrolled by the severe taste of Sparta, indulged a humour for drollery and sarcasm, which, though rougher than that of the Ionians, must have had its own flavour of raciness and fun. Roman satire maintained a strictly moral intention ; *facit indignatio versus* is the motto of Juvenal, while Horace holds the mirror of worldly philosophy to the follies and the vices of his age, and Persius applies the canons of Stoical Ethics to the phenomena of society as he observed them. This is the lead which our modern satirists—the Regnier of France, the Dryden or the Pope of England, have followed. Greek literature furnishes no specimen of this species of composition. Wherever in the Comedies of Aristophanes, or the Dialogues of Lucian, or the Epigrams of the Anthology, we meet with satire, we find the simple motives

of Archilochus and Simonides at work.[1] Personal animosity
gives a barb and a venom to the shaft : or the poet delineates
with more or less of comic wit the social anomalies that have
struck his fancy.   Of serious invective and of moral preaching,
the Greeks, in their satiric art at least, knew nothing.   Plato
himself is only accidentally a satirist in the sense of the term
which we moderns have adopted from the Romans.

  [1] I shall place a study of Herondas in the next volume. He adapted
the Choliambics of Hipponax to subjects which preserved something of
the manner of Sophron in what were called his Mimiambi.

CHAPTER X

THE LYRIC POETS

Various species of Greek lyric poetry.

To compress into a single chapter all that should be said about the Greek lyrical poets is impossible. Yet by eliminating the writers of elegies and iambics, who have been considered separately as gnomic poets and satirists, the field is somewhat narrowed. Simonides of Amorgos, Archilochus, Theognis, Solon, not to mention lesser names, are by this process legitimately excluded. The Æolian lyrists, with Sappho at their head, and the so-called Dorian lyrists, who culminate in Pindar, remain. Casting a glance backwards into the remote shadows of antiquity, we find that lyrical poetry, like all art in Greece, took its origin in connection with primitive Nature-worship. The song of Linus,[1] referred to by Homer in his

---

[1] τοῖσιν δ' ἐν μέσσοισι πάϊς φόρμιγγι λιγείη
ἱμερόεν κιθάριζε· λίνον δ' ὑπὸ καλὸν ἄειδεν
λεπταλέῃ φωνῇ.—*Iliad,* xviii. 569.

" A boy, amid them, from a clear-toned harp
Drew lovely music ; well his liquid voice
The strings accompanied."—*Lord Derby's Trans.*

description of the shield of Achilles, was a lament sung by reapers for the beautiful dead youth who symbolised the decay of summer's prime.[1] In the funeral chant for Adonis, women bewailed the fleeting splendour of the spring; and Hyacinthus, loved and slain by Phœbus, whom the Laconian youths and maidens honoured, was again a type of vernal loveliness deflowered. The Bacchic songs of alternating mirth and sadness, which gave birth, through the Dithyramb, to Tragedy, and through the Comus-hymn, to Comedy, marked the waxing and the waning of successive years, the pulses of the heart of Nature, to which men listened as the months passed over them. In their dim beginnings these elements of Greek poetry are hardly to be distinguished from the dirges and the raptures of Asiatic ceremonial, in which the dance and chant and song were mingled in a vague monotony—generation after generation expressing the same emotions according to traditions handed down from their forefathers. But the Greek genius was endowed with the faculty of distinguishing, differentiating, vitalising, what the Oriental nations left hazy and confused and inert. Therefore with the very earliest stirrings of conscious art in Greece we remark a powerful specialising tendency. Articulation succeeds to mere interjectional utterance. Separate forms of music and of metre are devoted, with the unerring instinct of a truly æsthetic race, to the expression of the several moods and passions of the soul. An unconscious psychology leads by intuitive analysis to the creation of distinct branches of composition, each accurately adapted to its special purpose.

[1] Bergk (*Poetæ Lyrici Græci*, 3 vols., Leipsic, 1866) gives an old Greek Linus-song on p. 1297 :—

> "O Linus, thee the gods did grace :
> For unto thee they gave, most dear,
> First among men the song to raise
> With shrill voice sounding high and clear ;
> And Phœbus thee in anger slays,
> And Muses mourn around thy bier."

Importance of form in Greek poetic art.

From the very first commencement of their literature, the Greeks thus determined separate styles and established critical canons, which, though empirically and spontaneously formed, were based on real relations between the moral and æsthetical sides of art, between feeling and expression, substance and form. The Hexameter was consecrated to epical narrative; the Elegy was confined to songs of lament or meditation; the Iambic assumed a satiric character. To have written a narrative in Iambics or a satire in Hexameters would have been odious to Greek taste: the stately march of the Dactylic metre seemed unfit for snarling and invective; the quick flight of the Iambic did not carry weight enough or volume to sustain a lengthy narrative. In the same way the infinite divisions of lyrical poetry had all their own peculiar proprieties. How could a poet have bewailed his loves or losses in the stately structure of the Pindaric ode? Conversely, a hymn to Phœbus required more sonorousness and elaboration than the recurring stanzas of the Sapphic or Alcaic offered. It was the business, therefore, of the Greek poet, after duly considering his subject, to select the special form of poetry consecrated by long usage for his particular purpose, to conform his language to some species of music inseparable from that style, and then, within the prescribed limits both of metre and of melody, to exercise his imagination as freely as he could, and to produce novelty. This amount of fixity in the forms of poetry and music arose from the exquisite tact and innate taste of the Greek race. It was far from being a piece of scholastic pedantry or of Chinese conservatism. No; the diction, metre, and music of an elegy or an ode tended to assume a certain form as naturally as the ingredients of a ruby or a sapphire crystallise into a crimson or an azure stone. The discrimination shown by the Greeks in all the technicalities of art remained in full vigour till the decline of their literature. It was not until the Alexandrian age that they began to confound these delicate distinctions, and to use the Idyllic Hexameter for all subjects, whether

narrative, descriptive, elegiac, encomiastic, hymeneal.[1] Then,
and not till then, the Greeks descended to that degradation of
art which prevailed, for instance, in England during what we
call the classic period of our literature. Under the influence
of Dryden and of Pope, an English poet used no metre but
the heroic couplet, whether he were writing a play, an epigram,
a satire, an epic, an eclogue, an elegy, or a didactic epistle;
thus losing all elasticity of style, all the force which appropriate
form communicates to thought.

To catalogue the minute subdivisions of the art of lyric
poetry in Greece, to show how wisely their several limits were
prescribed, how firmly adhered to, and to trace the connection
of choral song with all the affairs of public and private life,
would be a task of some magnitude. Colonel Mure, in a well-
known passage, writes:—"From Olympus down to the work-
shop or the sheepfold, from Jove and Apollo to the wandering
mendicant, every rank and degree of the Greek community,
divine or human, had its own proper allotment of poetical
celebration. The gods had their hymns, nomes, pæans,
dithyrambs; great men had their encomia and epinikia; the
votaries of pleasure their erotica and symposiaca; the mourner
his threnodia and elegies; the vine-dresser had his epilenia;
the herdsmen their bucolica; even the beggar his eiresione
and chelidonisma." Lyrical poetry in Greece was not produced, like poetry in modern times, for the student, by
men who find they have a taste for versifying. It was
intimately intertwined with actual life, and was so indispensable
that every town had its professional poets and choruses, just
as every church in Europe now has its organist, of greater or
less pretension. The mass of lyrical poetry which must have

Abundance of Greek lyric verse.

---

[1] Many poems of the Syracusan Idyllists are valuable historically as
adaptations of the Hexameter to subjects essentially lyrical. In the
Adoniazusæ, the Epithalamium Helenæ, Bion's Lament for Adonis, and
Moschus' Lament for Bion, etc., we trace a lyrical inspiration overlaid
by the Idyllic form. Theocritus must have worked on the lines of old
choral and dramatic poetry.

existed in Greece was probably enormous. We can only compare it to the quantity of church music that exists in Germany and Italy, in MS. and print, good, bad, and indifferent, unknown and unexplored, so voluminous that no one ventures to sift it or reduce it to order. Of this large mass we possess the fragments. Just as the rocky islands of the Ægean Archipelago testify to the existence of a submerged tract of mountain heights and valleys, whose summits alone appear above the waves, so the odes of Pindar, the waifs and strays of Sappho, Simonides, and others, are evidences of the loss we have sustained. They prove that beneath the ocean of time and oblivion remain for ever buried stores of poetry, which might have been sufficient to form the glory of a literature less rich in masterpieces than the Greek. To collect the fragments, to piece them together, to ponder over them until their scattered indications offer some suggestion of the whole which has been lost, is all that remains for the modern student. Like the mutilated marbles of Praxiteles, chips broken off from bas-reliefs and statues, which are disinterred from the ruins of Rome or Herculaneum, the minutest portions of the Greek lyrists have their value. We must be thankful for any two words of Sappho that survive in authentic juxtaposition, for any hemistich that may be veritably styled a relic of " some tender-hearted scroll of pure Simonides."

Disastrous fate of the Greek lyrists. Chance has wrought fantastically with these relics. The lyrists, even in classical days, fell comparatively early into neglect. They were too condensed in language, too difficult in style, too sublime in imagination for the pedants of the later Empire. Long before its close, Greek literature was oppressed with its own wealth; in the words of Livy, *magnitudine laboravit suâ*. Taste, too, began to change ; sophistic treatises, idyllic verses, novelettes in prose, neat epigrams, usurped upon the grander forms of composition. The stagnation, again, of civic life under imperial sway proved unfavourable to the composition of national odes and to choric celebrations in

which whole peoples took a part. So disdainful in her alms-
giving has Fortune been, that she has only flung to us the
Epinikian odes of Pindar; while his hymns to the gods, his
processional chants, and his funeral dirges, are lost. Young
Athens, Alexandria, and Byzantium cared, we may conceive,
for poems which shed lustre on athletic sports and horse-
racing. Trainers, boxers, riders, chariot-drivers — all the
muscular section of the public—had some interest in bygone
Pythian or Olympian victories. But who sought to preserve
the antiquated hymns to Phoebus and to Zeus, when the
rites of Isis and Serapis and the Phrygian mother were in
vogue? The outspoken boldness of the Erotic and Satiric
lyrists stood them in bad stead. When Theodora was exhibiting
her naked charms in the arena, who could commend the study
of Anacreon in the schoolroom? Degeneracy of public morals
and prudery of literary taste go not unfrequently together.
Therefore, the emperor Julian proscribed Archilochus; and
what Julian proscribed, the Christians sought to extirpate.
To destroy an ode of Sappho was a good work. Consequently,
we possess no complete edition of even a section of the works
of any lyrist except Pindar: what remains of the others has
been preserved in the works of critics, anecdote-mongers, and
grammarians; who cite tantalising passages to prove a rule in
syntax, to illustrate a legend or a custom, to exemplify a
canon of taste. Embedded in ponderous prose, these splintered
jewels escaped the iconoclastic zeal of the monks. Thanks be
to Athenæus above all men (the author of an imaginary
dialogue in fifteen bulky books on every topic of Greek
antiquity), to Longinus, to Philostratus, to Maximus Tyrius, to
Plutarch the moralist, to Stobæus, to Hephæstion, to Herodian,
and to the host of other Dryasdusts from whose heaps of
shot rubbish Bergk and his predecessors have sorted out the
fragments of extinguished stars! As a masterpiece of patient,
self-denying, scientific, exhaustive investigation, the three
volumes of Bergk are unrivalled. Every author of antiquity

has been laid under contribution, subjected to critical analysis, compared and confronted with his fellow-witnesses. The result, reduced to the smallest possible compass, yields a small glittering heap of pure gold-dust, a little handful of auriferous deposit sifted from numberless river-beds, crushed from huge masses of unfertile quartz. In our admiration of the scholar's ingenuity, we almost forget our sorrow for so much irreparable waste.

Various species of ; choral poetry.

Before proceeding to consider the justice of the time-honoured division of Greek Lyrics into Æolian and Dorian, it will be well to pass in review a few of the principal classes into which Greek choral poetry may be divided. Only thus can any idea of its richness and variety be formed. The old Homeric ὕμνοι, or hymns dedicated to special deities, were intended to be sung at festivals and rhapsodical contests. Their technical name was Proëmia, or preludes—preludes, that is, to a longer recitation ; and on this account, as they were chanted by the poet himself, they were written in hexameters. With them, therefore, we have nothing here to do. Processional hymns, or Prosodia, on the contrary, were strictly lyrical, and constituted a large portion of the poetry of Pindar, Alcman, and Stesichorus. They were sung at solemn festivals by troops of men and maidens walking, crowned with olive, myrtle, bay, or oleander, to the shrines. Their style varied with the occasion and the character of the deity to whom they were addressed. When Hecuba led her maidens in dire necessity to the shrine of Pallas, the Prosodion was solemn and earnest. When Sophocles, with lyre in hand, headed the chorus round the trophy of Salamis, it was victorious and martial. If we wish to present to our mind a picture of these processional ceremonies, we may study the frieze of the Parthenon preserved among the Elgin Marbles. Those long lines of maidens and young men, with baskets in their hands, with flowers and palm-branches, with censers and sacred emblems, are marching to the sound of flutes and

lyres, and to the stately rhythms of antiphonal chanting.
When they reach the altar of the god, a halt is made; the
libations are poured; and now the music changes to a solemn
and spondaic measure—for the term spondaic seems to be
derived from the fact that the libation-hymn was composed
in a grave and heavy metre of full feet. Hephæstion has
preserved a spondaic verse of Terpander which illustrates this
rhythm :—

> σπένδωμεν ταῖς Μνάμας
> παισὶν Μώσαις
> καὶ τῷ Μωσάρχῳ
> Λατοῦς υἱεῖ.[1]

In the age of Greek decadence the honours of the *The Pros-*
Prosodion were sometimes paid to men. Athenæus gives this *odion.*
lively description of the procession which greeted Demetrius
Poliorketes : "When Demetrius returned from Leucadia and
Corcyra to Athens, the Athenians received him not only with
incense and garlands and libations, but they even sent out
processional choruses, and greeted him with Ithyphallic hymns
and dances : stationed by his chariot-wheels, they sang and
danced and chanted that he alone was a real god; the rest were
sleeping, or were on a journey, or did not exist; they called
him son of Poseidon and Aphrodite, eminent for beauty,
universal in his goodness to mankind; then they prayed and
besought and supplicated him like a god." The hymn which
they sang may be read in Bergk, vol. iii. p. 1314. It is one
of the most interesting relics of antiquity.[2]

For the sake of its rare and curious metre alternating

---

[1] "Pour we libations to Memory's daughters, the Muses, and to the
Muse-leading son of Leto."

[2] Plutarch records with just indignation the honours of this sort paid
by Aratus to Antigonus : "He offered sacrifices, called Antigonea, in
honour of Antigonus, and sang pæans himself, with a garland on his head,
to the praise of *a wasted, consumptive Macedonian.*"—*Life of Cleomenes.*
The words in italics strongly express a true Greek sense of disgust for the
barbarian and the weakling.

the Iambic and Trochaic rhythms, I have faced the difficulties of translation, and have ventured on the following version :—

> " See how the mightiest gods, and best-beloved,
>   Towards our town are winging !
>   For lo, Demeter and Demetrius
>   This glad day is bringing !
>   She to perform her Daughter's solemn rites ;
>   Mystic pomps attend her :
>   He, joyous as a god should be, and blithe,
>   Comes with laughing splendour.
>   Show forth your triumph !   Friends all, troop around !
>   Let him shine above you !
>   Be you the stars to circle him with love ;
>   He's the sun to love you.
>   Hail, offspring of Poseidon, powerful god,
>   Child of Aphrodite !
>   The other deities keep far from earth ;
>   Have no ears, though mighty ;
>   They are not, or they will not hear us wail :
>   Thee our eye beholdeth ;
>   Not wood, not stone, but living, breathing, real,
>   Thee our prayer enfoldeth.
>   First give us peace !   Give, dearest, for Thou canst ;
>   Thou art Lord and Master !
>   The Sphinx, who not on Thebes, but on all Greece
>   Swoops to gloat and pasture ;
>   The Ætolian, he who sits upon his rock,
>   Like that old disaster ;
>   He feeds upon our flesh and blood, and we
>   Can no longer labour ;
>   For it was ever thus the Ætolian thief
>   Preyed upon his neighbour ;
>   Him punish Thou, or if not Thou, then send
>   Œdipus to harm him,
>   Who'll cast this Sphinx down from his cliff of pride,
>   Or to stone will charm him."

A special kind of prosodia were the Parthenia, or processional hymns of maidens ; such, for example, as the Athenian girls sang to Pallas while they climbed the staircase of the

Parthenon. Aristophanes has presented us with a beautiful Parthenia.
example of antiphonal Parthenia at the end of his *Lysistrata*,
where choruses of Athenian and Spartan girls sing turn and
turn about in rivalry. Alcman won his laurels at Sparta by
the composition of this kind of hymn. A fragment (Bergk,
p. 842) only remains to show what they were like: "No
more, ye honey-voiced, sweet-singing maidens, can my limbs
support me: oh, oh, that I were a cerylus, who skims the
flower of the sea with halcyons, of a dauntless heart, the sea-
blue bird of spring!" Such Parthenia, when addressed to
Phœbus, were called Daphnephorica; for the maidens carried
laurel-branches to his shrine. A more charming picture
cannot be conceived than that which is presented to our
fancy by these white-robed virgins, each with her rod of bay
and crown of laurel-leaves, ascending the marble steps of the
temple of the Dorian god. John Lyly, who had imbibed the
spirit of Greek life, has written a hymn, "Sing to Apollo,
god of day!" which might well have been used at such a
festival.

The Prosodia of which we have been speaking were ad- Pæan and Hyporchem.
dressed to all the gods. But there were other choric hymns
with special names, consecrated to the service of particular
deities. Of this sort was the Pæan, sung to Phœbus in his
double character of a victorious and a healing god. The
Pæan was both a song of war and of peace; it was the
proper accompaniment of the battle and the feast. In like
manner the Hyporchem, which, as its name implies, was
always accompanied by a dance, originally formed a portion
of the cult of Phœbus. The chorus described in the *Iliad*,
xviii. 590, and the glorious pageant of Olympus celebrated
in the Hymn to Apollo, 186, were, technically speaking,
Hyporchems. As the Pæan and the Hyporchem were originally consecrated to Apollo, so the Dithyramb and the Phallic
hymn belonged to Dionysus. The Dithyramb never lost the
tempestuous and enthusiastic character of Bacchic revelry;

but in time it grew from being a wild celebration of the
mystic sufferings of Bacchus into the sublime art of Tragedy.
Arion forms the point of this transition. He seems to have
thrown a greater reality of passion and dramatic action into
his choruses, which led to the introduction of dialogue, and
so by degrees to Tragedy proper. Meanwhile the Dithyramb,
as a tumultuous choric song, retained its individual existence.
As Arion had devoted his genius to the cultivation of the
Tragic or Cyclic chorus, Lasos, the master of Pindar, stamped
his own style upon the Dithyrambic ode as it continued to
be used at festive meetings. Every town in Greece had its
chorodidascalus, a functionary whom Aristophanes ridicules
in the person of Kinesias in the *Birds*.[1] He is introduced
warbling the wildest, windiest nonsense, and entreating to
have a pair of wings given him that he may chase his airy
ideas through the sky. The Phallic Hymn, from which in
like manner Comedy took its origin, was a mad outpour-
ing of purely animal exultation. Here the wine-god was
celebrated as the pleasure-loving, drunken, lascivious deity.
Aristophanes, again, our truest source of information respecting all the details of Greek life, supplies us with an instance
of one of these songs, and of the simple rites which accompanied its performance.[2] In the *Frogs*, also, the Master of
Comedy has presented us with an elaborate series of Bacchic
hymns.[3] Here the Phallic and Satyric element is combined
with something of the grandeur of the Dithyrambic Ode ;
the curious mixture of sarcasm, obscenity, and splendid
poetry offers a striking instance of Greek religious feeling,
so incomprehensible to modern minds. It is greatly to be
regretted that our information respecting the Dithyramb and
the Phallic Chorus has to be obtained from a dramatic poet
rather than from any perfect specimens of these compositions.

---

[1] See Frere, vol. ii. pp. 200, 201.

[2] See Tr. of *Acharnians*, Frere, vol. ii. p. 17.

[3] Frere's *Translation*, vol. ii. pp. 241-245.

Bergk's Collection, full as it is, yields nothing but hints and fragments.[1]

Passing to the Lyrics, which were connected with circum- Epinikia on
contests at
the games.
stances of human life, the first to be mentioned are Epinikia,
or odes sung in honour of victors at the games. Of these,
in the splendid series of Pindar and in the fragments of
Simonides, we have abundant examples. We are also able
to trace their development from the simple exclamation of
τήνελλα ὦ καλλίνικε[2] (Huzza ! thou conquering hero !), the
composition of which was ascribed to Archilochus, and which
Pindar looked back upon with scornful triumph. Indeed, in
his hands, to use the phrase of Wordsworth, "the thing
became a trumpet, whence he blew soul-animating strains."
The Epinikian Ode was the most costly and splendid flower
in the victor's wreath. Pindar compares the praise which
he pours forth for Diagoras the Rhodian to noblest wine foaming in the golden goblet, which a father gives to honour his
son-in-law, the prime and jewel of his treasure-house. The
occasions on which such odes were sung were various—either
when the victor was being crowned, or when he was returning
to his native city, or by torchlight during the evening of the
victorious day, or at a banquet after his reception in his
home. On one of these occasions the poet would appear
with his trained band of singers and musicians, and, taking
his stand by the altar of the god to whom the victor offered
a thanksgiving sacrifice, would guide the choric stream of
song through strophe and antistrophe and epode, in sonorous
labyrinths of eulogy and mythological allusion—prayer,
praise, and admonition mingling with the fumes of intoxicating poetry. Of all these occasions the most striking must
have been the commemoration of a victory in the temple of
Zeus at Altis, near Olympia, by moonlight. The contest has

---

[1] See, however, the interesting archaic hymns to Dionysus, pp. 1299,
1300.

[2] Bergk, p. 716 ; Pindar, *Olymp.* ix. 1.

taken place during the day; and the olive wreath has been placed upon the head, say of Myronides, from Thebes. Having rested from his labours, after the bath and the banquet, crowned with his victorious garland and with fillets bound about his hair, he stands surrounded by his friends. Zeus, in ivory and gold, looks down from his marble pedestal. Through the open roof shines a moon of the south, glancing aslant on statue and column and carved bas-relief; while below, the red glare of torches, paling her silver, flickers with fitful crimson on the glowing faces of young men. Then swells the choral hymn, with praise of Myronides and praise of Thebes, and stormy flights of fancy shooting beyond sun and stars. At its close follow libation, dedication, hands upraised in prayer to Zeus. Then the trampling of sandalled feet upon the marble floor, the procession with songs still sounding to the temple-gate, and on a sudden, lo! the full moon, the hills, and plain, and solemn night of stars. The band disperses, and the Comus succeeds to the thanksgiving.

Threnoi or funeral hymns.

As a contrast to the Epinikia we may take the different kinds of Threnoi, or funeral songs. The most primitive was called Epikedeion, a dirge or coronach, improvised by women over the bodies of the dead.[1] The lamentations of Helen and Andromache for Hector, and of the slave-girls for Patroclus, are Homeric instances of this species. Euripides imitates them in his tragedies—in the dirge sung by Antigone, for instance in the *Phœnissæ*, and in the wailings of Hecuba for Astyanax in the *Troades*. A different kind of Threnos were the songs of Linus, Hyacinth, Adonis, and others, to which I have already alluded in the beginning of this chapter. The finest extant specimen of this sort is Bion's Lament for

---

[1] It is interesting to observe that this custom of the funeral dirge, improvised with wild inspiration by women, has been preserved almost to the present day in Corsica. A collection of these coronachs, called *Voceri* in the language of the island, was published in 1855 at Bastia, by Cesare Fabiani.

Adonis, which, however, was composed in the Idyllic age, when the hexameter had been substituted for the richer and more splendid lyric metres. A third class of Threnos consisted of complex choral hymns composed by poets like Simonides or Pindar, to be sung at funeral solemnities. Many of our most precious lyric fragments, those which embody philosophical reflections on life and dim previsions of another world, belong to dirges of this elaborate kind.

Marriage festivals offered another occasion for lyric poetry. *Hymeneals.* The Hymeneal, sung during the wedding ceremony, the Epithalamium, chanted at the house of the bridegroom, and many other species, have been defined by the grammarians. Unfortunately we possess nothing but the merest *débris* of any true Greek ode of this kind. Sappho's are the best. We have to study the imitations of her style in Catullus, the marriage chorus at the end of the *Birds* of Aristophanes, and the Epithalamium of Helen by Theocritus, in order to form a remote conception of what a Sapphic marriage chorus might have been. In banquet songs we are more fortunate. *Drinking songs.* Abundant are the Parœnia of Alcæus, Anacreon, Theognis, and others. Scolia or catches, so called from their irregular metrical structure, were also in vogue at banquets; and of these popular songs a sufficient number are preserved. A drunken passage in the works of Aristophanes brings before us after a lively fashion the ceremonies with which the Scolion and the wine-cup circled the symposium together.[1] Of all these catches the most celebrated in ancient days was the panegyric of Harmodius and Aristogeiton, attributed to Callistratus. As I have the opportunity of printing from MS. a translation of this song by the late Professor Conington, I will introduce it here :—

> " In a wreath of myrtle I'll wear my glaive,
> Like Harmodius and Aristogeiton brave,

---

[1] Translated by Mitchell, vol. ii. p. 282, in his *Dicast turned Gentleman.*

> Who, striking the tyrant down,
> Made Athens a freeman's town.

> "Harmodius, our darling, thou art not dead !
> Thou liv'st in the isles of the blest, 'tis said,
> With Achilles first in speed,
> And Tydides Diomede.

> "In a wreath of myrtle I'll wear my glaive,
> Like Harmodius and Aristogeiton brave,
> When the twain on Athena's day
> Did the tyrant Hipparchus slay.

> "For aye shall your fame in the land be told,
> Harmodius and Aristogeiton bold,
> Who, striking the tyrant down,
> Made Athens a freeman's town."

Scolia. The whole collection of Scolia in Bergk (pp. 1287-1296) is full of interest, since these simple and popular songs carry us back more freshly than elaborate poems to the life of the Greeks. One of these, attributed to Simonides, sums up the qualities which a Greek most desired :—

> ὑγιαίνειν μὲν ἄριστον ἀνδρὶ θνατῷ,
> δεύτερον δὲ φυὰν καλὸν γενέσθαι,
> τὸ τρίτον δὲ πλουτεῖν ἀδόλως,
> καὶ τὸ τέταρτον ἡβᾶν μετὰ τῶν φίλων.[1]

Unlike Solomon, when asked what he would take from the Lord as a gift, the Greek poet does not answer Wisdom, but first Health, secondly Beauty, thirdly Wealth untainted by fraud, and fourthly Youth in the society of friends. The sentiment of Beauty being superior to Wealth was subjected to scornful criticism by the Comic dramatists. Still, it may be illustrated from the following tirade against riches in a lyrical fragment ascribed to Timocreon :—

---

[1] "To be in health is the best thing for mortal man ; the next best to be of form and nature beautiful ; the third, to enjoy wealth gotten without fraud ; and the fourth to be in youth's bloom among friends."

> " Would, blind Wealth, that thou hadst been
> Ne'er on land or ocean seen,
> Nowhere on this upper earth !
> Hell's black stream that gave thee birth
> Is the proper haunt for thee,
> Cause of all man's misery ! "

The last line of the Simonidean quatrain, celebrating the charm of youthful society, was expanded very beautifully in another Scolion :—

> σύν μοι πῖνε, συνήβα, συνέρα, συστεφανηφόρει,
> σύν μοι μαινομένῳ μαίνεο, σὺν σώφρονι σωφρόνει :

"Drink with me, be young with me, love with me, wear crowns with me, when I am mad be mad with me, be wise with me when I am wise." The verb συνηβᾶν (to enjoy the bloom of youth together) is almost untranslatable. Of another kind is the Scolion of Hybrias the Cretan, translated thus into English verse by Thomas Campbell :—

> " My wealth's a burly spear and brand,
> And a right good shield of hides untanned,
> Which on my arm I buckle :
> With these I plough, I reap, I sow,
> With these I make the sweet vintage flow,
> And all around me truckle.

> " But your wights that take no pride to wield
> A massy spear and well-made shield,
> Nor joy to draw the sword :
> Oh, I bring those heartless, hapless drones,
> Down in a trice on their marrow bones,
> To call me king and lord."

This catch brings before our eyes in a very lively picture the lawless Freiherr of early Dorian barbarism. Another species of the Scolion is more sentimental : " Would that I were a fair lyre of ivory, and that fair boys bore me to the Bacchic Choir; would that I were a fair, new, and mighty golden jar, and that a fair woman bore me with a pure heart."

Again we find moral precepts in these catches. "Whoso betrayeth not a friend hath great honour among men and gods, according to my mind."

Pindar's ode on Theoxenos. While on the subject of Scolia, it will not do to pass over the most splendid specimen we have in this order of composition. It is a fragment from Pindar (Bergk, p. 327), to translate which, I feel, is profanation :—

> " O soul, 'tis thine in season meet,
>   To pluck of love the blossom sweet,
>   When hearts are young :
>   But he who sees the blazing beams,
>   The light that from *that* forehead streams,
>   And is not stung ;—
>   Who is not storm-tost with desire,—
>   Lo ! he, I ween, with frozen fire,
>   Of adamant or stubborn steel,
>   Is forged in his cold heart that cannot feel.
>
> " Disowned, dishonoured, and denied
>   By Aphrodite glittering-eyed,
>   He either toils
>   All day for gold, a sordid gain,
>   Or bent beneath a woman's reign,
>   In petty broils,
>   Endures her insolence, a drudge,
>   Compelled the common path to trudge ;
>   But I, apart from this disease,
>   Wasting away like wax of holy bees,
>
> " Which the sun's splendour wounds, do pine,
>   Whene'er I see the young-limbed bloom divine
>   Of boys.   Lo ! look you well ; for here in Tenedos,
>   Grace and Persuasion dwell in young Theoxenos."

Of the many different kinds of lyric poetry consecrated to love and intended for recitation by single musicians, it is not possible to give a strict account. That the Greeks cultivated the serenade is clear from a passage in the *Ecclesiazusæ* of Aristophanes, which contains a graceful though gross specimen of this kind of song.

To illustrate this species I have attempted to compose an An Attic
irregularly - rhythmed ode, which might have been sung by   serenade.
an Athenian lover beneath the window of his beloved. It
is conceived in the style of the serenade from Aristophanes
alluded to above :—

" Arise ! arise !
See how the starry skies
Keep breathing through the night their breath of love !
The nightingale above,
In myrtle boughs
Close-shrouded, sleepeth not but sings ;
And on the faint air flings
The delicate rose her perfume.   Rouse
From slumber, darling, see,
I stand and wait for thee !
Come to thy lattice ; from thy curtained bed
Arise, and shed
Thy light of brightest eyes upon my head !

" Shine forth, my golden sun,
My little lovely one !
Sweet bud of beauty, nursling of heaven's grace !
Thou fairest face
Of all that bloom upon the smiling earth !
Why wilt thou shun
These words that wake thee to a happier birth,
Thou thoughtless one ?

" Nay, slay me not ! but rise !
And let thy living eyes
Be to me as the light
Which envious night
For all her clouds and shadows cannot chase away !
It is Melanthius cries :
Arise ! arise !
And beam upon him with thy spirit's day !
Nay, ere he dies,
Be pitiful, and ease
The languor of his love, Endiades ! "

The children's songs (Bergk, 1303-1307) about flowers,

tortoises, and hobgoblins are too curiously illustrative of Greek manners not to merit a passing notice, nor can I here omit a translation of the only Swallow - song preserved to us. Athenæus, to whom we owe this curious relic, localises the Chelidonisma in Rhodes, referring it particularly to the district of Lindus.[1] In springtime the children went round the town, collecting doles and presents from house to house, and singing as they went :—

> " She is here, she is here, the swallow !
> Fair seasons bringing, fair years to follow !
>> Her belly is white,
>> Her back black as night !
>> From your rich house
>> Roll forth to us
>> Tarts, wine, and cheese :
>> Or if not these,
>> Oatmeal and barley-cake
>> The swallow deigns to take.
> What shall we have ? or must we hence away ?
> Thanks, if you give ; if not, we'll make you pay !
>> The house-door hence we'll carry ;
>> Nor shall the lintel tarry ;
>> From hearth and home your wife we'll rob ;
>> She is so small,
>> To take her off will be an easy job !
> Whate'er you give, give largess free !
> Up ! open, open to the swallow's call !
> No grave old men, but merry children we ! "

After this lengthy, but far from exhaustive enumeration of the kinds and occasions of lyrical poetry in Greece, we may turn to consider the different parts played in their cultivation by the several chief families of Hellas. It is remarkable that all the great writers of elegies and iambics were Ionians ; Theognis of Megara is the only Dorian whose genuine poems are celebrated ; and against his we have to set the bulk of Solon, Mimnermus, Phocylides, Callinus, and Tyrtæus, all

[1] Athen. lib. viii. 360.

Ionians.[1] Not a single Dorian poet seems to have composed
iambics, the rigid discipline and strong sense of decorum in
a Dorian state probably rendering the cultivation of satire
impossible. We are told that the Spartans would not even
suffer Archilochus to lodge as a stranger among them. But
when we turn to lyric poetry—to the poetry of stanzas and
strophes—the two other families of the Greeks, the Æolians
and the Dorians, take the lead. As a Dorian was exceptional
among the elegists, so now an Ionian will be comparatively
rare among the lyrists. So great was the æsthetical conservatism of the Greeks that throughout their history their
primitive distinctions of dialect are never lost sight of. When
the Athenians developed Tragedy, they wrote their iambics in
pure Attic, but they preserved a Dorian tone in their choruses.
The epic hexameter and the elegy, on the other hand, retained an Ionian character to the last.

The paths struck out by the Æolians and Dorians in the
domain of lyric poetry were so different as to justify us
in speaking of two distinct species. When Milton, in the
Paradise Regained, catalogued the poetical achievements of the
Greeks, he assigned their true place to these two species in
the line—

> " Æolian charms and Dorian lyric odes."

The poets and poetesses of the Ægean Islands cultivated a
rapid and effusive style, polishing their passionate stanzas so
exquisitely that they well deserve the name of charms. The
Dorian poets, inspired by a graver and more sustained imagination, composed long and complex odes for the celebration of
gods and heroes. The Æolian singer dwelt on his own joys
and sorrows; the Dorian bard addressed some deity, or told
the tales of demigods and warriors. The Æolian chanted his
stanzas to the lyre or flute; the Dorian trained a chorus, who
gave utterance to his verse in dance and song.

Marginal note: Two species of lyric— Æolian and Dorian.

---

[1] This begs the question of the nationality of Tyrtæus, who, according
to antique tradition, was of Attic origin, but who writes like a Spartan.

Though the Æolians were the eldest family of the Hellenic stock, their language retaining more than any other dialect the primitive character of the Greek tongue, yet they never rose to such historical importance as the Dorians and Ionians. Geographically they were scattered in such a way as to have no definite centre. We find Æolians in Elis, in Bœotia, in Lesbos, and on the Asian sea-coast south of the Troad. But in course of time the Æolians of Elis and Bœotia were almost identified with the Dorians as allies of Sparta, while the Æolians of Lesbos and Asia merged themselves in the Athenian empire. Politically, mentally, and morally, they showed less activity than their cousins of the blood of Dorus and Ion. They produced no lawgivers like Lycurgus and Solon : they had no metropolis like Sparta and Athens ; they played no prominent part in the struggle with Persia, or in the Peloponnesian war. In the later days of Greece, Thebes, when Dorised by contact with the Spartans, for a short time headed Greece, and flourished with brief splendour. But it would not be accurate to give to the Æolian character the credit of the fame of Thebes at that advanced period. Yet, for a certain space of time, the Æolians occupied the very foreground of Greek literature, and blazed out with a brilliance of lyrical splendour that has never been surpassed. There seems to have been something passionate and intense in their temperament, which made the emotions of the Dorian and the Ionian feeble by comparison. Lesbos, the centre of Æolian culture, was the island of overmastering passions : the personality of the Greek race burned there with a fierce and steady flame of concentrated feeling. The energies which the Ionians divided between pleasure, politics, trade, legislation, science, and the arts, and which the Dorians turned to war and statecraft and social economy, were restrained by the Æolians within the sphere of individual emotions, ready to burst forth volcanically. Nowhere in any age of Greek history, or in any part of Hellas, did the love of physical beauty, the sensibility to radiant scenes of nature, the Lesbos. consuming fervour of personal feeling, assume such grand proportions and receive so illustrious an expression as they did in Lesbos. At first this passion blossomed into the most exquisite lyrical poetry that the world has known : this was the flower-time of the Æolians, their brief and brilliant spring. But the fruit it bore was bitter and rotten. Lesbos became a byword for corruption. The passions which for a moment had flamed into the gorgeousness of Art, burning their envelope of words and images, remained a mere furnace of sensuality, from which no expression of the divine in human life could be expected. In this the Lesbian poets were not unlike the Provençal troubadours, who made a literature of Love, or the Venetian painters, who based their art upon the beauty of colour, the voluptuous charms of the flesh. In each case the motive of enthusiastic passion sufficed to produce a dazzling result. But as soon as its freshness was exhausted there was nothing left for Art to live on, and mere decadence to sensuality ensued.

Several circumstances contributed to aid the development Æolian social of lyric poetry in Lesbos. The customs of the Æolians customs. permitted more social and domestic freedom than was common in Greece. Æolian women were not confined to the harem like Ionians, or subjected to the rigorous discipline of the Spartans. While mixing freely with male society, they were highly educated, and accustomed to express their senti- ments to an extent unknown elsewhere in history—until, indeed, the present time. The Lesbian ladies applied them- selves successfully to literature. They formed clubs for the cultivation of poetry and music. They studied the arts of beauty, and sought to refine metrical forms and diction. Nor did they confine themselves to the scientific side of art. Un- restrained by public opinion, and passionate for the beautiful, they cultivated their senses and emotions, and indulged their wildest passions. All the luxuries and elegances of life which

The Lesbian poetesses.

that climate and the rich valleys of Lesbos could afford, were at their disposal; exquisite gardens, where the rose and hyacinth spread perfume; river-beds ablaze with the oleander and wild pomegranate; olive-groves and fountains, where the cyclamen and violet flowered with feathery maiden-hair; pine-tree-shadowed coves, where they might bathe in the calm of a tideless sea; fruits such as only the southern sun and sea-wind can mature; marble cliffs, starred with jonquil and anemone in spring, aromatic with myrtle and lentisk and samphire and wild rosemary through all the months; nightingales that sang in May; temples dim with dusky gold and bright with ivory; statues and frescoes of heroic forms. In such scenes as these the Lesbian poets lived, and thought of Love. When we read their poems, we seem to have the perfumes, colours, sounds, and lights of that luxurious land distilled in verse. Nor was a brief but biting winter wanting to give tone to their nerves, and, by contrast with the summer, to prevent the palling of so much luxury on sated senses. The voluptuousness of Æolian poetry is not like that of Persian or Arabian art. It is Greek in its self-restraint, proportion, tact. We find nothing burdensome in its sweetness. All is so rhythmically and sublimely ordered in the poems of Sappho that supreme art lends solemnity and grandeur to the expression of unmitigated passion.

Sappho's poetry.

The world has suffered no greater literary loss than the loss of Sappho's poems. So perfect are the smallest fragments preserved in Bergk's Collection—the line, for example (p. 890), ἦρος ἄγγελος ἱμερόφωνος ἀήδων,[1] which Ben Jonson fancifully translated, " the dear good angel of the spring, the nightingale "—that we muse in a sad rapture of astonishment

---

[1] Compare Simonides (Bergk, vol. iii. p. 1143) :—

> ἄγγελε κλυτὰ ἔαρος ἁδυόδμου,
> κυανέα χελιδοῖ.

> "Blithe angel of the perfume-breathing spring,
> Dark-vested swallow."

to think what the complete poems must have been. Among the ancients Sappho enjoyed a unique renown. She was called "The Poetess," as Homer was called "The Poet." Aristotle quoted without question a judgment that placed her in the same rank as Homer and Archilochus. Plato in the *Phœdrus* mentioned her as the tenth Muse. Solon, hearing one of her poems, prayed that he might not see death till he had learned it. Strabo speaks of her genius with religious awe. Longinus cites her love-ode as a specimen of poetical sublimity. The epigrammatists call her Child of Aphrodite and Erôs, nursling of the Graces and Persuasion, pride of Hellas, peer of Muses, companion of Apollo. Nowhere is a hint whispered that her poetry was aught but perfect. As far as we can judge, these praises were strictly just. Of all the poets of the world, of all the illustrious artists of all literatures, Sappho is the one whose every word has a peculiar and unmistakable perfume, a seal of absolute perfection and inimitable grace. In her art she was unerring. Even Archilochus seems commonplace when compared with her exquisite rarity of phrase.

About her life—her brother Charaxus, her daughter Cleis, her rejection of Alcæus and her suit to Phaon, her love for Atthis and Anactoria, her leap from the Leucadian cliff—we know so very little, and that little is so confused with mythology and turbid with the scandal of the comic poets, that it is not worth while to rake up once again the old materials for hypothetical conclusions. There is enough of heart-devouring passion in Sappho's own verse without the legends of Phaon and the cliff of Leucas. The reality casts all fiction into the shade; for nowhere, except, perhaps, in some Persian or Provençal love-songs, can be found more ardent expressions of overmastering emotion. Whether addressing the maidens, whom even in Elysium, as Horace says, Sappho could not forget; or embodying the profounder yearnings of an intense soul after beauty, which has never on earth existed, but which

Her biography.

inflames the hearts of noblest poets, robbing their eyes of sleep and giving them the bitterness of tears to drink—these dazzling fragments—

> "Which still, like sparkles of Greek fire,
> Burn on through time and ne'er expire"

are the ultimate and finished forms of passionate utterance, diamonds, topazes, and blazing rubies, in which the fire of the soul is crystallised for ever. Adequately to translate Sappho was beyond the power of even Catullus: that love-ode, which Longinus called, "not one passion, but a congress of passions," and which a Greek physician copied into his book of diagnoses as a compendium of all the symptoms of corroding emotion, appears but languid in its Latin dress of "Ille mi par." Far less has any modern poet succeeded in the task: Rossetti, who deals so skilfully with Dante and Villon, is comparatively tame when he approaches Sappho. Instead of attempting, therefore, to interpret for English readers the charm of Sappho's style,[1] it is best to refer to pp. 874-924 of Bergk, where every vestige that is left of her is shrined.

Alcæus.   Beside Sappho, Alcæus pales. His drinking-songs and war-songs have indeed great beauty; but they are not to be named in the same breath, for perfection of style, with the stanzas of Sappho. Of his life we know a few not wholly uninteresting incidents. He was a noble of Mitylene, the capital of Lesbos, where he flourished as early as 611 B.C. Alcæus belonged to a family of distinguished men. His brothers Cicis and Antimenidas upheld the party of the oligarchy against the tyrant Melanchrus; and during the troubles which agitated Mitylene after the fall of this despot,

---

[1] Those who are curious in the matter of metres will find the Sapphic stanza reproduced in English, with perfect truth of cadence, in Swinburne's "Sapphics" (*Poems and Ballads*). The imitations by Horace are far less close to the original. A little volume published by H. T. Wharton (Stott, 1887) gives all the verses which English poets have composed in translation or imitation of Sappho's fragments. In that book will be found my own contributions to this literature.

while other petty tyrants—Myrsilus, Megalagyrus, and the Political Cleanactids—were attempting to subdue the island, the three career, exile, wanderings. brothers ranged themselves uniformly on the side of the aristocracy.   At first they seem to have been friendly with Pittacus.   It was while fighting at his side against the Athenians at Sigeum that Alcæus threw his shield away—an exploit which, like Archilochus, he celebrated in a poem without apparently damaging his reputation for valour.   Being a stout soldier, a violent partisan, the bard of revolutions, and the brother of a pair of heroes, he could trifle with this little accident, which less doughty warriors must have concealed. When Pittacus was chosen Æsymnetes, or dictator with despotic power for the preservation of public order, in 589 B.C., Alcæus and his brothers went into opposition and were exiled.   All three of them were what in modern politics we should call High Tories.   They could not endure the least approach to popular government, the slightest infringement of the rights of the nobility.   During his exile Alcæus employed his poetic faculty in vituperating Pittacus.   His satires were esteemed almost as pungent as those of Archilochus.   But the liberal-minded ruler did not resent them.   When Alcæus was on one occasion taken prisoner, he set him free, remarking that "forgiveness is better than revenge."   Alcæus lived to be reconciled with him and to recognise his merits.   As a trait in the domestic life and fortunes of the Greeks of this time, it is worth mentioning that Alcæus took refuge in Egypt during his banishment from Lesbos, and that his brother Antimenidas entered the service of the king of Babylon.   In the same way two Englishmen in the times of the Edwards might have travelled in Germany or become soldiers of the Republic of Florence.   Of the Greek oligarch who lent his sword to Nebuchadnezzar—in his wars perhaps against Jehoiakim or Pharaoh-Necho—we get a curious glimpse.   Alcæus greeted him on his return in a poem of which we possess a fragment, and which may be paraphrased thus :—

> " From the ends of the earth thou art come
> Back to thy home ;
> The ivory hilt of thy blade
> With gold is embossed and inlaid ;
> Since for Babylon's host a great deed
> Thou didst work in their need,
> Slaying a warrior, an athlete of might,
> Royal, whose height
> Lacked of five cubits one span—
> A terrible man."

The ivory
sword-hilt.

We can fancy with what delight and curiosity Alcæus, who, as may be gathered from his poems, was an amateur of armour, examined this sword-handle, wrought perhaps from Æthiopian tusks by Egyptian artists with lotos-flowers or patterns of crocodiles, monkeys, and lions. This story of the polished Greek citizen's adventure among the Jews and Egyptians, known to us through Holy Writ, touches our imagination with the same strange sense of novelty as when we read of the Persian poet Saadi, a slave in the camp of Richard Cœur de Lion's Crusaders.

Political and
military
poems.

Considering the life Alcæus led, it is not strange that he should have sung of arms and civic struggles. Many fragments, preserved in all probability from the *Stasiotica*, or Songs of Sedition, which were very popular among the ancients, throw light upon the stormier passages of his history. One of these pieces[1] describes the poet's armoury—his polished helmets and white horsehair plumes, the burnished brazen greaves that hang upon the wall, the linen breastplates and bucklers thrown in heaps about the floor, with Chalkidian blades, and girdles, and tunics. The most striking point about this fragment is its foppery. Alcæus spares no pains to make us know how bright his armour is, how carefully his greaves are fixed against the wall by pegs you cannot see (πασσάλοις κρύπτοισι περικείμεναι), how carelessly the girdles and small gear are tossed about in sumptuous disarray.

[1] Bergk, p. 935.

The poem seems to reveal a luxurious nature delighting in military millinery. No Dorian would have described his weapons from this point of view, but would have rather told us how often they had been used with effect in the field. The Æolian character is here tempered with Orientalism.

Of the erotic poems of Alcæus, only a very few and incon- *Erotic odes.* siderable fragments have survived. Horace says of them, addressing his lyre :—

> "Lesbio primum modulate civi,
>   Qui ferox bello, tamen inter arma,
>   Sive jactatam religârat udo
>   Littore navim,
> Liberum et Musas Veneremque et illi
>   Semper hærentem puerum canebat ;
>   Et Lycum nigris oculis nigroque
>   Crine decorum." [1]

Of Lycus we only know, on the authority of Cicero,[2] that *Lycus and* he had a wart upon the finger, which Alcæus praised in one *Sappho.* of his poems. It has also been conjectured that the line οἶνος, ὦ φίλε παῖ, καὶ ἀλάθεα, "wine, dear boy, and truth," which Theocritus quotes as a proverb at the beginning of his Æolic Idyll, was addressed to Lycus. An English version of this idyll made by me will be found in the appendix. A fragment of far greater interest is the couplet preserved by Hephæstion,[3] in which Alcæus calls on Sappho by her name : "Violet-crowned, pure, sweetly-smiling Sappho ! I want to say something, but shame prevents me." To this declaration Sappho replied : "If thy wishes were fair and noble, and thy

---

[1] *Carm.* i. 32, thus translated by Conington :—

> "Thou, strung by Lesbos' minstrel hand,
>   The bard, who 'mid the clash of steel,
> Or haply mooring to the strand,
>   His battered keel,
>
> "Of Bacchus and the Muses sung,
>   And Cupid, still at Venus' side,
> And Lycus, beautiful and young,
>   Dark-haired, dark-eyed."

[2] *De Nat. Deorum,* i. 28.   [3] *See* Bergk, p. 948.

tongue designed not to utter what is base, shame would not cloud thine eyes, but thou wouldst speak thy just desires." This is all we know about the love-passages between the greatest lyrists of the Æolian school. In this way do the ancient critics tantalise us. Aristotle,[1] in order to illustrate a moral proposition, Hephæstion, with a view to proving a metrical rule, fling these scraps of their wealth forth, little dreaming that after twenty centuries the men of new nations and other thoughts will eagerly collect the scraps, and long for more of that which might have been so freely lavished. Whether Sappho wrote her reply in maidenly modesty because the advances of Alcæus were really dishonourable, or whether she affected indignation to conceal a personal dislike for the poet, we cannot say. Aristotle or Hephæstion might probably have been able to tell us. But the one was only thinking of the signs of shame, while the attention of the other was riveted upon the " so-called *dodecasyllable Alcaic.*"

Drinking-songs.

The most considerable remains of the lyrics of Alcæus are drinking-songs — praises of wine, combined with reflections upon life and appropriate descriptions of the different seasons. No time was amiss for drinking, to his mind : the heat of summer, the cold of winter, the blazing dogstar and the driving tempest, twilight with its cheerful gleam of lamps, midday with its sunshine—all suggest reasons for indulging in the cup. Not that we are justified in fancying Alcæus to have been a vulgar toper : he retained Æolian sumptuousness in his pleasures and raised the art of drinking to an æsthetic altitude. One well-known piece from the *Parœnia* of Alcæus is capable of translation into Elizabethan rhymed verse, as follows :—

> " The rain of Zeus descends, and from high heaven
>   A storm is driven :
> And on the running water-brooks the cold
>   Lays icy hold :

---

[1] *Rhet.* i. 9.

Then up ! beat down the winter ; make the fire
    Blaze high and higher ;
Mix wine as sweet as honey of the bee
    Abundantly ;
Then drink with comfortable wool around
    Your temples bound.
We must not yield our hearts to woe, or wear
    With wasting care ;
For grief will profit us no whit, my friend,
    Nor nothing mend :
But this is our best medicine, with wine fraught
    To cast out thought."

The debt of Horace to Alcæus must have been immense. Horace and
Alcæus,
Catullus
and Sappho.
The fragment just translated is the original of the ninth ode
of the first book. The fragment on the death of Myrsilus,
νῦν χρὴ μεθύσθην (now it behoves us to drink deep), shows
where Horace found the model for the last ode of the first
book. Again, " O navis referent " (Hor. *Carm.* i. 14) is based
on an ode of the Lesbian poet of which we possess a fragment.[1] Between the temperaments of Horace and of Alcæus,
as between those of Catullus and of Sappho, there were
marked similarities and correspondences. The poetry of both
Horace and Alcæus was polished rather than profound,
admirably sketched rather than richly coloured, more graceful than intense, less passionate than reflective. In Sappho
and Catullus, on the other hand, we meet with richer and
more ardent natures : they are endowed with keener sensi-
bilities, with a sensuality more noble because of its intensity,
with emotions more profound, with a deeper faculty of
thought, that never loses itself in the shallows of " Stoic-
Epicurean acceptance," but simply and exquisitely apprehends
the facts of human life. Where Horace talks of Orcus and
the Urn, Catullus sings : [2]—

---

[1] Bergk, p. 936.

[2] Translated thus by Ben Jonson :—
        " Suns that set may rise again ;
        But if once we lose this light,
        'Tis with us perpetual night."

> " Soles occidere et redire possunt,
> Nobis cum semel occidit brevis lux
> Nox est perpetua una dormienda."

This contrast between the polished sententiousness of Horace
and the pathetic outcry of Catullus marks the difference
between two classes of poets to whom Horace and Alcæus,
Sappho and Catullus, respectively belong.

Erinna and
Damophila.

Of the other Lesbian poets, Erinna and Damophila, we
know but little : the one survives in a single epigram—if we
reject the epitaphs on Baucis : the other is a mere name. It
is noticeable that of the four Lesbian poets three are women.
We may remember that in Thebes, which was also an Æolian
city, Myrtis and Corinna rivalled Pindar.

Anacreon of
Teos.

To the list of Æolian poets Anacreon, though an Ionian by
birth and an Ionian in temperament, is generally added, because he cultivated the lyrical stanza of personal emotion.
Into the Æolian style Anacreon introduced a new and uncongenial element. His passion had none of Sappho's fiery
splendour, none of the haughtiness and restlessness which distinguished Alcæus. There was a vein of levity, almost of
vulgarity, in the Ionians, which removed them from the alti-
tudes of Dorian heroism and Æolian enthusiasm. This tincture of flippancy is discernible in Anacreon. Life and love
come easily to him. The roses keep no secrets for his ears,
such as they told to Sappho : they serve very well for garlands when he drinks, and have a pleasant smell—especially
in myrrh. The wine-cup does not suggest to him variety of
seasons,—the frozen streams of winter, the parched breath of
the Dog-star,—as with Alcæus : he tipples and gets drunk.
His loves too are facile—neither permanent nor tempestuous.
The girls and boys of whom he sings were flute-players and
cup-bearers, servants of a tyrant, *instrumenta libidinis*, chosen
for their looks, as the poet had been selected for the sweetness of his lyre with twenty chords. He never felt the
furnace of Sappho, whose love, however criminal in the

estimation of modern moralists, was serious and of the soul.
The difference between the lives of these three lyrists is very
striking. Alcæus was a politician and party leader. Sappho
was the centre of a free society of female poets. Anacreon The Court
was the courtier and laureate of tyrants. He won his first laureate.
fame with Polycrates, at whose death Hipparchus fetched
him to Athens in a trireme of fifty oars. Between Bacchus
and Venus he spent his days in palaces; and died at the ripe
age of eighty-five at Teos, choked, it is reported, by a grape-
stone—a hoary-headed *roué*, for whom the rhyme of the
Goliardic Archipoeta might have been written : [1]—

> " Meum est propositum,
>   In tabernâ mori," etc.

It need not be remarked that of the genuine poems of
Anacreon we possess but few (pp. 1011-1045 of Bergk). His
great popularity in Greece led to innumerable imitations of
his lighter style.[2] These are fully preserved in Bergk's
Collection (pp. 1046-1108).

The Dorian style offers a marked contrast to the Æolian.
In the case of the Ionian satirists and elegists, and in that of

---

[1] In the public-house to die
        Is my resolution ;
    Let wine to my lips be nigh
        At life's dissolution :
    That will make the angels cry,
        With glad elocution,
    "Grant this toper, God on high,
        Grace and absolution ! "

From *Wine, Women, and Song*, by J. A. Symonds (Chatto and
Windus, 1884).

[2] The people of Athens gave him a statue on their Acropolis. The
Teians struck his portrait on coins. Critias said that his poems would
last as long as the Cottabos in Hellas. He did in fact exactly represent
one side, and that the least heroic side, of the character of the Greeks—
their simple love of sensual pleasure. As mere Hedonism grew, so did
the songs and the style of Anacreon gain in popularity, whereas the
stormier passion of Sappho became unfashionable.

the Æolian lyrists, the national peculiarities of the art resulted from national qualities in the artists. This is not the case with the so-called Dorian poets. The great lyrists of this school are, with one exception, of extraction foreign to the Dorian tribe. Alcman was a Lydian; Stesichorus acknowledged an Ionian colony for his fatherland; Arion was a Lesbian; Simonides and Bacchylides were Ionian; Pindar was Bœotian; Ibycus of Rhegium alone was a Dorian. Why then is the style called Dorian? Because the poets, though not Dorian by birth, wrote for Dorian patrons in the land of Dorians, to add splendour to ceremonies and solemnities in vogue among the Dorians. The distinctive features of this, the most sublime branch of Greek lyrical poetry, have been already hinted at: these elaborate Choral Hymns, in which strophe answers to antistrophe, and epode to epode, chanted by bands of singers and accompanied at times by dancing, were designed to give expression, no longer to personal emotions, but to the feelings of great congregations of men engaged in the celebration of gods, and heroes, and illustrious mortals. Why this species of choral poetry received the patronage and name of the Dorian tribe may be seen by glancing at the institutions peculiar to this section of the Hellenic family. The Dorians, more than any other Greeks, lived in common and in public. Their children were educated, not at home, but in companies, beneath the supervision of state-officers. Girls as well as boys submitted to gymnastic training, and were taught to sacrifice domestic and personal to political and social interests. Tutored to merge the individual in the mass, habituated to associate together in large bodies, the Dorians felt no need of venting private feeling. Their personal emotions were stunted: they had no separate wants and wishes, aspirations and regrets, to utter. Yet the sense of melody and harmony which was rooted so profoundly in the Greek temperament, needed some outlet even here; while the gymnastic and athletic exercises practised by the Dorians rendered them peculiarly sensitive, not only to the beauties of the human body, but also to the refinements of rhythmical movement. The spiritual enthusiasm for great and glorious actions, which formed the soul of the Greek race, flamed with all the greater brilliancy among Dorians, because it was not narrowed, as among the Æolians, to the selfish passions of the individual, or diverted, as among Ionians, to meditation or satire ; but was concentrated on public interests, on religious and heroic traditions, on all the thoughts and feelings which stimulate a large political activity. The Dorians required a poetry which should be public, which should admit of the participation of many individuals, which should give utterance to national enthusiasms, which should combine the movements of men and women in choric evolutions with the melodies of music and the sublime words of inspired prophecy. In brief, the Dorians needed poets able—

" to inbreed and cherish in a great people the seeds of virtue and public civility, to allay the perturbations of the mind, and set the affections in right tune ; to celebrate in glorious and lofty hymns the throne and equipage of God's Almightiness, and what He works, and what He suffers to be wrought with high Providence. . . . Lastly, whatsoever in religion is holy and sublime, in virtue amiable or grave ; whatsoever hath passion or admiration in all the changes of that which is called fortune from without, or the wily subtleties and reflexes of man's thoughts from within ; all these things with a solid and treatable smoothness, to paint out and describe."

But here arose a difficulty. With all their need of the highest and most elaborate poetry, with all their sensibility to beauty, the Dorians thought it beneath the dignity of a citizen to practise the arts. Their education, almost exclusively military and gymnastic, unfitted them, at all events in Sparta, for studies indispensable towards gaining proficiency in any science so elaborate as that of choral poetry. Drilled to abstinence, obedience, and silence, dwelling in a camp, without privacy or leisure, how could a Spartan, that automaton of the State, be expected to produce poetry, or excel in any fine art? A

The Spartans employ foreigners to make their poetry.

Spartan king, on being shown the most distinguished musician of his age, pointed to his cook as the best maker of black broth. Music, if music they must have ; poetry, if poetry were required by some divinely implanted instinct ; dancing, if dancing were a necessary compliment to the Deity ; must be imported by these warriors from foreign lands. Thus the Spartans became the patrons of stranger artists, on whom they imposed their laws of taste. They pressed the flexible Ionian, the passionate Lesbian, the languid Lydian, the acute Athenian, into their service, and made them use the crabbed Dorian speech. They said : We want such and such odes for our choruses ; we wish to amuse our youths and maidens, and to honour the gods with pompous harmonies ; you, men of art, write for us, sing for us ; but be careful to comprehend our character ; and remember that, though you are Ionians or Lesbians, your inspiration must be Dorian. They got what they required. The so-called Dorian lyric is a genuine product of the Dorian race, although its greatest masters were foreigners and aliens. Much after the same fashion did England patronise Handel in the last century ; in the same way may Handel's oratorios be called English music; for though the English are not musicians, and are diffident in general of the artist class, yet neither Germans, nor Italians, nor French, have seen produced upon their soil such colossal works of art in the service of a highly intellectual religion.

Relation of the Dorians to the fine arts.

It is interesting to reflect upon the influence of the Dorian race in the evolution of Greek art. That, as a nation, they possessed the germs of artistic invention, and that their character expressed itself very clearly in æsthetic forms, is evident from the existence of the Dorian style in architecture, and the Dorian mood in music, both of which reflect their broad simplicity and strength disdaining ornament. The same stamp they impressed upon Greek poetry, through the instruments they selected from other tribes. Had it not been for the strict legislation of Lycurgus, which, by forcing Sparta into a purely political development, and establishing a complete community of life among the citizens, checked the emergence of that individuality which is so all-important to the artist, Sparta might have counted her great sculptors, poets, musicians, orators, and painters, in rivalry with Pheidias, Sophocles, Damon, Pericles, Polygnotus. As it was, though without hands to paint and carve, without lips to sing and plead, the stubborn Dorian race set its seal on a wide field of Greek art.[1]

The elaborate works of the choral lyrists may be regarded as the highly-wrought expansions of rudiments already existing among the Dorians. Alcman, Arion, and Stesichorus, the three masters who formed choral poetry from the materials indicated to us in the poems of Homer, and who had to blend in one harmonious whole the sister arts of dancing, music, and poetry, so as to present a pompous appeal to the intellect through speech, and through the ear and eye, found ready to their hands such simple songs as may be read in Bergk, pp. 1297-1303. The dithyramb of the women of Elis: "Come, hero, Dionysus, to the holy sea-temple, attended by the Graces, and rushing on with oxen-hoof! Holy ox! Holy ox!" The chorus of the old men, men, and boys at Sparta: "We once were stalwart youths: we are; if thou likest, try our strength: we shall be; and far better too!" The march-song of the Spartans in their rhythmic revels: "Advance, boys, set your feet forward, and dance in the reel better still."—From these had to be trained the complex and magnificent work of art, which culminated in a Pythian ode of Pindar! Alcman was a native of Sardis, and a slave of Agesilaus the Spartan. He flourished at Sparta between 671 and 631 B.C., composing Parthenia for the maidens of Taygetus. Who does not know

Rudiments of the choral ode.

---

[1] It is unhistorical to confound the Dorians with the Spartans, who were a specially-trained section of the Dorian stock. Yet it will be seen that, in relation at least to lyric poetry, Sparta fairly may be taken as *the* Dorian state.

Alcman and
Arion. his lines upon the valley of Eurotas? "Sleep holds the
mountain summits and ravines, the promontories and the
water-courses; leaves, and creeping things, and whatsoever
black earth breeds; and wild beasts of the hills, and bees,
and monsters in the hollows of the dark blue deep; and all
the wide-winged birds are sleeping." Junior to Alcman was
Arion, who spent most of his time with Periander at Corinth.
His contribution to choral poetry was the elaboration of the
Dithyramb. But of his work we have unfortunately not a
single fragment left. The piece that bears his name (Bergk,
p. 872) has to be ascribed to some tolerable poet of the
Euripidean period. His life is involved in mythology; most
beautiful is the oft-told tale of his salvation from the sea
waves by an enamoured dolphin—a fish, by the way, which
Athenæus dignified by the title of φιλῳδός τε καὶ φίλαυλος
(song-loving and flute-loving), and which Aristotle calls
φιλάνθρωπος (affectionate to men). Rather more is known
about Stesichorus. He was a native of Himera in Sicily, but
possibly a Locrian by descent. His parents called him Tisias,
but he took his more famous name from his profession.
Stesichorus. Stesichorus is a title that might have been given to any
chorus-master in a Greek city; but Tisias of Himera won
it by being emphatically the author of the choric system.
Antiquity recognised in him the inventor of Strophe, Antistrophe, and Epode, with the corresponding movements of the
dance, which were designated the Triad of Stesichorus. A
remark made by Quintilian about this poet—that he sustained
the burden of the Epos with his lyre—forms a valuable
criticism on his style. In the days of Stesichorus, the epic
proper had lost its vitality; but people still felt the liveliest
interest in heroic legends, and loved to connect the celebration of the past with their ceremonies. A lyrical poet had
therefore so to treat the myths of Hellas that choruses should
represent them in their odes and semi-dramatic dances. It is
probable that Stesichorus made far more use of mythical

material than Pindar, dealing with it less allusively and adhering more closely to the epic form of narrative. When we hear of his ode, the Orestea, being divided into three books (whatever that may mean), and read the titles of the rest—Cerberus, Cycnus, Scylla, Europa, the Sack of Troy, the Nostoi, and Geryonis, we are led to suspect that his choral compositions were not dissimilar to mediæval mystery plays—semi-lyrical, semi-dramatic poems, founded on the religious legends of the past. Stesichorus did not confine himself to this species of composition, but wrote hymns, encomia, and pæans, like other professional lyrists who succeeded him, and invented a curious kind of love-tale from real life. One of these romantic poems, called Calycé, was about a girl, who loved purely but unhappily, and died. Another, called Rhadina, told the forlorn tale of a Samian brother and sister put to death by a cruel tyrant. It is a pity that these early Greek novels in verse are lost. We might have found in them the fresh originals of Daphnis and Chloe, or of the romances of Tatius and Heliodorus. Finally, Stesichorus composed fables, such as the Horse and the Stag, and pastorals upon the death of Daphnis, in which he proved himself true to his Sicilian origin, and anticipated Theocritus. Enough has been said about Stesichorus to show that he was a richly inventive genius—one of those facile and abundant natures who excel in many branches of art, and who give hints by which posterity may profit. Yet with all his genius he was not thoroughly successful. His pastorals and romances were abandoned by his successors ; his epical lyrics were lost in the tragic drama. Like many other poets, he failed by coming at a wrong moment, or else by adhering to forms of art which could not long remain in vogue. In his attempt to reconcile the epical treatment of mythology with the choric system of his own invention, he proved that he had not fully grasped the capabilities of lyrical poetry. In his endeavour to create an idyllic and romantic species, he was far before his age.

Versatility of genius.

The remaining choral poets of the Dorian style, of whom the eldest, Ibycus, dates half a century later than Arion, received from their predecessors an instrument of poetical expression already nearly complete. It was their part to use it as skilfully as possible, and to introduce such changes as might render it more polished. Excellence of workmanship is particularly noticeable in what remains of Ibycus, Simonides, Bacchylides. These latter lyrists are no longer local poets : under the altered circumstances of Hellas at the time of the Persian war, art has become Panhellenic, the artists cease to be the servants of one state or of one deity ; they range from city to city, giving their services to all who seek for them, and embracing the various tribes and religious rites of the collected Greeks in their æsthetic sympathy. Now, for the first time, poets began to sell their songs of praise for money. Simonides introduced the practice, which had something shocking in it to Greek taste, and which Plato especially censures as sophistic and illiberal in his *Protagoras.* Now, too, poets became the friends and counsellors of princes, mixing freely in the politics of Samos, Syracuse, Agrigentum, Thessaly ; aiding the tyrants Polycrates, Hiero, Theron, the Scopads, with their advice. Simonides is said to have suspended hostilities between Theron and Hiero by his diplomatic intercession after their armies had been drawn up in battle-array. Petrarch did not occupy a more important place among the princes and republics of mediæval Italy. Under these new conditions, and with this expansion of the poet's calling, the old character of the Dorian lyric changed. The title Dorian is now merely nominal, and the dialect is a conventional language consecrated to this style.

Ibycus was a native of Rhegium, a colony of mixed Ionians and Dorians. To which of these families he belonged is not certain. If we judged by the internal evidence of his poems, we should call him an Ionian ; for they are distinguished by voluptuous sweetness, with a dash of almost Æolian intensity.

Ibycus was a poet-errant, carrying his songs from state to state. The beautiful story of the cranes who led to the discovery of his murder at Corinth, though probably mythical, like that of Arion's dolphin, illustrates the rude lives of these Greek troubadours, and shows in what respect the *sacer vates*, servant of the Muses and beloved of Phœbus, was held by the people. Ibycus was regarded by antiquity as a kind of male Sappho. His odes, composed for birthday festivals and banquets, were dedicated chiefly to the praise of beautiful youths ; and the legends which adorned them, like those of Ganymede or Tithonus, were appropriate to the erotic style. Aristophanes, in the *Thesmophoriazusæ*, makes Agathon connect him with Anacreon and Alcæus, as the three refiners of language. It is clear, therefore, that in his art Ibycus adapted the manner of Dorian poetry to the matter of Æolian or Ionian love-chants. Of his poetry we have but few fragments. The following seems to strike the keynote of his style : "Love once again looking upon me from his cloud-black brows, with languishing glances, drives me by enchantments of all kinds to the endless nets of Cypris : verily I tremble at his onset, as a chariot-horse, who hath won prizes, in old age goes grudgingly to try his speed in the swift race of cars." In another piece he compares the onset of Love to a downrush of the Thracian north wind armed with lightning. This fragment, numbered first in Bergk's Collection, is taken from Athenæus, who quotes it to prove the vehement emotion of the poet :—

> "In spring Cydonian apple-trees,
>   Watered by fountains ever flowing
>   Through crofts unmown of maiden goddesses,
> And young vines 'neath the shade
>   Of shooting tendrils, tranquilly are growing.
> Meanwhile for me Love never laid
>   In slumber, like a north-wind glowing
> With Thracian lightnings, still doth dart
> Blood-parching madness on my heart,

From Kupris hurtling, stormful, wild,
Lording the man as erst the child."

Poetical
idealisa-
tions of
amorous
passion.

We may turn aside to compare the different metaphors
whereby the early lyrists imaged the assaults of the Love-God.
Sappho describes him in one place as a youth arrayed with a
flame-coloured chlamys descending from heaven; in another
she calls him "a limb-dissolving, bitter-sweet, impracticable
wild beast;" again, she compares the state of her soul under
the influence of love to oak-trees torn and shaken by a mountain
whirlwind. Anacreon paints a fine picture of Love like a black-
smith, forging his soul and tempering it in icy torrents. The
dubious winged figure armed with a heavy sword, which is
carved upon the recently-discovered column from the Temple
of Ephesus, if he be the Love-God, and not, as some conjecture,
Death, seems to have been conceived in the spirit of these
energetic metaphors. The Greeks, at the period of Anacreon
and Ibycus, were far from having as yet imagined the baby
Cupid of Moschus, the Epigrammatists, and the Alexandrian
Anacreontics. He was still a terrible and passion-stirring power
—no mere malicious urchin coming by night with drenched
wings and unstrung bow to reward the poet's hospitality by
wounding him; no naughty boy who runs away from his mother
and steals honeycombs, no bee-like elf asleep in rosebuds.

Simonides
of Ceos.

Simonides is a far more brilliant representative than Ibycus,
both of Greek choral poetry in its prime, and also of the
whole literary life of Hellas during the period which immediately preceded and followed the Persian war. He was
born in the island of Ceos, of pure Ionian blood and breeding;
but the Ionians of Ceos were celebrated for their σωφροσύνη
(reserve, or self-restraint), a quality strongly marked in the
poems of Simonides. In his odes we do not trace that mixture of Æolian passion and that concentration upon personal
emotions which are noticeable in those of Ibycus, but rather a
Dorian solemnity of thought and feeling, qualifying Simonides
for the arduous functions to which he was called, of com-

memorating in elegy and epigram and funeral ode the achievements of Hellas against Persia. Simonides belonged to a family of professional poets; for the arts among the early Greeks were hereditary; a father taught the trade of flute-playing and chorus-leading and verse-making to his son, who, if he had original genius, became a great poet, as was the fate of Pindar; or, if he were endowed with commonplace abilities, remained a journeyman in art without discredit to himself, performing useful functions in his native place.[1] Simonides exercised his calling of chorus-teacher at Carthæa in Ceos, and lived at the χορηγεῖον, or resort of the chorus, near the temple *Life at courts.* of Apollo. But the greater portion of his life, after he had attained celebrity, was passed with patrons,—with Hipparchus, who invited him to Athens, where he dwelt in amity with Anacreon, and at enmity with Pindar's master Lasos—with the Scopads and Aleuads of Thessaly, for whom he composed the most touching threnoi and the most brilliant panegyrics, of which fragments have descended to us ;—finally, with Hiero of Syracuse, who honoured him exceedingly, and when he died, consigned him to the earth with princely funeral pomp. The relations of Simonides to these patrons may be gathered from numerous slight indications, none of which are very honourable to his character. For instance, after receiving the hospitality of Hipparchus, he composed an epigram for the statue of Harmodius, in which he calls the murder of the tyrant "a great light rising upon Athens." Again, he praised the brutal Scopas, son of Creon, in an ode which is celebrated, both as

---

[1] The Dramatic art was hereditary among the Athenians. Æschylus left a son, Euphorion, and two nephews, Philocles and Astydamas, who produced tragedies. The last is reported to have written no fewer than two hundred and forty plays. Iophon the son and Sophocles the grandson of the great Sophocles were dramatists of some repute at Athens. Euripides had a nephew of his own name, and Aristophanes two sons who followed the same calling. It is only from families like the Bachs that we can draw any modern parallel to this transmission of an art from father to son in the same race.

Panegyric of
the despot
Scopas.
being connected with the most dramatic incident in the poet's
life, and also as having furnished Plato with a theme for
argument, and Aristotle with an ethical quotation—" To be a
good man in very truth, a square without blame, is hard." This
proposition Plato discusses in the *Protagoras*, while Aristotle
cites the phrase, τετράγωνος ἄνευ ψόγου (four-square without
fault). From the general tenor of the fragments of this ode,
from Plato's criticism, and from what is known about the coarse
nature of Scopas, who is being praised, we must conjecture
that Simonides attempted to whitewash his patron's character
by depreciating the standard of morality. With Ionian facility
and courtly compliment, he made excuses for a bad man by
pleading that perfect goodness was unattainable. Scopas
refused to pay the price required by Simonides for the poem
in question, telling him to get half of it from the Dioscuri,
who had also been eulogised. This was at a banquet. While
the king was laughing at his own rude jest, a servant whispered
to the poet that two goodly youths waited without, desiring
earnestly to speak with him. Simonides left the palace, but
found no one. Even as he stood looking for his visitors, he
heard the crash of beams and the groans of dying men. Scopas
with his guests had been destroyed by the falling of the roof,
and Simonides had received a godlike guerdon from the two
sons of Tyndareus. This story belongs, perhaps, to the same
class as the cranes of Ibycus and the dolphin of Arion. Yet
there seems to be no doubt that the Scopad dynasty was
suddenly extinguished; for we hear nothing of them at the
time of the Persian war, and we know that Simonides composed
a threnos for the family.

The Persian
war.
The most splendid period of the life of Simonides was that
which he passed at Athens during the great wars with Persia.
Here he was the friend of Miltiades, Themistocles, and Pausanias. Here he composed his epigrams on Marathon, Thermopylæ, Salamis, Platæa—poems not destined to be merely
sung or consigned to parchment, but to be carved in marble or

engraved in letters of imperishable bronze upon the works of Epigrams by Simonides. the noblest architects and statuaries. The genius of Simonides is unique in this branch of monumental poetry. His couplets—calm, simple, terse, strong as the deeds they celebrate, enduring as the brass or stone which they adorned—animated succeeding generations of Greek patriots; they were transferred to the brains of statesmen like Pericles and Demosthenes, inscribed upon the fleshy tablets of the hearts of warriors like Cleomenes, Pelopidas, Epaminondas. We are thrice fortunate in possessing the entire collection of these epigrams, unrivalled for the magnitude of the events they celebrate, and for the circumstances under which they were composed. When we reflect what would have become of the civilisation of the world but for these Greek victories—when we remember that the events which these few couplets record, transcend in importance those of any other single period of history—we are almost appalled by the contrast between the brevity of the epigrams and the world-wide vastness of their matter. In reviewing the life of Simonides, after admitting that he was greedy of gain and not adverse to flattery, we are bound to confess that, as a poet, he proved himself adequate to the age of Marathon and Salamis. He was the voice of Hellas—the genius of Fame, sculpturing upon her brazen shield with a pen of adamant, in austere letters of indelible gold, the achievements to which the whole world owes its civilisation. Happy poet! Had ever any other man so splendid a heritage of song allotted to him?

In style Simonides is always pure and exquisitely polished. The style of Simonides. The ancients called him the sweet poet—Melicertes—*par excellence*. His σωφροσύνη, or tempered self-restraint, gives a mellow tone not merely to his philosophy and moral precepts, but also to his art. He has none of Pindar's rugged majesty, volcanic force, gorgeous exuberance : he does not, like Pindar, pour forth an inexhaustible torrent of poetical ideas, chafing against each other in the eddies of breathless inspiration. On the contrary, he works up a few thoughts, a few

carefully selected images, with patient skill, producing a
perfectly harmonious result, but one which is always border-
ing on the commonplace.   Like all correct poets, he is somewhat tame, though tender, delicate, and exquisitely beautiful.
Pindar electrifies his hearer, seizing him like the eagle in
Dante's vision, and bearing him breathless through the ether
of celestial flame.   Simonides leads us by the hand along the
banks of pleasant rivers, through laurel groves, and by the
porticoes of sunny temples.   What he possesses of quite
peculiar to his own genius is pathos—the pathos of romance.
This appears most remarkably in the fragment of a threnos
which describes Danaë afloat upon the waves at night.   It is
with the greatest diffidence that I offer a translation of what
remains one of the most perfect pieces of pathetic poetry in
any literature :—

The tale of Danaë.

    " When, in the carven chest,
      The winds that blew and waves in wild unrest
      Smote her with fear, she, not with cheeks unwet,
      Her arms of love round Perseus set,
        And said : O child, what grief is mine !
      But thou dost slumber, and thy baby breast
      Is sunk in rest,
      Here in the cheerless brass-bound bark,
      Tossed amid starless night and pitchy dark.
        Nor dost thou heed the scudding brine
      Of waves that wash above thy curls so deep,
      Nor the shrill winds that sweep,—
      Lapped in thy purple robe's embrace,
      Fair little face !
      But if this dread were dreadful too to thee,
      Then wouldst thou lend thy listening ear to me ;
      Therefore I cry,—Sleep babe, and sea be still,
      And slumber our unmeasured ill !
        Oh, may some change of fate, sire Zeus, from thee
      Descend, our woes to end !
      But if this prayer, too overbold, offend
      Thy justice, yet be merciful to me !"

The careful development of simple thoughts in Simonides

may best be illustrated by the fragment on the three hundred Spartans who died at Thermopylæ :—

"Of those who died at Thermopylæ glorious is the fate and fair the doom ; their grave is an altar ; instead of lamentation, they have endless fame ; their dirge is a chant of praise. Such winding-sheet as theirs no rust, no, nor all-conquering time, shall bring to nought. But this sepulchre of brave men hath taken for its habitant the glory of Hellas. Leonidas is witness, Sparta's king, who hath left a mighty crown of valour and undying fame."

The antitheses are wrought with consummate skill; the fate of the heroes is glorious, their doom honourable : so far the eulogy is commonplace ; then the same thought receives a bolder turn : their grave is an altar. We do not lament for them so much as hold them in eternal memory ; our very songs of sorrow become pæans of praise. What follows is a still further expansion of the leading theme : rust and time cannot affect their fame ; Hellas confides her glory to their tomb. Then generalities are quitted ; and Leonidas, the protagonist of Thermopylæ, appears.

In his threnoi Simonides has generally recourse to the common grounds of consolation, which the Ionian elegists repeat *ad nauseam,* dwelling upon the shortness and un-certainty and ills of life, and tending rather to depress the survivors on their own account than to comfort them for the dead.[1] In one he says, "Short is the strength of men, and vain are all their cares, and in their brief life trouble follows upon trouble ; and death, that no man shuns, is hung above our heads—for him both good and bad share equally." It is impossible, while reading this lachrymose lament, to forget the fragment of that mighty threnos of Pindar's which sounds like a trumpet-blast for immortality, and, trampling under

[1] The reputation gained by Simonides among the ancients for the sorrow of his song is proved by the phrase of Catullus,—"Mœstius lach-rymis Simonideis" (more sad than tears shed by Simonides).

feet the glories of this world, reveals the gladness of the souls
who have attained Elysium :—

> " For them the night all through,
>   In that broad realm below,
> The splendour of the sun spreads endless light ;
>   'Mid rosy meadows bright,
> Their city of the tombs with incense-trees,
>   And golden chalices
>   Of flowers, and fruitage fair,
>   Scenting the breezy air,
> Is laden.   There with horses and with play,
> With games and lyres, they while the hours away.
>
> " On every side around
>   Pure happiness is found,
> With all the blooming beauty of the world ;
>   There fragrant smoke, upcurled
> From altars where the blazing fire is dense
>   With perfumed frankincense,
>   Burned unto gods in heaven,
>   Through all the land is driven,
> Making its pleasant place odorous
> With scented gales and sweet airs amorous."

The same note of melancholy reflection upon transient
human life may be traced in the following fragment attributed to Simonides.   He is rebuking Cleobulus of Lindus
in Rhodes for an arrogant epigraph inscribed upon some
column :—

> " Those who are wise in heart and mind,
>   O Lindian Cleobulus, find
>   Naught in thy shallow vaunt aright ;
>   Who with the streams that flow for aye,
>   The vernal flowers that bloom and die,
>   The fiery sun, the moon's mild rays,
>   The strong sea's eddying water-ways,
>   Matchest a marble pillar's might.
>   Lo, all things that have being are
>   To the high gods inferior far ;
>   But carven stone may not withstand
>   Even a mortal's ruthless hand.

> Therefore thy words no wisdom teach
> More than an idiot's idle speech."

What has been said about Simonides applies in a great
measure also to Bacchylides, who was his nephew, pupil, and
faithful follower. The personality of Bacchylides, as a man
and a poet, is absorbed in that of his uncle—the greater bard,
the more distinguished actor on the theatre of the world.
While Simonides played his part in public life, Bacchylides
gave himself up to the elegant pleasures of society; while
Simonides celebrated in epigrams the military glories of the
Greeks, Bacchylides wrote wine-songs and congratulatory
odes. His descriptions of Bacchic intoxication and of the
charms of peace display the same careful word-painting as the
description by Simonides of Orpheus, with more luxuriance
of sensual suggestion. His threnoi exhibit the same Ionian
despondency and resignation—a dead settled calm, an elegant
stolidity of epicureanism. That this excellent, if somewhat
languid, lyrist may receive his due meed of attention, I have
selected his most important fragment, the *Praise of Peace*, for
translation (Bergk, vol. iii. p. 1230) :—

Bacchylides and his praise of peace.

> " To mortal men Peace giveth these good things :
>   Wealth, and the flowers of honey-throated song ;
>   The flame that springs
>   On carven altars from fat sheep and kine,
>   Slain to the gods in heaven ; and, all day long,
>   Games for glad youths, and flutes, and wreaths, and circling
>   wine.
>   Then in the steely shield swart-spiders weave
>   Their web and dusky woof :
>   Rust to the pointed spear and sword doth cleave ;
>   The brazen trump sounds no alarms ;
>   Nor is sleep harried from our eyes aloof,
>   But with sweet rest my bosom warms :
>   The streets are thronged with lovely men and young,
>   And hymns in praise of boys like flames to heaven are flung."

The tone common to Simonides and Bacchylides in funeral

poems will be illustrated by the four following fragments : [1]—

> "Being a man, say not what comes to-morrow,
> Nor, seeing one in bliss, how long 'twill last ;
> For wide-winged fly was ne'er of flight so fast
> As change to sorrow.

> "Nay, not those elder men, who lived of yore,
> Of sceptred gods the half-immortal seed,
> Not even they to prosperous old age wore
> A life from pain and death and danger freed.

> "Short is the strength of men, and vain their trouble,
> Through their brief age sorrows on sorrows double ;
> O'er each and all hangs death escaped by none ;
> Of him both good and bad an equal lot have won.

> "For mortal men not to be born is best,
> Nor e'er to see the bright beams of the day ;
> Since, as life rolls away,
> No man that breathes was ever alway blest."

Here we must stop short in the front of Pindar—the
Hamlet among these lesser actors, the Shakespeare among a
crowd of inferior poets.   To treat of Greek lyrical poetry and
to omit Pindar is a paradox in action.   Yet Pindar is so
colossal, so much apart, that he deserves a separate study,
and cannot be dragged in at the end of a bird's-eye view of a
period of literature.   At the time of Pindar poetry was sinking into mannerism.   He by the force of his native originality
gave it a wholly fresh direction, and created a style as novel
as it was inimitable.   Like some high mountain-peak, upon
the borderland of plain and lesser hills, he stands alone, sky-
piercing and tremendous in his solitary strength.

Before, however, entering upon the criticism of Pindar's
poetry, it will be of service to complete this review of the
Greek lyric by some specimens of those later artificial literary
odes, a few of which have been preserved for us by the
anthologists and grammarians.   The following Hymn to Virtue

[1] See Bergk, vol. iii. pp. 1128, 1129, 1132, 1227.

has a special interest, since it is ascribed to Aristotle, the philosopher, and makes allusion to his friend, the tyrant of Atarneus. The comparative dryness of the style is no less characteristic of the age in which the poem is supposed to have been written than its animating motive, the beauty of Virtue, is true to the Greek conception of morality and heroism :—

> " Virtue, to men thou bringest care and toil ;
>   Yet art thou life's best, fairest spoil !
>   O virgin goddess, for thy beauty's sake
>   To die is delicate in this our Greece,
>   Or to endure of pain the stern strong ache.
>   Such fruit for our soul's ease
> Of joys undying, dearer far than gold
> Or home or soft-eyed sleep, dost thou unfold !
>   It was for thee the seed of Zeus
> Stout Herakles, and Leda's twins, did choose
> Strength-draining deeds, to spread abroad thy name :
>   Smit with the love of thee,
>   Aias and Achileus went smilingly
> Down to Death's portal, crowned with deathless fame.
>   Now, since thou art so fair,
>   Leaving the lightsome air,
> Atarneus' hero hath died gloriously.
> Wherefore immortal praise shall be his guerdon :
> His goodness and his deeds are made the burden
>   Of songs divine
>   Sung by Memory's daughters nine,
> Hymning of hospitable Zeus the might
> And friendship firm as fate in fate's despite."

The next is a Hymn to Health, hardly less true to Greek feeling than the Hymn to Virtue. Simonides, it will be remembered, had said that the first and best possession to be desired by man is health. The ode is but a rhetorical expansion of this sentence, showing that none of the good things of human life can be enjoyed without physical well-being :—

> "Health ! Eldest, most august of all
>   The blessed gods, on thee I call !

Oh, let me spend with thee the rest
Of mortal life, securely blest !
Oh, mayst thou be my housemate still,
To shield and shelter me from ill !
If wealth have any grace,
If fair our children's face ;
If kinghood, lifting men to be
Peers with the high gods' empery ;
If young Love's flying feet
Through secret snares be sweet ;
If aught of all heaven's gifts to mortals sent,
If rest from care be dear, or calm content—
These goodly things, each, all of them, with thee
    Bloom everlastingly,
Blest Health ! yea, Beauty's year
Breaks into spring for thee, for only thee !
Without thee no man's life is aught but cold and drear."

Pæan to
Phœbus.

    As an example of the pæan or the prosodial hymn,
when it assumed a literary form, I may select an ode to
Phœbus, which bears the name of Dionysius. Apollo is here
addressed in his character of Light-giver, and leader of the
lesser powers of heaven. The stars and the moon are his
attendants, rejoicing in his music, and deriving from his
might their glory :—

" Let all wide heaven be still !
  Be silent vale and hill,
  Earth and whispering wind and sea,
  Voice of birds and echo shrill !
  For soon amid our choir will be
Phœbus with floating locks, the Lord of Minstrelsy :
  O father of the snow-browed morn :
  Thou who dost drive the rosy car
  Of day's wing-footed coursers, borne
  With gleaming curls of gold unshorn
  Over heaven's boundless vault afar ;
  Weaving the woof of myriad rays,
  Weath-scattering beams that burn and blaze,
  Enwinding them round earth in endless maze !
The rivers of thy fire undying
  Beget bright day, our heart's desire :

> The throng of stars to greet thee flying
> Through cloudless heaven, join choric dances,
> Hailing thee king with ceaseless crying
>   For joy of thy Phœbean lyre.
> In front the gray-eyed Moon advances
>   Drawn by her snow-white heifers o'er
>   Night's silent silvery dancing-floor:
> With gladness her mild bosom burns
> As round the dædal world she turns."

From these specimens we may infer the character of that semi-ethical, semi-religious lyric poetry which was produced so copiously in Greece, and of which we have lost all but accidental remnants. Though not to be compared for grandeur of style and abundance of grace with the odes of Pindar and the fragments of Simonides, they display a careful workmanship, a clear and harmonious development of ideas, that make us long, alas too vainly, for the treasures of a literature now buried in irrevocable oblivion.

CHAPTER XI

PINDAR

His Life—Legends connected with Him—The Qualities of his Poetry—
The Olympic Games—Pindar's Professional Character—His Morality—His Religious Belief—Doctrine of a Future State—Rewards
and Punishments—The Structure of his Odes—The Proëmia to his
Odes—His Difficulty and Tumidity of Style.

Descent and family of Pindar.

PINDAR, in spite of his great popularity among the Greeks, offers no exception to the rule that we know but little of the lives of the illustrious poets and artists of the world. His parents belonged to the town of Cynoscephalæ; but Pindar himself resided at Thebes, and spoke of Thebes as his native place—Θήβα μᾶτερ ἐμά (Thebes, mother mine!) That his father was called Daiphantus appears tolerably certain; and we may fix the date of his birth at about 522 B.C. He lived to the age of seventy-nine; so that the flourishing period of his life exactly coincides with the great Persian struggle, in which he lived to see Hellas victorious. He had three children—a son, Daiphantus, and two daughters, Eumetis and Protomache. His family was among the noblest and most illustrious of Thebes, forming a branch of the ancient house of the Ægeidæ, who settled both at Thebes and Sparta in heroic times, and offshoots from whom were colonists of Thera and Cyrene. Thus many of the heroes celebrated by Pindar, and many of the illustrious men to whom he dedicates his odes, were of his own kin. Genius for the art seems to have been hereditary in the family of Pindar, as it was in that of Stesichorus and of Simonides; therefore, when the youth showed an aptitude for poetry, his father readily acceded to his wishes, and sent him to Athens to learn the art of composing for the chorus from Lasos, the then famous but now forgotten antagonist of the bard of Ceos. Before his twentieth year, Pindar returned to Thebes and took, it is said, instruction from the poetesses Myrtis and Corinna. To this period of his artistic career belongs the oft-told tale, according to which Corinna bade her pupil interweave myths with his panegyrics, and when, following her advice, he produced an ode in which he had exhausted all the Theban legends, told him τῇ χειρὶ δεῖν σπείρειν, ἀλλὰ μὴ ὅλῳ τῷ θυλάκῳ, "that one ought to sow with the hand and not with the whole sack." Against both Myrtis and Corinna, Pindar entered the lists of poetical contest. Corinna is reported to have beaten him five times, and never to have been vanquished by her more illustrious rival. Pausanias hints that she owed her victories to her beauty, and to the fact that she wrote in a broad Æolic dialect, more suited to the ears of her judges than Pindar's Doric style. The same circumstance which ensured her this temporary triumph may have caused her ultimate neglect. The fragment we possess of Corinna—

The Theban poetesses.

> μεμφόμη δὲ κὴ λιγούραν Μούρτιδ ἰώνγα
> ὅτι βανὰ φοῦσ' ἔβα Πινδάροιο ποτ' ἔριν.

"I blame the clear-voiced Myrtis for that, a woman, she contended against Pindar," is curiously at variance with her own practice. Its Æolisms prove how local and provincial her language must have been.

The history of Pindar's life is the record of his poetical compositions. He was essentially a professional artist, taking no active part in politics, and studying to perfect his poetry all through the perilous days of Salamis and Platæa—like Michael Angelo, who went on modelling and hewing through the sack of Rome, the fall of Florence, the decline of Italian

Dedication to art.

freedom, with scarce a word to prove the anguish of his patriot soul. Pindar, unlike his fellow-countrymen, did not side with the Persians, but felt enthusiasm for Athens, the ἔρεισμα Ἑλλάδος (buttress of Hellas), as he calls her in a dithyramb [1] (fr. 4). For this he was made Proxenos of Athens, and received a present of 10,000 drachmas. It is said that the Thebans fined him for his implied reflections upon them, and that Athens paid the debt. These facts, if true, testify to the post of honour which a mighty poet occupied in Hellas, when the *vox et præterea nihil* (voice and naught besides) of a bard, inspired indeed by muses, but dependent on a patron for his bread, was listened to with jealous ears by the rulers of great cities. The last Isthmian ode shows in what a noble spirit Pindar felt the dangers of Hellas during her deadly strife with Persia, and how he could scarcely breathe for anxiety until the stone of Tantalus suspended over her had been arrested. In the Proemium he says :—

The Persian war.

"For Cleander and his prime of beauty let some one, O ye youths, bear the glorious meed of toil to the splendid portals of his sire Telesarchus, the revel-song, which pays him for his Isthmian victory and for his might in Nemean games. For him I too, though grieved in soul, am asked to call upon the golden muse. Freed as we are from mighty griefs, let us not fall into the bereavement of victorious crowns, nor nurse our cares : but ceasing from vain sorrows, spread we honeyed song abroad thus after our great trouble : forasmuch as of a truth some god hath turned aside the stone of Tantalus which hung above our heads—intolerable suffering for Hellas. Me verily the passing away of dread hath cured not of all care ; yet it is ever better to notice what is present : for treacherous time is hung above the lives of men, rolling the torrent of their days. Still, with freedom on our side, men can cure even these evils; and it is our duty to attend to wholesome hope."

Pindar passed his time chiefly at Thebes, where his home was. But he also visited the different parts of Greece, frequently staying at Delphi, where the iron chair on which he

---

[1] This and all references are made to Bergk's text of Pindar.

sat and sang was long preserved; and also journeying to the Pindar's
wanderings. houses of his patrons—Hiero of Syracuse, and presumably Theron of Agrigentum, and perhaps, too, Alexander of Macedon. Olympia must have often received him as a guest, as well as the island of Ægina, where he had many friends. Odes were sent by him to Cyrene, to Ceos, to Rhodes—on what tablets, we may wonder, adorned with what caligraphy from Pindar's stylus, in what casket worthy of the man who loved magnificence? The Rhodians inscribed his seventh Olympian—the most radiant panegyric of the sea-born isle of Helios—in letters of gold on the walls of their temple of the Lindian Athene. In the midst of his artistic labours, and while serving many patrons, Pindar, as we shall see, preserved his dignity and loftiness of moral character.

Pindar is said to have died in the theatre at Argos, in the His death
at Argos. arms of Theoxenos, a youth whom he loved passionately, and whom he has praised in the most sublime strains for his beauty in a Scolion, the fragment of which we possess.[1] Anacreon choked by a grape-stone, Sophocles breathing out his life together with the pathetic lamentations of Antigone, Æschylus killed on the sea-shore by the eagle whose flight he had watched, Empedocles committing his fiery but turbid spirit to the flames of Etna, Sappho drowning her sorrows in the surf of the Leucadian sea, Ibycus, the poet-errant, murdered by land robbers, Euripides torn to pieces like his own Pentheus, Archilochus honoured in his death by an oracle that cursed his battle-foe, Pindar amid the plaudits of the theatre sinking back into the arms of his Theoxenos and dying in a noontide blaze of glory—these are the appropriate and dramatic endings which the literary gossips among the Greeks, always inventively ingenious, ascribed to some of their chief poets. As the Italian proverb runs, "If they are not true, they are well invented."

Some purely legendary details show the estimation in

---

[1] See above, p. 286.

which Pindar was held by his countrymen. Multitudes of bees are said to have settled on his lips when he was an infant. Pan chose a hymn of his and sang it on the mountains, honouring a mortal poet with his divine voice. The Mother of the gods took up her dwelling at his door. Lastly, we have the famous story of the premonition of his death in dreams—a legend of peculiar significance, when we remember that Pindar, like Sir Thomas Browne, believed that "we are more than ourselves in our sleep," and wrote :—

> " All by happy fate attain
> The end that frees them from their pain ;
> And the body yields to death,
> But the shape of vital breath
> Still in life continueth ;
> It alone is heaven's conferring :
> Sleeps it when the limbs are stirring.
> But when they sleep, in many dreams it shows
> The coming consummation both of joys and woes." [1]

Just before his death, then, Pindar sent to inquire of the oracle of Ammon what was best for man; and the answer, which he had already himself anticipated in his commemoration of Trophonius and Agamedes, was—Death. Meanwhile Persephone appeared to him in his sleep, and told him that he should praise her in her own realm, although on earth he had left her, alone of the blest gods, unsung. Ten days afterwards he died. The hymn which Pindar composed for Persephone in Hades, was dictated to a Theban woman by his ghost—so runs the tale—and written down. After his death, Pindar received more than heroic honours. They kept his iron chair at Delphi ; and the priest of Phœbus, before he shut the temple gates, cried, "Let Pindar the poet go into the banquet of the god." At Athens his statue was erected at the public cost. At Thebes his house was spared in the ruin of two sieges :—

---

[1] Translated by Conington, from Fragment 2 of *Dirges*.

" Lift not thy spear against the Muses' bower ;
The great Emathian conqueror bid spare
The house of Pindarus, when temple and tower
Went to the ground."

At Rhodes, as we have seen, an ode of his was sculptured on
the temple walls of Pallas.   Throughout the future, so long as
Greek poetry endured, he was known emphatically by the
title of ὁ λυρικός (the lyrist).

Pindar was famous, as these semi-mythical stories about   The piety of
his infancy and old age indicate, for piety.   Unlike Horace,   Pindar.
who calls himself *Parcus deorum cultor et infrequens*, Pindar was
a devout and steadfast servant of his country's gods.   He
dedicated a shrine or ματρῷον near his own house to the
Mother of the gods, a statue to Zeus Ammon in Libya, and
one to Hermes in the Theban agora.   The whole of his poetry
is impregnated with a lively sense of the divine in the world.
Accepting the religious traditions of his ancestors with simple
faith, he adds more of spiritual severity and of mystical
morality than we find in Homer.   Yet he is not superstitious
or credulous.   He can afford to criticise the Myths like
Xenophanes and Plato, refusing to believe that a blessed god
could be a glutton.   In Pindar indeed we see the fine flower
of Hellenic religion, free from slavish subservience to creeds
and ceremonies, capable of extracting sublime morality from
mythical legends, and adding to the old glad joyousness of
the Homeric faith a deeper and more awful perception of
superhuman mysteries.   The philosophical scepticism which
in Greece, after the age of Pericles, corroded both the fabric of
mythology and the indistinct doctrines of theological monotheism, had scarcely yet begun to act.

Passing to the poetry of Pindar, we have a hard task before   His art.
us.   What can be said adequate to such a theme ?   What can
be left unsaid of the many thoughts that ought to be expressed ?   At the time of Pindar's youth, lyrical poetry in
Greece was sinking into mannerism.   He, by the force of his

originality, gave it a wholly new direction, and, coming last of the great Dorian lyrists, taught posterity what sort of thing an ode should be. The grand pre-eminence of Pindar as an artist was due in a great measure to his personality. Frigid, austere, and splendid ; not genial like that of Simonides, not passionate like that of Sappho, not acrid like that of Archilochus ; hard as adamant, rigid in moral firmness, glittering with the strong keen light of snow ; haughty, aristocratic, magnificent—the unique personality of the man Pindar, so irresistible in its influence, so hard to characterise, is felt in every strophé of his odes. In his isolation and elevation Pindar stands like some fabled heaven-aspiring peak, conspicuous from afar, girdled at the base with ice and snow, beaten by winds, wreathed round with steam and vapour, jutting a sharp and dazzling outline into cold blue ether. Few things that have life dare to visit him at his grand altitude. Glorious with sunlight and with stars, touched by rise and set of day with splendour, he shines when other lesser heights are dulled. Pindar among his peers is solitary. He had no communion with the poets of his day. He is the eagle ; Simonides and Bacchylides are jackdaws. He soars to the empyrean ; they haunt the valley mists. Noticing this rocky, barren, severe, glittering solitude of Pindar's soul, critics have not unfrequently complained that his poems are devoid of individual interest. Possibly they have failed to comprehend and appreciate the nature of this sublime and distant genius, whose character, in truth, is just as marked as that of Dante or of Michael Angelo.

Pindar's sublime personality.

The Theban Eagle.

Since I have indulged in one metaphor in the vain attempt to enter into some *rapport* with Pindar, let me proceed to illustrate the Pindaric influence—the impression produced by a sympathetic study of his odes upon the imagination saturated with all that is peculiar in his gorgeous style—by the deliberate expansion of some similes, which are by no means mere ornaments of rhetoric, but illustrations carefully selected from the multitude of images forced upon the mind during a detailed perusal of his poetry. One of the common names for Pindar is the Theban Eagle. This supplies us with the first image, which may be conveyed in the very words of Dante : [1]—

> " In dreams I seemed to see an eagle hovering in air on wings of gold, with pinions spread and ready to swoop. I thought I was on the spot where Ganymede was taken from his comrades and borne aloft to the celestial consistory. I pondered—peradventure the great bird only strikes this hill and peradventure scorns to snatch elsewhere his prey. Then it seemed to me that, after wheeling a while, it swooped, terrible like lightning, and caught me up into the sphere of flame ; and there I thought that it and I both burned ; and so fiercely did the fire in my imagination blaze, that sleep no longer could endure, but broke."

This simile describes the rapidity and fierceness of Pindar's spirit, the atmosphere of empyreal splendour into which he bears us with strong wings and clinging talons. Another image may be borrowed from Horace,[2] who says— *Stormy violence of song.*

> " Fervet immensusque ruit profundo
>   Pindarus ore ; "

likening the poet to a torrent, unrestrained, roaring to the woods and precipices with a thunderous voice. This image does not, like the other, fix our attention upon the quality peculiar to Pindar among all the poets of the world—splendour, fire, the blaze of pure effulgence. But it does suggest another characteristic, which is the stormy violence of his song, that chafes within its limits and seems unable to advance quickly enough in spite of its speed. This violence of Pindar's style, as of some snow-swollen Alpine stream, the hungry Arve or death-cold Lutschine, leaping and raging among granite

---

[1] *Purg.* ix. 19.
[2] *Carm.* iv. 2. Translated thus by Conington :—
> " Pindar, like torrent from the steep
> Which, swollen with rain, its banks o'erflows,
> With mouth unfathomably deep,
> Foams, thunders, glows."

boulders, has misled Horace into the notion that Pindar's odes are without metrical structure :—

> "numerisque fertur
> Lege solutis : "

whereas we know that, while pursuing his eagle-flight to the sun, or thundering along his torrent-path, Pindar steadily observed the laws of Strophé, Antistrophé, and Epode with consummate art. A third figure may be chosen from Pindar [1] himself.

Metaphors to express Pindar's style.

"As when a man takes from his wealthy hand a goblet foaming with the dew of the grape, and gives it with healths and pledges to his youthful son-in-law to bear from one home to the other home, golden, the crown of his possessions, gracing the feast and glorifying his kinsman, and makes him in the eyes of the assembled friends to be admired for his harmonious wedlock : so I, sending outpoured nectar, the Muses' gift, to conquering heroes, the sweet fruit of the soul, greet them like gods, victors at Olympia and Pytho."

Then too he adds : "With the lyre and with the various voices of flutes [2] I have come with Diagoras across the sea, chanting the wave-born daughter of the Cyprian goddess and the bride of Helios, island Rhodes." In this passage we get a lively impression of some of the marked qualities of Pindar. Reading his poetry is like quaffing wine that bubbles in a bowl of gold. Then too there is the picture of the poet, gorgeously attired, with his singing robes about him, erect upon the prow of a gilded galley, floating through dazzling summer-waves toward the island of his love, Rhodes, or Sicily, or Ægina. The lyre and the flute send their clear sounds across the sea. We pass temple and citadel on shore and promontory. The banks of oars sweep the flashing brine. Meanwhile the mighty poet stretches forth his golden cup of

[1] Seventh Ol.

[2] Compare this with the passage in Pythian, iii. 68, where Pindar describes himself Ἰονίαν τέμνων θάλασσαν (cleaving the Ionian Sea).

song to greet the princes and illustrious athletes who await Love of
splendour. him on the marble quays. Reading Pindar is a progress of this pompous kind. Pindar, as one of his critics remarks, was born and reared in splendour : splendour became his vital atmosphere. The epithet φιλάγλαος (splendour-loving), which he gives to Girgenti, suits himself. The splendour-loving Pindar is his name and title for all time. If we search the vocabulary of Pindar to find what phrases are most frequently upon his lips, we shall be struck with the great preponderance of all words that indicate radiance, magnificence, lustre. To Pindar's soul splendour was as elemental as harmony to Milton's. Of the Graces, Aglaia must have been his favourite. Nor, love as he did the gorgeousness of wealth, was it mere transitory pomp, the gauds and trappings of the world, which he admired. There must be something to stir the depths of his soul—beauty of person, or perfection of art, or moral radiance, or ideal grandeur. The blaze of real magnificence draws him as the sun attracts the eagle ; he does not flit moth-like about the glimmer of mere ephemeral lights.

After these three figures, which illustrate the fiery flight, Elemental
force and
magnetism. the torrent-fulness, the intoxicating charm of Pindar, one remains by which the magnetic force and tumult of his poetry may be faintly adumbrated. He who has watched a sunset attended by the passing of a thunderstorm in the outskirts of the Alps, who has seen the distant ranges of the mountains alternately obscured by cloud and blazing with the concentrated brightness of the sinking sun, while drifting scuds of hail and rain, tawny with sunlight, glistening with broken rainbows, clothe peak and precipice and forest in the golden veil of flame-irradiated vapour—who has heard the thunder bellow in the thwarting folds of hills, and watched the lightning, like a snake's tongue, flicker at intervals amid gloom and glory—knows in Nature's language what Pindar teaches with the voice of Art. It is only by a strained metaphor like this that any attempt to realise the *Sturm und Drang* of

Pindar's style can be communicated. In plainer language, Pindar, as an artist, combines the strong flight of the eagle, the irresistible force of the torrent, the richness of Greek wine, the majestic pageantry of Nature in one of her sublimer moods.

Pindar's victorious odes.

Like all the great lyrists of the Dorian School, Pindar composed odes of various species—Hymns, Prosodia, Parthenia, Threnoi, Scolia, Dithyrambs, as well as Epinikia. Of all but the Epinikian Odes we have only inconsiderable fragments left; yet these are sublime and beautiful enough to justify us in believing that Pindar surpassed his rivals in the Threnos and the Scolion as far as in the Epinikian Ode. Forty-four of his poems we possess entire—fourteen Olympians, twelve Pythians, eleven Nemeans, seven Isthmians. Of the occasions which led to the composition of these odes something must be said. The Olympian games were held in Elis once in five years, during the summer : their prize was a wreath of wild olive. The Pythian games were held in spring, on the Crissæan plain, once in five years : their prizes were a wreath of laurel and a palm. The Nemean games were held in the groves of Nemea, near Cleonæ, in Argolis, once in three years : their prize was a wreath of parsley. The Isthmian games were held at Corinth, once in three years : their prize was a wreath of pine, native to the spot. The Olympian festival honoured Zeus ; that of Pytho, Phœbus ; that of Nemea, Zeus ; that of the Isthmus, Poseidon. Originally they were all of the nature of a πανήγυρις or national assembly at the shrine of some deity local to the spot, or honoured there with more than ordinary reverence. The Isthmian games in particular retained a special character. Instituted for an Ionian deity, whose rites the men of Elis refused to acknowledge, they failed to unite the whole Greek race. The Greek games, like the Schwing-feste and shooting matches of Switzerland, served as recurring occasions of reunion and fellowship. Their influence in preserving a Panhellenic feeling was very

marked. During the time of the feast, and before and after,
for a sufficient number of days to allow of travellers journeying to and from Olympia and Delphi, hostilities were suspended
throughout Hellas; safe-conduct was given through all states
to pilgrims. One common feeling animated all the Greeks
at these seasons : they met in rivalry, not of arms on the
battlefield, but of personal prowess in the lists. And though
the various families of the Hellenic stock were never united,
yet their games gave them a common object, and tended to
the diffusion of national ideas.

Let us pause to imagine the scene which the neighbourhood *The games*
of Olympia must have presented, as the great recurring festival *at Olympia.*
of the Greek race approached—a festival in the fullest sense
of the word popular, but at the same time consecrated by
religion, dignified by patriotic pride, adorned with Art. The
full blaze of summer is overhead ; plain and hillside yield no
shade but what the spare branches of the olive and a few
spreading pines afford. Along the road throng pilgrims and
deputies, private persons journeying modestly, and public
ambassadors gorgeously equipped at the expense of their
state. Strangers from Sicily, or Cyrene, or Magna Græcia,
land from galleys on the coast of Elis. Then there are the
athletes with their trainers—men who have been in rude
exercise for the prescribed ten months, and whose limbs are
in the bloom of manly or of boyish strength. Sages, like
Gorgias, or Prodicus, or Protagoras, are on their way, escorted
by bands of disciples, eager to engage each other in debate
beneath the porticoes of the Olympian Zeus. Thales or
Anaxagoras arrives, big with a new theory of the universe.
Historians like Herodotus are carrying their scrolls to read
before assembled Hellas. Epic poets and rhapsodes are
furnished with tales of heroes, freshly coined from their own
brains, or conned with care from Homer. Rich men bring
chariots for racing or display ; the more a man spends at
Olympia, the more he honours his native city. Women, we

need not doubt, are also on the road—Hetairæ from Corinth, and Cyprus, and Ionia.   Sculptors show models of their skill. Potters exhibit new shapes of vases, with scrolls of honey-suckle wreathing round the pictured image of some handsome boy, to attract the eyes of buyers.   Painters have their tablets and colours ready.   Apart from these more gay and giddy servants of the public taste, are statesmen and diplo-matists, plenipotentiaries despatched to feel the pulse of Hellas, negotiators seeking opportunities for safe discussion of the affairs of rival cities.   Every active brain, or curious eye, or wanton heart, or well-trained limb, or skilful hand, or knavish wit may find its fit employment here.

The influx of pilgrims and travellers.   As they approached Olympia, a splendid scene burst upon the travellers' eyes—the plain of Elis, rich, deep-meadowed, hoary with olive-trees.   One cried to the other, There is the hill of Cronion!   There is the grove of Altis !   Thither flows Alpheus to the sea !   Those white and glittering statues are the portraits of the victors !   That temple is the house of everlasting Zeus ; beneath its roof sits the Thunderer of Pheidias !   Every step made the journey more exciting.   By the bed of the Alpheus, tawny in midsummer with dusty oleander-blossoms, the pilgrims passed.   At last they enter the precincts of Olympian Zeus : the sacred enclosure is alive with men ; the statues among the trees are scarcely more wonder-worthy in their glittering marble than are the bodies. of the athletes moving beneath them.   The first preoccupation of every Greek who visited Olympia was to see the statue of Zeus.   Not to have gazed upon this masterpiece of Pheidias was, according to a Greek proverb, the unhappiness of life. In this, his greatest work, the Athenian sculptor touched the highest point of art, and incarnated the most sublime concep-tion of Greek religious thought.   The god was seated on his throne ; but, even so, the image rose to the height of forty feet, wrought of pure ivory and gold.   At his feet stood figures symbolical of victory in the Olympian games : among

them the portrait of Pantarkes, himself a victor, the youth
whom Pheidias loved. In designing his great statue the
sculptor had in mind those lines of Homer which describe
Zeus nodding his ambrosial locks, and shaking Olympus.
That he had succeeded in presenting to the eye all that
the Greek race could imagine of godlike power and holiness
and peace, was attested not only by the universal voice of
Hellas, but also by the Romans who gazed as conquerors
upon the god. Lucius Paulus Æmilius, we are told, after
the battle of Pydna, swept Greece, and coming to Olympia,
saw the Pheidian Zeus. He shuddered, and exclaimed that
he had set mortal eyes upon the deity incarnate. Yet Paulus
was a Roman trampling with his legionaries the subject states
of fallen Hellas. Cicero proclaimed that Pheidias had copied
nothing human, but had carved the ideal image existing in
an inspired mind.

Zeus, it must be remembered, was the supreme god of the
Aryan race, the purest divinity of the Greek cultus. He was
called Father, Sire of gods and men. Therefore his presence
in the Panhellenic temple was peculiarly appropriate and
awe-inspiring. We may imagine the feelings of an athlete
coming to struggle for the fame of his own city, when he first
approached this statue in the august Olympian shrine. The
games were held at the time of a full moon; through the
hypæthral opening of the temple-roof fell the silver rays
aslant upon those solemn lineaments, making the glow of
ivory and gold more solemn in the dimness of a wondrous
gloom.

The Zeus of Pheidias.

Presidents chosen from the people of Elis and named
Hellanodikai, awarded the prizes and controlled the conduct
of the games. From their decision, in cases of doubt, there
was a final appeal to the assembly of Elis. In the morning
the heralds opened the lists with this proclamation:[1] "Now
begins the contest that dispenses noblest prizes; time tells

Conduct of the games.

[1] Bergk, *Poetæ Lyrici*, p. 1301.

you to delay no longer." When the runners were ready, the heralds started them with these words, "Put your feet to the line and run." At the end of the day they cried, "Now ceases the contest that dispenses noblest prizes; time tells you to delay no longer." The victor was crowned with wild olive, and led by his friends to the temple of Zeus. On the way they shouted the old Archilochian chorus, τήνελλα καλλίνικε, to which Pindar alludes in the beginning of his ninth Olympian : "The song of Archilochus uttered at Olympia, the triple cry of Hail Victorious! was enough to conduct Epharmostus, leading the revel to the Cronian hill with his comrades. But now, from the far-darting bows of the Muses, approach Zeus of the blazing thunder and the holy jutting land of Elis with these mightier shafts." Sacrifice and banquet took place in the evening; and happy was the athlete who, in this supreme moment, was greeted by Pindar with attendant chorus and musicians of the flute and lyre. Three Olympians, which seem to have been composed and chanted on the spot, survive—the fourth, the eighth, the tenth. The Proëmia to these odes, two of which are remarkably short, indicating the haste in which they had been prepared, sufficiently establish this fact. "Supreme hurler of the thunderbolt that never tires, Zeus! Thy festival recurring with the season brings me with sound of lyre and song to witness august games." "Parent of golden-crowned contests, Olympia, mistress of truth," etc. But it could not be expected that the more elaborate of Pindar's compositions should be ready on such occasions. It usually happened that the victor either found Pindar at Olympia, or sent a message to him at Thebes, and bespoke an ode, adding gifts in accordance with the poet's rank and fame. Then Pindar composed his Epinikian, which was sung when the conqueror returned to his own city. The ode would be repeated on successive anniversaries at banquets, sacrificial festivals, and processions in honour of the victory. The ninth Olympian, which has been already quoted, was, for example, sung at a banquet in honour of Epharmostus of Opus, after the altar of Ajax, son of Oïleus, had been crowned. Pindar, as we find from frequent allusions in the odes, had such a press of work that he often delayed sending his poems at the proper time, and had to excuse himself for neglect. In the second Isthmian he records a delay of two years. We may add that he did not disdain to accept money for his toil. In the eleventh Pythian he says : "Muse, it is thy part, since thou hast contracted to give thy voice for gold, to set it going in various ways." In the Proëmium to the second Isthmian he somewhat bitterly laments the necessity that made him sell his songs :—

> "The men of old, Thrasybulus, who climbed the chariot of the gold-crowned Muses, and received a famous lyre, lightly shot their arrows of honey-voiced hymns in praise of boys, of him whose beauty kept the summer bloom of youth, that sweetest souvenir of Aphrodite throned in joy. For the Muse as yet loved not gain, nor worked for hire, nor were sweet and tender songs with silvered faces sold by Terpsichore. But now she bids us keep the Argive's speech in mind ; and verily it hits the truth ; that Money, Money, Money makes the man. He spoke it when deserted of his riches and his friends."

Yet we must not suppose that Pindar sang slavishly the praise of every bidder. He was never fulsome in his pane-gyric. He knew how to mingle eulogy with admonition. If his theme be the wealth of a tyrant like Hiero, he reminds him of the dangers of ambition and the crime of avarice. Arcesi-laus of Cyrene is warned [1] to remit his sentence of banish-ment in favour of a powerful exile. Victors, puffed up with the pride of their achievements, hear from him how variable is the life of man, how all men are mere creatures of a day. Handsome youths are admonished to beware of lawless-ness and shun incontinence. Thus Pindar, while suiting his praises to the persons celebrated, always interweaves an appropriate precept of morality. There was nothing that he hated more than flattery and avarice, and grasping after higher

Eulogy and warning.

[1] Pyth. iv. 263.

honours than became his station.   In him more than in any
other poet were apparent the Greek virtues of εὐκοσμία,
σωφροσύνη (orderly behaviour, self-restraint) and all the
moral and artistic qualities which were summed up in the
Ideal of life. motto μηδὲν ἄγαν (nothing in excess).[1]   Those who are
curious to learn Pindar's opinions on these points may consult
the following passages :[2]—Nem. viii. 32 ; Nem. vii. 65 ; Pyth.
xi. 50 ; Isthm. vii. 40 ; Isthm. v. 14 ; and lastly, Pyth. x. 22,
which contains this truly beautiful description of a thoroughly
successful life, as imagined by a Greek :—

"That man is happy and songworthy by the skilled, who,
victorious by might of hand or vigour of foot, achieves the greatest
prizes with daring and with strength ; and who in his lifetime sees
his son, while yet a boy, crowned happily with Pythian wreaths.

---

[1] These pregnant words imply self-government and self-restraint in
obedience to a high ideal of order and symmetry, as opposed to the perils
and the uncomeliness of extravagance.

[2] "Hateful of a truth, even in days of old, was treacherous blandish-
ment, attendant of wily words, designing guile, mischief making slander,
which loves to wrest the splendour of fame and to maintain the unreal
honours of ignoble men.   Never may such be my temper, Zeus, our father !
but may I follow the plain paths of life, that, dying, I may leave no foul fame
to my children.   Some pray for gold, and some for vast lands ; but I to
please my countrymen, and so to hide my limbs beneath the earth, praising
where praise is due, and sowing blame for sinful men.   Virtue grows and
blooms, like a tree that shoots up under fostering dews, when skilled men
and just raise it towards the liquid air." . . . "Among my fellow-
citizens I look with brightness in my eye, not having overstepped due
bounds, and having removed from before my feet all violence.   May future
time come kindly to me." . . . "May I obtain from heaven the desire
of what is right, aiming at things within my powers in my prime of life.
For finding, as I do, that the middle status in a city flourishes with more
lasting prosperity, I deprecate the lot of kings." . . . "Passing the
pleasure of the days I gently glide towards old age and man's destined end :
for all alike we die : yet is our fortune unequal ; and if a man seek far,
short is his strength to reach the brazen seat of the gods : verily winged
Pegasus cast his lord Bellerophon, who sought to come into the dwellings
of the heaven, unto the company of Zeus." . . . "Seek not to be Zeus
. . . mortal fortunes are for mortal men."

The brazen heaven, it is true, is inaccessible to him ; but whatsoever joys we race of mortals touch, he reaches to the farthest voyage."

With this we may compare the story of happy lives told by Crœsus to Solon, and the celebrated four lines of Simonides : —"Health is best for a mortal man ; next beauty ; thirdly, well-gotten wealth ; fourthly, the pleasure of youth among friends."

Closely connected with Pindar's ethical beliefs were his religious notions, which were both peculiar and profound. Two things with regard to his theology deserve especial notice—its conscious criticism of existing legends, and its strong Pythagorean bias, both combined with true Hellenic orthodoxy in all essentials. One of the greatest difficulties in forming an exact estimate of the creed of a philosophical Greek intellect, is to know how to value the admixture of scientific scepticism on the one hand, and of purer theism on the other. About Pindar's time the body of Hellenic mythology was being invaded by a double process of destructive and constructive criticism. Xenophanes, for example, very plainly denounced as absurd the anthropomorphic Pantheon made in the image of man, while he endeavoured to substitute a cult of the One God, indivisible and incognisable. Plato still further developed the elements suggested by Xenophanes. But there was some inherent incapacity in the Greek intellect for arriving at monotheism by a process of rarefaction and purification. The destructive criticism which in Xenophanes, Pindar, and Plato, had assailed the grosser myths, dwindled into unfruitful scepticism. The attempts at constructing a rational theosophy ended in metaphysics. Morality was studied as a separate branch of investigation, independent of destructive criticism and religious construction. Meanwhile the popular polytheism continued to flourish, though enfeebled, degenerate, and disconnected from the nobler impulses of poetry and art. In Pindar the

Pindar's religion.

process of decadence had not begun. He stood at the very highest point which it was possible for a religious Greek to reach—combining the æsthetically ennobling enthusiasm for the old Greek deities with so much critical activity as enabled him to reject the grosser myths, and with that moderate amount of theological mysticism which the unassisted intellect of the Greeks seemed capable of receiving without degeneracy into puerile superstition. The first Olympian ode contains the most decided passages in illustration of his critical independence of judgment :—

Critique of vulgar beliefs.

> " Impossible is it for me to call one of the blessed ones a glutton : I stand aloof : loss hath often overtaken evil speakers."

Again :—

> " Truly many things are wonderful ; and it may be that in some cases fables dressed up with cunning fictions beyond the true account falsify the traditions of men. But Beauty, which is the author of all delicious things for mortals, by giving to these myths acceptance, ofttimes makes even what is incredible to be credible : but succeeding time gives the most certain evidence of truth ; and for a man to speak nobly of the gods is seemly ; for so the blame is less."

These two passages suffice to prove how freely Pindar handled the myths, not indeed exposing them to the corrosive action of mere scepticism, but testing them [1] by the higher standard of the healthy human conscience. When he refuses to believe that the immortals were cannibals and ate the limbs of Pelops, he is like a rationalist avowing his disbelief in the savage doctrine of eternal damnation. His doubt does not proceed from irreligion, but from faith in the immutable holiness of the gods, who set the ideal standard of human morality. What seems to him false in the myths, he attributes to the accretions of ignorant opinion and vain fancy round the truth.

The mystical element of Pindar's creed, whether we call it

---

[1] Compare for a similar freedom of judgment Antigone's famous speech on the unwritten Laws.

Orphic or Pythagorean, is remarkable for a definite belief in Mystic ele-
ments in
Pindar's
creed. the future life, including a system of rewards and punishments, for the assertion of the supreme tribunal of conscience,[1] and finally, for a reliance on rites of purification. The most splendid passage in which these opinions are expressed by Pindar is that portion of the second Olympian in which he describes the torments of the wicked and the blessings of the just beyond the grave :—

"Among the dead, sinful souls at once pay penalty, and the crimes done in this realm of Zeus are judged beneath the earth by one who gives sentence under dire necessity.

"But the good, enjoying perpetual sunlight equally by night and day, receive a life more free from woes than this of ours ; they trouble not the earth with strength of hand, nor the water of the sea for scanty sustenance ; but with the honoured of the gods, all they who delighted in the keeping of their oath pass a tearless age : the others suffer woe on which no eye can bear to look. Those who have thrice endured on either side the grave to keep their spirits wholly free from crime, journey on the road of Zeus to the tower of Cronos : where round the islands blow breezes ocean-borne : and flowers of gold burn some on the land from radiant trees, and others the wave feeds : with necklaces whereof they twine their hands and brows, in the just decrees of Rhadamanthus, whom father Cronos has for a perpetual colleague, he who is spouse of Rhea throned above all gods.

"Peleus and Cadmus are numbered among these : and thither was Achilles brought by his mother when she swayed the heart of Zeus with prayer : he who slew Hector, the invincible firm pillar of Troy, and gave Cycnus to death and Eo's Æthiopian son."

---

[1] The conscience forms a strong point in the ethical systems of many of the ancients, especially of Plato, of Lucretius, of Persius—authors otherwise dissimilar enough as representing three distinct species of thought. In Mythology it receives an imperfect embodiment in the Erinnyes, who, however, are spiritual forces acting from without, rather than from within, upon the criminal. Purifying rites belong to the Mysteries or τελεταί ; they formed a prominent feature in the Ethics of Empedocles and Pythagoras, and an integral part of the cult of Apollo and the nether deities. Philosophers like Plato rejected them as pertaining to ceremonial superstition.

The following fragments from Threnoi [1] translated by Professor Conington further illustrate Pindar's belief in a future state of weal or woe :—

> " They from whom Persephone
>   Due atonement shall receive
>   For the things that made to grieve,
> To the upper sunlight she
> Sendeth back their souls once more,
> Soon as winters eight are o'er.
> From those blessed spirits spring
> Many a great and goodly king,
> Many a man of glowing might,
> Many a wise and learned wight :
> And while after-days endure,
> Men esteem them heroes pure."

And again :—

> " Shines for them the sun's warm glow
> When 'tis darkness here below :
> And the ground before their towers,
> Meadow-land with purple flowers,
> Teems with incense-bearing treen,
> Teems with fruit of golden sheen.
> Some in steed and wrestling feat,
> Some in dice take pleasure sweet,
> Some in harping : at their side
> Blooms the spring in all her pride.
> Fragrance all about is blown
>   O'er that country of desire,
> Ever as rich gifts are thrown
>   Freely on the far-seen fire,
> Blazing from the altar-stone.

·   ·   ·   ·   ·

> But the souls of the profane,
>   Far from heaven removed below,
> Flit on earth in murderous pain
>   'Neath the unyielding yoke of woe ;
> While pious spirits tenanting the sky
> Chant praises to the mighty one on high."

---

[1] Bunsen's *God in History*, vol. ii. pp. 144 and 136.

For Pindar's conception of the destinies of frail humanity, *Ephemeral frailty of human life.* take this sublime but melancholy ending to an ode [1] which has been full of triumphant exultation : "Brief is the growing-time of joy for mortals, and briefly too doth its flower fall to earth shaken by fell fate. Things of a day ! what are we—and what are we not ! A shadow's dream is man. But when the splendour that God gives descends, then there remains a radiant light and gladsome life for mortals." Compare with this the opening of the sixth Nemean :—

"One is the race of men, and one the race of gods ; from one mother we both draw breath. But a total difference of force divides us, since man's might is nought, while brazen heaven abideth a sure seat for aye. Nevertheless, we are not all unlike immortals either in our mighty soul or strength of limb, though we know not to what goal of night or day fate hath written down for us to run."

Passing to the consideration of Pindar purely as an artist, *Pindar's treatment of his themes.* we may first examine the structure of his odes, and then illustrate the qualities of his poetry by reference to some of the more splendid Proëmia and descriptions. The task which lay before him when he undertook to celebrate a victory at one of the Greek games, was this. Some rich man had won a race with his chariot and horses, or some strong man had conquered his competitors by activity or force of limb. Pindar had to praise the rich man for his wealth and liberality, the strong man for his endurance of training and personal courage or dexterity. In both cases the victor might be felicitated on his good fortune—on the piece of luck which had befallen him ; and if he were of comely person or illustrious blood, these also offered topics for congratulation. The three chief commonplaces of Pindar, therefore, are ὄλβος, ἀρετή, εὐτυχία, wealth or prosperity, manliness or spirit, and blessings independent of both, god-given, not acquired. But it could not be that a great poet should ring the changes only on these three subjects, or content himself with describing the actual contest,

[1] Pyth. viii.

which probably he had not witnessed. Consequently Pindar
illustrates his odes with myths or stories bearing more or less
closely on the circumstances of his hero. Sometimes he celebrates the victor's ancestry, as in the famous sixth Olympian,
in which the history of the Iamidæ is given; sometimes his
city, as in the seventh Olympian, where he describes the birthplace of Diagoras, the island Rhodes; sometimes he dwells
upon an incident in the hero's life, as when in the third
Pythian the illness of Hiero suggests the legend of Asclepius
and Cheiron; sometimes a recent event, like the eruption of
Etna, alluded to in the first Pythian, gives colour to his ode;
sometimes, as in the case of the last Pythian, where the story
of Medusa is narrated, the legendary matter is introduced
to specialise the nature of the contest. The victory itself is
hardly touched upon : the allusions to prosperity, excellence of
manhood, advantages of fortune, though frequent and interwoven with the texture of the ode, are brief : the whole
poetic fabric is so designed as to be appropriate to the occasion
and yet independent of it. Therefore Pindar's odes have not
perished with the memory of the events to which they owed
their composition.

Translation
of the
twelfth
Pythian.

Pindar's peculiar treatment of the Epinikian ode may best
be illustrated by analysing the structure of one or two of his
poems. But first take this translation of one of the shorter
and simpler of the series—the twelfth Pythian :—

> " To thee, fairest of earthly towns, I pray—
> Thou splendour-lover, throne of Proserpine,
> Piled o'er Girgenti's slopes, that feed alway
> Fat sheep !—with grace of gods and men incline,
> Great queen, to take this Pythian crown and own
> Midas ; for he of all the Greeks, thy son,
> Hath triumphed in the art which Pallas won,
> Weaving of fierce Gorgonian throats the dolorous moan.

> " She from the snake-encircled hideous head
> Of maidens heard the wailful dirges flow,
> What time the third of those fell Sisters bled

By Perseus' hand, who brought the destined woe
To vexed Seriphos.   He on Phorkys' brood
ｊWrought ruin, and on Polydectes laid
Stern penance for his mother's servitude,
And for her forceful wedlock, when he slew the maid

" Medusa.   He by living gold, they say,
Was got on Danaë : but Pallas bore
Her hero through those toils, and wrought the lay
Of full-voiced flutes to mock the ghastly roar
Of those strong jaws of grim Euryale :
A goddess made and gave to men the flute,
The fountain-head of many a strain to be,
That ne'er at game or nation's feast it might be mute,

" Sounding through subtle brass and voiceful reeds,
Which near the city of the Graces spring
By fair Cephisus, faithful to the needs
Of dancers.   Lo ! there cometh no good thing
Apart from toils to mortals, though to-day
Heaven crown their deeds : yet shun we not the laws
Of Fate ; for times impend when chance withdraws
What most we hoped, and what we hoped not gives for aye. "

Here it will be seen that Pindar introduces his subject with *Analysis of various odes.* a panegyric of Girgenti, his hero's birthplace.   Then he names Midas, and tells the kind of triumph he has gained.   This leads him to the legend of Medusa.   The whole is concluded with moral reflections on the influence of Fate over human destinies.   The structure of the sixth Pythian is also very simple.   "I build an indestructible treasure-house of praise for Xenocrates (lines 1-18), which Thrasybulus, his son, gained for him ; as Antilochus died for Nestor (19-43), so Thrasybulus has done what a son could do for his father (44-46) ; wise and fair is he in his youth ; his company is sweeter than the honeycomb" (47-54).   One of the longest odes, the fourth Pythian, is constructed thus : "Muse ! celebrate Arcesilaus (1-5).   Cyrene, Arcesilaus' home ; its foundation and the oracle given to Battus (5-69).   The tale of the Argonauts, ancestors of the founders of Thera and of Cyrene (69-262).

Advice to Arcesilaus in the interest of Demophilus " (263-299).
Here the victory at Pytho is but once briefly alluded to (64).
The whole ode consists of pedigree and political admonition,
either directly administered at the end, or covertly conveyed
through the example of Pelias. The sixth Olympian, which
contains the pedigree of the Iamidæ, is framed on similar
principles. The third Pythian introduces its mythology by a
different method : " I wish I could restore Cheiron, the healer
and the tutor of Asclepius, to life (1-7). The story of Coronis,
her son Asclepius, and Hippolytus (7-58). Moral, to be content and submit to morality (58-62). Yet would that Cheiron
might return and heal Hiero (62-76) ! I will pray ; and do
you, Hiero, remember that Heaven gives one blessing and two
curses, and that not even Cadmus and Peleus were always
fortunate (17-106). May I suit myself always to my fortune ! "
(107-115). The whole of this ode relates to Hiero's illness,
and warns him of vicissitudes : even the episode of Coronis
and Asclepius contains a covert warning against arrogance,
while it gracefully alludes to Hiero's health.

The open-
ings or
Proëms.   The originality and splendour of Pindar are most noticeable
in the openings of his odes—the Proëmia, as they are technically called. It would appear that he possessed an inexhaustible
storehouse of radiant imagery, from which to draw new thoughts
for the commencement of his poems. In this region, which
most poets find but barren, he displayed the fullest vigour
and fertility of fancy. Sometimes, but rarely, the opening is
simple, as in the second Olympian : " Hymns that rule the
lyre ! what god, what hero, what man shall we make famous ? "
Or the ninth Pythian : " I wish to proclaim, by help of the
deep - girdled Graces, brazen - shielded Telesicrates, Pythian
victor," etc. Rather more complex are the following :—Nem.
iv. " The joy of the feast is the best physician after toil ; but
songs, the wise daughters of the Muses, soothe the victor with
their touch : warm water does not so refresh and supple weary
limbs as praise attended by the lyre ; " or again : Ol. xi. " There

is a time when men have greatest need of winds; there is when heaven's showers of rain, children of the cloud, are sorest sought for. But if a man achieves a victory with toil, then sweet-voiced hymns arise as the beginning of future fame," etc. etc. But soon we pass into a more gorgeous region. "As when with golden columns reared beneath the well-walled palace-porch we build a splendid hall, so will I build my song. At the beginning of the work we must make the portal radiant." [1] Or again: "No carver of statues am I, to fashion figures stationary on their pedestal; but come, sweet song! on every argosy and skiff set forth from Ægina to proclaim that Pytheas, Lampon's son, by strength of might is victor in Nemean games, upon whose chin and cheek you see not yet the tender mother of the vine-flower, summer's bloom." [2] Or again: "Hallowed bloom of youth, herald of Aphrodite's ambrosial pleasures, who, resting on the eyelids of maidens and of boys, bearest one aloft with gentle hands of violence, but another rudely!" [3] Or once again, in a still grander style :—

"Listen! for verily it is of beauty's queen, or of the Graces, that we turn the glebe, approaching the rocky centre of the deep-voiced earth : where for the blest Emmenidæ and stream-washed Acragas, yea, and for Zenocrates is built a treasure-house of Pythian hymns in the golden Apollonian vale. This, no rain of winter, driving on the wings of wind, the pitiless army of the rushing cloud, no hurricane, shall toss, storm-lashed with pebbles of the uptorn beach, into the briny ocean caves : but in pure light its glorious face shall speak the victory that brings a common fame on thy sire, Thrasybulus, and thy race, remaining in the windings of Crisæan valleys." [4]

We have already seen how Pindar compares his odes to arrows, to sun-soaring eagles, to flowers of the Muses, to wine in golden goblets, to water, to a shrine which no years will fret away. Another strange figure [5] may be quoted from the third Nemean (line 76): "I send to thee this honey mingled

Lyrical imagery.

---

[1] Ol. vi.   [2] Nem. v.   [3] Nem. viii.   [4] Pyth. vi.
[5] Compare, too, Nem. vii. 11, 62, 77.

with white milk ; the dew of their mingling hangs around the
bowl, a draught of song, flowing through the Æolian breath
of flutes." It will be perceived that to what is called confusion of metaphors Pindar shows a lordly indifference. Swift
and sudden lustre, the luminousness of a meteor, marks this
monarch of lyric song. He grasps an image, gives it a form
of bronze, irradiates it with the fire of flame or down-poured
sunlight.

Pindar's
power of
narration.

To do justice to Pindar's power of narrative by extracts
and translations is impossible. No author suffers more by
mutilation and by the attempt to express in another language
and another rhythm what he has elaborately fashioned. Yet
it may be allowed me to direct attention to the rapidity with
which the burning of Coronis (Pyth. iii. 38), and the birth of
Rhodes from the sea (Ol. vii. 54), are told in words the
grandest, simplest, and most energetic that could be found.
This is the birth of Iamos (Ol. vi. 39) :—

> " Nor could she hide from Æpytus the seed
>   Divine : but he to Pytho, chewing care,
> Journeyed to gain for this great woe some rede ;
>   She loosening her crimson girdle fair,
> And setting on the ground her silver jar,
>   Beneath the darksome thicket bare a son,
> Within whose soul flamed godhead like a star ;
>   And to her aid the golden-haired sent down
> Mild Eleithuia and the awful Fates,
> Who stood beside, while from the yearning gates

> " Of childbirth, with a brief and joyous pain,
>   Came Iamos into the light, whom she therewith
> Sore-grieving left upon the grass : amain
>   By gods' decree two bright-eyed serpents lithe
> Tended, and with the harmless venom fed
>   Of bees, the boy ; nor ceased they to provide
> Due nurture. But the king, what time he sped
>   Homeward from rocky Pytho, to his side
> Called all his household, asking of the son
> Born of Evadne, for he said that none

" But Phœbus was the sire, and he should be
    Chief for his prophecy 'mid mortal men,
Nor should his children's seed have end.   Thus he
    Uttered the words oracular : and then
They swore they had not heard or seen the child,
    Now five days old ; but he within the reed
And thick-entangled woodland boskage wild,
    His limbs 'mid golden beams and purple brede
Of gillyflowers deep-sunken, lay ; wherefore
He by his mother's wish for all time bore

" That deathless name.   But when he plucked the flower
    Of golden-wreathéd youth, he went and stood
Midmost Alphëus, at the midnight hour,
    And called upon the ruler of the flood,
His ancestor Poseidon, and the lord
    Of god-built Delos, praying that he might
Rear up some race to greatness.   Then the word
    Responsive of his sire upon the night
Sounded :—' Arise, my son, go forth and fare
Unto the land whereof all men shall share ! '

" So came they to the high untrodden mound
    Of Cronion ; and there a double meed
Of prophecy on Iamos was bound,
    Both from the voice that knows no lie to heed
Immortal words, and next, when Heracles,
    Bold in his counsels, unto Pisa came,
Founding the festivals of sacred peace
    And mighty combats for his father's fame,
Then on the topmost altar of Jove's hill,
The seat of sooth oracular to fill."

After so much praise of Pindar's style it must be confessed
that he has faults.   One of these is notoriously tumidity—an
overblown exaggeration of phrase.   For example, when he
wants to express that he cannot enlarge on the fame of
Ægina, but will relate as quickly as he can the achievements
of Aristomenes which he has undertaken, he says : " But I
am not at leisure to consecrate the whole long tale to the
lyre and delicate voice, lest satiety should come and cause
annoy : but that which is before my feet shall go at running

Drawbacks of the Pindaric style.

speed—thy affair, my boy—the latest of the noble deeds made winged by means of my art." [1] The imaginative force which enabled him to create epithets like φιλάγλαος, παμπόρφυρος (splendour-loving, all-purple), and to put them exactly in their proper places, like blocks of gleaming alabaster or of glowing porphyry—for the architectural power over language is eminent in Pindar—the Titanic faculty of language which produced such phrases as ἐξ ἀδάμαντος ἢ σιδάρου κεχάλκευται μέλαιναν καρδίαν ψυχρᾷ φλογί (from adamant or steel hath been forged in his dark heart with frigid fire) did also betray him into expressions as pompous and frigid as these— ποικιλοφόρμιγγος ἀοιδᾶς . . . σχοινοτενεία τ' ἀοιδὰ διθυράμβων (song accompanied by varied notes of the stringed lyre . . . the linkéd long-drawn melodies of dithyrambic song). These, poured forth by Pindar in the insolence of prodigality, when imitated by inferior poets, produced that inflated manner of lyrical diction which Aristophanes ridicules in Kinesias. The same may be said about his mixed metaphors, whereof the following are fair examples : [2]—

δόξαν ἔχω τιν' ἐπὶ γλώσσᾳ ἀκόνας λιγυρᾶς
ἅ μ' ἐθέλοντα προσέλκει καλλιρόοισι πνοαῖς.—Ol. vi. 82.

Κώπαν σχάσον ταχὺ δ' ἄγκυραν ἔρεισον χθονὶ
πρῴραθε χοιράδος ἄλκαρ πέτρας.
ἐγκωμίων γὰρ ἄωτος ὕμνων
ἐπ' ἄλλοτ' ἄλλον ὦτε μέλισσα θύνει λόγον.—Pyth. x. 51.

Apparent incoherence, mixed metaphors.

Nor are these the worst, perhaps, of the sort which might be chosen : for Pindar uses images like precious stones, setting them together in a mass, without caring to sort them, so long

---

[1] Pyth. viii. 30.

[2] " I seem to have upon my tongue the feeling as of a shrill-sounding whetstone, which draws me willingly along on gently-flowing airs."

"Check the oar, and quickly cast anchor from the prow to keep our ship from running on the sunken reef : for the flower of my encomiastic songs, like a bee, is darting from one theme to another."

as they produce a gorgeous show. Apparent incoherences,
involving difficulty to the reader, and producing a superficial
effect of obscurity, constitute another class of his alleged
faults—due partly to his allusive and elliptical style, partly
to his sudden transitions, partly to the mixture of his images.
Incapable of what is commonplace, too fiery to trudge, like
Simonides, along the path of rhetorical development, infinitely
more anxious to realise by audacity the thought that seizes
him than to make it easy to his hearer, Pindar is obscure to
all who are unwilling to assimilate their fancy to his own.
La Harpe called the Divine Comedy *une amplification stupide-
ment barbare:* what, if he had found occasion to speak the
truth of his French mind, would he have said about the Odes
of Pindar? Another difficulty, apart from these of verbal style
and imagination, is derived from the fact that the mechanism
of Pindar's poetry, carefully as it is planned, is no less carefully concealed. He seems to take delight in trying to solve
the problem of how slight a suggestion can be made to
introduce a lengthy narrative. The student is obliged to
maintain his attention at the straining point if an ode of
Pindar's, even after patient analysis, is to present more than
a mass of confused thoughts and images to his mind. But
when he has caught the poet's drift, how delicate is the
machinery, how beautiful is the art, which governs this most
sensitive fabric of linked melodies! What the hearers made
of these odes—the athletes for whom they were written, the
handsome youths praised in them, the rich men at whose
tables they were chanted—remains an impenetrable mystery.
Had the Greek race perceptions infinitely finer than ours?
Or did the classic harmonies of Pindar sweep over their souls,
ruffling the surface merely, but leaving the deeps untouched,
as the soliloquies of *Hamlet* or the profound philosophy of
Troilus and Cressida must have been lost upon the groundlings
of Elizabeth's days, who caught with eagerness at the queen's
poisoned goblet or the byplay of Sir Pandarus? That is a

Difficulty of
the Pindaric
style.

problem we cannot solve. All we know for certain is, that allowing for the currency of Pindar's language, and for the familiarity of his audience with the circumstances under which his odes were composed, as well as with their mythological allusions, these poems must at all times have been more difficult to follow than is Bach's fugue in G minor to a man who cannot play the organ.

CHAPTER XII

ÆSCHYLUS

Life of Æschylus—Nature of his Inspiration—The Theory of Art in the *Ion* of Plato—Æschylus and Sophocles—What Æschylus accomplished for the Attic Drama—His Demiurgic Genius—Colossal Scale of his Work—Marlowe—Oriental Imagery—Absence of Love as a Motive in his Plays—The Organic Vitality of his Art—Opening Scenes—Messenger—Chorus—His Theology—Destiny in Æschylus—The Domestic Curse—His Character-drawing—Clytemnestra—Difficulty of Dealing with the *Prometheus*—What was his Fault?—How was Zeus Justified?—Shelley's Opinion—The Lost Trilogy of *Prometheus*—Middle Plays in Trilogies—Attempt to reconstruct a *Prometheus*—The Part of Herakles—Obscurity of the Promethean Legend—The Free Handling of Myths permitted to the Dramatist—The *Oresteia*—Its Subject—The Structure of the Three Plays—The *Agamemnon*—Its Imagery—Cassandra—The Cry of the King—The Chorus—Iphigeneia at the Altar—Menelaus abandoned by Helen—The Dead Soldiers on the Plains of Troy—The *Persæ*—The Crime of Xerxes—Irony of the Situation—The Description of the Battle of Salamis—The Style of Æschylus—His Religious Feeling.

ÆSCHYLUS, son of Euphorion, was born at Eleusis, in 525 B.C. When he was thirty-five years of age, just ten years after the production of his first tragedy, he fought at Marathon. This fact is significant in its bearings on his art and on his life. Æschylus belonged to a family distinguished during the decisive actions of the Persian war by their personal bravery. Ameinias, his brother, gained the *aristeia*, or reward for valour, at the battle of Salamis; and there was an old picture in the theatre of Dionysus at Athens which represented the great deeds of the poet and his brother Cynægeirus at Marathon. Of his military achievements he was more proud than of his poetical success; for he mentions the former and is silent about the latter in the epitaph he wrote for his own tomb. Of his actual life at Athens, we only know this much, that he sided with the old aristocratic party. His retirement to Sicily after his defeat by Sophocles in 468 B.C. arose probably from the fact that Cimon, who adjudged the prize, was leader of the democratic opposition, and was felt to have allowed political leanings to influence a purely critical decision. His second retirement to Sicily in 453 B.C., after the production of the *Oresteia*, in which he unsuccessfully supported the Areiopagus against Pericles, was due, perhaps, in like manner to his disagreement with the rising powers in the State. That at some period of his career he was publicly accused of impiety, because he had either divulged the mysteries of Demeter, or had offended popular taste by his presentation of the *Furies* on the stage, rests upon sufficient antique testimony. Such charges were not uncommon at Athens, as might be proved by the biographies of Anaxagoras and Socrates. But the exact nature of the prosecution directed against Æschylus is not known; we cannot connect it with any of his extant works for certain, or determine how far it affected his action. He died at Gela, in 456 B.C., aged sixty-nine, having spent his life partly at Athens and partly at the court of Hiero, pursuing in both places his profession of tragic poet and chorus-master.

Pausanias tells a story of his early vocation to dramatic art:—" When he was a boy he was set to watch grapes in the country, and there fell asleep. In his slumber Dionysus appeared to him, and ordered him to apply himself to tragedy. At daybreak he made the attempt, and succeeded very easily." There is no reason that this legend should not have been based on truth. It was the general opinion of antiquity that

Æschylus was a poet possessed by the deity, working less by
artistic method than by immediate inspiration. Athenæus
asserts crudely that he composed his tragedies while drunk
with wine (μεθύων γοῦν ἔγραφε τὰς τραγῳδίας), and
Sophocles is reported to have told him that, " He did what
he ought to do, but did it without knowing." Longinus, in
like manner, after praising Æschylus for the audacity of his
imagination and the heroic grandeur of his conceptions, adds
that his plays were frequently unpolished, unrefined, ill-
digested, and rough in style. Similar expressions of opinion
might be quoted from Quintilian, who describes his style as
" sublime and weighty, and grandiloquent often to a fault,
but in most of his compositions rude and wanting in order."
He adds, that "the Athenians allowed later poets to correct
his dramas and to bring them into competition under new
forms, when many of them gained prizes." Æschylus seems,
therefore, to have impressed critics of antiquity with the
god-intoxicated passion of his genius rather than with the
perfection of his style or the consummate beauty of his
art. It is possible that he received less justice from his
fellow-countrymen than we, who have been educated by the
Shakespearean drama, can now pay him.

Æschylus might be selected to illustrate the artistic
psychology of Plato. In the *Phædrus* Plato lays down the
doctrine that poetic inspiration is akin to madness — an
efflation from the Muses, a divine mania analogous to love.
In the *Ion* he further develops this position, and asserts that
"all good poets compose their beautiful poems not as works
of art, but because they are inspired and possessed." The
analogy which he selects is drawn from the behaviour of
Bacchantes under the influence of Dionysus. He wishes to
distinguish between the mental operations of the poet and
the philosopher, to show that the regions of poetry and science
are separate, and to prove that rule and method are less sure
guides than instinct when the work to be produced is a poem.

Plato's theory of poetic inspiration

"The poet is a light and winged and holy thing, and there is no invention in him until he has been inspired and is out of his senses, and the mind is no longer in him; when he has not attained to this state, he is powerless and is unable to utter his oracles." The final dictum of the *Ion* is, "inspiration, not art," θεῖον καὶ μὴ τεχνικόν. It is curious to find a Greek of the best age, himself in early days a poet, and throughout distinguished by genius allied to the poetic, thus boldly and roundly stating a theory which corresponds to the vulgar notion that poetry comes by nature, untutored and untaught, and which seems to contradict the practice and opinion of supreme authorities like Sophocles and Goethe. The truth is, that among artists we find two broadly differentiated types. The one kind produce their best work when all their faculties are simultaneously excited, and when the generative impulse takes possession of them. They seem to obey the dictates of a power superior to their ordinary faculties. The other kind are always conscious of their methods and their aims; they do nothing, as it were, by accident; they avoid improvisation, and subordinate their creative faculty to reason. The laws of art may be just as fully appreciated by the more instinctive artists, and may have equally determined their choice of form and their calculation of effects; but at the moment of production these rules are thrust into the background, whereas they are continually present to the minds of the deliberate workers. It may be said in passing, that this distinction enables us to understand some phrases which the Italians, acutely sensitive to artistic conditions, have reserved for passionate and highly-inspired workers; they speak, for instance, of painting a picture or blocking out a statue *con furia*, when the artist is a Tintoretto or a Michael Angelo. If there is any truth at all in this analysis, we are justified in believing that Æschylus belonged to the former, and Sophocles to the latter class of poets, and that this is the secret of the criticism passed by Sophocles upon his predecessor. The

Two types of the artistic temperament.

account which Æschylus himself gave of his tragedies throws
no light upon his method ; he is reported to have said that
they were "fragments picked up from the mighty feasts of
Homer." The value he attached to them is proved by his
saying that he dedicated what he wrote to Time.

Though the ancients may have been right in regarding
Æschylus as an enthusiastic writer, obeying the impulse of
the god within him rather than the rules of reason, no
dramatic poet ever had a higher sense of the æsthetic unity
which tragedy demands. Each of his masterpieces presents
to the imagination a coherent and completely organised
whole ; every part is penetrated with the dominant thought
and passion that inspired it. He had, moreover, the strongest
sense of the formal requirements of his art. Tragedy had
scarcely passed beyond the dithyrambic stage when he received it from the hands of Phrynichus. Æschylus gave it
the form which, with comparatively unimportant alterations,
it maintained throughout the brilliant period of Attic culture.
It was he who curtailed the function of the Chorus and
developed dialogue, thus expanding the old Thespian elements
of tragedy in accordance with the true spirit of the drama.
By adding a second actor, by attending diligently to the
choric songs and dances, by inventing the cothurnus and the
tragic mask, and by devising machinery and scenes adapted
to the large scale of the Athenian stage, he gave its permanent
form to the dramatic art of the Greeks. However god-
possessed he may have been during the act of composition,
he was therefore a wise critic and a potent founder in all
matters pertaining to the theatre. Yet though Æschylus in
this way made the drama, the style in which he worked went
out of date in his own lifetime. So rapid was the evolution
of intelligence at Athens that during a single generation his
tragedies became, we will not say old-fashioned, but archaic.
They were duly put upon the stage ; a chorus at the public
expense was provided for their representation, and the MS.

Æschylus as a dramatic artist and creator.

which authorised their canon and their text was regarded as
a public treasure. Yet the Athenians already had come to
love and respect them in the same way as the English race
love and respect the Oratorios of Handel. They praised
them for their unapproachable magnificence; they knew that
no man of the latter days could match them in their own
kind; but they criticised their antique form and obsolete
embellishments. The poet who in his youth had played the
part of innovator, and who had shocked the public by his
realistic presentation of the Furies, depended in the heyday
of the fame of Aristophanes upon conservative support and
favour.

His demiur-
gic energy.

Æschylus was essentially the demiurge of ancient art.
The purely creative faculty has never been exhibited upon a
greater scale, or applied to material more utterly beyond the
range of feebler poets. He possessed in the highest degree
the power of giving life and form to the vast, the incorporeal,
and the ideal. In his dramas, mountains were made to speak;
Oceanus received shape, conversing face to face with the
Titan Prometheus, while his daughters, nurslings of the waves
and winds, were gathered on the Scythian crags in groups to
listen to their argument. The old intangible, half-mystical,
half-superstitious, fears of the Greek conscience became
substantial realities in his mind. Justice and Insolence and
Até no longer floated, dreamlike, in the background of religious thought: he gave them a pedigree, connected them
in a terrible series, and established them as ministers of
supreme Zeus. The Eumenides, whom the Greeks before
him had not dared to figure to their fancy, assumed a form
more hideous than that of Gorgons or Harpies. Their
symbolic torches, their snake-entwined tresses, their dreadful
eyes, and nostrils snorting fiery breath, were shown for the
first time visibly in the trilogy of *Orestes*. It was a revelation
which Greek art accepted as decisive. Thus the imagination
of Æschylus added new deities to the Athenian Pantheon.

The same creative faculty enabled him to inform elemental
substances, fire, water, air, with personal vitality. The
heaven, in his verse, yearns to wound the earth with love-
embraces; the falling rain impregnates the rich soil. The
throes of Ætna are a Titan's groaning. The fire that leaps
from Ida to the Hermæan crags of Lemnos, from Ægiplanctus
to the Arachnæan height, has life within it. There is nothing
dead, devoid of soul, in the world of this arch-mythopoet.
Even the ghosts and phantoms, dreams and omens, on which
he loves to dwell, are substantial. Their reality exists outside the soul they dominate.

As befits a demiurgic nature, Æschylus conceived and
executed upon a stupendous scale. His outlines are huge ; his
figures are colossal; his style is broad and sweeping—like a
river in its fulness and its might. Each of his plays might be
compared to a gigantic statue, whereof the several parts, taken
separately, are beautiful, while the whole is put together with
majestic harmony. But as the sculptor in modelling a colossus,
cannot afford to introduce the details which would grace a
chimney ornament, so Æschylus was forced to sacrifice the
working-out of minor motives. His imagination, penetrated
through and through with the spirit of his subject as a whole,
was more employed in presenting a series of great situations,
wrought together and combined into a single action, than in
elaborating the minutiæ of characters and plots. The result
has been that those students who delight in detail, have
complained of a certain disproportion between his huge design
and his insufficient execution. It has too frequently been implied that he could rough-hew like a Cyclops, but that he
could not finish like a Praxiteles ; that he was more capable of
sketching in an outline than of filling up its parts. Fortunately
we possess the means of laying bare the misconception upon
which these complaints are founded. There still remains one,
but only one, of his colossal works entire. The *Oresteia* is
sufficient to prove that we gain no insight into his method as

*Vast scale
and breadth
of his artistic
productions.*

an artist if we consider only single plays. He thought and wrote in Trilogies. Sophocles, with whom it is usual to compare Æschylus, somewhat to the disadvantage of the latter, abandoned the large scale, the uncial letters, of the trilogy. Each separate Sophoclean drama is a studied whole. In order to do Æschylus the very barest justice, we ought therefore to contrast, not the *Agamemnon* alone, but the entire *Oresteia* with the *Œdipus* or the *Antigone*. It will then be seen that the one poet, designing colossi, gave to them the style and finish and the unity which suit a statue larger than life-size : the other, restricting himself within more narrow limits, was free to lavish labour on the slightest details of his model. Such elaboration, on the scale adopted by Æschylus, would have produced a bewildering and painful effect of complexity. The vast design which it was the artist's object to throw into the utmost possible relief, would inevitably have suffered from excess of finish.

Æschylus and Marlowe.

Few dramatists have ventured, like Æschylus, to wield the chisel of a Titan, or to knead whole mountains into statues corresponding to the superhuman grandeur of their thought. Few indeed can have felt that this was their true province, that to this they had the thews and sinews adequate. He stands alone in his triumphant use of the large manner, and this solitude is prejudicial to his fame with students whose taste has been formed in the school of Sophocles. Surveying the long roll of illustrious tragedians, there is but one, until we come to Victor Hugo, in whom the Æschylean spirit found fresh incarnation : and he had fallen upon days disadvantageous to his full development ; his life was cut short in its earliest bloom, and the conditions under which he had to work, obscure and outcast from society, were adverse to the highest production. This poet is our own Christopher Marlowe. Like Æschylus, Marlowe's imagination was at home in the illimitable ; like Æschylus, he apprehended immaterial and elemental forces—lusts, ambitions, and audacities of soul—as though they were substantial entities, and gave them shape and form ; like Æschylus, he was the

master of a "mighty line," the maker of a new celestial music
for his race, the founder and creator of an art which ruled his
century, the mystagogue of pomps and pageants and things
terrible and things superb in shrines unvisited by earlier poets
of his age and clime; like Æschylus, he stands arraigned of
emptiness, extravagance, and "sound and fury," because the
scale on which he wrought was vast, because he set no verbal
limit to the presentation of the passion or the thought in view.
Comparing Æschylus to Marlowe is comparing the monarch of
the pine forest to the sapling fir, the full-grown lion to the
lion's whelp, the achievement of the hero to the promise of the
stripling.   Yet Herakles in his cradle, when he strangled Hera's
serpents, already revealed the firm hand and unflinching nerve
of him who plucked the golden fruit of the Hesperides.   Even
so Marlowe's work betrays the style and spirit of a youthful
Titan; it is the labour of a beardless Æschylus, the first-fruit
of Apollo's laurel-bough untimely burned, the libation of a consecrated priest who, while a boy, already stood "chin-deep in
the Pierian flood."   If we contrast the *Supplices*, which Æschylus
can hardly have written before the age at which Marlowe died,
with *Tamburlaine*, which was certainly produced before Marlowe
was twenty-six, the most immature work of the Greek with the
most immature work of the English dramatist, we obtain a
standard for estimating the height to which the author of
Faustus might have grown if he had lived to write his *Oresteia*
in the fulness of a vigorous maturity.

Much that has been described as Asiatic in the genius of
Æschylus may be referred to what I have called his demiurgic
force.   No mere citation of Oriental similes will account for
the impression of hugeness left upon our memory, for the
images enormous as those of farthest Ind, yet shaped with
true Hellenic symmetry, for the visions vast as those of
Ezekiel, yet conveyed withal in rich and radiant Greek.   The
so-called Asiatic element in Æschylus was something which
he held in common with the poets and prophets of the East—

The Asiatic
strain in
Æschylus.

a sense of life more mystic and more deep, a power to seize it and discover it more real and plastic than is often given to the nations of the West. This determination towards the hitherto invisible, unshaped, and unbelieved, to which he must give form, and for which he would fain win credence, may

Absence of love as the leading motive in his drama.

possibly help to explain the absence of human love as a main motive in his tragedies. There is plenty of Ares—too much, indeed, unless we recollect that the poet was a man of Marathon—but of Aphrodite nothing in his inspiration. It would seem that this passion, which formed the theme of Euripides' best work, and which Sophocles in the *Antigone* used to enhance the tragic situation brought about through the self-will of the heroine, had no attraction for Æschylus. Among the fragments of his plays there is, indeed, one passage in which he speaks of Love as a cosmical force, controlling the elemental powers of heaven and earth, and producing the flocks and fruits which sustain mortal life. The lines in question are put into the mouth of Aphrodite. The lost *Myrmidones*, again, described the love of Achilles for Patroclus, which Æschylus seems to have portrayed with a strength of passion that riveted the attention of antiquity. The plot of the *Supplices*, in like manner, implies the lawless desire of the sons of Ægyptus for the daughters of Danaus; and the adultery of Clytemnestra with Ægisthus lies in the background of the *Agamemnon*. But of love, in the more romantic modern sense of the word, we find no trace either in the complete plays or in the fragments of Æschylus. It lay, perhaps, too close at hand for him to care to choose it as the theme of tragic poetry ; and, had he so selected it, he could hardly have avoided dwelling on its aberrations. The general feeling of the Greeks about love, as well as his own temper, would have made this necessary. It did not occur to the Greeks to separate love in its healthy and simple manifestations by any sharp line of demarcation from the other emotions of humanity. The brotherly, filial, and wifely feelings—those which owe their ascendency to use and to the sanctities of domestic life—appeared in their eyes more important than the affection of youth for maid unwedded. When love ceased to be the expression on the one side of a physical need, and on the other the binding tie that kept the family together, the Greeks regarded it as a disease, a madness. Plato, who treated it with seriousness, classed it among the μάνιαι. Euripides portrayed it as a god-sent curse on Phædra. Viewed in this light, it may be urged that the love of Zeus for Io, in the *Prometheus*, is an example of a passion which became an unbearable burden and source of misery to its victim ; but of what we understand by love there is here in reality no question. The tale of Io rather resembles the survival of some mystic Oriental myth of incarnation.

The organic vitality which Æschylus, by the exercise of his creative power, communicated to the structure of his tragedies, is further noticeable in his power of conducting a drama without prologue and without narration. In Æschylus, the information that is necessary in order to place the spectators at the proper point of view is conveyed as part of the action. He does not, like Euripides, compose a formal and preliminary speech, or, like Shakespeare, introduce two or three superfluous characters in conversation. In this respect the openings of the *Agamemnon*, the *Prometheus*, and the *Eumenides* are masterpieces of the most consummate art. Not only are we plunged *in medias res*, without the slightest sacrifice of clearness ; but the spectacle presented to our imagination is stirring in the highest degree. The fire has leapt from mountain peak to peak until at last it blazes on the watchman's eyes ; Hephæstus and his satellites are actually engaged in nailing down the Titan to his bed of pain ; the Furies are slumbering within the sacred Delphian shrine, and the ghost of Clytemnestra moves among them, rousing each in turn from her deep trance. Euripides, proceeding less by immediate vision than by patient thought, prefixed a monologue,

Simplicity of construction.

which contained a programme of preceding events, and prepared the spectator for what would follow in the play. These
narratives are often frigid, and not unfrequently are placed,
without propriety, in the mouth of one of the actors. We
feel that a wholly detached prologue would have been more
artistic.

No prologue
and no
messenger.
　　The same is true about the speeches of the Messenger.
The art of Æschylus was far too highly organised to be
obliged to have recourse to such rude methods. It is true
that, when he pleased, as in the *Persæ*, he gave the principal
part to the Messenger. The actors in that play are little
better than spectators; and the same might be said about the
Seven against Thebes. But the Messenger, though employed as
here for special purposes, was no integral part of his dramatic
machinery; nor did he ever commit the decisive event of the
drama to narration. His master-stroke as a dramatic poet—
the cry of Agamemnon, following close upon the prophecies
of Cassandra, and breaking the silence like a clap of doom, in
that awful moment when the scene is left empty and the
Chorus tremble with the apprehension of a coming woe—
would probably have yielded in the hands of Euripides to the
speech of a servant. It was not that the later poet would not
willingly have employed every means in his power for stirring
the emotions of his audience; but he had not the creative
imagination of his predecessor; he could not grasp his subject
as a whole so perfectly as to dispense with artificial and
mechanical devices. He fell back, therefore, upon narrative,
in which he was a supreme master.

Participa-
tion of the
Chorus in
the action.
　　Equally remarkable from this point of view is the Æschylean treatment of the Chorus. It is never really separated
from the action of the play. In the *Prometheus*, for example,
the Oceanidæ actually share the doom of the protagonist. In
the *Supplices* the daughters of Danaus may be termed the protagonist; for upon them converges the whole interest of the
drama. In the *Seven against Thebes* the participation of the

Chorus in the fate of the chief actors is proved by half of them siding with Ismene and the other half with Antigone at the conclusion. In the *Persœ* they represent the nation which has suffered through the folly of Xerxes. In the *Agamemnon* the elders of Mycenæ assume an attitude directly hostile to Ægisthus and Clytemnestra. In the *Choëphorœ* the women who sympathise with Electra, further the scheme of Orestes by putting Ægisthus off the track of danger and sending him unarmed to meet his murderers. In the *Eumenides* the Furies play a part at least equal in importance to that of Orestes. They, like the protagonist, stand before the judgment-seat of Pallas and accept the verdict of the Areiopagus. Thus, in each of the extant plays of Æschylus, even the Chorus, which was subsequently so far separated from the action as to become a mere commentator and spectator, is vitally important in the conduct of the drama. Euripides, by formalising the several elements of the tragic art, by detaching the Chorus, introducing a prologue, and expanding the functions of the Messenger, sacrificed that higher kind of unity which we admire in the harmonious working of complex parts. What he gained was the opportunity of concentrating attention upon the conflict of motives, occasions for the psychological analysis of character, and scope for ethical reflection and rhetorical description.

I have hitherto been occupied by what appear to me the essential features of the genius of Æschylus—its demiurgic faculty of creativeness, and its capacity of dealing with heroic rather than merely human forms. To pass to the consideration of his theology would at this point be natural and easy. I do not, however, wish to dwell on what is called the prophetic aspect of his tragedy at present. It is enough to say that, here, as in the sphere of pure art, he was in the truest sense creative. Without exactly removing the old landmarks, he elevated the current conception of Zeus regarded as the supreme deity, and introduced a novel life and depth of meaning into the moral fabric of the Greek religion. Much as he rejoiced in

Theology and high conception of Zeus.

the delineation of Titanic and primæval powers, he paid but slight attention to the minor gods of the Pantheon; his creed was monotheism detached upon a pantheistic background, to which the forms of polytheism gave variety and colour. Zeus was all in all for Æschylus far more than for his predecessors, Homer and Hesiod. The most remarkable point about the Æschylean theology is that, in spite of its originality, it seems to have but little affected the substance of serious Greek thought. Plato, for example, talks of Prometheus in the *Protagoras* as if no new conception of his character had been revealed to him by Æschylus. We are not, therefore, justified in regarding the dramatic poet as in any strict sense a prophet, and the oracles he uttered are chiefly valuable as indications of his own peculiar ways of thinking; nor ought we, even so, perhaps, to demand from Æschylus too much consistency. The *Supplices*, for instance, cannot without due reservation be used to illustrate the *Prometheus ;* since the dramatic situation in the two tragedies is so different as to account for any apparent divergence of opinion.

Destiny and Nemesis. There is, however, one point in the morality of Æschylus concerning fate and freewill which calls for special comment, since we run a danger here of doing real violence to his art by overstating some one theory about his supposed philosophical intention. I allude, of course, to his conception of Destiny. If we adopt the fatalistic explanation of Greek tragedy propounded by Schlegel, we can hardly avoid coarsening and demoralising fables which owe their interest not to the asphyxiating force of destiny, but to the action and passion of human beings. If, on the other hand, we overstrain the theological doctrine of Nemesis, we run a risk of trying to find sermons in works of art, and of exaggerating the importance of details which support our favourite hypothesis. It should never be forgotten that whatever view we take of the moral and religious purpose of Greek tragedy has been gained by subsequent analysis. It was not in any case present to the consciousness of the poet as a necessary condition of his art as art. His first business was to provide for the dramatic presentation of his subject : his philosophy, whether ethical or theological, transpired in the heat and stress of production, not because he sought to give it deliberate expression, but because it formed an integral part of the fabric of his mind. Æschylus, in common with the Greeks of his age, firmly believed in the indissoluble connection between acts and consequences, and in the continuation of these consequences through successive generations. "Whatsoever a man soweth that shall he also reap," "the fathers have eaten a sour grape and the children's teeth are set on edge," formed the ground-work of his view of human life. This sort of fatalism he coloured with religious theories adopted from the antique theology of his race, but strongly moralised, and developed in the light of his own reason. The importance attributed by the Greeks to hereditary curses even in the common affairs of life, is proved by the familiar example of the proclamation by the Spartans against Pericles in the first year of the Pelo-ponnesian War. Much of elder superstition, therefore, clings about his ethics, and an awful sense of guilt and doom attaches to acts in themselves apparently indifferent; nor can we fail to recognise a belief in fate as fate ($\tau\grave{o}$ $\pi\epsilon\pi\rho\omega\mu\acute{e}\nu o\nu$) superior to all besides. The realm of tragic terror lies precisely in this borderland between inexorable reason and unreasoned fear. It has nothing to do with pure science or pure religion : they speak each for themselves, with their own voice ; but it is not the voice of the dramatist. On the one hand, logical fatalism offers no freedom for the play of character, no turning-points of choice, no revolutions which may rouse our sympathy and stir us with the sense of self-determined ruin. On the other hand, theology, in its methodic form, supplies, indeed, the text of sermons, admonitions, and commandments, but not the subject-matter for a work of art. Where the necessity of circumstance or the will of the Deity is paramount, human

The realm of tragic passion and dread.

action sinks into insignificance; the canons of inevitable
sequence and of obedience under pain of penalty supersede
the casuistry of balanced motives, and the poet is swallowed
up in the divine or the logician. Somewhere between the
two, in the intermediate darkness, or μεταίχμιος σκότος
(darkness between two armies), where all the ways of life are
perilous, and where no clear light reveals the pitfalls of fate
and the gins of religious duty, lies the track of the tragedian.
His men and women are free; yet their action is overruled by
destiny. They err against the law of heaven and flourish for
a season; but the law pursues them and enacts its penalty.
While terror and pity are stirred by the pervading sense of
human helplessness, scope is still left for the exercise of the
moral judgment; nor is the poet precluded from teaching his
audience by precept and example. These remarks apply to
the domestic curse which played so prominent a part in all
Greek tragedy, and especially in the dramas of Æschylus. It
was no mere avalanche of doom falling from above and crushing the innocent and the criminal alike; nor, again, can it
justly be paralleled by what it most resembles, the taint of
hereditary disease. It partook of the blind force of fate; it
was propagated from generation to generation by laws analogous to those which govern madness; yet it contained another
element, inasmuch as the transgression of each successive
victim was a necessary condition of its prolongation. Sin alone,
however, was not sufficient to establish its mysterious power;
for all men are liable to offend against the divine law, and yet
all families are not afflicted with a curse. In order to appreciate its nature, all these factors must be taken into account;
their sum total, notwithstanding the exactitude of our calculation, remains within the realm of mystery. The undiscovered
residuum, or rather the resolution of all these elements in a
power which is all of them and more than all, is fate. Students
who are curious to appreciate the value attached by the Greeks
themselves to the several elements implicit in the notion of

Nature of the domestic curse in Greek tragedy.

domestic Até, should attentively peruse the longer of the two arguments to the *Seven against Thebes*, while the play itself sets forth more energetically than any other the terrible lesson of the Æschylean Nemesis. The protagonist Eteocles is a curse-intoxicated man, driven by the doom of his race and by the imprecations of his father on a dreadful shoal of fate. He walks open-eyed to meet his destiny—to slay his brother and be slain. Still, helpless as he seems, he is not innocent. His own rebellious and selfish nature, by rousing the fury of Œdipus, kindles afresh the smouldering flame of the ancestral Até. Thus the fate which overwhelms him is compounded of hereditary guilt, personal transgression, and the courage-quelling terror of a father's curse. But it is more than all this: it is an irresistible compelling force. He cannot avoid it, since action has been thrust upon him by the strength of circumstance. The tragic horror of his situation arises from the necessity under which he labours of going forward, though he knows that the next step leads to a bottomless abyss.

In estimating the characters of Æschylus what has already been said about his art in general must be taken into account. He was occupied with the task of exhibiting a great action, a δρᾶμα in the strictest sense of the Greek phrase ; and this action was frequently so colossal in its relations as to preclude the niceties of merely personal character. Persons had to become types in order to play their part efficiently. The underlying moral and religious idea was blent with the æsthetic purpose of the poet, and penetrated with the interest pertaining to the clash of conflicting principles : the total effect produced sometimes seems to defy analysis of character in detail. The psychology of his chief characters is, therefore, inherent in their action, and is only calculable in connection with their momentary environments. We have to infer their specific quality less from what they say than from their bearing and their conduct in the crisis of the

Conception of character.

drama. Only after profound study of the situation of each tragedy, after steeping our imagination in the elementary conditions selected by the poet, can we realise the fulness of their individuality. In this respect Æschylus resembles Homer. Like Homer, he repeats the work of nature, and creates men and women entire. He does not strive to lay bare the conscious workings of the mind piecemeal. He has none of the long speeches on which Euripides relied for setting forth the flux and reflux of contending motives, or for making clear the attitude adopted by his *dramatis personæ*. There is no revelation of the anatomical method in his art;

The plastic fulness and unity of his creations. nor, again, can we detect the *ars celandi artem* (art of concealing art) to which poets of a more reflective age are forced to have recourse. Everything with Æschylus is organic; each part is subordinated to the whole which pre-existed in his mind, and which has been evolved in its essential unity from his imagination. Even the weighty sentences and gnomic judgments upon human affairs, uttered by his actors, are necessitated by the straits in which they find themselves. Severed from their context, they lose half their value; whereas the similar reflections in Euripides may be detached without injury, and read like extracts from a commonplace book. Perhaps sufficient stress has not been laid by critics upon this quality of absolute creativeness, which distinguishes the Homeric, Æschylean, and Shakespearean poets from those who proceed from mental analysis to artistic presentation. It is easy to render an account of characters that have first been thought out as ethical specimens, and then provided with a suitable exterior. It is very difficult to dissect those which started into being by an act of intuitive invention, and which, dissociated from the texture of circumstance woven round them, appear at first sight to elude our intellectual grasp. Yet the latter are found in the long run to be cast in the more vital mould. Once apprehended, they haunt the memory like real persons, and we may fancy, if we choose, innumerable series of events through which they would maintain their individuality intact. They are, in fact, living creatures, and not puppets of the poet's brain.

Of the characters of Æschylus, those which have been Clytemnestra.
wrought with the greatest care, and which leave the most profound impression on the memory, are Clytemnestra and Prometheus. Considering how slight were the outlines of the Homeric picture of Clytemnestra, it may be said that Æschylus created her. What is still more remarkable than his creation of Clytemnestra, is that he should have realised her far more vividly than any of the men whom he has drawn. This proves that Æschylus, at least among the Attic Greeks, gave a full share to women in the affairs of the great world of public action. As a woman, she stands outside the decencies and duties of womanhood, supporting herself by the sole strength of her powerful nature and indomitable will. The self-sufficingness of Clytemnestra is the main point in her portrait. Her force of character is revealed by the sustained repression of her real feelings and the conceal-ment of her murderous purpose, which enable her to compass Agamemnon's death. During the critical moments when she receives her husband in state, and leads him to the bath within the palace, she remains calm and collected. The deed that she has plotted must, if ever, be done at once. A single word from the Chorus, who are aware of her relations to Ægisthus, would spoil all her preparations. Yet she shows no fear, and can command the fairest flowers of rhetoric to greet the king with feigned congratulations. The same strength is displayed in her treatment of Cassandra, on whom she wastes no words, expends no irritable energy, although she hates and has the mind to murder her. Studied craft and cold disdain mark her bearing at the supreme crisis. When the death-blow has been given to Agamemnon, she breathes freely ; her language reveals the exhilaration of one who expands his lungs and opens wide his nostrils to snuff

the elastic air of liberty. The blood upon her raiment is as pleasant to her as a shower of rain on thirsty cornfields; she shouts like soldiers when the foemen turn to fly. Æschylus has sustained the impression of her force of character by the radiant speech with which he gifts her. This splendour of rhetoric belongs by nature to the magnificent and lawless woman, who rejoices in her shame. It is like the superb colours of a venomous lily. The contrast between the serpent-coils of her sophistic speech to Agamemnon at the palace-gate and the short sentences in which she describes his murder— true tiger-leaps of utterance—is a triumph of dramatic art.

Murder of Agamemnon.

As regards her motive for killing the king, I see no reason to suppose that Æschylus intended to diverge from the Homeric tradition. Clytemnestra has lived in adultery with Ægisthus; she dares not face a public discovery of her fault, nor is she willing to forego her paramour. The passage in the *Choëphoræ*, where she argues with Orestes before her own murder, proves that she has no other valid reason to set forth. Her son tells her she shall be slain and laid by the side of Ægisthus, seeing that in life she preferred him to her lord. All her answer is: "Child, in your father's absence I was sorely tried." The same is clear from the allusions in the *Agamemnon* to the nerveless lion, who tumbles in the royal couch, and is a sorry housekeeper for the departed king. Æschylus, however, with the instinct of a great poet, has not suffered our minds to dwell wholly upon this adulterous motive. He makes Clytemnestra put forth other pleas, and intends us to believe in their validity, as lending her self-confidence in the commission of her crime, and as suggesting reasons for our sympathy. Revenge for Iphigeneia's sacrifice, the superstitious sense of the Erinnys of the house of Atreus, jealousy of Chryseis and Cassandra, mingle with the master impulse in her mind, and furnish her with specious arguments. The solidity of Clytemnestra's character is impressed upon us with a force and a reality of presentation that have never been surpassed. She maintains the same *aplomb*, the same

cold glittering energy of speech, the same presence of mind
and unswerving firmness of nerve, whether she bandies words
of bitter irony with the Chorus, or ceremoniously receives the
king, or curls the lip of scorn at Cassandra, or defies the
Argives after Agamemnon's death. She loves power, and
despises show. When the deed is done, and fair words are
no longer needed, her hypocrisy is cast aside. At the same
time she defends herself with a moral impudence which is
only equalled by her intellectual skill, and rises at last to the
sublimity of arrogance when she asserts her right to be re-
garded as the incarnate dæmon of the house. Clytemnestra Clytemnes-
tra and Lady
Macbeth.
has been frequently compared to Lady Macbeth; nor is it
easy to think of the one without being reminded of the other.
Clytemnestra, however, is a less elastic character than Lady
Macbeth : she is cast in metal of a tougher temper, and the
springs which move her are more simple. Lady Macbeth has
not in reality so much force and fibre : she does not design
Duncan's death many months beforehand ; she acts from overmastering impulse under the temptation of opportunity, and
when her husband and herself are sunk chin-deep in blood she
cannot bear the load of guilt upon her conscience. Shakespeare has conceived and analysed a woman more sensitive,
and therefore more liable to nervous failure, than Clytemnestra. Clytemnestra never breaks down. Her sin feeds and
nourishes her nature, instead of starving and palsying it ; her
soul grows fat and prospers, nor does she know what conscience means. She is never more imposing in her pride of
intellectual strength than when she receives the feigned news
of Orestes' death. Just as the superior nature of Lady
Macbeth is enhanced by contrast with her weaker husband,
so Clytemnestra appears to the greatest advantage by the side
of Ægisthus. Ægisthus in the last scene of the *Agamemnon*
brags and blusters : Clytemnestra utters no superfluous syllable.
Ægisthus insults the corpse of the king; Clytemnestra is
satisfied with having slain him. Nothing shakes her courage

or weakens her determination.	When Orestes turns his sword
against her in the *Choëphorœ* her first impulse is to call aloud :
" Reach me with all speed an axe of weight to tire a man,
that we may know at once the issue of this combat." She
will measure weapons with her son.	And when his blade is
already at her breasts, she has the nerve to bare them and
exclaim : "My son, behold where thou didst lie ; these
nipples gave thee milk." There is no groaning in her last
life-struggle. She dies, as she lived, self-sustained and equal
to all emergencies. This terrible personality endures even in
the grave. When she rises in the *Eumenides*, a ghost from
Hades, it is with bitter taunts and a most biting tongue that
she stirs up the Furies to revenge. If we are to seek a

Clytemnes-
tra and Vit-
toria Corom-
bona.

parallel for Clytemnestra in our own dramatic literature, I
should be inclined to look for it in the *Vittoria Corombona* of
Webster. The modern poet has not developed his "white
devil of Italy " with the care that Æschylus bestowed on
Clytemnestra. Her portrait remains a sketch rather than a
finished picture ; and the circumstances of her tragedy are
infinitely less impressive than those which place the Queen of
Mycenæ on so eminent a pinnacle of crime. But Vittoria is
cast in the same mould. Like Clytemnestra, she has the
fascination and the force of sin, self-satisfied and self-contained
to face the world with brazen arrogance, and browbeat truth
before the judgment-seat of gods or men.

The
Prometheus.

Of all the masterpieces of Greek tragedy which have been
preserved to us, the *Prometheus* of Æschylus presents by far
the greatest difficulty, and involves at the same time by far
the most enticing problems. Its paramount interest lies in the
fact that the dramatic action is removed beyond and above the
sphere of humanity, and that the poet, who was also the chief
prophet of Hellas in the very prime of Athenian culture, is
dealing with the mystery of God's relation to the world and
man. In the trilogy of the *Oresteia* he is concerned with
heroes ; in the *Prometheus* with gods, Titans, and demigods.

The *dramatis personæ* are Prometheus, Hephæstus and his comrade Force, Hermes, the herald of Zeus, Io, the victim of the love of Zeus, and Oceanus, the ruler of the streams and seas. The Chorus is composed of Oceanides, the maiden daughters of the deep, cloud-bearing dews and mists, who gather round the Scythian crags, where Prometheus lies, chained, and exposed to fiery heat by day and freezing cold by night. The only mortal who visits him is Io ; and she bears within her the child of Zeus. Thus everything in the tragedy is conceived upon a vast and visionary scale. It is no episode of real or legendary history which forms the subject-matter of the play. The powers of heaven and earth are in action. The destinies of Olympian Zeus and of the whole human race are at stake. In this lofty region of the imagination the genius of Æschylus moves freely. The scenery of his drama is in harmony with its stupendous subject. Barren mountain summits, the sea outspread beneath, the sky with all its stars above, silently falling snowflakes and tempestuous winds, thunder, and earthquake, and riven precipices, are the images which crowd upon the mind. In like manner the duration of time is indefinitely extended. Not years, but centuries, measure the continuance of the struggle between the sovereign will of Zeus and the stubborn resistance of the Titan.

At the opening of the play Prometheus appears in the midst of the desert which is designed for his prison-home. *Opening of Prometheus Bound.* Hephæstus and his satellites chain him down with adamantine rivets, so that he may neither bend the knee nor rest in slumber, but must cling, crucified in wakeful torment, to the unyielding rock. While they are at their work, Prometheus utters not a word or groan. He is gifted with unerring foresight, and knows surely that his doom must be borne, and also that his doom must have an end. He defies the power of Zeus in frigid silence—not sullenly, because, when sympathy has loosed his lips, he proves that a warm heart beats within his breast— but proudly and indignantly. Hephæstus and Titanic Force leave him alone in his misery, when their task is finished. Then at last he speaks. It is to the kindred powers of elemental nature, to the Sun and Sea and nourishing Earth, his brethren and his mother, that he addresses his complaint: "See you how I, a god, suffer at the hands of God ; and for what crime? —*for having given fire to mortal man.*"

The sin or tragic error of Prometheus.

This, then, is the sin of Prometheus. He found humanity abject and forsaken by the gods. Zeus, who had recently seized upon the empire of the universe, designed to extirpate men from the world, and to create a new race after his own heart. Prometheus took pity upon them, saved them from destruction, gifted them with fire, the mother of all arts, taught them carpentry and husbandry, revealed to them the stars, whereby they knew the order of the seasons and recurrences of crops, instructed them in letters, showed them how to tame the horse and ox, and how to plough the sea with ships, then taught them medicine and the cure of wounds, then divination and the sacrifice of victims to propitiate the gods, and lastly how to smelt the ore contained within the bowels of the earth. All these good things Prometheus gave to men. And here, in passing, we may notice how accurately Æschylus has sketched the primitive conditions of mankind in its emergence from the state of savagery. The picture is indeed poetical, but subsequent knowledge has only strengthened the outlines and filled them in with details, not altered or erased them.

Position of Zeus.

Now, however, we ask, In what true sense was Prometheus criminal? What right had Zeus, who is invariably represented by Æschylus in all his other dramas as a just and wise ruler, to impose these trials on the benefactor of the human race? Æschylus, in this play, clearly desires to rouse our sympathy for Prometheus. He makes all the principal actors speak of Zeus as a forceful tyrant, newly come to power, which he abuses for his selfish ends, subverting the old order of the world, oppressing the old powers, who are his kindred, yet substituting nothing but his own ill-regulated and capricious will. On the

other hand, Æschylus has indicated that Prometheus is in the
wrong; that he regards his disobedience to Zeus as the cause
of merited punishment.   The Chorus points this moral by
asserting, in spite of their tender feeling for the Titan, that they
only are sane and righteous who bow to necessity and accept
the law of their superior.   Oceanus in like manner advises his
kinsman to submit; and reminds him that, though the rule of
Zeus is a novelty, it is not intolerable, and that acquiescence is
always prudent.

The chief difficulty of the play consists, therefore, in understanding the error of the protagonist, and in reconciling the
character of Zeus, as here depicted, with the theology elsewhere
expressed by Æschylus.   The most probable solution of the
problem is suggested by the ideal to which Greek tragedy
aspired.   It was the object of the Athenian dramatists not to
represent a simple study of character, or to set forth a merely
stirring action, but to depict a hero worthy of all respect and
admirable, exposed to suffering or ruin by some fault of temperament.   We are probably meant to look upon Prometheus
as having erred, though nobly, through self-will, because he
would not obey the ruler of the world for the time being, nor
abide the working out of the law of fate in patience, but tried
to take that law into his own hands, and to anticipate the evolution of events.   At the same time the play seems to convict
supreme Zeus himself of a tyrannical exercise of a forcefully
acquired power; he also, through a like self-will, appears to be
kicking against the pricks of immutable destiny; and it is prophesied that in his turn he will be superseded by a more
righteous ruler.   The secret of the revolution in Olympus,
whereby Zeus will be deposed, is possessed by Prometheus
and withheld by him from his tormentor.   Thus the knowledge of the future enables the hero of the drama to endure,
while Zeus upon his throne suffers through the consciousness
that fate cannot be resisted.   Therefore the *Prometheus*, as
we possess it, presents the spectacle of two stubborn wills in

*The clash of
wills in Zeus
and Prome-
theus*

conflict. The action is suspended. The conclusion cannot
be foreseen. Owing to its very excellence as a work of art, it
contains no indication of the ultimate solution; we are only
told by Prometheus that, after he has been liberated, and
not till then, he may reveal the means by which the ruin of
Zeus shall be averted. We are left to conjecture that Æschylus
intended to harmonise the wills of the Titan and his oppressor
through the final submission of both alike to the laws of destiny
which are supreme. Prometheus, when once his pride has
given way, will reveal the secret which he holds, and Zeus,
made acquiescent by the lapse of time, will accept it.

Shelley's
judgment of
the cata-
strophe.
The chief obstacle to the satisfactory interpretation of the
Prometheus springs, as I have hinted, from the difficulty of
understanding how Prometheus was guilty and Zeus justified.
The transgression of the hero, if it deserves the name at all,
was eminently noble. His punishment appears extravagant
in its severity. At first sight we can hardly avoid the conclusion that the final alliance between the two conflicting
actors in this drama was a kind of political compromise, unworthy of the protagonist. To this judgment Shelley was
led by his hatred of despotism, and by his inability to imagine
a dignified termination to the dispute that enlisted his sympathies so strongly on the side of the disinterested hero. "I
was averse," he says in the Preface to *Prometheus Unbound*,
"from a catastrophe so feeble as that of reconciling the
Champion with the Oppressor of mankind. The moral
interest of the fable, which is so powerfully sustained by the
sufferings and endurance of Prometheus, would be annihilated
if we could conceive of him as unsaying his high language
and quailing before his successful and perfidious adversary."
Those, however, who have learned to respect the lofty
theosophy of Æschylus, no less than to admire his imperial
artistic faculty, will be slow to accept the conclusion of
Shelley, or to believe that the catastrophe prepared by the
Greek poet was feeble. They will rather mistrust their

powers of judgment, or suspect that the key to the riddle
has been lost. The truth is, that we have no means of
settling what the catastrophe really was; and at this point it
is necessary to give some account of the relation of this drama
to the entire scheme of Æschylus.

The *Prometheus Bound* (δεσμώτης) was probably the second
of a trilogy, or series of three tragedies, of which the first
was called *Prometheus the Fire-bearer* (πυρφόρος), and the third
Prometheus Unbound (λυόμενος). *Prometheus the Fire-bearer*
and *Prometheus Unbound* have disappeared; it seems that they
were not even known to the Greek scholiast, for he does not
mention them in his argument to the *Prometheus Bound*. At
the same time the argument prefixed to the *Persæ* informs us
that that play was the second in a series, of which the *Phineus*
was first, the *Glaucus Potnieus* third, and a so-called *Prometheus*
fourth. It has been conjectured that the *Prometheus*, which
formed the fourth or satyric drama in this tetralogy, was distinguished by the title *Fire-kindler* (πυρκαεύς), a name which
is mentioned in an obscure passage of Pollux; and that consequently four plays altogether by Æschylus bore the title of
Prometheus. It cannot, however, be proved beyond doubt
that the *Fire-kindler* existed independent of the *Fire-bearer*;
or, if so, that the former was the last play in the tetralogy of
the *Persæ*, the latter the first in the trilogy of the *Prometheus
Bound*. Both arguments to the only *Prometheus* we possess
entire are unfortunately silent about the plays which accompanied it; and it is only from allusions to a lost tragedy
called *Prometheus Unbound* that we are at all justified in
assuming the disappearance of the first drama of the series,
and in calling it the *Fire-bearer*. It should be added that the
learned editor of the Greek Scenic Poets is inclined to
identify the *Fire-bearer* and the *Fire-kindler*, and to regard this
play as the satyric drama attached to the tetralogy of the
Persæ. By so doing he leaves the *Prometheus Bound* and *Unbound* without a proper dramatic introduction.

Probable trilogy to which Prometheus Bound belonged.

In spite of the uncertainty which surrounds the criticism of this play, no students familiar with the style of Æschylus will fail to recognise in the *Prometheus Unbound* the second drama of a trilogy. It has the stationary character which belongs to the *Choëphorœ*, the *Persœ*, and the *Supplices*. The dramatic action is not helped forward in these second pieces; they develop the situation to which affairs have been brought by the events of a previous drama, and which in its turn must lead to the conclusive action of the third piece. It was only in this way that a series of three dramas on the same subject could be connected into true artistic unity. The catastrophe of the first play produced a combination of events, which required such expansion in a second that a new action, involving a final catastrophe, should be unfolded in the third, and the whole series should in the end be seen to have coherence. Now the *Prometheus Unbound* is unintelligible, except as the result of a preceding action, while its conclusion leaves the fate of the hero still undetermined: the events which brought the hero to his dreadful doom, and the events which will deliver him, are alluded to as things of the past and of the future; in the present there is no drama, no doing, but only a development of the intermediate and transitional situation. We have, therefore, the right to assume the antecedence of a play which must, according to the data given in our extant tragedy, have turned upon the hero's theft of fire.[1]

We may now attempt to reconstruct the whole trilogy, and see if, having done so, any new conditions are supplied for the solution of the difficulty as originally stated. In the *Fire-bearer*, for the subject-matter of which we have to rely on the allusions of the *Bound*, Zeus has recently acquired the empire of the universe by imprisoning his father Cronos, and by defeating the giants who rose up in arms against him. Prometheus, knowing, through the inspiration of his mother

[1] See line 107.

Earth, or Themis, that Zeus will prevail, has taken his side, Attempt to reconstruct the trilogy. and has materially helped him in the conflict. But the sympathies of Prometheus are less with Zeus than with the race of men who, at that primitive period of the world's history, existed in the lowest state of wretchedness. Zeus, intent on getting his new kingdom into order, entertains the notion of destroying mankind, and planting a better stock of mortal beings on the earth. Prometheus opposes this design, and enables men to raise themselves above their savage condition into comparative power and comfort. It is just at this point that the lost drama would probably have revealed the true nature of his offence, or ἁμαρτία. In the Hesiodic legend he is punished for having taught men to deceive the powers of heaven; and though it is clear that Æschylus did not closely follow that version of the myth, we may conjecture that he represented the benefactor of humanity as a rebel against the ruler of Olympus. Against the express command of Zeus, Prometheus gave men fire; and though this act seems innocent enough, we must remember that, according to Genesis, Adam lost Eden by merely plucking an apple. Satisfied with his own sense of justice, and hardened in his pride by the foreknowledge of the future, Prometheus resisted a power that he regarded as tyrannical, and had to be treated by Zeus with the same severity as Atlas or Typhœus.

In the *Prometheus Bound* we see the beginning of his The secret possessed by Prometheus. punishment. The Titan, in whose person, as it were, the whole race of mortals suffer, is crucified on a barren cliff of Scythia. Meanwhile he makes two prophecies—first, that a descendant of Io is destined to deliver him; and, secondly, that Zeus will marry and beget a son, who shall sway the universe in his place. At the same time he declares that he knows how Zeus may avoid this danger. Zeus, anxious to possess this secret, sends down Hermes, and endeavours to wrest it from his prisoner with threats; but Prometheus abides, scornful and unyielding; his pain may be increased, yet it cannot last for ever; he is immortal, and Zeus will in the end be humiliated. To requite his contumacy, Zeus rends the mountains, hell is opened, and Prometheus descends to the lowest pit of Tartarus.

Sympathy excited for the protagonist.

It is clear that, whatever may have been the fault of Prometheus in the *Fire-bearer*, the poet has done all in his power to excite our sympathy for him in the second drama of the trilogy. He draws the character of Oceanus as a trimmer and time-server, who inspires contempt. He introduces Io suffering as a wretched victim of the selfish love of her almighty master. He makes the Oceanides willing in the end to share the doom of the Titan; while all the human sympathies of the audience are powerfully affected by the spectacle of a martyrdom incurred for their sake. This play is, therefore, the triumph of the protagonist; his offence is hidden; his heroic resistance is idealised; we are made to feel sure that, when at last he is reconciled with Zeus, it will be through no unworthy weakness on his part.

Part played by Herakles in the solution.

In the third drama of the trilogy, parts of which, translated into Latin by Cicero, have been preserved to us, Prometheus has been raised from Tartarus, and is again crucified on Caucasus. A vulture sent by Zeus daily gnaws his liver, which daily growing, supplies continually fresh food for the tormentor. The tension of the situation is still protracted. Prometheus has not given way. Zeus has not relented. Meanwhile the seasons have revolved through thirteen generations of the race of men, and the deliverer appears. It is Herakles who cuts the Gordian knot. He destroys the vulture, and persuades his father Zeus to suffer Cheiron, the Centaur, whom he had smitten with a poisoned arrow, and who is weary of continued life, to take the place of the Titan in Hades. Then Prometheus is liberated. He declares that Zeus, if he would avoid the coming doom, must refrain from marriage with Thetis. He binds the willow of repentance

round his forehead, and places the iron ring of necessity upon
his finger. His will is made at last concordant with that of
his enemy. Thetis is given in wedlock to the mortal Peleus,
and Achilles is born.[1]

From this last drama of the trilogy it would appear that
the honours of the whole series were reserved for Herakles.
Herakles is the offspring of Zeus by a mortal woman. He
occupies, therefore, a middle place between the two contending
parties, and is able to effect their reconciliation. We may
fairly conclude that herein lay the solution designed by
Æschylus. In order to mediate between Zeus and Prometheus,
a third agency was imperatively demanded. The heroic demigod, who is the son of the Olympian, and at the same time a
scion of oppressed humanity, prompted by no decree of his
father, but following the instincts of his generous humanity,
will not allow the torments of Prometheus to continue. By
killing the vulture, he resolves the justice of Zeus in an act
of mercy; at the same time, he touches the heart of the
Titan, and draws his secret from him, working a revolution
in the stubborn nature of Prometheus similar to that which
Neoptolemus effected in Philoctetes by his humane uprightness.
It is thoroughly in accordance with the spirit of Greek tragedy
that the scales should thus have fallen from the eyes of
Prometheus. He saw at last that Zeus, though severe, was
really justified; and, as a makepeace-offering, he rendered up
the secret which brought the ruler into harmony with the
immutable laws of fate. According to this solution of the
plot the final concession of Prometheus would have been as
noble as his intermediate resistance; the $\pi\epsilon\rho\iota\pi\acute{\epsilon}\tau\epsilon\iota\alpha$, or
revolution, which was imperatively required before the drama
could have been conducted to an issue, would have taken

Mediation between Zeus and Prometheus.

[1] It should be said that the subject-matter of the *Prometheus Unbound*
has to be gathered partly from fragments of the play, partly from prophecies in the *Prometheus Bound*, and partly from later versions of the
legend.

place within the protagonist's soul, while Herakles, by introducing a new element into the action, furnished the efficient cause of its conclusion. It may be argued on the other hand that Prometheus foreknew the advent of Herakles, and prophesied of him to Io in the second drama of the trilogy. To this I should answer that he could not then have calculated on the change which would be wrought in his own character by the deliverer.

Æschylean
conception
of Zeus. How Æschylus handled the subject-matter of the *Prometheus Unbound* we cannot say. It seems, however, certain that, unless he falsified his otherwise consistent conception of Zeus, as the just and wise, though stern, lord of the universe, and unless he satisfied himself with a catastrophe which Shelley would have been justified in calling "feeble," he must, through Herakles, have introduced a factor capable of solving the problem, by revealing to Prometheus the nature of his original offence, and thus rendering it dignified for him to bow to Zeus.

Divine
justice. If this reading of the *Prometheus* be accepted, it will be seen that the whole trilogy involved the deepest interests, the mightiest collision of wills, the most pathetic situations, and the most sublime of reconciliations. Zeus, in the second drama of the series, is purposely exposed to misrepresentation in order that his true character in the climax as

$$τὸν\ φρονεῖν\ βροτοὺς\ ὁδώσαντα,\ τὸν\ πάθη\ μάθος$$
$$θέντα\ κυρίως\ ἔχειν\ ^1$$

may be established. The divine justice personified in Zeus is displayed irreconcilably opposed to the natural will personified in Prometheus, until the hero who partakes of both, the active and unselfish Herakles, atones them. We are even justified in conjecturing that, as Prometheus occupied the foreground of the second drama, so Zeus must have been paramount in the first, and that the two antithetical proposi-

---

[1] " Him who leads men in the ways of wisdom, who has ordained that suffering should teach.'

tions having thus been stated, the chief part of the third play was assigned to Herakles. What strengthens the interpretation now advanced is the peculiar nature of the punishment of Prometheus. The liver, according to antique psychology, was the seat of the passions; consequently Prometheus suffered through the organ of his sin.

That Æschylus intended to describe the protagonist of his trilogy as a transgressor, though offending in a noble cause, while Zeus was acting in accordance with real justice, however hard to comprehend, is further indicated by the series of events which are supposed to have taken place between the termination of the *Fire-bearer* and the climax of the *Unbound*. All this while Prometheus in his obstinacy is suffering on Caucasus and in the depth of Tartarus; but the way of salvation is meantime being wrought out on earth. By the commerce of the Olympian deities with the daughters of men the heroic race is generated; and not only is the deliverer and reconciler, Herakles, sent forth to purge the world of monstrous wrong, but the better age of equity and justice, foreseen by the Titan and ordained by the Fates, is being prepared. The marriage of Thetis to Peleus is the proper inauguration of the heroic age; it not only confirms Zeus in his sovereignty, but it also provides for humanity the greatest actor in the drama of the Trojan war—the first historical event of Hellas.

Advent of the heroes.

If the character ascribed to Zeus in the *Prometheus Bound* still seems to offer difficulties; if, in other words, we are not satisfied with assuming that his conduct must have been justified by the evolution of events in the *Prometheus Unbound*, the following considerations may be adduced by way of further explanation. In the first place, at the supposed time of the *Prometheus Bound*, Zeus was but just seated on his throne, and had to deal with unruly and insurgent powers. The punishment of Prometheus was an episode in the Titanomachy. It was the business, therefore, of Æschylus to exhibit the

The Titans and Destiny.

firmness and force of government of the new ruler, not to draw the picture of a kind paternal monarch. In the second place, the speakers who describe Zeus as despotic, belonged by kinship to the old order of the Titans, or were closely related through friendship to Prometheus. Dramatic propriety required that they should calumniate the new king, or at least misunderstand his motives. In the third place, Io, whose fate appeared so hard, became the mother of a mighty nation, and received tenfold for all her sufferings at the hand of Zeus.[1] Here, therefore, his inscrutable ways were in the end proved righteous; nor is it probable that if Æschylus justified Zeus in his dealings with the unoffending Io, he would leave his treatment of Prometheus unexplained. In the fourth place, the theology of the Greeks was not absolute, like that to which we are accustomed through Christianity. The power ascribed to their deities was political and economical.

Fate and Necessity.
Fate and necessity determined the action of even Zeus, who was himself an outgrowth from an earlier and ruder order. They also imagined a gradual development in the moral order of the universe. The intellectual powers of Olympus had superseded the old nature-forces of the Titanic cosmogony. There was, therefore, nothing ridiculous to the Greek mind in the notion that Zeus might be conceived as growing in wisdom and in righteousness. In the fifth place, we must remember that the Athenian audience, familiar with the Hesiodic legend of Prometheus, were better prepared than we are, after listening to the invectives against Zeus in the second drama of the trilogy, to accept his triumphant justification in the third.

Not only is the trilogy of Æschylus—if, indeed, he composed a Promethean trilogy at all—now irrecoverable except by hazardous conjecture, but what is more unfortunate, the whole mythus on which it was based has descended to us in hopelessly mutilated fragments. We can clearly perceive

[1] See *Supplices*, 524-599.

that it enshrined the deepest speculations of the Greeks concerning the origin of humanity, the relation of deified intelligence to material nature and to abstract necessity, the kinship between the human soul and the divine spirit, and the consciousness of sin, which implies a division between the will and the reason. Furthermore, there are hints implied in it of purification through punishment, of ultimate reconciliation, and of vicarious suffering. But the fabric of the legend is so ruined that to reconstruct these elements of a theological morality is now impossible. Moreover, the very conditions under which the mythus flourished, tended to divert the minds of the Greeks themselves away from the underlying meaning to the romantic presentation. The story could not fail to usurp upon the doctrine. Like the Glaucus of Greek mythology, whom Plato used as a parable in the *Republic*, the idea which takes shape in a legend during the first ages of human speculation, gathers an accretion of the sea-weeds and the shells of fancy round it, lying at the bottom of the ocean of the human mind through centuries, so that, when it emerges into the light of critical inquiry, the original lineaments of the conception are deformed and overgrown, and to strip it bare and see it clearly is no easy matter. Far more difficult is the task when only the maimed fragments, the *disjecta membra*, of the myth remain to us.

However freely Æschylus may have dealt with the tale of Prometheus, however he may have employed it as a vehicle for rational theology, he cannot have wholly eliminated those qualities which belonged to it as a Saga rather than as an episode of religious tradition. Indeed, by dramatising, he was probably impelled to accentuate the legendary outline at the expense of philosophical coherence. This consideration may explain some of the apparent incongruities in his fable, to which attention has not been yet directed in this chapter. One of these concerns the position of the human race between Zeus, their apparent oppressor, and Prometheus, their avowed champion.

It was for the sake of mankind that Prometheus disobeyed Zeus; it was through severity towards mankind that Zeus placed himself at variance with justice. Yet we find Zeus seeking a mortal bride among the daughters of the men he had sought to destroy; nor is there any reason why, when he could crucify their champion, he should not have annihilated the whole race outright. Perhaps, however, we ought to conjecture that, at this point, the episode of Deucalion and his restoration of mankind after the deluge was understood to have intervened.

Discrepancies in the Promethean legend.

Other discrepancies may be stated briefly. In the elder version of the fable presented by Hesiod, Prometheus is almost identified with humanity, while some later fragments of the legend make him the father of Deucalion. In Æschylus he is an immortal god, whose sympathy with men proceeds from generosity and pity. Hesiod describes him as the son of the Titan Iapetos by Asia. Æschylus places him in the first rank of Titanic agencies, by making him the son of Earth or Themis; he is married to Hesione, daughter of Oceanus. Hesiod names his brother Epimetheus; and herein we trace the remnants of an antique psychological analysis, whereof Æschylus has made no use. It is clear, therefore, that the Attic poet dealt freely with the mythus, selecting for artistic purposes only such points in the Hellenic fable as would fit the framework of his drama.

Summary.

The only sure ground, amid so much that is both shifting and uncertain, is that the race of men had sinned against God, and that Prometheus was a responsible co-agent in their crime. This in itself is a strong argument in favour of the view which has been urged throughout this chapter. This view may be resumed in the following positions. First, it is probable that the *Prometheus Bound* is only the second drama of a trilogy. Secondly, the vilification of Zeus as a despot must be understood in a dramatic sense; it was appropriate to the situation of the actors, and intended to enhance the pathos of the protagonist's suffering. Thirdly, if we possessed the trilogy entire, we should see that Prometheus had been really and gravely in the wrong, and that his obstinacy was in the highest sense tragic according to the Greek conception, inasmuch as it displayed the aberration of a sublime character. Fourthly, the occasion of a worthy reconciliation between Zeus and Prometheus, wherein the former should forego his anger and the latter bend the proud neck of his will, was furnished by Herakles, who held an intermediate position between God and men, and who was recognised as the redresser of wrongs and saviour by the Greeks at large.

The Trilogy of the *Oresteia* is at the same time the master-piece of Æschylus as a dramatic poet, and also the surest source that we possess for forming a theory of his theological opinions. I do not propose to consider it from the second of these points of view, but rather to concentrate attention upon its greatness as a connected poem in three stupendous parts—as "the majestic image of a high and stately tragedy, shutting up and intermingling her solemn scenes and acts with a sevenfold chorus of hallelujahs and harping symphonies." In the *Oresteia* Æschylus plucked the last fruit upon the Upas-tree of crime which flourished in the palace of Mycenæ. The murder of Agamemnon, after his return in pomp and power from Troy, forms the subject of the first play. By selecting this point for the overture to the series, the poet was able to allude in choric songs to the ancestral curse of the house, and also to the special crimes of Agamemnon, in his sacrifice of Iphigeneia, in the protracted sufferings of the Argives before Troy, and in his fatal pride. The vaticinations of Cassandra opened a terrific vista of the horrors accumulated upon the family of Thyestes. Thus the past was connected with the present, and the intolerable account of guilt which Orestes, the chief actor, was destined in the end, by the help of Heaven, to discharge, was vividly pre-sented to the minds of the audience. Agamemnon is murdered,

The *Oresteia*
—murder of
Agamem-
non.

and the tragedy closes with Clytemnestra's pæan of triumph and defiance. She glories in her act, pretending that she has duly revenged the death of Iphigeneia, and suppressing her own adultery with Ægisthus—a criminal motive more than enough to vitiate its character of retributive justice.

The Chorus, who are hostile to her and her paramour, call upon her, if she really slew her husband for Iphigeneia's sake, to leave the palace and seek purification. This was her duty according to Greek etiquette. But she refuses ; and no Furies haunt her for her crime, seeing that the Furies take account of none but kindred blood, and Clytemnestra killed a man who was no relative by birth, but only by marriage. Such is the strange doctrine which the Eumenides themselves, in the third play of the series, propound before the judgment-seat of Pallas. In a deeper sense it was artistically fitting that Clytemnestra should remain unvisited by the dread goddesses. They were the deities of remorse, and she had steeled her soul against the stings of conscience. Neither from the blood of a slain husband could they rise ; nor was there in her own heart harbourage for their grim choir. But though Clytemnestra escaped the spiritual visitings of the Erinnyes, she knew what fear was. Orestes, as the Chorus told her, was still living.

The *Choëphorœ* continues the tale of blood and vengeance. Orestes returns to Mycenæ. He recognises his sister Electra by their father's tomb, deludes Clytemnestra with a false tale of his own death, and then succeeds in killing her together with Ægisthus on the spot where they had murdered Agamemnon. Once more the palace is thrown open ; instead of Agamemnon and Cassandra, Clytemnestra and Ægisthus lie prostrate before the desecrated altars, and Orestes exhibits to the Argives the robe in which his father had been caught and tangled ere the axe descended on his head. Then, when the song of joy is rising from Electra and the Chorus, while they are crying that the ancient Fury of the house has been

Position of Clytemnestra.

The Choëphorœ— murder of Clytemnestra.

appeased, at that very moment the eyes of Orestes dilate with
horror, his hair bristles, and he trembles with madness.   He
sees what none around him may discern.   The Erinnyes of
his mother are upon him, and he flies.   Like all the middle
plays of a trilogy, the *Choëphoræ* is somewhat stationary in its
action.   But this closing scene is tremendous.   It powerfully
affected the imagination of the Greeks, and continued,
through the period of Græco-Roman art, to form a favourite subject for sepulchral bas-reliefs.   Some of these have
been preserved to us, the finest being one in the Capitoline
Museum.

By the termination of the *Choëphoræ* we are prepared for
yet another tragedy, the last of the series.   The *Eumenides*
opens with a scene which represents the temple of Phœbus at
Delphi.   Orestes has taken refuge with the god who bade him
slay his mother, and who must now purify him.   He lies
breathless at the altar-steps, with the branch of suppliant
wool-enwoven olive in his hand.   Not far away are stretched
the Furies, hideous, and snorting in their slumber.   Phœbus,
while they yet sleep, bids his client rise and speed to Athens,
to await the verdict of Pallas in his case.   So much we learn,
partly from the speech of the Pythia, and partly from the lips
of the god himself.   Then, when Orestes has started on his
way, the phantom of Clytemnestra appears and bids the sleeping Furies rise.   One by one they start, and groan like hounds
disturbed in the midst of dreamings of the chase.   When they
see their prey has escaped, they break into full cry—a brazen-
throated chorus, accompanied by brazen-footed tramplings.
Phœbus, however, drives them forth with scorn from his sun-
bright shrine.   Why linger they in those hypæthral temple-
chambers, resonant with song, and gladdened by the feet of
youths and maidens bearing bays ?   Their haunts should
rather be the charnel-house, the shambles, the gallows, the
torture-chamber of barbarians.   The scene is now changed to
Athens, where Pallas presides over the court of the Areiopagus

The
Eumenides—
position of
Orestes.

assembled to decide between the Furies who prosecute Orestes, and Phœbus who defends his suppliant. There is no doubt about the deed : Clytemnestra was slain by her own son ;

Trial and acquittal of Orestes.

the question to settle is, whether circumstance could justify so unnatural an act. The Furies represent the blind instinct of repulsion for the shedding of maternal blood, which no *primâ facie* argument can excuse, and which cannot be covered. Phœbus is the holy and pure power, who will not suffer moral abominations, like the unpunished insolence of the murderess Clytemnestra, to abide. Pallas stands for reason, capable of weighing motives, of disengaging a necessary act of retributive justice from brute murder. In the breasts of the human judges, these three faculties—the instinct which condemns matricide, the instinct which sanctions under any circumstance the punishment of crime, and the reason which holds the balance of impulses—are active. After much angry pleading by the advocates on both sides, the votes are taken. Half decide against Orestes ; half acquit him. Pallas, by her casting vote, determines the verdict in his favour. The Eumenides, disappointed of their prey, threaten vengeance against Athens ; but Pallas appeases them, and assigns them a place of honour in her city for ever.

Connection of motives in the *Oresteia*.

It is clear that the three plays of this trilogy are closely bound together, and that their connection is that of thesis, antithesis, and synthesis. The *Agamemnon* sets forth the crime of Clytemnestra ; the *Choëphorœ* exhibits the exceptional conduct of Orestes with regard to that crime ; the *Eumenides* contains his exculpation. The third play offers a reconciliation of the agencies at warfare in the first and second ; the curse of the house of Atreus is worked out and set at rest by the hero whose awful duty it was to revenge a father's murder on a mother. His justification lay in his submission to the divine will. Had he taken the matricidal office on himself in haste or anger, he must have added another link to the chain of crime that hitherto had bound his family through generations.

What he did, however, was done with a clear conscience; and, though he suffered the maddening anguish of so terrible an act, he found rest and peace for his soul at last. Thus a new power, unrealised in the *Agamemnon* and the *Choëphorœ*, was needed for the solution presented in the *Eumenides*.

Passing from the internal structure of these dramas to their form, we may notice how Æschylus provided theatrical variety consistent with the varying subject. It was requisite that the action of the two first should take place at Mycenæ; so the scene was not altered, but the Chorus was changed, in order that the pathos of Electra's situation might be made more clear in the *Choëphorœ*. The *Eumenides* admitted not only of a new Chorus, but also of a total change of scene; it may be added that this third drama violates the unities alike of place and time.

Treatment of the Chorus.

Of the three plays of the trilogy, the *Agamemnon* is unquestionably the noblest. It is the masterpiece of Æschylus, and to one who has conquered its difficulties and imbibed its spirit it offers a spectacle of tragic grandeur not to be surpassed, hardly to be equalled, by anything which even Shakespeare produced. What some modern critics might regard as defects—the lengthy choric passages, abstract in their thought, though splendid in their imagery—the concentration of the poet's powers on one terrific climax—for each word that Agamemnon, Clytemnestra, and Cassandra utter, leads up to the death-cry of the King—contribute to the excellence of a drama of this style. If we lack the variety and subtlety that charm us in a work like *Hamlet;* if, after reading the play over and over again, and testing it in many crucibles of critical analysis, we do not, as in the case of Shakespeare's tragedies, discover new and delicate beauties in the minor parts, but learn each time, and by each process, to admire the vigour of the poet's main conception, the god-like energy with which he has developed it; that may be taken as the strongest proof of its perfection as a monument of classic art.

Perfection of the Agamemnon.

Passion of the *Agamemnon*. There is, in the *Agamemnon*, an oppressive sense of multitudinous crimes, of sins gathering and swelling to produce a tempest. The air we breathe is loaded with them. No escape is possible. The marshalled thunderclouds roll ever onward, nearer and more near, and far more swiftly than the foot can flee. At last the accumulated storm bursts in the murder of Agamemnon, the majestic and unconscious victim felled like a steer at the stall; in the murder of Cassandra, who foresees her fate, and goes to meet it with the shrinking of some dumb creature, and with the helplessness of one who knows that doom may not be shunned; in the lightning-flash of Clytemnestra's arrogance, who hitherto has been a glittering hypocrite, but now proclaims herself a fiend incarnate. As the Chorus cries, the rain of blood, that hitherto has fallen drop by drop, descends in torrents on the house of Atreus. But the end is not yet. The whole tragedy becomes yet more sinister when we regard it as the prelude to ensuing tragedies, as the overture to fresh symphonies and similar catastrophes. Wave after wave of passion gathers and breaks in these stupendous scenes; the ninth wave mightier than all, with a crest whereof the spray is blood, falls foaming; over the outspread surf of gore and ruin the curtain drops, to rise upon the self-same theatre of new woes.

Imagery of the *Agamemnon*. The imagery of the *Agamemnon* most powerfully contributes to heighten the tragic impression of the plot. At one time the ancestral Fury of the doomed house is likened to a dæmon leaping on it from above, by a metaphor which vividly suggests Blake's design of Satan pouring flame upon the dwelling of Job's sons. At another it is compared to a cormorant brooding upon its battlements; and yet again, by a stroke of irony peculiarly impressive to the Greeks, it is likened to a band of revellers. The repetition of the same class of metaphors, the frequent references to the net in which Agamemnon was to be caught, to the axe with which he and

Cassandra were to be slaughtered, to the smoke and scent
of blood which was to bathe the altar of the household Zeus
with sacrifice unhallowed, assail the imagination with por-
tentous monotony.

Of all the terrors in this tragedy none is so awful in itself, Cassandra's
prophecy.
or so artistically heightened, as Cassandra's prophecy. Accom-
panying her lord and master, she has approached the palace
of Mycenæ. Clytemnestra has greeted the King with a set
oration, admirable for its rhetoric, covering by dark innuendoes
her foul thought. Spreading upon the threshold purple
raiment and mantles suited to the service of the gods—such
embroidered garments, we may fancy, as Athenian ladies
wrought for Pallas—she exclaims : "Descend from this thy
chariot ; nor set on earth, dread monarch, thy foot that
trampled upon Troy." It is as though a mediæval wife
should bid her lord, returning from the East, to tread on
altar-cloths and sacerdotal vestments. Agamemnon shrinks
from the sacrilege, but she overrules his scruples, and he
complies. All this while Cassandra is seated, patient, in her
car. Like a statue sculptured in monumental alabaster, with
hands upon her knees, and head bowed on her breast, she
waits unmoved. Then the conqueror is led in to his doom—
a doom which the Chorus, in one of their wild eddying
hymns of woe, seem almost to anticipate. Still Cassandra
tarries ; and now Clytemnestra comes again, with taunts and
dreadful irony : "Happy are you, princess though you be, to
have such rich and prosperous masters ; enter the palace, the
sacrifice is ready at the altar, and to this, as a slave of the
house, you too are bidden." But Cassandra will not move.
In her soul, where, though a slave, she still retains the gift
of oracular vision, she foresees her doom. She knows what
the riches of the house of Atreus mean, what the prosperity
of Agamemnon really is, what the sacrifice to which she too
is bidden will be. Clytemnestra leaves her, half in scorn and
half in anger. Then, at length, Cassandra lifts her head, and

Cassandra
and Apollo.
stirs herself, and groans. The first word she utters is,
"Apollo! oh! Apollo!" This rouses the Chorus, and they
ask: "What cry of wailing hast thou shrieked about Apollo?
He is not a god to be greeted with dirges." Phœbus was, in
truth, the deity of brightness and music, not of the funeral
groan or death-lament. Still Cassandra, with the same
ill-omened utterance, reverberates the name: "Apollo!
ah, Apollo! lo, a second time hast thou undone me!" To
Phœbus she had promised her virginity; the promise was
not kept, and he requited her with prophecy that none might
heed or understand. No tragic portion is more piteous than
this of her who was the clear-eyed seer of coming woes, the
unwilling mouthpiece of dread oracles, doomed alike to knowledge worse than ignorance, and to the scorn that falls on
idle babblers. Now, once again, descending on her with the
might of prophecy, the god compels her to predict her own
swift-coming fate. Little by little, at the intercession of the
Chorus, Cassandra becomes more articulate. She calls the
house before her "the shambles of a man, a pavement blood-
bedabbled." There stands the stately palace-front; its marble
steps are covered with tapestry, the statues of its protective
gods are crowned with flowers; while the lonely prophetess
is shuddering at so fair a frontispiece to a tragedy within so
frightful, now to be accomplished on her master and herself.
Meantime the Chorus also wait, involved in their own anxiety;
the mysterious anguish of the weird woman, whom they
know to have the hand of God laid heavily upon her, makes
them tremble. "What mean you," they exclaim, "by scent-
Her vision.
ing like a dog for blood upon this royal threshold!" Cassandra
only answers: "Are not these children wailing for their death
enough? Is not their flesh, tasted by their father at their
uncle's board, my witness?" She points to phantoms which
the Chorus cannot see, the ghosts of the children of Thyestes.
They reply sullenly, for they know the story of the house:
"We want no soothsayers." Then Cassandra breaks forth

afresh, this time vaticinating imminent calamity : "What is
she plotting, what doom unbearable ? and there is none to
aid !" The Chorus take up their strain : "Here indeed you
are a riddler; what you meant before was common talk."
But Cassandra heeds them not. Her second-sight pierces the
palace-walls, and she shrieks : "Mad woman, are you decking
your husband for the bath ? The end draws near. Hand
stretches forth to hand. Is it a net of Hell ? Keep the ox from
the heifer ! she hath caught him in her robe and slays him.
I tell you he is falling, falling in the trough of death." The
Chorus are puzzled by these hurried and ecstatic exclamations ;
but their very fear seems to keep them from the apprehension
of the truth. Then Cassandra changes her tone, and bewails
her own misfortunes, her coming death, and the crime of
Paris which brought her to this doom, employing throughout
these prophecies a lyric metre suited to their pregnant
brevity. At last, when she has well-nigh worn out the
patience of the Chorus, she assumes the regular iambic of
common speech : "Now, then, at length shall the oracle gaze
upon you free from veils like a bride. The Furies are in
this house; blood-surfeited, but not assuaged, they hold
perpetual revel here. It is the crime of Atreus and of
Thyestes which they hunt, and woe will fall on woe." The
Chorus can only wonder that she, a foreign princess, should
know the secrets of the fated race; but she tells them the
story of Apollo's love, and how she deceived him, and what
he wrought to punish her. Then, even as she speaks, the
pang of inspiration thrills her. Perhaps the speech that
follows, through its ghastly blending of visions evoked from
the past with insight piercing into the immediate future,
affects the imagination more intensely than any other piece
of tragic declamation. Even the sleep-mutterings of Lady
Macbeth, though they form a curious modern counterpart to
the broken exclamations of Cassandra, are less appalling ; for
hers reveal a guilty conscience maddened by one crime, while

Her sense of the imminent murder

Cassandra's outcry sums up the history of a whole accursed race, and expresses at the same time the agony of an innocent victim :—

> "Woe, woe !   Ah, ah ! what pain !
> Again the dreadful pangs oracular
> Shoot through me, tempesting my soul with preludes.
> See you those children seated on the house-roof ?
> Babes are they, like unto the shapes of dreams ;
> Yea, children seem they, slaughtered by their kin,
> Whose hands are filled with meat of their own flesh ;
> Their very hearts and entrails, piteous load,
> I see them bear, whereof their father tasted !
> Wherefore I say, vengeance for this is plotting
> A lion, thewless, amid pillows lapped,
> House-guard, alas ! for my returning master—
> Mine : for I needs must bear the yoke, a slave.
> But he, the admiral, Ilion's overthrower,
> Knows not what things the tongue of that lewd bitch.
> With speeches and with long-drawn fawning fairness, like
> A lurking Até, by ill-luck will do.
> Thus, then, she dares : she, woman, slays a man ;
> Yea, slays.   What loathsome reptile can I name her,
> Nor miss my mark ?—foul amphisbæna, Scylla
> That dwells in rocks, the ship-borne seaman's bane,
> Raging mother of Hell, a truceless strife
> Belching on friend and kindred !   How she shouted
> With daring swollen, as when the foemen scatter !
> Now of these things I care not if I gain
> No credence.   What ?   What will be, comes ; and thou
> Wilt stand and pity and call me too true prophet."

Her declaration of the murderers.

No translation can do justice to the appalling fury of the original, since it is only in Greek—a language usually sedate and harmonised by sense of beauty—that such phrases as θύουσαν 'Αΐδου μητέρ' have their full value.   The Chorus are shaken from their incredulity, as much by the intensity of Cassandra's conviction as by the desperate calm of her last words.   Is Agamemnon really to be slain ?   Yes, she answers, and, pray or not as you may choose, they there inside the house are slaying.   Then once more the rage of divination seizes her,

and the scene of her own death, like that of Agamemnon's, Prediction of her own murder.
flames upon her soul. The second speech has more of pathos
than the first, less of fury ; but it is scarcely less awful :—

"Ah, ah ! the fire ! lo, how it comes upon me !
Phœbus Lycæan, ho ! Ah, woe is me !
She, too, this two-foot lioness that couches
With the wolf, what time the lion is away,
Will slay me, slay me ! Like a poison-brewer
She'll mix my death-wage with her broth of hell ;
Yea, and she swears, sharpening the knife to slay him,
Her lord shall pay with blood for bringing me.
Why wear I, then, these gauds to laugh me down—
This rod, these necklace-wreaths oracular ?
You, ere my death, at least I will destroy :—
Go ; fall ; away, and perish : I shall follow.
Make rich some other curse of men than me.
Lo, you ! Apollo's self is stripping me
Of this prophetic raiment—he who saw me
Even in these robes jeered at 'mid friends by foemen,
Who scorned in chorus with one voice of vain scorn.
Yea, when I was called beggar, vagabond,
Poor, wretched, starveling, speechless, I endured :
Now he who made me prophetess, the prophet,
Himself hath brought me to these straits of death.
No altar of my fathers waits for me,
But that red block where I must reeking wallow.
Nay, but not unavenged of heaven we perish !
For yet another in our cause shall come,
Avenger, matricide, his father's champion :
Though exiled, wandering from this land a stranger,
He shall return to crown the curse of kindred :
For gods in heaven have sworn a mighty oath
That the sire's prostrate corse shall bring him home.
Why wait I, then, lamenting thus, an alien ?—
I, who beheld of old proud Ilion
Fare as she fared, and they who dwelt therein
Receive such measure from the gods of judgment,
I, too, will rise and dare, myself, to perish.
Therefore I greet these gates as gates of Hades,
Praying a full fair stroke may be my due,
That thus with blood that gently flows to waste,
Torn by no death-pangs, I these eyes may close."

Cassandra
enters the
palace of
Mycenæ.

The draught of prophecy is now drained to the very dregs. Nothing remains but for Cassandra to enter the palace-doors of Hades. She approaches them step by step, bewailing, after the fashion of Greek tragedy, her own woes, and those of Priam's family. Suddenly she starts. The scent of blood assails her nostrils, and, like a steer that shivers at the gory shambles, she draws back. The Chorus say, " It is only the smell of sacrifice upon the hearth." But the weird woman discovers a very different odour of coming slaughter : " To me the reek is like the breath of charnels." Still forward, though shrinking from the unseen, unavoidable doom, she must advance, invoking the avenger of herself and Agamemnon, and calling on the all-seeing sun. Her last words are uttered in the same spirit as Macbeth's soliloquy upon the point of battle ; they intensify and elevate the tragic moment by drawing the whole destiny of mortals into harmony with her own doom :—

> " Ah, lives of men ! When prosperous, they glitter
> Like a fair picture ; when misfortune comes,
> A wet sponge at one blow hath blurred the painting."

Thus, at the last, tranquil and stately, she touches the door, enters, and it shuts behind her. For a while the Chorus stand alone, and sing a low, brief chant of terror. The scene is empty, and the palace-front towers up into calm light. Then, when our nerves have been strained to the cracking-point of expectation by Cassandra's prophecy and by the silence that succeeds it, from within the house is heard the deep-chested

Agamem-
non's death-
cry.

cry of Agamemnon : " O me, I am stricken with a stroke of death ! " This shriek is the most terrible incident in all tragedy, owing to its absolute and awful timeliness, its adequacy to the situation. The whole dramatic apparatus of the play has been, as it were, constructed with a view to it ; yet, though we expect it, our heart stops when at last it comes. The stillness, apparently of home repose, but really of death,

which broods upon the house during those last moments, while
every second brings the hero nearer to his fate, has in it a
concentrated awfulness that surpasses even the knocking at
the gate in *Macbeth.* Then comes the cry of Agamemnon,
and the whole structure of terror descends upon us. It is
as though an avalanche had been gathering above our heads
and gradually loosening—loosening with fearfully accelerated
ratio of movement as the minutes fly—until a single word will
be enough to make it crumble. That word, uttered from
behind the stately palace - walls, startling the guilty and
oppressive silence, intimating that the workers have done
working, that the victim has been taken in their toils, is
nothing less than the shriek of the smitten King. It sounds
once for the death-blow given ; and once again it sounds, to
mark a second stroke. Then shriek and silence are alike Final scenes.
forgotten in the downfall of the mass of dread. The Chorus
are torn asunder by hurried and conflicting counsels, eddying
like dead leaves caught and tossed in the clutches of a
tempest. Horror huddles upon horror, as the spectacle of
slaughter is itself revealed—the King's corpse smoking in the
silver bath, Cassandra motionless in death beside him. Above
them stands Clytemnestra, shouldering her murderous axe,
with open nostrils and dilated eyes, glorying in her deed,
cherishing the blood-drops on her arms and dress and sprinkled
bosom ; while, invisible to mortal eyes, the blood-swilled
dæmon of the house sits eyeing her as its next victim.
Ægisthus—craven, but spiteful—slinks forth, hyena-like, after
the accomplished act, to trample on the hero and insult his
grave.

Some such spectacle as this was revealed to the Athenians
by the rolling forward of the eccyclema at the end of the
Agamemnon. The triumph of adulterous Clytemnestra and
cowardly Ægisthus would, however, have been far from tragic
in its utter moral baseness, did we not know that this drama
was to be succeeded by another which should right the

balance. Perhaps this is the reason why the *Oresteia* is the only extant trilogy. Its three parts are so closely interlinked that to separate them was impossible. The preservers of the *Agamemnon* were forced to preserve the *Choëphorœ;* the preservers of the *Choëphorœ* could not dispense with the *Eumenides.*

The Chorus in the *Aga-memnon.* The Chorus of the *Agamemnon* demands separate criticism. The Chorus in all Greek tragedy performs, it has been often said, the part of an ideal spectator. It comments on the plot, not daring so much actively to interfere, as uttering reflections on the conduct of the *dramatis personœ*, and referring all obscure events to the arbitrament of Heaven. Thus the Chorus is a mirror of the poet's mind, an index to the moral which he inculcates, an inspired critic of each movement in the play. The choric odes, introduced at turning-points in the main action, are lyrical interbreathings that connect the past and future with the present. In the plays of Æschylus the Chorus, as I have already shown, is, moreover, personally interested in the drama. In the case of the *Agamemnon* the fortunes of the burghers of Mycenæ are engaged in the success or failure of Clytemnestra's scheme. At the same time, knowing the whole dark history of the house of Atreus, they foresee the perils which their master, as a member of that family, must run. It follows that their songs embody the moral teaching of the tragedy itself without lapsing into mere sententiousness. Their sympathies, antipathies, and interests add vital importance to their utterance. The burden of all these odes is that punishment for crime, however long delayed or tortuous in its operation, is inevitable. The grandeur of the whole work depends in a great measure on the force with which this idea is wrought out lyrically, sometimes by bold images, sometimes by dark innuendoes, repeated like a mystic rede, or tossed upon the eddies of a wizard chaunt. From beginning to ending these ancient men are adverse to the sons of Atreus, gloomily conscious that

they cannot prosper.   While recognising the justice of their
cause against Paris, who had transgressed the laws of
hospitable Zeus, they yet remember Agamemnon's swiftness
to shed his daughter's blood, the old Erinnys which pursues
the race, the wholesale slaughter of Achaian citizens before
Troy's walls.   These recollections inspire them with uneasiness
before the Messenger appears.   Their doubts are confirmed
by his news that the altars of the Trojans had been dishonoured, while their mistrust of Clytemnestra adds yet a
deeper hue to their alarm.   Then comes the scene with
Cassandra.   No more doubt remains; and the only question
is how to act.   Even at the last moment the Chorus do not
lose their faith.   They defy Clytemnestra, telling her to
her face that her crime must be avenged, that the curse must
be worked out to the full, and that justice cannot fail to
triumph.   At the very end they rise to prophecy: you,
yourself, unfriended in the end shall fall; the doer, when
Zeus wills, shall suffer for his deed; remember, therefore,
that Orestes lives.

The Choric interludes of the *Agamemnon*, though burdened
with the mystery of sin and fate, and tuned to music stern
and lofty, abound in strains of pathetic and of tender poetry,
deep-reaching to the very fount of tears, unmatched by aught
else in the Greek language.   The demiurge who gave a shape
to Titans and to Furies, mingled tears with the clay of the
men he wrought, and star-fire with the beauty of his women;
while even for the birds of the air and the wild creatures of
the woods he felt a sympathy half human, half divine.   In
the first Chorus, Æschylus compares the Atreidæ to eagles
robbed of their young, whose cries are answered by Zeus,
Phœbus, or Pan.   "Hearing the shrill clamour of these airy
citizens, he sendeth after-vengeance on the robbers."   And,
again, Artemis exacts penalty for the hare whom the eagles
bore off to their nests, a prey.   "So kindly disposed is the
fair goddess to the tender young of fierce lions, and to the

Poetry of the Choric songs.

suckling brood of all beasts that range the fields and forest."
Thus the large philosophy of the poet includes justice for all
living things, and even dumb creatures have their rights,
which men may not infringe.

Iphigeneia and Mene- laus. The depth of his human pathos no mere plummet-line of
scholarship or criticism can fathom. Before the vision of
Iphigeneia at the altar we must needs be silent: "Letting
fall her saffron-coloured skirts to earth, she smote each slayer
with a piteous arrow from her eyes, eloquent as in a picture,
desiring speech, since oftentimes beside the well-spread board
within her father's hall she sang, and maidenly, with chaste
voice, honoured the pæan raised in happy times at festal
sacrifice of her dear sire." We do not need the sententious
moral of Lucretius uttered four centuries later, *tantum relligio
potuit suadere malorum* (so many evils has religion been able
to instil into the human breast) to point the pathos which
Æschylus, with a profounder instinct, draws by one touch
from the contrast between then and now. In the same strain
is the description of Menelaus abandoned in his home by
Helen: "She, leaving to her fellow-citizens the din of shielded
hosts, and armings of the fleet with spears, bringing to Ilion
destruction for a dower, went lightly through the doors,
dishonourably brave; and many a sigh was uttered by the
bards of the palace, while they sang—O house! O house,
and rulers! O marriage bed, and pressure on the pillows of
her head who loved her lord!—He stands by in silence,
dishonoured, but without reproaches, noting with anguish of
soul that she is fled. Yea, in his longing after her who is
beyond the sea, a phantom will seem to rule his house. The
grace of goodly statues hath grown irksome to his gaze, and
in his widowhood of weary eyes all beauty fades away. But
dreams that glide in sleep with sorrow, visit him, conveying
a vain joy; for vain it is, when one hath seemed to see good
things, and lo, escaping through his hands, the vision flies
apace on wings that follow on the paths of sleep."

To read the Greek aright in this wonderful lyric, so concentrated in its imagery, and so direct in its conveyance of the very soul of passion, is no light task; but far more difficult it is to render it into another language. Yet, even thus, we feel that this poem of defrauded desire and ever-lasting farewell, of vain outgoings of the spirit after vanished joy, is written not merely for Menelaus and the Greeks, but for all who stretch forth empty hands to clasp the dreams of dear ones, and then turn away, face-downward on the pillow, from the dawn, to weep or strain hot eyes that shed no tears. Touched by the same truth of feeling, which includes all human nature in its sympathy, is the lament, shortly after uttered by the Chorus, for the numberless fair men who died before Troy town. Ares, the grim gold-exchanger, who barters the bodies of men, sends home a little dust shut up within a narrow urn, and wife and father water this with tears, and cry—Behold, he perished nobly in a far land, fighting for a woman, for another's wife. And others there are who come not even thus again to their old home; but barrows on Troy plain enclose their fair young flesh, and an alien soil is their sepulchre. This picture of beautiful dead men, warriors and horsemen, in the prime of manhood, lying stark and cold, with the dishonour of the grave upon their comely hair, and with the bruises of the battle on limbs made for love, is not meant merely for Achaians, but for all—for us, perchance, whose dearest moulder on Crimean shores or Indian plains, for whom the glorious faces shine no more; but at best some tokens, locks of hair, or books, or letters, come to stay our hunger unassuaged. How truly and how faithfully the Greek poet sang for all ages, and for all manner of men, may be seen by comparing the strophes of this Chorus with the last rhapsody but one of the chaunts outpoured in America by Walt Whitman, to commemorate the events of the great war. The pathos which unites these poets, other-wise so different in aim and sentiment, is deep as nature, real as life; but from this common root of feeling springs in the one verse a spotless lily of pure Hellenic form, in the other a mystical thick growth of fancy, where thoughts brood and nestle amid tufted branches; for the powers of classic and of modern singers upon the same substance of humanity are diverse.

The *Persæ*.   The *Persæ* is certainly one of the earliest among the extant tragedies of Æschylus, since it was produced upon the stage in 473 B.C., seven years after the battle of Salamis. This drama can scarcely be called a tragedy in the common sense of the word. It is rather a tragic show, designed to grace a national festival and to preserve the memory of a great victory. That purpose it fulfilled effectively; the events it celebrates were still recent; the author of the play had fought himself at Salamis, and the whole Athenian people were glowing with the patriotic impulse that had placed them first among the States of Hellas. Æschylus was, however, too deeply conscious of the spirit of his art to let the *Persæ* sink into the rank of pageantry or triumph. The defeat of Xerxes and his host supplied him with a splendid tragic instance of pride humbled, and greatness brought to nothing, through one man's impiety and pride. The moral that the poet wished to draw is put into the mouth of Darius, whose ghost, evoked by Atossa and the Chorus, completes the tale of Persian disasters by predicting the battle of Platæa. "Swiftly are the oracles accomplished. I looked for length of days; but when a man hastes, God helps to urge him on. It was my son's insolence, in chaining the holy Hellespont, and thinking he could stay the Bosporus, the stream divine, from flowing, which brought these woes. He thought to make a path for his army, to hold Poseidon and the powers of heaven in bondage—he, a mortal, and they gods! Few of his great host shall return again to Susa. In Hellas they must pay the penalty of arrogance and godless hearts. Coming to that land, they thought it no shame to rob the statues of the gods and burn the shrines; the altars were cast down, the temples overthrown. Therefore, as they did evil, evil shall they suffer. Heaps of dead upon Platæa's plain shall tell to the third generation, by speechless signs appealing to the eyes of men, that no man mortal may dare raise his heart too high. For insolence blooms forth and bears the crop of disaster, whence one reaps a harvest of tears. Seeing which payment for these crimes, remember Hellas and Athens. Nor let a man, in scorn of his own lot, desire another's good, and spill much wealth; for Zeus, in sooth, stands high above, a grievous schoolmaster, to tame excessive lifting-up of hearts." Nowhere else, it may be said, has Æschylus thought fit so decidedly to moralise his dramatic motive, or so clearly to state in simple words his philosophy of Nemesis. The ghost of Darius, as may be conjectured from this address, does not belong to the same race as the Banquos and Hamlets of our stage. He is a political phantom, a monarch evoked from his mausoleum to give sage counsel, and well informed about the affairs of his empire.

By laying the scene of this drama at Susa, the ancient capital of the Persian kings, Æschylus was enabled to adopt a style of treatment peculiarly flattering to his Greek audience. The Persians are made to bewail their own misfortunes, to betray the rottenness of their vast empire, and to lament the wretchedness of nations subject to the caprice of irresponsible and selfish princes. Inured to slavery, they hug their chains; and, though in rags, Xerxes is still to them a demigod. The servility of Oriental courtiers, the pomp and pride of Oriental princes, the obsequious ceremonies and the inflated flatteries of barbarians, are translated for Greek ears and eyes into gorgeous forms by the poet, whose own genius had something Asiatic in its tone and temper. Many occasions for grim irony are afforded by this mode of handling; whereof the famous speech of Atossa on the clothes of Xerxes, if that, indeed, be genuine, and the inability of the Chorus, through

Greek conception of Asiatic splendour.

servile shyness, to address the ghost of Darius, furnish the most obvious examples. A finer and subtler note is struck in the dialogue between Atossa and the Chorus just before the news of the defeat at Salamis arrives. She asks where Athens may be found :—

κεῖνα δ' ἐκμαθεῖν θέλω,
ὦ φίλοι, ποῦ τὰς Ἀθήνας φασὶν ἱδρῦσθαι χθονός ;

"And this I fain would learn,
Friends, where on earth is Athens said to be?"

Description of Athens. This offers the poet an opportunity for putting into the mouth of the Persian coryphæus a flattering account of his own nation : No monarch have they, few are they, but all men of might, and strong enough to rout the myriad bowmen of the Persian host with spear and shield. The *naïveté* of the description—in itself highly complimentary to the Athenians—must have made it effective on the stage. We may fancy how the cheering of the men of Marathon re-echoed from the Dionysian theatre, and filled Athene's hill "song-wise" with sound, as each triumphant trochaic leapt forth from the Persian lips. At the same time the tragic irony is terrible, for the queen is on the point of hearing from the Messenger that this mere handful of spearmen crushed her son's host, countless as the stars, in one day upon sea and shore. The real point of that fierce duel of two nations, which decided the future of the human race—the contrast between barbarians and men in whom the spirit was alive, between slaves driven to the fight like sheep, and freemen acting consciously as their own will determined, between the brute force of multitudes and the inspired courage of a few heroes—has never been expressed more radiantly than in this play. No language of criticism can do justice to the incomparable brilliancy and vigour with which the tale of Salamis is told. We must remember, in reading the speeches of the Messenger, that this is absolutely the first page of Greek history. It came before Herodotus, and the soldier-poet, who had seen what he narrated, was no less conscious than we are, after all our study, of the real issues, of the momentous interests at stake. Never elsewhere has contemporary history been written thus. In these triumphant declamations Æschylus did not choose to maintain a bare dramatic propriety. The herald is relating disaster after disaster ; yet the elation of the poet pulses through his speech, and he cannot be sad. We feel that, while he is dinning into the ears of the barbarian empress and her courtiers this panegyric of Hellenic heroism, he is really speaking to an Attic audience. The situation is, however, sufficiently sustained for theatrical purposes by the dignity wherewith Atossa meets her ruin. She shows herself a queen in spite of all, and the front she presents to "the sea of troubles" (κακῶν πέλαγος) breaking over the whole Asian empire is fully adequate to the magnitude of the calamity. It is difficult to believe that the speech written for her by Æschylus, when she returns with the libations for Darius, was not intended, by its grandly decorative style, to convey the impression of calmness in the midst of sorrow. Atossa is great enough to be self-possessed, and to dwell with tender thoughtfulness upon the gifts of nature beloved by the powers of darkness. The lines are these : [1]—

> βοός τ' ἀφ' ἀγνῆς λευκὸν εὔποτον γάλα,
> τῆς τ' ἀνθεμουργοῦ στάγμα, παμφαὲς μέλι,
> λιβάσιν ὑδρηλαῖς παρθένου πηγῆς μέτα·
> ἀκήρατόν τε μητρὸς ἀγρίας ἄπο
> ποτὸν παλαιᾶς ἀμπέλου γάνος τόδε·
> τῆς δ' αἰὲν ἐν φύλλοισι θαλλούσης ἴσον
> ξανθῆς ἐλαίας καρπὸς εὐώδης πάρα,
> ἄνθη τε πλεκτὰ παμφόρου γαίας τέκνα.

---

[1] "White delicious milk drawn from an unsullied cow, and the blossom-worker's distillation, translucent honey, with watery tricklings from a virgin spring ; also the unblemished liquor gushing from a rustic mother, this quickening draught of the old vine ; nor lacks there fragrant fruit of her, the fair-haired olive-tree, whose foliage flourishes alike the whole year round, together with wreaths of flowers, the children of all-generating earth."

This passage is a fair example of the "mighty line" of
Æschylus, employed for purposes of pure adornment. The
pomp and circumstance of tragic style, which he so well knew
how to use, gave unrivalled dignity to his narration. Yet
this style, even in the days of Aristophanes, had come to
sound extravagant, while its occasional bombast, as in the
famous periphrasis for dust,

κάσις
πηλοῦ ξύνουρος διψία κόνις,

"Thirsty dust twin-brother of mud,"

reminds a modern reader too much of the padding of the
actors' chests, the cothurnus, brazen mouthpiece, and heightened
mask required by the huge size of the Athenian theatre. The
phrases invented in the *Frogs* to express the peculiarities
of the Æschylean exaggeration, κομποφακελορρήμονα, or
ἱππολόφων λόγων κορυθαίολα νείκη, or, again,

φρίξας δ' αὐτοκόμου λοφιᾶς λασιαύχενα χαίταν
δεινὸν ἐπισκύνιον ξυνάγων βρυχώμενος ἥσει
ῥήματα γομφοπαγῆ πινακηδὸν ἀποσπῶν
γηγενεῖ φυσήματι

very cleverly parody the effect of the more tumid passages.[1]
Yet when Æschylus chose to be simple he combined majesty
with grace, strength with beauty, and speed with volume, in a
style which soars higher and reaches farther than the polished
perfection of Sophocles or the artistic elegance of Euripides.
The descriptions of Ionia and Doria drawing Xerxes' chariot
in Atossa's dream, and of the education of mankind in the
Prometheus, belong to his more pure and chastened manner.
The famous speech in which Clytemnestra tells of the leaping
up of watchfire after watchfire from Troy to Mycenæ, of Ida
flashing the flame to the Hermæan cliff of Lemnos, of Athos

---

[1] It is idle to attempt a translation of these Aristophanic lines, which
owe the whole of their force to the exactitude with which the peculiar
qualities of the style of Æschylus are reproduced.

taking it up and sending it with joy across the gulf to far
Makistus, of the Messapian warders lighting their dry heath
and speeding the herald-blaze in brightness like the moon to
Cithæron, and thence, by peak and promontory, over fen and
plain and flickering armlet of the sea, onward to Agamemnon's
palace-tower—this brilliant picture, glittering with the rarest
jewels of imaginative insight, can only be coupled with the
Salaminian speeches of the *Persœ*.   They stand in a place
apart.   Purity, lucidity, rapidity, energy, elevation, and fiery
intensity of style are here divinely mingled.   There is no
language and no metre equal to the Greek and the iambic for
such resonant, elastic, leaping periods as these.   The firm
grasp upon reality preserved by Æschylus, even in his most
passionate and most imaginative moments, adds force unrivalled to these descriptive passages.

At the same time he surpassed all the poets of his nation
in a certain Shakespearean concentration of phrase.   The invectives uttered by Cassandra against Clytemnestra, and her
broken exclamations, abound in examples of energetic, almost
grotesque, imagery, not to be paralleled in Greek literature.
The whole of the *Seven against Thebes*, and in particular that
choric ode which describes the capture and sack of a town,
might be cited with a similar intention.   But perhaps the
strongest instance of this more than Greek vehemence of
expression is the denunciation hurled by Phœbus at the Furies
in his Delphian shrine :—

> "Away, I bid you !   Leave my palace halls :
> Quit these pure shrines oracular with speed !
> Lest haply some winged glistening serpent sent
> From the gold-twisted bow-wire bite your flesh,
> And ye, pain-stricken, vomit gory froth,
> The clotted spilth of man's blood ye have supped.
> Nay, these gates are not yours !   *There* is your dwelling,
> Where heads are chopped, eyes gouged in savage justice,
> Throats cut, and bloom of boys unnameably
> Is mangled ; there where nose and ears are slithered,

> With stonings, and the piteous smothered moan
> Of slaves impaled.   Hence !   Hear ye not whereby,
> Loving like ghouls these banquets, ye're become
> To gods abominable ?   Lo, your shape
> Bewrays your spirit.   Blood-swilled lions' dens
> Are fit for you to live in, not the seat
> Of sooth oracular, which you pollute.
> Go, heifers grazing without herdsmen, go !
> To herd like yours no face of god is kindly."

Bold meta-
phors.

Another Shakespearean quality in the Æschylean use of
language and of imagery might be illustrated from his metaphors.   He calls the ocean a forest—πόντιον ἄλσος or
ἁλίρρυτον ἄλσος (sea-forest, or wood of the surging wave)—
as though he would remind us of the great sea-beasts that
roam like wolves or lions down beneath the waves.   The
gryphons are ὀξύστομοι Ζηνὸς ἀκραγεῖς κύνες (sharp-voiced
dogs of Zeus that bark not).   The eagle is Διὸς πτηνὸς
κύων δαφοινός (the winged blood-boltered hound of Zeus).
The Furies of Clytemnestra are μητρὸς ἔγκοτοι κύνες (a
mother's vengeful sleuth-hounds).   The Argives who poured
forth from the Wooden Horse to plunder Troy are called
Ἀργεῖον δάκος, ἵππου νεοσσὸς, ἀσπιδηφόρος λεώς (the
savage beast of Argos, youngling of the horse, the lion
charged with shields).   The flame of the thunderbolt becomes
πυρὸς ἀμφήκης βόστρυχος (the forked tress of fire).   The
beacon-flame on Ægiplanctus is a huge beard, φλογὸς μέγαν
πώγωνα (great beard of fire).   In all these metaphors we
trace an imaginative energy which the Greek poets usually
sought to curb.   When we speak of the mighty line of
Æschylus, we naturally remember verses like these :—

> ἀλλ' οὗ καρανιστῆρες ὀφθαλμωρύχοι,

and,

> φαιοχίτωνες καὶ πεπλεκτανημέναι
> πυκνοῖς δράκουσιν,

which carry with them a massive weight not only of sound and

words, but also of meaning and of imagery.[1] No wonder that
Aristophanes jestingly compared the gravity of the style of
Æschylus with that of Euripides in balances. A single phrase
of the former's causes a score of the latter's to kick the beam ;
and as the sonorous nouns, flanked by their polysyllabic
epithets, advance, the earth is seen to shake as though bat-
talions were hurrying to the charge, and squadrons of cavalry
with thundering horses' hoofs and waving plumes were prancing
on the plain.

The difficulty of Æschylus, when it is not due, as in the
Suppliants and in the choric odes of the *Agamemnon*, to a
ruined text, may be ascribed to the rapidity of his transition
from one thought to another, to the piling up of images
and metaphors, and to the remote and mystic nature of the
ideas he is seeking for the first time to express in language.
Where even simple prose could scarcely convey his meaning,
he presents a cloud of highly poetic figures to our mind. This
kind of difficulty, however, like that which the student has to
meet in Pindar, is straightforward. You know when you are at
fault, and why, and how alone you can arrive at a solution of
the problem. The difficulty of Sophocles is more insidious.
It is possible to think you understand him, when you really
do not ; to feel his drift, and yet to find it hard to construe
his language.   In this case the difficulty arises from the
poet's desire to convey his meaning in a subtle, many-sided,
pregnant, and yet smooth style. The more you think over
it, the more you get from it. Euripides belonged to an age
of facile speech, fixed phraseology, and critical analysis ; it
therefore follows that he presents fewer obvious difficulties to
the reader ; and this, perhaps, was one reason for his popularity among the early scholars of the modern age. At any
rate, he does not share with Æschylus the difficulty that
arose when a poet of intense feeling and sublime imagination

Difficulties of the Æschylean style.

[1] These lines lose their force in translation, it being impossible to
reproduce the effect of their ponderous polysyllabic words.

strove to grapple with deep and intricate thoughts before language had become a scientific instrument.

Profound moral teaching.

In conclusion I would once again return to that doctrine of παθήματα μαθήματα (to learn by suffering), connected with a definite conception of the divine government, and based upon a well-considered theory of human responsibility, which may be traced throughout the plays of Æschylus. To this morality his drama owes its unity and vigour, inasmuch as all the plots constructed by the poet both presuppose and illustrate it. The conviction that what a man sows he will reap, and that the world is not ruled by blind chance, is, in one sense or another, the most solid ethical acquisition of humanity. Amid so much else that seems to shift in morals and in religion, it affords firm ground for action. This vital moral faith the Greeks held as securely, at least, as we do; and the theology with which their highest teachers—men like Æschylus, Pindar, Plato—sought to connect it, tended to weaken its effect far less than any other systems of divinity have done. We are too apt to forget this, while we fix our attention upon the unrivalled beauty of Greek art. In reality there are few nations whose fine literature combines so much æsthetic splendour with direct, sound, moral doctrine; and this, not because the poets strove to preach, but because their minds were healthily imbued with human wisdom. Except in the works of Milton, we English, for example, can show no poetical exposition of a moral theory at all equal to that of Æschylus. But while Milton sets forth his doctrine as a portion of divine revelation, and vitiates it with the dross of dogmatism, Æschylus shows the law implicit in the history of men and heroes : it is inferred by him intuitively from the facts of spiritual life, as apprehended by the consciousness of the Greeks in their best age.

CHAPTER XIII

SOPHOCLES

SOPHOCLES, the son of Sophilus, was born at Colonus, a village
about one mile to the north-west of Athens, in the year 495 B.C.
This date makes him thirty years younger than Æschylus, and
fifteen older than Euripides. His father was a man of substance, capable of giving the best education, intellectual and
physical, to his son; and the education in vogue at Athens
when Sophocles was a boy was that which Aristophanes
praised so glowingly in the speeches of the Dikaios Logos.
Therefore, in the case of this most perfect poet, the best
conditions of training (τροφή) were added to the advantages

Birth of Sophocles.

of nature (φύσις), and these two essential elements of a noble manhood, upon which the theorists of Greece loved to speculate, were realised by him conjointly in felicitous completeness. Early in life Sophocles showed that nature had endowed him with personal qualities peculiarly capable of conferring lustre on a Greek artist of the highest type. He was exceedingly beautiful and well-formed, and so accomplished in music and gymnastics that he gained public prizes in both these branches of a Greek boy's education. His physical grace and skill in dancing caused him to be chosen, in his sixteenth year, to lead the choir in celebration of the victory of Salamis. According to Athenian custom, he appeared on this occasion naked, crowned, and holding in his hand a lyre: —

> εἴθε λύρα καλὴ γενοίμην ἐλεφαντίνη,
> καί με καλοὶ παῖδες φέροιεν Διονύσιον ἐς χορόν.[1]

Perfect balance of his nature.

These facts are not unimportant, for no Greek poet was more thoroughly, consistently, and practically εὐφυής, according to the comprehensive meaning of that term, which denotes physical, as well as moral and intellectual, distinction. The art of Sophocles is characterised above all things by its faultless symmetry, its grace and rhythm, and harmonious equipoise of strength and beauty. In his own person the poet realised the ideal combination of varied excellences which his tragedies exhibit. The artist and the man were one in Sophocles. In his healthful youth and sober manhood, no less than in his serene poetry, he exhibited the pure and tempered virtues of εὐφυία (essential goodness of nature). We cannot but think of him as specially created to represent Greek art in its most refined and exquisitely balanced perfection. It is impossible to imagine a more plastic nature, a genius more adapted to its special function, more fittingly provided with all things

---

[1] "Fain would I be a fair lyre of ivory, and fair boys carrying me to Dionysus' choir."

needful to its full development, born at a happier moment in the history of the world, and more liberally endowed with physical qualities suited to its intellectual capacity.

In 468 B.C. Sophocles first appeared as a tragic poet in contest with Æschylus. The advent of the consummate artist was both auspicious and dramatic. His fame, as a gloriously endowed youth, had been spread far and wide. The supremacy of his mighty predecessor remained as yet unchallenged. Therefore the day on which they met in rivalry was a great national occasion. Party feeling ran so high that Apsephion, the Archon Eponymus, who had to name the judges, chose no meaner umpires than the general Cimon and his colleagues, just returned from Scyros, bringing with them the bones of the Attic hero, Theseus. Their dignity and their recent absence from the city were supposed to render them fair critics in a matter of such moment. Cimon awarded the victory to Sophocles. It is greatly to be regretted that we have lost the tragedies which were exhibited on this occasion; we do not know, indeed, with any certainty, their titles. As Welcker has remarked, the judges were called to decide, not so much between two poets as between two styles of tragedy; and if Plutarch's assertion, that Æschylus retired to Sicily in consequence of the verdict given against him, be well founded, we may also believe that two rival policies in the city were opposed, two types of national character in collision. Æschylus belonged to the old order. Sophocles was essentially a man of the new age, of the age of Pericles, and Pheidias, and Thucydides. The incomparable intellectual qualities of the Athenians of that brief blossom-time have so far dazzled modern critics that we have come to identify their spirit with the spirit itself of the Greek race. Undoubtedly the glories of Hellas, her special genius in art, and thought, and statecraft, attained at that moment to maturity through the felicitous combination of external circumstances, and through the prodigious mental greatness of the men who made Athens so

First contest with Æschylus.

The age of Pericles.

splendid and so powerful. Yet we must not forget that
Themistocles preceded Pericles, while Cleon followed after;
that Herodotus came before Thucydides, and that Aristotle, at
a later date, philosophised on history; that Æschylus and
Euripides have each a shrine in the same temple with
Sophocles. And all these men, whose names are notes
of differences deep and wide, were Greeks, almost contemporaneous. The latter and the earlier groups in this triple
series are, perhaps, even more illustrative of Greece at large;
while the Periclean trio represent Athenian society in a
special and narrow sense at its most luminous and brilliant,
most isolated and artificial, most self-centred and consummate
point of αὐταρκεία, or internal adequacy. Sophocles was
the poet of this transient phase of Attic culture, unexampled
in the history of the world for its clear and flawless character,
its purity of intellectual type, its absolute clairvoyance, and
its plenitude of powers matured, but unimpaired, by use.

Further
events in
the life of
Sophocles.

From the date 468 to the year of his death, at the age of
ninety, Sophocles composed one hundred and thirteen plays.
In twenty contests he gained the first prize; he never fell below
the second place. After Æschlyus he only met one formidable
rival, Euripides. What we know about his life is closely connected with the history of his works. In 440 B.C., after the
production of the *Antigone*, he was chosen, on account of his
political wisdom, as one of the generals associated with Pericles
in the expedition to Samos. But Sophocles was not, like
Æschylus, a soldier; nor was he in any sense a man of action.
The stories told about his military service turn wholly upon
his genial temperament, serene spirits, unaffected modesty,
and pleasure-loving personality. So great, however, was the
esteem in which his character for wisdom and moderation was
held by his fellow-citizens that they elected him in 413 B.C.
one of the ten commissioners of Public Safety, or πρόβουλοι,
after the failure of the Syracusan expedition. In this capacity
he gave his assent to the formation of the governing council

of the Four Hundred two years later, thus voting away the constitutional liberties of Athens. It is recorded that he said this measure was not a good one, but the best under bad circumstances. It should, however, be added that doubt has been thrown over this part of the poet's career; it is not certain that the Sophocles in question was in truth the author of *Antigone*.

One of the best-authenticated and best-known episodes in the life of Sophocles is connected with the *Œdipus Coloneüs*. As an old man, he had to meet a lawsuit brought against him by his legitimate son Iophon, who accused him of wishing to alienate his property to the child of his natural son Ariston. This boy, called Sophocles, was the darling of his later years. The poet was arraigned before a jury of his tribe, and the plea set up by Iophon consisted of an accusation of senile incapacity. The poet, preserving his habitual calmness, recited the famous chorus which contains the praises of Colonus. Whereupon the judges rose and conducted him with honour to his house, refusing for a moment to consider so frivolous and unwarranted a charge.

Iophon's lawsuit.

Personally Sophocles was renowned for his geniality and equability of temper; εὔκολος μὲν ἐνθάδ᾽ εὔκολος δ᾽ ἐκεῖ (good-natured in the world above, and good-natured here below) is the terse and emphatic description of his character by Aristophanes. That he was not averse to pleasures of the sense, is proved by evidence as good as that on which such biographical details of the ancients generally rest. To slur these stories over because they offend modern notions of propriety is feeble, though, of course, it is always open to the critic to call in question the authorities; and in this particular instance the witnesses are far from clear. The point, however, to be remembered is that, supposing them true to fact, Sophocles would himself have smiled at such unphilosophical partisanship as seeks to overthrow them in the interest of his reputation. That a poet, distinguished for his physical beauty,

Personal qualities.

should refrain from sensual enjoyments in the flower of his age, is not a Greek, but a Christian notion. Such abstinence would have indicated in Sophocles mere want of inclination. The words of Pindar are here much to the purpose—

χρῆν μὲν κατὰ καιρὸν ἐρώτων δρέπεσθαι, θυμέ, σὺν ἁλικίᾳ.[1]

All turned upon the κατὰ καιρὸν (in due season), and no one had surely a better sense of the καιρὸς, the proper time and season for all things, than Sophocles. He showed his moderation—which quality, not total abstinence, was virtue in such matters for the Greeks—by knowing how to use his passions, and when to refrain from their indulgence. The whole matter is summed up in this passage from the *Republic* of Plato : "How well I remember the aged poet Sophocles, when, in answer to the question, 'How does love suit with age, Sophocles—are you still the man you were ?' 'Peace,' he replied ; 'most gladly have I escaped from that, and I feel as if I had escaped from a mad and furious master.'"

Was Sophocles avaricious?

A more serious defect in the character of Sophocles is implied in the hint given by Aristophanes, that he was too fond of money. The same charge was brought against many Greek poets. We may account for it by remembering that the increased splendour of Athenian life, and the luxuriously refined tastes of the tragedian, must have tempted him to do what the Greeks very much disliked—make profit by the offspring of his brain. To modern notions nothing can sound stranger than the invectives of the philosophers against sophists who sold their wisdom ; it can only be paralleled by their deeply-rooted misconceptions about interest on capital, which even Aristotle regarded as unnatural and criminal. That Sophocles was in any deeper sense avaricious or miserly we cannot believe : it would contradict the whole tenor of the tales about his geniality and kindness.

[1] "Soul of mine, in due season it is meet to gather love, when life is young."

Unlike Æschylus and Euripides, Sophocles never quitted *His pro-*
Athens, except on military service.   He lived and wrote there *longed re-*
sidence in
through his long career of laborious devotion to the highest art. *Athens.*
We have, therefore, every right, on this account also, to accept
his tragedies as the purest mirror of the Athenian mind at its
most brilliant period.   Athens, in the age of Pericles, was
adequate to the social and intellectual requirements of her
greatest sons ; and a poet whose earliest memories were connected with Salamis may well have felt that even the hardships
of the Peloponnesian War were easier to bear within the
sacred walls of the city than exile under the most favourable
conditions.   No other centre of so much social and political
activity existed.   Athens was the Paris of Greece, and
Sophocles and Socrates were the Parisians of Athens.   At the
same time the stirring events of his own lifetime do not appear
to have disturbed the tranquillity of Sophocles.   True to his
destiny, he remained an artist ; and to this immersion in his
special work he owed the happiness which Phrynichus recorded
in these famous lines :—

> μάκαρ Σοφοκλέης ὃς πολὺν χρόνον βιοὺς
> ἀπέθανεν εὐδαίμων ἀνὴρ καὶ δεξιός·
> πολλὰς ποιήσας καὶ καλὰς τραγῳδίας
> καλῶς ἐτελεύτησ᾽ οὐδὲν ὑπομείνας κακόν.

> "Thrice happy Sophocles ! in good old age,
>   Blessed as a man, and as a craftsman blessed,
> He died : his many tragedies were fair,
>   And fair his end, nor knew he any sorrow."

The change effected by Sophocles in tragedy tended to *Changes in*
the form of
mature the drama as a work of pure art, and to free it further *the drama.*
from the Dionysiac traditions.   He broke up the Trilogy into
separate plays, exhibiting three tragedies and a satyric drama,
like Æschylus before him, but undoing the link by which they
were connected, so that he was able to make each an independent poem.   He added a third actor, and enlarged the number
of the Chorus, while he limited its function as a motive force

in the drama. These innovations had the effect of reducing the scale upon which Æschylus had planned his tragedies, and afforded opportunities for the elaboration of detail. It was more easy for Sophocles than it had been for Æschylus to exhibit play of character through the interaction of the *dramatis personæ*. Tragedy left the remote and mystic sphere of Æschylean theosophy, and confined herself to purely human arguments. Attention was concentrated on the dialogue, in which the passions of men in action were displayed. The dithyrambic element was lost; the choric odes providing a relief from violent excitement, instead of embodying the very soul and spirit of the poet's teaching. While limiting the activity of the Chorus, Sophocles did not, like Euripides, proceed to disconnect it from the tragic interest, or pay less attention than his predecessors to its songs. On the contrary, his choric interludes are models of perfection in this style of lyric poetry, while their subject-matter is invariably connected with the chief concerns and moral lessons of the drama.

The style of Sophocles.

All the extant plays of Sophocles belong to a date later than the year 440 B.C. They may safely be said to represent the period of his finished style; or, in the language of art criticism, his third manner. What this means will appear from a valuable passage in Plutarch: "Sophocles used to say that, when he had put aside the tragic pomp of Æschylus, and then the harsh and artificial manner of his own elaborate style, he arrived in the third place at a form of speech which is best suited to portray the characters of men, and is the most excellent." Thus it would appear that Sophocles had begun his career as a dramatist by the study of the language of Æschylus; finding that too turgid and emphatic, he had fallen into affectation and refinement; and finally had struck the just medium between the rugged majesty of his master and the mannered elegance which was in vogue among the sophists. The result was that peculiar mixture of grace, dignity, and natural eloquence which scholars know as Sophoclean. It is interest-

ing to notice that the first among the extant tragedies of
Sophocles, the *Antigone*, is more remarkable for studied phrase
and verbal subtleties than his later plays. The *Œdipus Coloneüs*,
which is the last of the whole series, exhibits the style of the
poet in its perfect purity and freedom. A curious critical
passage in Plutarch seems to indicate that the ancients themselves observed the occasional euphuism of the Sophoclean
style as a blemish. It runs thus : μέμψαιτο δ᾽ ἄν τις Ἀρχι-
λόχου μὲν τὴν ὑπόθεσιν . . . Εὐριπίδου δὲ τὴν λαλιάν,
Σοφοκλέους δὲ τὴν ἀνωμαλίαν.[1] "One might censure the Antique
garrulity of Euripides and the inequality of Sophocles." I am   criticism.
not, however, certain whether this or "linguistic irregularity"
is the right meaning of the word ἀνωμαλία. Another censure,
passed by Longinus upon Sophocles, points out a defect which
is the very last to be observed in any of the extant tragedies :—
"Pindar and Sophocles at one time burn everything before
them in their fiery flight, but often strangely lack the flame of
inspiration, and fall most grievously to earth." [2] Then he adds :
"Certainly no wise critic would value all the plays of Ion put
together at the same rate as the single tragedy of *Œdipus.*"
The importance of these critiques is to prove that the ancients
regarded Sophocles as an unequal, and in some respects a cen-
surable poet, whence we may infer that only masterpieces
belonging to his later style have been preserved to us, since
nothing, to a modern student, is more obvious than the uniform
sustained perfection of our seven inestimably precious tragedies.
A certain tameness in the *Trachiniœ*, and a relaxation of dramatic interest in the last act of the *Ajax*, are all the faults it is
possible to find with Sophocles.

What Sophocles is reported to have said about his style will
apply to his whole art. The great achievement of Sophocles
was to introduce regularity of proportion, moderation of
tone, and proper balance into tragedy. The Greek phrases
συμμετρία, σωφροσύνη, μετριότης—proportion of parts, self-

[1] *De Aud. Poet.* p. 16 C.   [2] *De Subl.* xxxiii. 5.

restraint, and moderation—sum up the qualities of his drama
when compared with that of Æschylus. Æschylus rough-
hewed like a Cyclops, but he could not at the same time finish
like Praxiteles. What the truth of this saying is, I have
already tried to show.[1] Sophocles attempted neither Cyclopean
nor Praxitelean work. He attained to the perfection of
Pheidias. Thus we miss in his tragedies the colossal scale
and terrible effects of Æschylean art. His plays are not so
striking at first sight, because it was his aim to put all the parts
of his composition in their proper places, and to produce a
harmony which should not agitate or startle, but which upon
due meditation should be found complete. The σωφροσύνη,
or moderation, exhibited in all his work, implies by its very
nature the sacrifice of something—the sacrifice of passion and
impetuosity to higher laws of equability and temper. So
perfect is the beauty of Sophocles, that, as in the case of
Raphael or Mozart, it seems to conceal the strength and fire
which animate his art.

　　Aristotle, in the *Poetics*, observes that "Poetry is the proper
affair of either artistic or enthusiastic natures," εὐφυοῦς ἢ
μανικοῦ. Now Æschylus exactly answers to the notion of the
μανικός, while Sophocles corresponds to that of the εὐφυής.
To this distinction between the two types of genius we may
refer the partiality of Aristotle for the younger dramatist. The
work of the artistic poet is more instructive, and offers more
matter for profitable analysis, for precept and example, than
that of the divinely inspired enthusiast. Where creative intelligence has been used consciously and effectively to a certain
end, critical intelligence can follow. It is clear that in the
Poetics, which we may regard as a practical text-book for
students, the philosopher is using the tragedy of Sophocles, and
in particular the *Œdipus Tyrannus*, as the standard of perfection.
Whatever he has to say about the handling of character, the
treatment of the fable, the ethics of the drama, the catastrophes

---

[1] See above, chap. xii.

and recognitions (περιπέτειαι and ἀναγνωρίσεις), that absorbed so large a part of his dramatic analysis, he points by references to *Œdipus*. In Sophocles Aristotle found the μεσότης, or intermediate quality, between two extremes, which, in æsthetics as in morals, seemed to his Greek mind most excellent. Consequently he notes all deflections from the Sophoclean norm as faulty ; and since in his day Euripides led the taste of the Athenians, he frequently shows how tragic art had suffered by a deviation from the principles Sophocles illustrated. The chief point on which he insists is the morality of the drama. "The tragedies of the younger poets for the most part are unethical." With his use of the word ἦθος, we must be careful not to confound the modern notion of morality : ἦθος means, indeed, with Aristotle as with us, the determination of the character to goodness or badness ; but it also includes considerations of what is appropriate to sex and quality and circumstance in the persons of a work of fiction. The best modern equivalent for ἦθος, therefore, is character. Since tragedy is an imitation of men acting according to their character, ἦθος, in this wide sense, is the whole stuff of the dramatist, and a proper command of ἦθος implies real knowledge of mankind. Therefore, when Aristotle accuses the tragedies of Euripides and his school of being "unethical," he does not merely mean that they were prejudicial to good manners, but also that they were false to human nature, unscientific, and therefore inartistic ; exceptional or morbid, wavering in their conception and unequal in their execution. The truly great poet, Sophocles, shows his artistic tact and taste by only selecting such characters as are suitable to tragedy. He depicts men, but men of heroic mould, men as they ought to be.[1] When Sophocles said that he portrayed

Dramatic character.

---

[1] Notice the phrases βελτίονες (better) in *Poet.*, Cap. ii., as compared with καθ' ἡμᾶς (after our sort), and again ὁμοίους ποιοῦντες, καλλίους γράφουσιν (while making them resemblant, paint them fairer) in Cap. xv., together with the whole analogy of painting in both of these places.

men as tragedy required them to be, whereas Euripides drew
them just as they are, he indicated the real solution of the
tragic problem.[1] The point here raised by Aristotle has
an intimate connection with its whole theory of tragedy.
Tragic poetry must purify the passions of fear and pity ; in
other words, it must teach men not to fear when fear is vile,
or to pity where pity would be thrown away. By exhibiting a
spectacle that may excite the fear of really dreadful calamity,
and compassion for truly terrible misfortune, tragedy exalts the
soul above the ordinary miseries of life, and nerves it to face the
darker evils to which humanity in its blindness, sin, and self-
pride is exposed. Now this lesson cannot be taught by drawing
men as they exist around us. That method drags the mind
back to the trivialities of every day.

Ethical
quality of
his ideal.

What Aristotle says about the ἤθη of tragedy may be
applied to point the differences between Sophocles and
Æschylus. He has not himself drawn the comparison ; but
it is clear that, as Euripides deflects on the one hand from the
purely ethical standard, so also does Æschylus upon the other.
Æschylus keeps us in the high and mystic region of religious
fatalism. Sophocles transports us into the more human region
of morality. His problem is to exhibit the complexities of
life—" whatsoever has passion or admiration in all the changes
of that which is called fortune from without, or the wily
subtleties and reflexes of man's thoughts from within "—and to
set forth men of noble mental stature acting in subjection to
the laws appointed for the order of the world. His men and
women are like ourselves, only larger and better in so far as
they are simpler and more beautiful. Like the characters of
Æschylus, they suffer for their sins ; but we feel that the
justice that condemns them is less mystic in its operation,
more capable of philosophical analysis and scientific demon-
stration.

It must not be, therefore, thought that Sophocles is less

_____
[1] Cap. xxvi.

religious than Æschylus.   On the contrary, he shows how the Relation of
Sophocles.
will and passion of men are inevitably and invariably related
to divine justice.   Human affairs can only be understood by
reference to the deity ; for the decrees of Zeus, or of that
power which is above Zeus, and which he also obeys, give their
moral complexion to the motives and the acts of men.   Yet,
while Æschylus brings his theosophy in detail prominently
forward, Sophocles prefers to maintain a sense of the divine
background.   He spiritualises religion, while he makes it more
indefinite.   By the same process it is rendered more impreg-
nable within its stronghold of the human heart and reason,
less exposed to the attacks of logic or the changes of opinion.
The keynote to his tragic morality is found in these two
passages : [1]—

> "Oh ! that my lot may lead me in the path of holy innocence
> of word and deed, the path which august laws ordain, laws that in
> the highest empyrean had their birth, of which heaven is the father
> alone, neither did the race of mortal men beget them, nor shall
> oblivion ever put them to sleep.   The power of God is mighty in
> them, and groweth not old."

The second is like unto the first in spirit :—

> " It was no Zeus who thus commanded me,
>   Nor Justice, dread mate of the nether powers,—
>   For they, too, gave these rules to govern men.
>   Nor did I fondly deem thy proclamations
>   Were so infallible that any mortal
>   Might overleap the sure unwritten laws
>   Of gods.   These neither now nor yesterday,
>   Nay, but from everlasting without end,
>   Live on, and no man knows when they were issued."

The religious instinct in Sophocles has made a long step
toward independence since the days of Æschylus.   No
more upon Olympus or at Delphi alone will the Greek poet
worship.   He has learned that "God is a spirit, and they

---

[1] *Œd. Tyr.* 863 ; *Ant.* 450.   The first translation is borrowed from
Mr. M. Arnold.

Spirituality
of his faith
in God. that worship Him must worship Him in spirit and in truth."
The voice that speaks within him is the deity he recognises.
At the same time the Chorus of the *Œdipus*, part of which
has just been quoted, and that of the *Antigone*, which bewails
the old doom of the house of Labdacus, might, but for their
greater calmness, have been written by Æschylus. The
moral doctrine of Greek tragedy has not been changed, but
humanised. We have got rid in a great measure of ancient
dæmons, and brass-footed Furies, and the greed of earth for
blood in recompense for blood. We have passed, as it were,
from the shadow cast by the sun, into the sunlight itself.
And, in consequence of this transfiguration, the morality of
Sophocles is imperishable. "Not of to-day nor of yesterday,
but fixed from everlasting," are his laws. We may all learn
of him now, as when Antigone first stood before the throne
of Creon on the Attic stage. The deep insight into human
life, that most precious gift of the Greek genius, which produced their greatest contributions to the education of the
world, is in Sophocles obscured no longer by mystical mythology and local superstition. His wisdom is the common heritage of human nature.

Philosophy
of human
life. The moral judgments of Æschylus were severe. Those
of Sophocles, implicit in his tragic situations rather than
expressed, are not less firm ; but he seems to feel a more
tender pity for humanity in its weakness and its blindness.
The philosophy of life, profoundly sad upon the one side, but
cheerful on the other, which draws lessons of sobriety and
tempered joy from the consideration of human impotence
and ignorance, is truly Greek. We find it nowhere more
strongly set forth than by Sophocles and Aristophanes—by
the comic poet in the Parabasis of the *Birds*, and in the songs
of the Mystæ in the *Frogs*, by the tragic poet in his choruses,
and also in what is called his irony.

All that has been said about the art of Sophocles up to
this point has tended to establish one position. His innate

and unerring tact, his sense of harmony and measure, pro- <small>Sophocles as artist.</small>
duced at Athens a new style of drama, distinguished for
finish of language, for careful elaboration of motives, for
sharp and delicate character-drawing, and for balance of parts.
If we do not find in Sophocles anything to match the passion
of Cassandra, the cry of Agamemnon, or the opening of the
Eumenides, there is yet in his plays a combination of quite
sufficient boldness and inventiveness with more exquisite
workmanship than Æschylus could give.   The breadth of the
whole is not lost through the minuteness of the details.
Unlike Æschylus, Sophocles opens very quietly, with conversations, for the most part, which reveal the characters of
the chief persons or explain the situation.   The passion grows
with the development of the plot, and it is only when the
play is finished that justice can be done to any separate part.
Each of the seven tragedies presents one person, who dominates
the drama, and in whom its interest is principally concentrated.
Œdipus in his two plays, Antigone in hers, Philoctetes in
his, Deianeira in the *Trachiniæ*, Electra in her play, and Ajax
in his, stand forth in powerful and prominent relief.   Then
come figures on the second plane, no less accurately conceived
and conscientiously delineated, but used with a view to
supporting the chief personages, and educing their decisive
action.[1]   A *rôle* of this kind is given to Orestes in the *Electra*,
to Neoptolemus in the *Philoctetes*, to Teucer in the *Ajax*, to
Creon in the *Antigone*, to Teiresias in the *Œdipus*.   Clytemnestra and Tecmessa, Odysseus and Theseus, play similar
parts.   Again, there is a third plane for characters still more
subordinate, but no less artistically important, such as Jocasta,
Ismene, Chrysothemis, Ægisthus, Hyllus.   Then follow the
numerous accessory persons — *instrumenta dramatis* — the
guardian of the corpse of Polyneices, the shepherd of Laius,
the tutor of Orestes, messengers and servants, all of whom

---

[1] See what Goethe says about the importance of Creon and Ismene in
the *Antigone* (Eckermann, vol. i.)

receive their special physiognomy from the great master. In this way Sophocles made true æsthetic use of the three agonistæ. The principle on which these parts were distributed in his tragedies will be found to have deep and subtle analogies with the laws of bas-relief in sculpture. Poetry, however, being a far more independent art than sculpture, may employ a greater multiplicity of parts, and produce a far more complex effect than can be realised in bas-relief.

The *Philoctetes* might be selected as an example of the power in handling motives possessed by Sophocles. The amount of interest he has concentrated by a careful manipulation of one point—the contest for the bow of Herakles—upon so slight and stationary a plot, is truly wonderful. Not less admirable is the contrast between the youthful generosity of Neoptolemus and the worldly wisdom of Odysseus —the young man pliant at first to the crafty persuasions of the elder, but restored to his sense of honour by the compassion which Philoctetes stirs, and by the trust he places in him. Nothing more beautiful can be conceived than this moral revolution in the character of Neoptolemus. It suited the fine taste and exquisite skill of Sophocles not only to exhibit changes in circumstance and character, but also to compel a change of sympathy and of opinion in his audience. Thus, in the *Ajax*, he contrives to reverse the whole situation, by showing in the end Ajax sublime and Odysseus generous, though at first the one seemed sunk below humanity, and the other hateful in his vulgar scorn of a fallen rival. The art which works out psychological problems of the subtle kind, and which invests a plot like that of the *Philoctetes* with intense interest, is very far removed from the method of Æschylus. The difference between the two styles may, however, be appreciated best by a comparison of the *Electra* with the *Choëphoræ*. In these two tragedies very nearly the same motives are employed ; but what was simple and straightforward in Æschylus, becomes complex and involved in The *Electra*. Sophocles. Instead of Orestes telling the tale of his own death, we have the narrative of his tutor, confirmed and ratified by himself in person. Instead of Electra at once recognising her brother, she is brought at first to the verge of despair by hearing of his death. Then Chrysothemis informs her of the lock of hair. This, however, cannot reassure Electra in the face of the tutor's message. So the situation is admirably protracted. Æschylus misses all that is gained for the development of character by the resolve of Electra, stung to desperation by her brother's death, to murder Ægisthus, and by the contrast between her single-hearted daring and the feebler acquiescent temper of Chrysothemis. Also the peripeteia whereby Electra is made to bewail the urn of Orestes, and then to discover him alive before her, is a stroke of supreme art which was missed in the *Choëphorœ*. The pathos of the situation is almost too heart-rending; at one moment its intensity verges upon discord; but the resolution of the discord comes in that long cadence of triumphant harmony when the anagnorisis at length arrives. Nor is the ingenuity of Sophocles, in continuing and sustaining the interest of this one set of motives, yet exhausted. While the brother and sister are rejoicing together, the action waits, and every moment becomes more critical, until at last the tutor reappears and warns them of their perilous imprudence. To take another point: the dream of Clytemnestra is more mysterious and doubtful in the *Electra* than in the *Choëphorœ*; while her appearance on the stage at the beginning of the play, her arguments with Electra, her guarded prayers to Phœbus, and her reception of the tutor's message, enable Sophocles fully to develop his conception of her character. On the other hand, Sophocles has sacrificed the most brilliant features of the *Choëphorœ*—the dreadful scene of Clytemnestra's death, than which there is nothing more passionately piteous and

spirit-quelling in all tragedy, and the descent of his mother's
furies on the murderer. It was the object of Sophocles not
so much to dwell upon the action of Orestes, as to exhibit
the character of Electra; therefore, at the supreme moment,
when the cry of the queen is heard within the palace, he
shows his heroine tremendous in her righteous hatred and
implacable desire for vengeance. Such complete and exhaustive elaboration of motives, characters, and situations, as
forms the chief artistic merit of the *Electra*, would, perhaps,
have been out of place in the *Choëphorœ*, which was only the
second play in a trilogy, and had therefore to be simple and
stationary, according to the principles of Æschylean art. The
character of Clytemnestra, for example, needed no development, seeing that she had taken the first part in the
Agamemnon. Again, it was necessary for Æschylus to insist
upon the action of Orestes more than Sophocles was forced
to do, in order that the climax of the *Choëphorœ* might produce the subject of the *Eumenides*. In comparing Sophocles
with his predecessor, we must never forget that we are comparing single plays with trilogies. This does not, however,
make the Sophoclean mastery of motives and of plots the
less admirable; it only fixes our attention on the real nature
of the innovations adopted by the younger dramatist.

Climax of
*Œdipus
Coloneüs.*

Another instance of the art wherewith Sophocles prepared
a tragic situation, and graduated all the motives which should
conduct the action to a final point, may be selected from the
Œdipus Coloneüs. It was necessary to describe the death of
Œdipus, since the fable selected for treatment precluded
anything approaching to a presentation on the stage of this
supreme event. Œdipus is bound to die alone mysteriously,
delivering his secret first in solitude to Theseus. A Messenger's
speech was therefore imperatively demanded, and to render
that the climax of the drama taxed all the resources of the
poet. First comes thunder, the acknowledged signal of the
end. Then the speech of Œdipus, who says that now, though

blind, he will direct his steps unhelped. Theseus is to follow
and to learn. Œdipus rises from his seat; his daughters and
the king attend him. They quit the stage, and the Chorus
is left alone to sing. Then comes the Messenger, and gives
the sublime narration of his disappearance. We hear the
voice that called—

> ὦ οὗτος οὗτος Οἰδίπους τί μέλλομεν
> χωρεῖν; πάλαι δὴ τἀπὸ σοῦ βραδύνεται.[1]

We see the old man descending the mysterious stairs,
Antigone and Ismene grouped above, and last, the kneeling
king, who shrouds his eyes before a sight intolerable. All
this, as in a picture, passes before our imagination. To
convey the desired effect otherwise than by a narrative would
have been impossible, and the narrative, owing to the expectation previously raised, is adequate.

To compare Sophocles with Euripides, after having said
so much about the points of contrast between him and
Æschylus, and to determine how much he may have owed
in his later plays to the influence of the younger poet, would
be an interesting exercise of criticism. That, however,
belongs rather to an essay dealing directly with the third
Greek dramatist in detail. It is sufficient here to notice a
few points in which Sophocles seems to have prepared the
way for Euripides. In the first place he developed the part
of the Messenger, and made far more of picturesque description than Æschylus had done. Then, again, his openings
suggested the device of the prologue by their abandonment
of the eminently scenic effects with which Æschylus preferred
to introduce a drama. The separation of the Chorus from
the action was another point in which Sophocles led onward
to Euripides. So also was the device of the *deus ex machinâ*
in the *Philoctetes*, unless, indeed, we are to regard this as an

Sophocles and Euripides.

---

[1] "Ho, Œdipus, Œdipus! why linger we from going? Long, long have
you already kept us waiting."

invention adopted from Euripides.[1] Nor, in this connection, is it insignificant that Aristotle credits Sophocles with the invention of σκηνογραφία, or scene-painting. The abuse of scenical resources to the detriment of real dramatic unity and solidity was one of the chief defects of Euripidean art.

Motive of love in the Trachiniæ.

It may here be noticed that Sophocles in the *Trachiniæ* took up the theme of love as a main motive for a drama. By doing so he broke ground in a region that had been avoided, as far as we can judge from extant plays, by Æschylus, and in which Euripides was destined to achieve his greatest triumphs. It is, indeed, difficult to decide the question of precedence between Sophocles and Euripides in the matter. Except on this account the *Trachiniæ* is the least interesting of his tragedies. The whole play seems like a somewhat dull, though conscientious, handling of a fable, in which the poet took but a slight interest. Compared with Medea or with Phædra, Deianeira is tame and lifeless. She makes one fatal and foolish mistake through jealousy, and all is over. Hyllus, too, is a mere *silhouette*, while the contention between him and Herakles about the marriage with Iole, at the end, is frigid. Here, if anywhere, we detect the force of the critique quoted above from Longinus. At the same time the *Trachiniæ* offers many points of interest to the student of Greek sentiment. The phrase ταύτης ὁ δεινὸς ἵμερος (the grievous yearning after her) is significant, as expressing the pain and forceful energy which the Greeks attributed to passion : nor is the contrast drawn by Deianeira between πόσις (lawful husband) and ἀνήρ (paramour) without value. The motive used by Sophocles in this tragedy was developed by Euripides with a comprehension so far deeper, and with a fulness so far more satisfactory, that the *Hippolytus* and the *Medea* must always take rank above it.

[1] Our imperfect knowledge of the Attic drama prevents our forming any opinion as to the employment of the *deus ex machinâ* by the earlier tragedians.

The deepest and most decisive quality in which the tragic art of Sophocles resembled that of Euripides is rhetoric. Sophoclean rhetoric. Sophocles was the first to give its full value to dramatic casuistry, to introduce sophistic altercations, and to set forth all that could be well said in support of a poor argument. A passage on this subject may be quoted from "Eckermann's Conversations with Goethe:"[1]—

"That is the very thing," said Goethe, "in which Sophocles is a master; and in which consists the very life of the dramatic in general. His characters all possess this gift of eloquence, and know how to explain the motives for their action so convincingly that the hearer is almost always on the side of the last speaker. One can see that in his youth he enjoyed an excellent rhetorical education, by which he became trained to look for all the reasons and seeming reasons of things. Still, his great talent in this respect betrayed him into faults, as he sometimes went too far."

The special point selected by Goethe for criticism is the celebrated last speech of Antigone :—

"At last, when she is led to death, she brings forward a motive which is quite unworthy, and almost borders on the comic. She says that if she had been a mother she would not have done either for her dead children or for her dead husband what she has done for her brother. 'For,' says she, 'if my husband died I could have had another, and if my children died I could have had others by my new husband. But with my brother the case is different. I cannot have another brother ; for since my mother and father are dead there is none to beget one.' This is at least the bare sense of the passage, which, in my opinion, when placed in the mouth of a heroine going to her death, disturbs the tragic tone, and appears to me very far-fetched—to savour too much of dialectical calculation. As I said, I should like a philologist to show us that the passage is spurious."

In truth this last speech of Antigone is exactly what the severer critics of Euripides would have selected in a play of his for condemnation. It exhibits, after all allowance for peculiar Greek sentiments, the rhetorical development of a

---

[1] English Translation, vol. i. p. 371.

sophistic thesis. In the simple thought there is pathos. But its elaboration makes it frigid.

Sophocles, though he made the subsequent method of Euripides not only possible but natural by the law of progressive evolution, was very far indeed from disintegrating the tragic structure as Euripides was destined to do. The *deus ex machinâ* of the *Philoctetes*, for example, was only employed because there was absolutely no other way to solve the situation. Rhetoric and wrangling matches were never introduced for their own sake. The choric odes did not degenerate into mere musical interludes. Description and narration in no case took the place of action, by substituting pictures to the ear under conditions where true art required dramatic presentation. It remains the everlasting glory of Sophocles that he realised the mean between Æschylus and Euripides, sacrificing for the sake of his ideal the passionate and enthusiastic extremities of the older dramatist, without imperilling the fabric of Greek tragedy by the suicidal innovations of Euripides. He and he alone knew how to use all forms of art, to express all motives, and to hazard all varieties, with the single purpose of maintaining artistic unity.

What remains to be said about Sophocles, and in particular about his delineation of character, may be introduced in the course of an analysis of his tragedies upon the tale of Thebes.

These three plays do not, like the three plays of Æschylus upon the tale of the Atreidæ, form a trilogy. That is to say, they are not so connected in subject as to form one continued series. A drama, for example, similar to the *Seven against Thebes* might be interpolated between the *Œdipus Coloneüs* and *Antigone;* while the *Œdipus Tyrannus* might have been followed by a tragedy upon the subject of the king's expulsion from Thebes. Nor, again, are they artistically designed as a trilogy. There is no change of form, suggesting the beginning, middle, and ending of a calculated work of art, like that which we notice in the *Oresteia*. More-

over, the protagonist is absent from the *Antigone*, and therefore to call the three plays an *Œdipodeia* is impossible. Finally,
they were composed at different periods : the *Antigone* is the
first extant tragedy of Sophocles ; the *Œdipus Coloneüs* is the
last.

So much it was necessary to premise in order to avoid *Three plays,*
the imputation of having treated the three masterpieces of *not an*
Sophocles as in any true sense a trilogy. The temptation to *Oresteia.*
do so is at first sight almost irresistible ; for they are written
on the same legend, and the same characters are throughout
sustained with firmness, proving that, though Sophocles composed the last play of the series first and the second last of
all, he had conceived them in his brain before he undertook
to work them out in detail. Or, if this assumption seems
unwarranted, we may at least affirm with certainty that at
some point of time anterior to the production of the *Antigone*,
he had subjected the whole legend of the house of Laius to
his plastic imagination, and had given it coherence in his
mind. In other words, it was impossible for him to change
his point of view about this mythus in the same way as
Euripides when he handled that of Helen according to two
different versions. It so happens, moreover, that the climax
of the *Œdipus Tyrannus* prepares us, by the revolution in the
character of the protagonist, for the *Œdipus Coloneüs*, while
the last act of the second tragedy, by the prominence given
to Antigone, serves as a prelude to the third and final play.

The house of Laius was scarcely less famous among the *The house*
Greeks than the house of Atreus for its overwhelming dis- *of Laius.*
asters, the consequences of an awful curse which rested on
the family. Laius, the son of Labdacus, was supposed to
have introduced an unnatural vice into Hellas ; and from this
first crime sprang all the subsequent disasters of his progeny.
He took in marriage Jocasta, the sister of Prince Creon, and
swayed the State of Thebes. To him an oracle was given
that a son of his by Jocasta should kill him. Yet he did not

therefore, in obedience to the divine warning, put away his wife or live in chastity. A boy was born to the royal pair, who gave him to one of their shepherds, after piercing his feet and tying them together, and bound the hind to expose him on Cithæron. Thus they hoped to defeat the will of Heaven. The shepherd, moved by pity, saved the baby's life and handed him over to a friend of his, who used to feed his master's sheep upon the same hill-pastures. This man carried the infant, named Œdipus because of his wounded and swollen feet, to Polybus of Corinth, a childless king, who brought him up as his own son. Œdipus, when he had grown to manhood, was taunted with his obscure birth by his comrades in Corinth. Thereupon he journeyed alone to Delphi to make inquiry concerning his parentage from Phœbus. Phœbus told him nought thereof, but bade him take heed lest he slay his father and wed his mother. Œdipus, deeming that Polybus was his father and Merope his mother, determined to return to Corinth no more. At that time Thebes was troubled with the visitation of the Sphinx, and no man might rede her riddle. Œdipus, passing through the Theban land, was met in a narrow path, where three roads joined, by an old man on a chariot attended by servants. The old man spoke rudely to him, commanding him to make way for his horses, and one of the servants struck him. Whereupon Œdipus slew the master, knowing not that he was his own father Laius, and the men too, all but one, who fled. Thereafter he passed on to Thebes, and solved that riddle of the Sphinx, and the Thebans made him their king, and gave him the lady Jocasta to be his wife. Thus were both the oracles accomplished, and yet Œdipus and Jocasta remained ignorant of their doom. For many years Œdipus ruled Thebes like a great and warlike prince; and to him and Jocasta in wedlock were born two daughters and two sons—Antigone and Ismene, Polyneices and Eteocles. These grew to youth, and a seeming calm of fair weather and

prosperity abode upon their house. Yet the gods were
mindful of the abomination, and in course of time a plague
was sent, which ravaged the people of Thebes. Sorely
pressed by calamity, Œdipus sent his brother-in-law Creon to
inquire at Delphi of the causes of the plague and of the means
of staying it. This brings us to the opening of *Œdipus the
King*. At this point something should be said about the
mythus itself and about the position of the several persons at
the commencement of the tragedy.

The fable is obviously one of those which Max Müller and
his school describe as solar. Œdipus, who slays his father
and weds his mother, may stand for the sun, who slays the
night and is married to the dawn. We know how all
legends can fall into this mould, and how easy it is to clap
the Dawn on to the end of every Greek tale, like the ληκύθιον
ἀπώλεσεν (lost a little oil-flask) of the *Frogs*. This, however,
is nothing to our purpose; for Sophocles had never heard
of solar myths. The tale of Thebes supplied him with the
subject of three dramas; he used it as a story well suited
for displaying passions in their strongest and most tragic
workings. As usual, he was not contented with merely
following the traditional version of the legend, nor did he
insist upon its superstitious elements. That the gods had a
grudge against the Labdacidæ, that the oracles given to Laius
and Œdipus were not warnings so much as sinister predictions
of a doom inevitable, that the very powers who uttered them
were bent on blinding the victims of fate to their true import,
were thoroughly Greek notions, consistent with the divine
φθόνος or envy of Herodotus, and not wholly inconsistent
with the gloomy theology of Æschylus. But it was no part
of the method of Sophocles to emphasise this horrible doctrine
of destiny. On the contrary, he moralised it. While preserving all the essential features of the myth, he made it clear
that the characters of men constitute their fatality.

As our own Fletcher has nobly written :—

Ancestral curse of the Labdacidæ.

> " Man is his own star, and the soul that can
>   Render an honest and a perfect man,
>   Commands all light, all influence, all fate ;
>   Nothing to him falls early or too late ;
>   Our acts our angels are, or good or ill,
>   Our fatal shadows that walk by us still."

Moralisation of Fate.

What to the vulgar apprehension appears like doom, and to the theologian like the direct interposition of the deity, is to the tragic poet but the natural consequence of moral, physical, and intellectual qualities. These it is his function to set forth in high and stately scenes, commingling with his psychological analysis and forcible dramatic presentation somewhat of the old religious awe.

It may be urged that this is only shifting the burden of necessity, not removing it. It is, perhaps, impossible scientifically to avoid a fatalistic theory of some sort, since in one sense it is true that

> " A fishwife hath a fate, and so have I—
>   But far above your finding."

Yet practically we do not act upon such theories, and, from the point of view of ethics, there is all the difference in the world between showing how the faults and sins of men must lead them to fearful ends, and painting them in the grip of a remorseless and malignant deity.

Infatuation of the chief actors in these tragedies.

Laius was warned that his son by Jocasta would kill him. Yet he begat a son ; and in his presumptuous disregard of heaven, thinking, forsooth, that by mere barbarity a man may cheat the omnipotent, and that the all-seeing cannot save a child of prophecy and doom, he exposed this son upon Cithæron. The boy lived. Thus the crime of Laius is want of self-restraint in the first instance, contempt of God in the second, and cruelty in the third. After this, Œdipus appears upon the theatre of events. He, too, receives oracular warning —that he will slay his sire and wed his mother. Yet, though well aware of the doubt which rests upon his own birth—for it was just on this account that he went to Delphi—he is satisfied with avoiding his supposed parents. The first man whom he meets, while the words of the oracle are still ringing in his ears, he slays; the first woman who is offered to him in marriage, though old enough to be his mother, he weds. His crime is haste of temper, heat of blood, blind carelessness of the divine decrees. Jocasta shows her guilty infatuation in another form. Not only does she participate in the first sin of Laius; but she forgets the oracle which announced that Laius should be slain by his own son. She makes no inquiry into the causes of his death. She does not investigate the previous history of Œdipus, or observe the marks upon his feet, but weds him heedlessly. Here, indeed, the legend itself *Improba-* involves monstrous improbabilities—as, for instance, that *the legend.* Jocasta, while a widow of a few days, should have been thus wedded to a stranger young enough to be her son, that the Thebans should have made no strict search for the murderer of their king, that Œdipus himself should have heard nothing about the death and funeral of Laius, but should have stepped incuriously into his place and sat upon his throne without asking further questions either of his wife or of his subjects. Previous to the opening of *Œdipus the King* there is, there-fore, a whole tissue of absurdities; and to these Aristotle is probably referring when he says : ἄλογον δὲ μηδὲν εἶναι ἐν τοῖς¹ πράγμασιν, εἰ δὲ μὴ, ἔξω τῆς τραγῳδίας, οἷον τὰ ἐν τῷ Οἰδίποδι τῷ Σοφοκλέους.¹

Granting this, the vigorous logic wherewith the conclusions *Œdipus the* are wrought out by Sophocles leaves nothing to be desired *King.* on the score of truth to nature. There is, indeed, no work of tragic art which can be compared with the *Œdipus* for the closeness and consistency of the plot. To use the critical terms of the *Poetics*, it would rank first among tragedies for its μῦθος

---

¹ "There ought to be nothing irrational in the events, or at any rate only outside the action of the tragedy itself, as is the case with those in the *Œdipus* of Sophocles."

(plot), and for the σύστασις πραγμάτων (construction), even were its ἤθη (characters) far less firmly traced. The triumph of Sophocles has been, however, so to connect the ἤθη of his persons with the πράγματα, characters with plot, as to make the latter depend upon the former; and in this kind of ethical causality lies the chief force of his tragic art.

Ethical errors of Œdipus and Jocasta.

If questioned concerning the situation of events previous to the play of *Œdipus*, it is possible that Sophocles would have pointed out that the ἁμαρτία or error common to all the *dramatis personœ* was an unwarrantable self-confidence. One and all they consult the oracle, and then are satisfied with taking the affairs they had referred to Phœbus into their own hands. Unlike the Orestes of Æschylus, they do not endeavour to act up to the divine commands, and, having done so, place themselves once more beneath the guidance of the god. The oracle is all-important in the three plays on the tale of Thebes, and Sophocles seems to have intended to inculcate a special lesson with regard to the submission of the human will. Those who inquire of a god, and who attempt to thwart his decrees by human skill and foresight, will not prosper. The apparent success of their shifty schemes may cause them to exclaim: "The oracle was false; how weak are those who look for its accomplishment!" Thus they are lured by their self-conceit into impiety. In the end, too, the oracle is found to be fearfully exact. Those, therefore, who take the step of consulting Phœbus, must hold themselves responsible to him, must expect the fulfilment of his prophecy; or if they seek to avert the promised evils, they must, at all events, not do so by criminal contrivances and petty lawlessness, such as man thinks that he may practise upon man. It was thus that Sophocles conceived of the relation of human beings to the deity. He delights in exhibiting the blindness of arrogance and self-confidence, and in showing that characters determined by these qualities rush recklessly to their own doom. At the same time he draws a clear distinction between the man who is hardened in

godless folly and one who errs through simple haste. The
impiety of Jocasta ends in suicide. Œdipus, who has been
impetuous and self-willed, finds a place for repentance, and
survives his worst calamities, to die a god-protected and god-
honoured hero.

The opening scene of the *Œdipus* serves a double purpose.
While it places the spectators at the exact point in the legend
selected by the poet for treatment, it impresses them with the
greatness and the majesty of the King. Thebes is worn out
with plague. The hand of heaven lies heavily upon the citizens. Therefore the priest of Zeus approaches the hero who
once before had saved them from the Sphinx, and who may
now—fit representative of God on earth—find out a remedy
for this intolerable evil. Œdipus appears upon the stage, a
confident and careful ruler, sublime in the strength of manhood and the consciousness of vast capacity, tender for the
afflictions of his people, yet undismayed by their calamity.
He is just the man to sustain a commonwealth by his firm
character and favouring fortune. Flawless in force of will
and singleness of purpose, he seems incapable of failure. To
connect the notions of disgrace or guilt or shame with such
a king is utterly impossible. Yet, even so, Sophocles has
hinted in the speech of Œdipus a something overmuch of
confidence and courage :—

Opening of the play.

> " Well I know
> That ye all suffer, yet, thus suffering, I
> More than you all in overmeasure suffer :
> For that which wounds you strikes at each man singly,
> At each and not another ; while my soul
> For Thebes, for me, for you, feels one huge sorrow."

Even here the irony, for which the play is famous, begins
to transpire. Œdipus believes that his grief is sympathy for
a vexed people committed to his charge. Little does he know
that, while he is pluming himself upon his watchful care for
others, he himself is the head and front of all offending. In

Irony of the situation.

the word κἀμὲ (me too), almost negligently uttered, lies the kernel of the future revelation. While he is informing the suppliants that Creon has gone to Delphi for advice, the prince arrives. A garland of good augury is on his brow; and in this sign of an auspicious embassy we discern another stroke of tragic irony. Phœbus has declared that the presence in Thebes of the hitherto unpunished, unregarded murderer of Laius is the cause of the plague. Œdipus, when he fully understands the matter, swears to discover the offender. The curse which he pronounces on this guilty man is terrible —terrible in its energy of interdiction and excommunication from all rites of hospitality, from human sympathy, from earth and air and water and the fruits of the field—but still more terrible through the fact that all these maledictions are uttered on his own head. The irony of the situation—if we are justified in giving this word to the contrast between what seems and what really is—between Œdipus as he appears to the burghers, and Œdipus as he is known to us—rises in the emphatic eloquence of his denunciation to a truly awful height. At the same time his obvious sincerity enlists our sympathy upon his side. We feel beforehand that the man who speaks thus, will, when his eyes are opened, submit to his self-imprecated doom. It now remains to detect the murderer. Thinking that his faculty of divination may be useful, Œdipus has already sent for the blind seer Teiresias. Teiresias is one of the great creations of Sophocles. Twice he appears, once in this play, once in the *Antigone*, each time in conflict with infatuated kings. He is so aged, and the soul within him is so fixed on things invisible, that he seems scarcely human. We think of him as of one who dwells apart, not communing in ordinary social ways with men, but listening to the unspoken words of God, and uttering his wisdom in dark parable to those who heed him not. The Greek poets frequently exhibited the indifference of prosperous persons to divine monitions. Cassandra's prophecies were not attended

The blind seer Teiresias.

to; the Delphic oracle spoke in vain; and Teiresias is only honoured when it is too late. Sophocles, while maintaining the mysterious fascination of the soothsayer, has marked his character by some strong touches of humanity. He is proud and irritable to excess. His power of sarcasm is appalling, and his indignation is inexorable. Between two stubborn and unyielding natures like the seer and King, sparks of anger could not fail to be struck; the explosion that follows on their meeting serves to display the choleric temper of Œdipus, which formed the main trait of his character, the pith of his ἁμαρτία (fault).

Œdipus greets Teiresias courteously, telling him that he, the King, is doing all he can to find the murderer of Laius, and that the soothsayer must spare no pains. To this generous patronage and protective welcome, Teiresias, upon whose sightless soul the truth has suddenly flashed, answers with deep sighs, and requests to be led home again. This naturally nettles Œdipus. The hastiness that drew him into his first fault renders him now ungovernable. Teiresias keeps saying it will be better for the King to remain ignorant, and the King retorts that he is only a blind dotard; were he not blind, he, and no other, might be suspected of the murder. This provokes an oracular response :— Œdipus and Teiresias.

> " Ay ! Is it so ? I bid thee, then, abide
> By thy first ordinance, and from this day
> Join not in converse with these men or me,
> Being thyself this land's impure defiler."

Thus the real state of affairs is suddenly disclosed; and were Œdipus of a submissive temper he would immediately have proceeded to the discovery of the truth. This would, however, have destroyed the drama, and have prevented the unfolding of the character of the King. Instead, therefore, of heeding the seer's words, Œdipus rushes at once to the conclusion that Creon and Teiresias are plotting to overthrow him in his tyranny. The quarrel waxes hot. Each word Blindness of Œdipus.

uttered by Teiresias is pregnant with terrific revelation. The whole context of events, past, present, and future, is painted with intense lucidity in speech that has the trenchant force of oracular conviction ; yet Œdipus remains so firmly rooted in his own integrity and in the belief which he has suddenly assumed of Creon's treason, that he turns deaf ears and a blind soul to the truth. At last the seer leaves him with this denunciation :—

> " I tell thee this : the man whom thou so long
> Seekest with threats and mandates for the murder
> Of Laius, that very man is here,
> By name an alien, but in season due
> He shall be shown true Theban, and small joy
> Shall have therein ; for, blind, instead of seeing,
> And poor, who once was rich, he shall go forth,
> Staff-guided, groping, o'er a foreign land.
> He shall be shown to be with his own children
> Brother and sire in one, of her who bore him
> Husband at once and offspring, of his father
> Bedmate and murderer. Go ; take now these words
> Within, and weigh them ; if thou find me false,
> Say then that divination taught me nothing."

Œdipus and Creon.

The next scene is one of altercation between Œdipus and Creon. Œdipus, full of rage, still haunted by the suspicion of treason, yet stung to the quick by some of the dark speeches of the prophet, vehemently assails the prince, and condemns him to exile. Creon—who, of course, is innocent, but who is not meant to have a generous or lofty soul—defends himself in a dry and argumentative manner, until Jocasta comes forth from the palace and seeks to quell their conflict. Œdipus tells her haughtily that he is accused of being the murderer of Laius. She begins her answer with a frivolous and impious assertion that all oracles are nonsense. The oracle uttered against Laius came to nothing, for his son died on Mount Cithæron, and robbers slew him near Thebes long afterwards, where three ways meet. These words, ἐν τριπλαῖς ἁμαξιτοῖς (at the meeting of three roads), stir suspicion in the mind of Œdipus.

He asks at once : "Where was the spot ?"   "In Phokis, where
one goes to Delphi and to Daulia."   "What was Laius like ?"
"Not unlike you in shape," says Jocasta, "but white-haired."
"Who were with him ?"   "Five men, and he rode a chariot."
"Who told you all this ?"   "One who escaped, and who
begged me afterwards to send him from the palace, and who
now keeps a farm of ours in the country."   Each answer
adds to the certainty in the mind of Œdipus that it was Laius
whom he slew.   The only hope left is to send for the servant,
and to find out whether he adheres to his story of there
having been more robbers than one.   If he remains firm upon
this point, and does not confess that it was one solitary man
who slew his master and his comrades, then there is a chance
that he, the King, may not be guilty.   Jocasta, with her
usual levity, comforts him by insisting that he spoke of
robbers in the plural, and that he must not be suffered to
retract his words.

While they are waiting for the servant, a messenger arrives   The messenger from
from Corinth with good news.   Polybus, the king, is dead, and   Corinth.
Œdipus is proclaimed his successor.   "Where now," shouts
impious Jocasta, "are your oracles—that you should slay your
father ?   See you not how foolish it is to trust to Phœbus and
to auguries of birds ?   Chance is the lord of all.   Let us, therefore, live our lives as best we can."   Awful is the irony of these
short-sighted jubilations ; and awful, as Aristotle has pointed
out,[1] is the irony which makes this messenger of apparently
good tidings add the last link to the chain of evidence that
will overwhelm Œdipus with ruin.   Œdipus exclaims :
"Though my father is dead, I may not return to Corinth :
Merope still lives."   "What," says the messenger, "do you
fear her because she is your mother ?   Set your mind at ease.
She is no mother of yours, nor was Polybus your father.   I
gave you to them as a gift when you were yet an infant."
"Where did you find me ?" cries the King.   "Upon Cithæron :

[1] *Poetics*, xi.

a shepherd of the house of Laius gave you to me; your feet were pierced, and I believe that you were born in the royal household." Terrible word, Cithæron! It echoes through this tragedy with horror—its scaurs and pastures, the scene of the first crime. And now those two hinds, who had met there once apparently by chance with the child of doom between them, are being again, as though by chance, brought face to face with the man of doom between them, in order to make good the words of Teiresias :—

> βοῆς δὲ τῆς σῆς ποῖος οὐκ ἔσται λιμήν,
> ποῖος Κιθαιρὼν οὐχὶ σύμφωνος τάχα; [1]

Jocasta before her suicide.

Jocasta is struck dumb by the answers of the messenger. She, and she alone, knows now at last the whole truth; but she does not speak, while Œdipus continues asking who the shepherd of the house of Laius was. Then she utters words of fearful import, praying the King to go no farther, nor to seek what, found, will plunge his soul into despair like hers. After this, finding her suit ineffectual, she retires into the palace. The Chorus are struck by the wildness of her gestures, and hint their dread that she is going to her doom of suicide. But Œdipus, not yet fully enlightened, and preoccupied with the problem which interests himself so deeply, only imagines that she shrinks from the possible proof of his base birth. As yet he does not suspect that he is the own son of Laius; and here, it may be said in passing, the sole weakness of the plot transpires. Neither the oracle first given to him at Delphi, nor the plain speech of Teiresias, nor the news of the Corinthian messenger, nor the pleadings of Jocasta, are sufficient to suggest the real truth to his mind. Such profundity of blindness is dramatically improbable. He is, however, soon destined to receive illumination. The servant of Laius, who gave Jocasta intelligence of the manner of her husband's

---

[1] "What place shall not re-echo to thy cries, what Cithæron shall not soon be ringing with thy lamentations?"

death, is now brought upon the stage ; and in him the Corin- The cata-
strophe.
thian messenger recognises the same shepherd who had given
him the infant on Cithæron.   Though reluctant to confess the
truth so long concealed, the shepherd is at last forced to reveal
all he knows ; and in this supreme moment Œdipus discovers
that he is not only the murderer of his own father, but also
that Jocasta is his mother.   In the madness of this revelation
he rushes to the palace.   The Chorus are left alone to moralise
upon these terrible events.   Then the dramatic Messenger
arrives.   Jocasta has hanged herself within her bedchamber.
Œdipus, breaking bars and bolts in the fire of his despair, has
followed her.   Around him were the servants, drawn together
by the tumult.   None, however, dared approach him.   Led by
an inner impulse, he found the place where his wife and mother
hung, released the corpse, and tearing from her dress the golden
buckles, cut out both his eyes, crying aloud that no longer
should they look upon the light or be witness to his woe, seeing
that when they might have aided him they were as good as
blind.   Thus one day turned the prosperity of Œdipus to
" wailing, woe, death, disgrace, all evils that have name—not
one is absent."   The speech of the Messenger narrating these
events is a splendid instance of the energy of Sophocles, when
he chooses to describe a terrible event appallingly.   It does
not convey the Æschylean mystery of brooding horror ; but
the scene is realised in all its incidents, briefly, vividly, with
ghastly clearness.   Meanwhile, the voice of Œdipus himself is
heard.   He bids the palace-doors be opened, in order that
all Thebes may see the parricide, the monster of unhallowed Climax of
the tragedy.
indescribable abominations.   So the gates are rolled asunder :
and there lies dead Jocasta ; and sightless Œdipus, with bloody
cheeks and beard, stands over her, and the halls are filled with
wailing women and woe-stricken men.

Here, if this had been a modern tragedy, the play of
Œdipus Tyrannus might have ended ; but so abrupt and
scenical a conclusion did not suit the art of Sophocles.   He

had still further to develop the character of Œdipus, and to offer the prospect of that future reconciliation between the fate and the passions of his hero which he had in store. For this purpose the last two hundred lines of the drama, though they do not continue the plot, but rather suggest a new and secondary subject of interest, are invaluable. Hitherto we have seen Œdipus in the pride of monarchy and manhood, hasty, arrogant, yet withal a just and able ruler. He is now, through a περιπέτεια, or revolution of circumstances, more complete than any other in Greek tragedy, revealed in the very depths of his calamity, still dignified. There is no resistance left in the once so strong and stubborn man. The hand of God, weighing heavily upon him, has bowed his head, and he is humble as a little child. Yet the vehemence that marked his former phase persists. It finds vent in the passionate lucidity wherewith he examines all the details of the pollution he has unwittingly incurred, and in the rage with which he demands to have his own curse carried out against him. Let him be cast from the city, sent forth to wander on the fells of Cithæron—οὑμὸς Κιθαίρων οὗτος (that Cithæron which is my own place). It was the highest achievement of tragic art to exhibit so suddenly and by so sharp a transition this new development of the King's nature. Saul of Tarsus, when blinded by the vision, was not more immediately converted from one mood into another, more contrite in profound sincerity of sorrow. Still in the altered Œdipus we see the same man, the same temperament; though all internal and external circumstances have been changed, so that henceforward he will never tread the paths of life as once he did. The completeness of his self-abandonment appears most vividly in the dialogue with Creon, upon whose will his immediate fate depends. When Creon, whom he had lately misjudged and treated with violent harshness, comes and greets him kindly, the wretched King tastes the very bitterness of degradation, yet he is not abject. He only prays once more, with intensest urgency of pleading, to have the uttermost of the excommunication he had vowed, executed upon his head. Thinking less of himself than of the miserable beings associated with him in disaster, he beseeches Creon to inter the Queen, and, for his boys, to give them only a fair chance in life—they will be men, and may carve out their own fortunes in the world ; but for his two poor girls, left desolate, a scorn and mockery to all men, he can only pray that they may come to him, be near him, bear the burden of their misery by their father's side. The tenderness of Œdipus for Ismene and Antigone, his yearning to clasp them, is terribly—almost painfully—touching, when we remember who they were, how born, the children of what curses. The words with which the King addresses them are even hazardous in their directness. Yet it was needful that humanity should by some such strain of passion be made to emerge from this tempest of soul-shattering woes ; and thus, too, a glimpse of that future is provided which remained for Œdipus, if sorrowful, assuaged at least by filial love. In reply to all his eloquent supplications Creon answers that he will not take upon himself the responsibility of dealing with his case. Nothing can be done without consulting the oracle at Delphi. Œdipus has, therefore, to be patient and endure. The strong hero, who saved Thebes from the Sphinx and swayed the city, is now in the hands of tutors and governors awaiting his doom. He submits quietly, and the tragedy is ended.

The effect of such a tragedy as *Œdipus the King* is to make men feel that the earth is shaken underneath them, and that the heavens above are big with thunder. Compassion and fear are agitated in the highest degree ; old landmarks seem to vanish ; the mightiest have fallen, and the most impious, convinced of God, have been goaded to self-murder. Great indeed is the tragic poet's genius who can make us feel that the one sure point amid this confusion is the firmness of its principal foredestined victim. That is the triumph of Sophocles. Out of the chaos of the *Œdipus Tyrannus* springs the new order of

the *Œdipus Coloneüs :* and here it may be said that perhaps
the most valid argument in favour of the Æschylean trilogy
as a supreme work of dramatic art is this—that such a
tragedy as the first Œdipus demanded such another as the
second. The new motives suggested in the last act were
not sufficiently worked out to their conclusion ; much that
happened in the climax of the *Tyrannus* seemed to necessitate
the *Coloneüs.*

Transition
to the
Coloneüs.

The interest of the *Œdipus Tyrannus* centres in its plot,
and that is my only excuse for having dwelt so long on the
structure of a play familiar to every student. That of the
Œdipus Coloneüs is different. It has, roughly speaking, no
plot. It owes its perfect, almost superhuman, beauty to the
atmosphere which bathes it, as with peace after tempest,
with the lucid splendours of sunset succeeding to a storm-
vexed and tumultuous day. The scene is laid, as the name
indicates, in the village birthplace of the poet. Years are
supposed to have elapsed since the conclusion of the former
tragedy ; Œdipus, after being detained in Thebes against his
will at first, has now been driven forth by Creon, and has
wandered many miles in blindness, led by his daughter's
hand. The ethical interest of the play, so far as it is not
absorbed by Œdipus himself, centres principally in Antigone,
whereby we are prepared for her emergence into fullest
prominence in the tragedy which bears her name. Always
keeping in mind that these three plays are not a trilogy, I
cannot but insist again that much is lost, especially in all
that concerns the unfolding of Antigone's character, by not
reading them in the order suggested by the fable. At the
same time, though Antigone engrosses our sympathy and
attention, Sophocles has varied the drama by a more than
usual number of persons. The generous energy of Theseus
forms a fine contrast to the inactivity forced upon Œdipus
by the conditions of the drama, and also to the meanness of
Creon ; while the episodes of Ismene's arrival, of Antigone's

abduction, and of the visit of Polyneices, add movement to what might else have been too stationary. It should also be said that all these subsidiary sources of interest are used with subtle art by Sophocles for enhancing the dignity of Œdipus, for arousing our sympathy with him, and for bringing into prominence the chief features of his character. None can, therefore, be regarded as superfluous, though, strictly speaking, they might have been detached without absolute destruction of the drama, which is more than can be said about the slightest incidents of *Œdipus Tyrannus*. As regards Œdipus himself, that modification of his fiery temperament which Sophocles revealed at the end of the first tragedy, has now become permanent. He is schooled into submission ; yet he has not lost the old impetuosity that formed the groundwork of his nature. He is still quick to anger and vehement in speech, but both his anger and his vehemence are justified by the occasion. Something, moreover, of fateful and mysterious, severing him from the common race of men and shrouding him within the seclusion of his dread calamity, has been added. The terror of his dreadful past, and the prospect of his august future, environ him with more than kingly dignity. The skill of Sophocles as a dramatic poet is displayed in all its splendour by the new light thrown upon the central figure of Œdipus. The effect of unity is not destroyed : those painful shocks to our sense of probability, so frequent when inferior dramatists—poets of the rank of Fletcher or of Jonson—attempt to depict a nature altered by internal reformation or by force of circumstance, do not occur. The Œdipus of both the tragedies remains one man ; we understand the change that has been wrought in him ; and while we feel that it is adequate and natural, we marvel at the wisdom of the poet who could vary his design with so much firmness.

The oracle, which continues to play an important part in this tale of Thebes, has warned Œdipus that he will end his

Construction of the *Coloneüs*.

The new phase of the hero's character.

days within the precincts of the Semnai Theai, or august goddesses of retribution. In his new phase the man of haste and wrath is no longer heedless of oracles; nor does he let their words lie idle in his mind. It is, therefore, with a strong presentiment of approaching death that he discovers early in this play that his feet, led by Antigone, have rested in the grove of the Furies at Colonus. The place itself is fair. There are here no Harpy-Gorgons with bloodshot eyes, and vipers twining in their matted hair. The meadows are dewy, with crocus-flowers and narcissus; in the thickets of olive and laurel nightingales keep singing; and rivulets spread coolness in the midst of summer's heat. The whole wood is hushed, and very fresh and wild. A solemn stillness broods there; for the feet of the profane keep far away, and none may tread the valley-lawns but those who have been purified. The ransomed of the Lord walk there. This solemnity of peace pervades the whole play, forming, to borrow a phrase from painting, the silver-gray harmony of the picture. In thus bringing Œdipus to die among the unshowered meadows of those Dread Ladies, whom in his troubled life he found so terrible, but whom in his sublime passage from the world he is about to greet resignedly, we may trace peculiar depth of meaning. The thought of death, calm but austere, tempers every scene in the drama. We are in the presence of one whose life is ended, who is about to merge the fever of existence in the tranquillity beyond. This impression of solemnity is heightened when we remember that the poet wrote the *Coloneüs* in extreme old age. Over him too the genius of everlasting repose already spread wings in the twilight, and the mysteries of the grave were nearer to him and more daily present than to other men.

A country fellow, who perceives Œdipus seated by his daughter on a marble bench within the sacred precinct, bids them quit the spot; for it is hallowed. Œdipus, however, knowing that his doom shall be fulfilled, asks that he may

be confronted with the elders of the place.   They come and
gaze with mingled feelings of distrust and awe on the blind
hero, august in desolation.   Before they can converse with
him, Œdipus has to quit the recesses of the grove, and gain a
spot where speech and traffic are permitted.   Then, in answer
to their questions, he informs them who he is—Œdipus.   At
that name they start back in horror, demanding that he
shall carry the abomination of his presence from their land.
This affords the occasion for a splendid speech from the old
man, one of the most telling passages of eloquence in Sophocles,
in which he appeals to the time-long hospitality and fame
for generosity of Athens.   Athens was never known to spurn
the suppliant or expel the stranger, and the deeds of Œdipus
they so much dread, are sufferings rather :—

$$\epsilon\pi\epsilon\grave{\iota}\ \tau\acute{a}\ \gamma'\ \acute{\epsilon}\rho\gamma a\ \mu o \upsilon$$
$$\pi\epsilon\pi o\nu\theta\acute{o}\tau'\ \acute{\epsilon}\sigma\tau\grave{\iota}\ \mu\hat{a}\lambda\lambda o\nu\ \mathring{\eta}\ \delta\epsilon\delta\rho a\kappa\acute{o}\tau a.[1]$$

The Chorus, moved by the mingled impetuosity and sound   Appeal to
reasoning of their suitor, perceive that the case is too grave   Theseus.
for them to decide.   Accordingly, they send a messenger for
Theseus ; but before he can be summoned, Ismene arrives
on horseback with the news that her brothers are quarrel-
ling about the throne of Thebes.   Eteocles, the younger, has
usurped the sovereignty, while Polyneices has fled to Argos
to engage the chiefs of the Achaians in his cause.   Both
parties, meantime, are eager to secure the person of Œdipus,
since an oracle has proclaimed that with him will victory
abide.   Œdipus, hearing these tidings, bursts into a strain
of passionate denunciation, which proves that the old fire of
his temper is smouldering still unquenched.   When he was
forlorn and in misery, his unnatural sons took no thought of
him.   They sent him forth to roam, a pariah upon the earth,
leaving to his daughters the care and burden of supporting

---

[1] "Seeing that my actions are rather things I suffered than deeds
which I performed."

him. Now, basely anxious for their selfish profit, they come to claim possession of his old, world-wearied flesh. Instead of blessings, they shall meet with curses. Instead of the fair land of Thebes to lord it over, they shall barely get enough ground to die and be buried in. He, meanwhile, will abide at Athens, and bequeath a heritage of help and honour to her soil.

Arrival of Theseus. The Chorus now call upon Œdipus to perform the rites of purification required by the Eumenides—rites which Sophocles has described with the loving minuteness of one to whom the customs of Colonus were from boyhood sacred. Ismene goes to carry out their instructions, and in her absence Theseus arrives upon the scene. Theseus, throughout the drama, plays toward Œdipus the part of a good-hearted, hospitable friend. His generosity is ethically contrasted with the meanness of Creon and the selfishness of Polyneices, while, artistically, the practical energy of his character serves for a foil to the stationary dignity of the chief actor. Sophocles has thus contrived to give weight and importance to a personage who might, in weaker hands, have been degraded into a mere instrument. Œdipus assures the Attic king that he will prove no useless and unserviceable denizen. The children of Erechtheus, whose interests rank first in the mind of Theseus, will find him in the future a powerful and god-protected sojourner within their borders. His natural sympathy for the persecuted and oppressed having been thus strengthened by the prospect of reciprocal advantage, Theseus formally accepts Œdipus as a suppliant, and promises him full protection. At this point, forming as it were a halting-place in the action of the play, Sophocles introduced that famous song about Colonus, which no one has yet succeeded in translating, but which, for modern ears, has received new value from the music of Mendelssohn.

What follows, before the final climax of the drama, consists of the efforts made by Creon, on the part of Eteocles, and by Polyneices, to enlist Œdipus respectively upon their sides in

the war of succession to the Theban throne. Creon displays Action of Creon
his heartless, cunning, impudent, sophistical, and forceful
character, while Œdipus opposes indignation and contempt,
unmasking his hypocrisy, and stripping his specious arguments
of all that hides their naked selfishness. In this scene we feel
that Sophocles is verging upon the Euripidean manner. A
little more would make the altercation between Creon and
Œdipus pass over into a forensic wrangling-match. As it is,
the chief dramatic value of the episode is to exhibit the grandeur
of the wrath of Œdipus in its righteous heat, when contrasted
with the wretched shifts of a mere rhetorical sophist.

After Creon, by the help of Theseus, has been thwarted in Polyneices.
his attempt to carry off Antigone, Polyneices approaches with
crocodile tears, fawning intercessions, and fictitious sorrow
for his father's desolation. Œdipus flashes upon his covert
egotism the same light of clear unclouded insight which had
unmasked Creon. "What," he asks, "is the value of tears
now, of prayers now? Dry were your eyes, hard as stone
your heart, dumb your lips, when I went forth from Thebes
unfriended. Here is your guerdon : before Thebes' walls you
shall die, pierced by your brother's hand, and your brother by
yours." The imprecation of the father upon the son would be
unnatural, were it not for the son's falseness, who behaved
like a Regan to Œdipus in his calamity, and who now, when
the old man has become a mysteriously important personage,
seeks to make the most of him for his own uses.

The protracted dialogues with Creon and Polyneices serve Mystical sacredness of the hero.
to enhance the sublimity of Œdipus. He, all the while, is
seated, a blind, travel-stained, neglected mendicant, upon the
marble bench of the Eumenides. There is horror in his very
aspect. Hellas rings with the abominations connected with
his name. Yet, to this poor pariah, to this apparent object
of pity and loathing, come princes and warriors capable
of stirring all the States of Greece in conflict. He rejects
them, firm in his consciousness of heaven-appointed destiny.

Sophocles seems bent on showing how the wrath of God may be turned aside from its most signal and notorious victims by real purity of heart and nobleness of soul; how, from the depths of degradation and affliction, the spirit of man may rise; and how the lot of demigods may be reserved for those whom the world ignorantly judges worthy of its scorn. Œdipus of late stood like the lightning-blasted tree that travellers dread—the *evitandum bidental* of Roman superstition. His withered limbs have now more health and healing in them than the leaf-embowered forest oak.

The curse of Œdipus.

The treatment of Polyneices in the *Œdipus Coloneüs* supplies a good example of the Sophoclean tendency to humanise the ancient myths of Hellas. The curse pronounced by Œdipus formed an integral element of that portion of the legend which suggested to Æschylus the *Seven against Thebes*. By its force, the whole weight of the doom that overhangs the house of Laius is brought to bear upon the suicidal brethren, both of whom rush helplessly, with eyes open, to meet inevitable fate.

> ὦ Ζεῦ τε καὶ Γῆ καὶ πολισσοῦχοι θεοί,
> Ἀρά τ' Ἐρινὺς πατρὸς ἡ μεγασθενής [1]

are the opening words of the prayer of Eteocles in that tragedy; while phrases like these, ὦ πόνοι δόμων νέοι παλαιοῖσι συμμιγεῖς κακοῖς and ὦ μέλαινα καὶ τελεία γένεος Οἰδίπου τ' ἀρά,[2] from the burden of the choric songs. Sophocles does not seek to make the wrath of Œdipus less terrible; he adheres to the old outline of the story, and heightens the tragic horror of the curse by framing for it words intense by reason of their very calculated calmness (1383-96). At the same time he shows how the obstinate temper of Polyneices, and his sense of honour, are necessary to its operation. After the dreadful sentence, dooming him

[1] "O Zeus and Earth and gods that guard the city,
   And the fell puissance of a father's curse!"
[2] "O troubles of the ancient house, new miseries commingled with the old!" and "O dark and fateful curse of the whole race and Œdipus!"

to self-murder by his brother's spear, has been pronounced, Polyneices stands before his father and his sister like one stunned. Antigone, with a woman's instinct, entreats him to choose the only way still left of safety. He may disband the army, and retire from the adventure against Thebes. To this her brother answers :—

> ἀλλ' οὐχ οἷόν τε. πῶς γὰρ αὖθις ἂν πάλιν
> στράτευμ' ἄγοιμι ταὐτὸν εἰσάπαξ τρέσας ; [1]

When she persists, he repeats μὴ πεῖθ' ἃ μὴ δεῖ (persuade me not to my dishonour). Thus, instead of bringing into strong relief the operation of blind fate, Sophocles places in the foreground the human agencies which contribute to the undoing of Polyneices. His crime of unfilial egotism, his dread of being thought a coward, and his honour rooted in dishonour, drive him through the tempest of his father's curse upon the rock of doom. The part played by Antigone in this awful scene of altercation between her father and her brother, first interceding for mercy, and then striving to break the stubborn will of the rebellious youth,[2] prepares our minds for the tragedy in which she will appear as protagonist. Hitherto she has been remarkable for filial love. She now shows herself a gentle and tender sister to one who had deeply wronged her. The absolute unselfishness, which gives to her the beauty as of some clear flawless jewel, shines forth by anticipation in the *Coloneüs*, enlisting our warmest sympathies upon her side and tempering the impression of hardness that might be produced by a simple study of the *Antigone*.

The obstinacy of Polyneices.

When Polyneices, with the curse still ringing in his ears, has fled forth, Cain-like, from the presence of his father, thunder is heard, and the end approaches. The chief actors, led by the blind hero, move from the stage in order suited to

Climax of the Coloneüs.

---

[1] " Nay, but I cannot. How could I again
     Lead the same troops forth, having once turned tail ? "
[2] See especially 1181-1203, 1414-43.

the processional gravity of the Greek theatre, while the speech of the Messenger, conveying to the Chorus the news of the last minutes in the life of Œdipus, prepares the spectators for the reappearance of his daughters on the scene. As in the *Œdipus Tyrannus*, so now a new motive of interest is introduced in the last act of the drama. The *Antigone* is imperatively demanded as a sequel. Our attention is riveted upon Antigone, who in losing her father has lost all. Her first thought is that he died nobly, peacefully, at one with God. Her next thought is that she shall never see him again, never more bear the sweet burden of anxiety and pain for him, never even have access to his hidden tomb. Her third thought is a longing to be dead with him, enfolded in oblivion of the fate which persecutes her kith and kin. Life stretches before her boundless, homeless, comfortless, nor has she now a single memory for him whose love might have consoled a woman of less stubborn soul, for Hæmon. It is characteristic of his whole conception of Antigone that Sophocles introduced no allusion to that underplot of love at this point. When Theseus reproves her for despair, she awakes to fresh unselfishness : "Send me to Thebes," she cries, "that I may stay, if possible, my brothers' strife." Throughout this final scene the single-hearted heat and firm will of Antigone, her desire for action, and her readiness to accept responsibility are contrasted with Ismene's yielding temper and passivity. We are thus prepared for the opening of the third drama, which, though written first by Sophocles, is the artistic close and climax of the tale of Thebes.

Position of Antigone.

The character of Antigone.

The most perfect female character in Greek poetry is Antigone. She is purely Greek, unlike any woman of modern fiction, except perhaps the Fedalma of George Eliot. In her filial piety, in her intercession for Polyneices at the knees of Œdipus, in her grief when her father is taken from her, she does indeed resemble the women whom most men among us have learned to honour in their sisters or their daughters or their mother. Of such women the Greek maiden, with her pure calm face and virginal straight lines of classic drapery, is still the saint and patroness. But what shall we say of the Antigone of this last drama, of the sister who is willing, lest her brother lie unburied on the Theban plain, to lay her own life down, disobeying the law of her sovereign, defying Creon to the face, appealing against unjust tribunals to the judgment-seat of powers more ancient than the throne of Zeus himself, and marching to her living tomb with dauntless strength in order that the curse-attainted ghost of Polyneices shall have rest in Hades? To the modern mind she appears a being from another sphere. A strain of unearthly music seems to announce her entrance and her exit on the stage. That the sacrifice of the sister's very life, the breaking of her plighted troth to Hæmon, should follow upon the sprinkling of those few hand-fuls of dust—that she should give that life up smilingly, nor ever in her last hours breathe her lover's name—is a tragic circumstance for which our sympathies are not prepared : we can neither divest our minds of the fixed modern prejudice that the first duty of a woman is to her husband, nor can we fully enter into the antique superstition of defrauded sepulture. Yet it is necessary to do both of these things, to sequester Antigone from the sphere of modern obligations, and to enter hand in hand with her the inner sanctuary of antique piety, in order to do justice to the conception of Sophocles. This effort of the imagination may be facilitated by remembering first, that Antigone inherited her father's proud self-will—

Tragic sublimity of the heroine.

> δηλοῖ τὸ γέννημ' ὠμὸν ἐξ ὠμοῦ πατρὸς
> τῆς παιδός· εἴκειν δ' οὐκ ἐπίσταται κακοῖς [1]—

and secondly, that disaster after disaster, the loss of Œdipus, the death of her two brothers, has come huddling upon her in a storm of fate, so that life is in a manner over for her, and she feels isolated in a cold and cruel world. This combination

---

[1] " How in the daughter the sire's temper stern
    Shows sternly ! Bend she will not, rather breaks ! "

of her character and her circumstances renders her action in the *Antigone* conceivable. Without the hardness she inherited from Œdipus, she could not have gone through her tragic part. Without the vow she registered above her father's grave, to bring help to her brethren, seeing that they alone were left, the sentiment of her last speech would sound rhetorical. Moreover, the poet who breathed into her form a breath of life so fiery, has himself justified us in regarding her act as one removed from the plain path of virtue. Antigone was no Hindhu widow to die upon a husband's pyre. Her heroism, her resistance offered to the will of Creon, had in it a splendid criminality. It was just the casuistry of the conflict between public and private obligations, between the dictates of her conscience and the commands of her sovereign, that enabled Sophocles to render the peculiar stoicism of her character pathetic. In spite of all these considerations, it is probable that she will strike a modern reader at the first as frigid. Especially if he have failed to observe the *nuances* of her portrait in the *Œdipus Coloneüs*, he will be inclined to wish that Sophocles had softened here and there the outlines of her adamantine statue. Yet, after long contemplation of those perfect lineaments, we come to recognise in her a purity of passion, a fixity of purpose, a loyalty of kinship, a sublime enthusiasm for duty, simply conceived and self-justified in spite of all conventions to the contrary, which soar above the strain of modern tragic sentiment. Even Alfieri, in the noble drawing he has sketched from the Sophoclean picture, could not abstain from violating its perfection by this sentimental touch of common feeling :—

Conflict of duties.

> " Emone, ah ! tutto io sento,
> Tutto l' amor, che a te portava : io sento
> Il dolor tutto, a cui ti lascio." [1]

---

[1] " Hæmon !　Ah me !　I feel it all,
　　Feel all the love I bore thee ; yea, I feel
　　All the despair to which I leave thee ! "

No such words are to be found in Sophocles upon the lips of Hæmon.
the dying Antigone. She is all for her father and her brothers.
The tragedy of Hæmon belongs to Creon, not to her. Her
furthest concessions to the sympathies which might have
swayed a weaker woman, are found in this line—

ὦ φίλταθ' Αἷμον, ὥς σ' ἀτιμάζει πατήρ,[1]

and in the passage of the Kommos where she bewails her
luckless lot of maidenhood. For the rest, Sophocles has sustained her character as that of one "whom, like sparkling
steel, the strokes of chance made hard and firm." This steely
durability, this crystalline sparkle, divide her not only from
the ideal raised by romance for womanhood, but distinguish
her as the daughter of Œdipus from the general sisterhood
even of Greek heroines.

The peculiar qualities of Antigone are brought into sharp Ismene.
relief by the milder virtues of Ismene, who thinks it right to
obey Creon, and who has no spirit for the deed of daring, but
who is afterwards eager to share the punishment of her sister.
Antigone repels her very sternly, herein displaying the force
of her nature under its less amiable aspect: "Have courage!
Thou livest, but my soul long since hath died." The glory of
the act is hers alone. Ismene has no right to share it when
the risks are past, the penalty is paid. Antigone's repulsion
of her sister seems to supply the key to her own heroism.
"Œdipus," she says, "is dead; my brethren are dead: for
them I lived, and in their death I died to life; but you—your
heart is not shut up within your father's and your brothers'
grave; it is still warm, still eager for love and the joys of this
world. Live, then. For me it would be no more possible to live
such life as yours, than for the clay-cold corpse upon the bier."

The character of Creon, darkened in its tone and shadow Creon.
to the utmost with a view to affording a foil of another species
for Antigone, was thought worthy of minute and careful

[1] "Ah, dearest Hæmon, how doth thy sire misrate thee!"

treatment by Sophocles. In the *Œdipus Tyrannus* he is wronged rather than wronging. While suffering from the unjust suspicion and hasty language of the King, he pleads his cause with decent gravity and shows no sign of either arrogance or cowardice. At the end, when Œdipus has fallen, his own behaviour is such as would not disgrace a generous as well as prudent prince. The neutrality for good or evil which distinguishes Creon in this play, marking him out in contrast with the fiery heat of Œdipus, the impious irony of Jocasta, is, to say the least, respectable. In the *Œdipus Coloneüs* he plays a consistently mean and odious part; his pragmatical display of rhetoric before the burghers of Colonus, when tested by his violent and cruel conduct toward Antigone, proves him to be a hollow-hearted and specious hypocrite. The light here reflected back upon his respectability in the *Tyrannus* is decidedly unfavourable. In the *Antigone* Creon becomes, if possible, still more odious; only our animosity against him is tempered by contempt. To the faults of egotism, hardness, and hypocritical prating, are now added the infatuation of self-will and the godless hatred of a dead foe. There is, indeed, a show of right in the decree published concerning the two brothers, one of whom had brought a foreign army against Thebes; but it would be sophistry to maintain that Creon was actuated by patriotic motives. The defeat and death of Polyneices were punishment enough. By pursuing his personal spite beyond the grave Creon insults the common instincts of humanity, the sympathies of the people, and the supposed feelings of the gods, who cannot bear to gaze upon abominations. The pathetic self-devotion of Antigone, the voice of the city, the remonstrances of Hæmon, and the warnings of Teiresias are all thrown away upon his stubborn and conceited obstinacy. He shows himself, in short, to be a tyrant of the orthodox sort. Like a tyrant, he is moreover absurdly suspicious: the guardian has, he thinks, been bought; Ismene must be hatching treason; Hæmon prefers a woman to his duty; Teiresias

Develop-
ment of
Creon's
character.

is plotting for the sake of gain against him. When it is just too late, he gives way helplessly and feebly, moved to terror by the dark words of the seer. Creon is, therefore, a mixed character, great neither for good nor for evil, weak through wilfulness, plausible in words and wavering in his determinations, a man who might have passed for excellent if he had never had to wield a kingdom's power. His own description of himself—μάταιον ἄνδρα (a man of naught)—suits him not only in the utter collapse of his character and ruin of his fortunes, but also in the height of his prosperity and fulness of his seeming strength.

Sophocles might fairly be censured for having made the misery of Creon the climax of a drama which ought to have had its whole interest centred in Antigone. Our sympathies have not been sufficiently enlisted on the side of Hæmon to make us care much about his death. For Eurydice it is impossible to rouse more than a languid pity. Creon, we feel, gets no more than he deserves; instead of being sorry for him, we are only angry that he was not swept away into the dust-heap of oblivion sooner. It was surely a mistake to divert the attention of the audience, at the very end of the tragedy, from its heroine to a character which, like that of Creon, rouses impatient scorn as well as antipathy. That Sophocles had artistic reasons for not concluding this play with the death of Antigone, may be readily granted by those who have made the crises of the *Ajax*, the *Œdipus Tyrannus*, and the *Œdipus Coloneüs* the subject of special study. He preferred, it seems, to relax the strained sympathies of his audience by a prolongation of the drama on an altered theme. Yet this scarcely justifies the shifting of the centre of interest attempted in the *Antigone*. We have to imagine that the inculcation of a moral lesson upon the crime of ἀσέβεια (impiety) was the poet's paramount object.[1] If so, he sacrificed dramatic effect to ethics.

The last scenes of the Antigone.

[1] The last six lines spoken by the Chorus seem to justify this view.

Ethical pro-
blem of the
Antigone.

It should be noticed that Antigone, in whom the fate of the family of Laius is finally accomplished, falls an innocent victim. Her tragedy is no immediate consequence of the Œdipodean curse. While her brethren were wilfully involved in the doom of their house, she perished in the cause of divine charity. Finding that the immutable ordinances of heaven clashed with the arbitrary volition of a ruler, she preferred to obey the law of conscience and to die at the behest of a pride-maddened tyrant. She is technically dis-obedient, morally most duteous. Thus the *Antigone* carries us beyond the region of hereditary disaster into the more universal sphere of ethical casuistry. Its tragic interest depends less upon the evolution of the law of ancestral guilt than on the conflict of two duties. By suggesting the casuistical question to his audience, while he freed his heroine from all doubt upon the subject, Sophocles maintained the sublime simplicity which distinguishes Antigone above all women of romance. The retribution that falls on Creon furnishes a powerful example of the Greek doctrine of Nemesis; but over Antigone herself Nemesis exerts no sway. In her action there was nothing unconsidered; in her doom there was nothing unforeseen.

A couplet from the *Pheræi* of Moschion might be inscribed as a motto upon the *Antigone* :—

κενὸν θανόντος ἀνδρὸς αἰκίζειν σκιάν·
ζῶντας κολάζειν οὐ θανόντας εὐσεβές.

"'Tis vain to vilify a dead man's shadow;
To scourge the living, not the dead, is righteous."

END OF VOL. I

Printed by R. & R. CLARK, LIMITED, *Edinburgh*